Praise for
Is Atheism Dead?

"With great oratorical skill and irrepressible humor, Metaxas engages lay readers with the story of how recent discoveries have made atheism scientifically, historically, and philosophically untenable."

—**HUGH ROSS, Ph.D.**, astrophysicist and founder and president of Reasons to Believe

"When Eric Metaxas comes out with a new book, I have a problem: I know I will have to read it. I have read all his books—because I learn an immense amount from them and because they are difficult to put down. This latest book features Metaxas versus atheism. It's not a fair fight. Read *Is Atheism Dead?* and you'll understand why."

—**DENNIS PRAGER,** nationally syndicated radio talk show host, founder of Prager University, and bestselling author

"*Is Atheism Dead?* displays the wonders of the universe, the chemistry of life, the vast archaeological evidence, and the thoughts and writings of great thinkers.... Yet another all-engaging Metaxas book."

—**JAMES M. TOUR, Ph.D.**, professor of chemistry, computer science, materials science, and nanoengineering at Rice University

"A beautifully written, highly readable compendium of scientific, archaeological, and historical evidence.... Highly recommended for anyone wrestling with the big questions!"

—**STEPHEN C. MEYER, Ph.D.**, director of the Center for Science and Culture at the Discovery Institute and author of *Return of the God Hypothesis*

"Is atheism dead? Metaxas answers this question meticulously and engagingly, addressing the most pressing questions and ostensibly the most compelling arguments for atheism. A must-read."

—**SARAH SALVIANDER, Ph.D.**, astrophysicist and author

Over a half century ago, while I was still a child, I recall hearing a number of old people offer the following explanation for the great disasters that had befallen Russia: "Men have forgotten God; that's why all this has happened." Since then I have spent well-nigh fifty years working on the history of our revolution; in the process I have read hundreds of books, collected hundreds of personal testimonies, and have already contributed eight volumes of my own toward the effort of clearing away the rubble left by that upheaval. But if I were asked today to formulate as concisely as possible the main cause of the ruinous revolution that swallowed up some sixty million of our people, I could not put it more accurately than to repeat: "Men have forgotten God; that's why all this has happened."

—Aleksandr Solzhenitsyn

Is Atheism Dead?

IS ATHEISM DEAD?

ERIC METAXAS

SALEM
BOOKS

an imprint of Regnery Publishing
Washington, D.C.

Salem Books™ is a trademark of Salem Communications Holding Corporation
Regnery® is a registered trademark and its colophon is a trademark of Salem Communications Holding Corporation

Cataloging-in-Publication data on file with the Library of Congress

ISBN: 978-1-68451-173-0
eISBN: 978-1-68451-209-6

Library of Congress Control Number: 2021943439

Published in the United States by
Salem Books
An Imprint of Regnery Publishing
A Division of Salem Media Group
Washington, D.C.
www.SalemBooks.com

Manufactured in the United States of America

10 9 8 7 6 5 4

Books are available in quantity for promotional or premium use. For information on discounts and terms, please visit our website: www.SalemBooks.com.

This book is dedicated to the memory of two of the greatest minds and dearest souls imaginable, my beloved friends, of whom this world was not worthy,

John Rankin and Thomas Howard.

How I long to see you again, my brothers, when we three will "round the tent of God like lambs rejoice"!

CONTENTS

Acknowledgments

In the course of writing this book I have felt an indebtedness to several people, all of whom I have the high honor of calling friends and whom it is my joy here to acknowledge and thank.

For example, it was in 1990 that my eyes lit on the books of Dr. Hugh Ross, who introduced me to the notion of the fine-tuned universe and who first enabled me to goggle at the breathtaking and soaring *pas de deux* of Science and Faith.

My friend Dr. Stephen Meyer also has proved to be an invaluable source of kindness, information, and wisdom, as has the extraordinary Dr. John Lennox, whose own books and spoken observations have had the effect of impishly haunting much of what I myself write and think.

I am also indebted to my friend Elizabeth Blakemore for her generous introduction to her Houston friend Dr. James Tour, and to Dr. Tour for his prodigal and withering critique of abiogenesis; and I am indebted to my friend Skip Heitzig for his generous introduction to his Albuquerque friend Dr. Steven Collins, and to Dr. Collins for his indefatigable trust in the Hebrew Scriptures, which extended to his following their lead not only to the Kikkar

Plain, but all the way down to the Destruction Matrix level at what we now know to be biblical Sodom.

I would also like to thank my publisher, Tim Peterson at Salem Books, for believing in me and what I have to say in a way that has been profoundly encouraging; and for Salem's editorial director, Karla Dial, whose cheerfulness and helpfulness has been entirely unparalleled in my experience with editors. I'm also grateful to Salem's assistant managing editor, Kathryn Riggs; and to Salem's senior marketing manager, Jennifer Valk.

I also here must very heartily thank my own team—Elisa Leberis, Katie Madonna, Janille Hawkins, Annalisa Pesek, and Sarah Luebkemann—for their support generally. I am especially indebted to Elisa for her extreme dedication in tracking down citations and photos for this book, which makes me not merely grateful, but grateful to the point of embarrassment.

And finally, I thank my agents on this book, Esther Fedorkevich of the Fedd Agency, and Elisa Leberis, for making it possible that this book could be published and eventually find its way to you, the reader, whom I thank last but not at all least, for as you know it was you I was writing to all along, and none other, and to whom I am writing even now.

PART I

Does Science Point to God?

The Grand Counter-Narrative

We are living in unprecedentedly exciting times. But most of us don't know it yet. That's essentially the point of this book, to share the news that what many people have dreamt of—and others have believed could never happen—has happened, or at any rate is happening this very minute and has been happening for some time. By this I mean the emergence of inescapably compelling evidence for God's existence.

Although such evidence has been appearing for decades, the culture hasn't much noticed it or spoken of it. And more recently, such evidence has been accelerating. But we are generally still stuck in the secular narrative that reached its apogee in the 1966 *Time* magazine cover article with the infamous title, "Is God Dead?" That was essentially the high-water mark for evidence that God had never existed, and as a result of that cultural moment, most of us have carried on with that idea ever since. We have likely heard little to disprove it and have mostly assumed the question was settled.

More importantly, our rather disproportionately secular cultural leaders were quite sure it was settled. So when any evidence came their way to the contrary, they tended to ignore it, since it so clearly defied the trend toward secularization that everyone had already accepted. It is more than anything because of this that the rest of us haven't heard much.

But while all of us were sleeping through the decades and assuming the religious tide was going further and further out, never to return, something happened. The wind shifted. And for some time now the tide has been returning, slowly but steadily. So those for whom this is somehow bad news will feel like sunbathers who have drifted off to blissful sleep on the beach, only to leap awake hours later to see waves gurgling over their blankets and soaking their Hermann Hesse paperbacks. And then they realize they are badly sunburnt too!

I was myself awakened to this idea about seven years ago, when I wrote my book *Miracles*, in which I talked about the scientific evidence for God via the argument for "fine-tuning," which is the idea that many things in our universe are calibrated so perfectly that they cannot have just happened, but rather overwhelmingly seem to point to some Designer. Over the years I had read about this and other evidence, but the sheer scope of it had never hit me until I was writing my book. Because the "fine-tuning" argument struck me as so compelling, I put it front and center in the book. When my publisher at Penguin asked me to write an op-ed to publicize the book, I thought this to be the most miraculous and surprising story of all, and so I wrote about it, sending eight hundred words to the *Wall Street Journal*. I initially titled it "Is Science Leading Us to God?" but the editors changed it to "Science Increasingly Makes the Case for God." They seem to have known what they were doing, because no sooner did it appear than it went viral—to use that cliché—and then some.[1] Actually, it was astonishing to watch—but I did watch it, with more interest than I had watched anything in some time.

The article went online on Christmas Eve in 2014 and appeared in the print edition on Christmas Day. Only hours afterward, it had been shared on Facebook thousands of times, with hundreds of comments. And it kept on going at an impossible rate. As my family and I drove to Vermont for a few

---

[1] You may read the original article in the Appendix.

days' skiing, we kept checking the link. It seemed there was a bizarre level of interest. This continued the next day—and the next, too. While having breakfast in a Vermont diner three days after it appeared, a young man approached.

"Are you Eric Metaxas?" he asked. He worked in banking in Boston and had read the article, found me online, and recognized me. He seemed thrilled by what he had read in the article, and of course I was thrilled that he was thrilled. What was going on?

Soon the Facebook shares hit one hundred thousand. When would the interest end? But it didn't even slow. It kept charging ahead until it hit two hundred thousand—and kept going. An editor I knew at the *Journal* told me that the most Facebook shares any article had ever gotten was three hundred thousand, so if we passed that, the article would have the record—albeit unofficially, since they couldn't comment on such things publicly. A few days later it hit that number—and kept going. A few months later it hit over six hundred thousand shares, after which the *Journal* ceased publishing those metrics for the public.

I realized that what I was watching was evidence for something I had believed for some time: People were hungry for answers to the big questions—or rather, the Big Questions—such as whether there is a God, or if there is a God, can we know it rationally? And of course everyone wondered what science might have to say about all of this. But because we live in a world that generally avoids such questions, we rarely hear these things discussed in any public forum. Good answers therefore elude us, which can be frustrating. So when my essay appeared, was it any wonder many readers responded as they did? Finally, they were getting some answers for these questions no one ever seemed to talk about. And those answers were the very opposite of what the general cultural conversation had led them to believe.

My article was just a tiny trickle of water in the middle of a cultural desert, but who could blame people dying of thirst for getting excited? But it is because of the response to that article that I have written this book. The evidence for "fine-tuning" has only been growing since that article appeared. And other evidence in other areas has come out too, changing much of what we once felt so sure of. So I thought it was about time someone blew the trumpet about this—or sounded the alarm, depending on whether you think this news is generally good or bad.

It seems extraordinary to think that roughly when *Time* in 1966 asked "Is God Dead?"—at the moment of what we must now regard as premature secularist triumph—things were already beginning to shift. The evidence began to come in slowly, but steadily as we have said, and has only increased as the years and decades have passed. Those hostile to such evidence and those friendly to it were equally oblivious. Somehow over the years I have had the good fortune to stumble across books in which bits of this evidence have appeared, and have quietly been making mental notes. But it is only recently that I've realized the sheer amount of such evidence and thought I ought to share this little-known but paradigm-shifting news. Since the *Time* article in 1966, roughly five things have arisen to challenge—and I will argue, to overturn—the secular consensus that formed in the wake of that article.

The first is the discovery of what we call the Big Bang—and the proof of the Big Bang, which settled the question once and for all whether the universe always existed or didn't. In discovering that the universe had a clear beginning, we realized there was a point at which all the laws of physics—and all of matter and energy—did not exist. It was the paradigm-smashing concept to end all paradigm-smashing concepts, one whose effects—like those of the Big Bang itself—continue to ripple onward and outward. One corollary to this is that we now know not just that the universe began, but when it began, and therefore, we know the age of the universe. Before we knew this, we could always say the emergence of life out of non-life had an infinite amount of time to happen; and theoretically, given infinity, anything could happen. But suddenly that infinity shrank to 13.8 billion years, and there was no longer forever for life to emerge. The breathing room of an infinite past had vanished.

The second thing—which we have already mentioned—is our discovery in the last decades of the increasingly overwhelming evidence of so-called "fine-tuning" in the universe. This was already observed in the 1950s, but things didn't begin to look seriously troubling for atheists until about the 1990s. But since then, because of scientific advances, we can look much more closely at the nature of things and can see more clearly than ever that things in our universe and on this earth could not have emerged by chance, as we once so easily believed. Some of the elements of fine-tuning are, as we shall see, astonishing.

The third major shift in the last decades has to do with our views on how life emerged from non-life on the early earth, often called "Abiogenesis." The more closely we can examine cells, for example, the more we can see how stupefyingly complex they are. We once thought they were very simple and imagined that they could have randomly assembled themselves in the primordial oceans. Thanks also to the world's premier nanoscientist, James Tour of Rice University, we know how difficult it is to create molecules under even the best-controlled conditions, so the idea of life emerging from non-life—which once seemed at least theoretically possible—has with the progress of science seemed less and less so, until now it seems so far beyond the realm of possibility that we need to go back to our drawing boards on the whole subject. If the facts on this have not led most scientists in the field all the way to God, they have certainly led many to awe and wonder.

The fourth thing that has happened over the last decades concerns archaeological discoveries in the Middle East. The field has matured to the point where almost every month someone uncovers another small or large piece to add to the jigsaw picture of the Bible as an historically accurate guidebook to the past. Although this trend has been in motion since biblical archaeology began in the mid-nineteenth century, it too has accelerated in the last decades, with astonishing recent discoveries such as the Tel Dan stele, which mentions the monarchy of King David; the discovery and identification of biblical Sodom; and very recently, the discovery of Jesus's childhood home in Nazareth. Taken together, these things make it impossible for any serious person to continue to regard the Bible as a collection of folktales.

The fifth thing that has changed in recent years is our knowledge of what atheism is, both theoretically and practically. For example, we have had the time to observe the lives of various atheists, such as Jean-Paul Sartre, Albert Camus, and Antony Flew, to see whether any of them were able to live out their philosophies in a way that was inspiring or even merely logical; we have had the opportunity to see which of them most honestly grappled with the eternal question of God's existence and what they eventually came to believe. We also have had the opportunity to watch the decades-long careers of atheist states like the former Soviet Union, China, Nazi Germany, and North Korea, and we have seen the inhuman horrors attending that worldview so that anyone with any respect for human rights or freedom must conclude that state-sponsored—and enforced—atheism must rank as the most wicked form of oppression in human history. Which must say something about those nations, and about atheism generally as well.

In this book we will deal with all of these five subjects, although there is no particular reason for the reader to feel compelled to take the chapters in the order in which they appear. Each of them may more or less stand alone, so if someone prefers, for example, to read all of the chapters on biblical archaeology first, or all the chapters on science, that should not affect the flow of the larger argument.

Finally, we should be clear that in this book we have set the bar rather low in not expecting to convince anyone of anything beyond the larger point: that the belief that there is no God has—at least in recent decades—become untenable. So we won't wade into anything much beyond that, and anyone looking for an explanation of the Trinity, or proof of the Resurrection, or for eye-popping photos of the Ark—or of the fossil of a serpent with a larynx—will be disappointed. These and many other things are outside the scope of this book, but the claims of atheism are not.

Atheism declares that there is no God, and it claims that this is a rational position; but atheism does not attempt to do much beyond convincing people of this idea. So although I might not be able to convince the reader of specific details of the Bible or of the truth of some of the doctrines of faith, I can certainly hope and even expect to convince any rational person that atheism is no longer an option for those wishing to be regarded as intellectually honest. We may all have excellent questions and may doubt many things, and we may even be hostile to many expressions of faith and might reasonably call ourselves agnostics. But the idea that anyone can at this juncture say they believe there is no God—much less know such a thing—must henceforth be regarded as willful unreason or as mere affectation, or perhaps both. But I hope that this will become self-evident to the reader in due course.

CHAPTER ONE

In the Beginning Was the Big Bang

The story of the Big Bang—what it is and how we came to know it happened—is appropriately as big a story as they come. It starts near the beginning of the twentieth century in 1911, when in the midst of a world drifting from the idea of God, a certain German genius came up with what we call the Theory of Relativity. And it essentially ends in 1964 with the discovery of the background radiation from the early universe, although it ends utterly and as decisively as anyone could have hoped—or feared—in the 1990s, when NASA's Cosmic Background Explorer (COBE) satellite fleshed out the contours of that radiation in extraordinary and indisputable detail. The story about the Big Bang is really many stories, but it is perhaps best told through the story of one of the world's greatest scientists, an American astronomer named Allan Sandage.

I first heard about Sandage from Dr. Stephen Meyer during a Socrates in the City[1] event in Dallas in 2019. Meyer was telling the story of a conference he

---

[1] Socrates in the City is a Manhattan-based conversation series on "Life, God, and other Small Topics" that I began in 2000 in order to explore what are often called the "Big Questions." It has featured authors (Mark Helprin, Malcolm Gladwell, Dana Gioia, and Mary Norris), scientists (Sir John Polkinghorne, Dr. Francis Collins, Dr. Gerald Schroeder, and Dr. Owen Gingerich), public intellectuals (Sir Roger Scruton, Dr. John Lennox, Rabbi Sir Jonathan Sacks, Dame Alice von

Allan R. Sandage (1926–2010) was among the most influential astronomers of the twentieth century.

had attended back in February 1985, when he had first stumbled across the changing narrative in science and had begun wondering if the idea of God was making a comeback.[2] The conference featured a veritable Who's Who of scientists, including Sandage, who was one of those mythical figures one hardly expected to see in the same room. But it was what Sandage did during the conference that especially stunned Meyer and first made him wonder if the strict atheistic consensus he expected at such gatherings was changing.

It happened at the end of the conference, when the scientists were asked to "vote" whether they believed there was a God or wasn't by standing on one side of the stage or another. Meyer was hardly alone in being astounded to see the legendary Sandage walk to the side of the stage representing belief in God. Here was one of the greatest scientists in the world publicly standing with those convinced the universe could not have come into being apart from some unfathomable Mind, whom Sandage at that time already understood to be the God of the Bible.

The story of Sandage is superbly told in *Lonely Hearts of the Cosmos: The Story of the Scientific Quest for the Secret of the Universe*, by *New York Times* science writer Dennis Overbye. It is filled with many stories and personages, but Sandage emerges as the most significant. "Few men are handed the keys to heaven," Overbye says, "but Allan Sandage was one." Overbye tells about a 1954 *Fortune* magazine article in which the twenty-eight-year-old Sandage is portrayed as one of "ten promising

---

Hildebrand, Os Guinness, and N. T. Wright), politicians and activists (Baroness Caroline Cox), entrepreneurs (Peter Thiel), and celebrities (Dick Cavett and Caroline Kennedy), among many others. For further information, visit www.SocratesintheCity.com.

[2] This is the subject of his recent book, *Return of the God Hypothesis*.

young scientists" and was "photographed leaning against the base of a famous 200-inch telescope on Palomar Mountain. He looked lean and Jimmy Stewartish, wearing a bomber jacket and grinning with dimpled cheeks, a spit of curl hanging over his high forehead." Overbye explains that Sandage "had become the first person in history whose job description was to determine the fate of the universe."

Science writer Dennis Overbye.

What Sandage did for thirty years after that photograph was operate the telescope he is pictured leaning on. It was probably the most famous scientific instrument of the twentieth century, and Overbye says Sandage operated it "as if it were his backyard spyglass, measuring and remeasuring the universe, scraping from the shadows of photographic plates and enigmatic spectra and mathematical drudge-work clues to the size and fate of the universe." To be clear, the young Sandage had been handed the job of carrying on the world-changing work of the legendary Edwin Hubble, whose name most of us today recognize because of the Hubble Space Telescope.

Hubble himself began looking at the heavens in 1919, using the newly completed one-hundred-inch telescope on Mount Wilson in the mountains north of Los Angeles. It was the largest telescope in the world, and through it in 1924 he saw something astonishing. No one else had ever seen it, nor would have believed it if they had. The universe, Hubble noticed, was expanding. The whole thing. And all the stars and galaxies in our universe—like the raisins in a raisin cake—were moving farther and farther away from each other as it expanded. Sandage became Hubble's protégé, and when Hubble died in 1953, he took over the job of methodically observing the expanding universe and trying to figure out where it was headed. Would it expand outward forever, or would it only expand to a certain perimeter, and then begin returning the way it had come? And which way *had* it come?

Before Hubble and his one-hundred-inch telescope, everyone believed that what we call the Milky Way was not a mere galaxy, as we now know it to be, but was the whole universe. Galileo had trained his new telescope on the Milky Way in 1610, so he was the first to see that what looked like a cloud-like

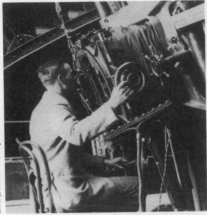

Edwin Powell Hubble at the one-hundred-inch reflecting telescope, Mount Wilson Observatory, 1922.

haze to our naked eyes was—upon closer inspection—actually comprised of stars. But in the decades and centuries after Galileo, some astronomers saw that what looked like stars to Galileo were in fact "nebulae"—hazy clouds comprised of ionized gasses and dust. But when Hubble started out in 1919, he saw that some of these nebulae were not located within our own Milky Way galaxy, but were in fact galaxies themselves, impossibly far away. Suddenly, the universe was wildly beyond what we had believed. It was astonishingly vast. And then in 1924, Hubble saw something perhaps even more astounding, and more to our point here: the universe—always believed to be static—was in fact expanding, and at an inconceivable speed.

In order to explain the larger story of what Hubble saw—and what Sandage continued to see and document—we must go back to Albert Einstein and the mathematical calculations that led to his Theory of Relativity. Based on his initial calculations in 1911, Einstein eventually formulated the theory that light would be affected by gravity, which didn't make sense beyond his equations. Anyone familiar with Einstein's $e = mc^2$ understands that Einstein had shown that energy (e) and matter (m) were related—that they were actually different forms of the same thing. So energy could be transformed into matter, and matter could be transformed into energy. But Einstein's other conclusion—that the mass and gravity of a planet or star would have an effect on beams of light—is more complicated. If light and the photons that carry light are weightless and massless, how could gravity have any effect on them? Yet this is what Einstein's calculations showed. But then the question arose: Could we somehow actually observe this strange phenomenon to see if the calculations were correct?

During the First World War, a Quaker Christian named Sir Arthur Eddington set out to do just that; it was because of his faith—which made him

Hooker one-hundred-inch reflecting telescope, circa 1940. Photo by Edison Hoge.

a pacifist—that he was able to do it, and for two reasons. First, even though he was English and his country was at war with Germany, Eddington could not, as a Quaker Christian, think of himself as a dedicated enemy of everything German. He was therefore not hostile to the "German" Theory of Relativity, which had emerged from the German mind of Albert Einstein. So Eddison was virtually alone in England in being open to the strange "German" theory. He was also one of the extremely few people in the world who understood the math behind it. So when in 1915 Einstein himself proposed the idea that a solar eclipse would provide the perfect opportunity to test the theory, Eddington leapt at the chance to oversee the experiment. What was necessary was to observe the position of a star that looked to be near the sun from our earth-bound point of view. If the position was off from what we knew to be correct, it would show that the sun's gravity affected the light. But the brightness of the sun made such observations impossible. Except, of course, during a solar eclipse, in which the sun's light is covered. It just so happened that a perfect solar eclipse would take place on May 29, 1919. It would even last almost seven minutes, longer than any solar eclipse since 1416.

As a Quaker, Eddington was able to stay out of fighting in the First World War, and instead served his country by continuing his scientific studies, which

Professor Arthur S. Eddington, circa 1900.

were deemed of national interest. So it was because of his Christian faith that he was able to perform this historic experiment. In fact, it was his desire to conduct this very experiment that was the decisive factor in his being allowed to forgo fighting, even though the war ended before he could do so. The first attempt in 1918 failed due to clouds, but in spring 1919 Eddington—then director of the Observatory at Cambridge—sailed for the coast of West Africa to try again. Although clouds just before the eclipse once again threatened to scotch his best-laid plans, they parted in time, and Eddington observed with his eyes precisely what Einstein's mathematical calculations predicted. The news of this exploded around the world, instantly making Eddington famous and catapulting Einstein into that highest orbit of fame from which he would never return. Thanks to Eddington, Einstein's extraordinary—and to many, utterly outlandish-sounding—theory had been demonstrated to be correct.

To follow our Big Bang narrative, we must return to Einstein's 1915 paper, whose equations indicated that the universe was expanding—or was perhaps collapsing in on itself—neither of which option he found at all palatable. The "settled science" during this period was that the universe was eternal and unchanging. It had no beginning, and time had no beginning. So when his calculations directly challenged this idea, Einstein balked. Like many lesser geniuses, he desperately feared challenging the establishment view. So rather than let the math and physics say what they said and imply what they implied, Einstein decided to punt. He would remedy the troubling issue in advance by fudging things, and in 1917, as a prophylactic hedge against the embarrassing notion of an expanding universe, he fatefully and fatally introduced into his equations what he called "the Cosmological Constant." That would put an end to the embarrassing implications. Except that it didn't.

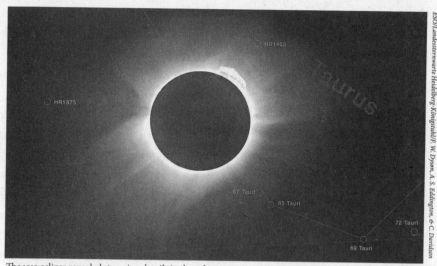

ESO/Landessternwarte Heidelberg-Königstuhl/F. W. Dyson, A. S. Eddington, & C. Davidson

The 1919 eclipse revealed stunning details in the solar corona, a giant prominence emerging right, and stars in the Taurus constellation that were used to confirm Einstein's relativity predictions.

In 1922, the Russian physicist Alexander Friedmann showed via his own equations that Einstein's equations worked perfectly well with an expanding universe. He also showed that the universe really was expanding. Einstein was understandably vexed, but what could he do? Then in 1927 a Belgian Catholic priest, Father Georges Lemaître, discovered that not only were Einstein's equations consonant with the idea of an expanding universe, but showed that they actually proved it. Lemaître even went so far as to show the rate at which he thought the universe was expanding. For complicated reasons this rate came to be known as the "Hubble Constant," but Lemaître got there first.

Einstein could not find fault with Lemaître's mathematics, but he peevishly told him: "Your calculations are correct, but your physics are atrocious." But Lemaître's physics were proved correct too. So by the time Edwin Hubble saw that the universe was expanding through his brand-new Hooker telescope—he published these findings in 1929—the jig was up. Just as Eddington through his telescope had seen that gravity actually did bend light as Einstein's calculations showed, Hubble saw through his telescope what Einstein and others had predicted in their calculations: the universe really was expanding.

Father Lemaître took things a step further in 1931 when he was the first to postulate that the entire universe had expanded from an initial point, which he called "the primeval atom." If one ran the film of the expanding universe in reverse, so to speak, the outward explosion of space and time would lead backwards down to a single point—literally a point of infinite density, whatever that meant. The Belgian priest's shocking idea eventually came to be known as "the Big Bang theory."

But Einstein didn't like this idea at all. He felt that it smacked not of science, but of religion, and sniped that Lemaître's "primeval atom hypothesis" was "inspired by the Christian dogma of creation," and was "totally unjustified from the physical point of view." Of course Einstein should have known that the Christian dogma of creation was really the Hebrew dogma of creation too, and he should have known that if a scientific theory happened to support what ancient scriptures said, this could hardly constitute a logical objection to the theory. It was an early example of how modern science was revealing the prescience and accuracy of texts written three thousand years before Newton, at a time when the Egyptians were worshiping cats and dung beetles. But it was dumbfounding to many, because more than a century ago, the erroneous idea that faith and science were enemies was already operating powerfully.

Einstein eventually had no choice but to see there was no escaping what his calculations showed about the expanding universe. The Russian Friedmann, the Belgian Lemaître, and the American Hubble had all been right on the money. At a conference in Pasadena, California, Einstein finally admitted as much. Not long after this he also conceded that introducing his "Cosmological Constant" was not merely an error, but "the greatest stupidity of my life." He knew that if he had not acted out of fear of the scientific consensus—and in reaction against what smacked of "faith"—he would have been the one credited for discovering that the universe was expanding, many years before anyone else had done so. It is a sobering lesson that even the greatest scientists may yield to the temptation to bow to the crippling consensus of the herd, especially if it involves the widespread bias against "religion."

Albert Einstein, Edwin Powell Hubble, and others standing in front of the Mount Wilson Observatory, January 29, 1931.

So the story of the expanding universe—or "Big Bang"—would inevitably lead scientists backward to a beginning for time and space, but as we continue telling the larger story, we must say more about why many scientists found the idea so distressing.

CHAPTER TWO

Where Science Cannot Go: The Big Bang and Other Singularities

Scientists had several objections to the Big Bang, which are not unrelated. The first is that it is like a heavy portcullis crashing down and closing off any possibilities of infinite time. Infinite time was the darling of many atheists who maintained that "with enough time" anything was possible, and therefore the idea of God was unnecessary. Whenever anyone objected that certain things could not have happened randomly and without some "Designer" or "Creator," those wed to the atheist-materialist position would object that "given enough time" anything could happen. Life could arise randomly out of non-life in the primordial oceans. Amoebas could become redwoods. Aquatic creatures could become flying mammals. It was only a matter of having enough time, for time covered a multitude of sins.

This creaky argument was wheeled out whenever necessary and usually sufficiently quieted those on the other side, so for many decades atheists clutched the notion of infinite time to themselves the way Linus clutched his blanket. It was extremely comforting, especially when other facts arose to challenge their theses. But the eventual consensus about the Big Bang ended this forever, forcing everyone to grow up and face the ugly fact that past time was finite. In fact, we came to know precisely how finite. So whatever one proposed as happening randomly over·great periods of time—whether the emergence of life from non-life, or the evolution from amphibians to orangutans—needed to happen within that limited time frame.

But the second problem some had with the Big Bang was that it came across like a large sign that said: "Science Not Admitted." It was where time and space—and science—did not exist. But the idea that we could go back in time to this literal point of infinite density and infinite temperature—out of which time and space and our universe had been born—seemed absurd. As Robert Frost said, "Something there is that does not love a wall," and for scientists the singularity from which the universe emerged in the Big Bang was precisely that. Overbye writes that a singularity "could be a cosmic dead end, where particles and energy simply went out of existence, a free-fire zone where anything was permitted and possible." He also tells us that "Einstein himself reluctantly admitted that singularities were *mathematically* possible . . . but thought they were nonsense as far as the real world was concerned. After all, a real physical object could never be squeezed down to a point, could it?"

As it happens, it could. Nonetheless when we who live in this physical universe think about singularities, we cannot help but be hornswoggled. Perhaps this is because thinking about the Big Bang makes us wonder if there might be other singularities. The idea of that single singularity—even if it existed safely back 13.8 billion years in the past—made a hash of all science. If we know the laws of physics were crushed out of existence once, why couldn't they be crushed out of existence another time? And another? If the laws of physics do not exist independently of the universe forever, they can cease to exist anywhere and anytime, at least theoretically. This idea put science on a leash, and some scientists didn't like that at all, as it defied their sometimes-deified versions of themselves as the ultimate arbiters of truth and knowledge, as the priests of the new religion that was beyond religion. So it could be humbling and embarrassing.

What's the Opposite of a Bang?

As the twentieth century wore on, some physicists actually did postulate the existence of other singularities, and eventually realized that they already existed, and in great numbers, deep in outer space. This began in 1939, three decades before anyone saw where it would lead. J. Robert Oppenheimer—the future head of the Manhattan Project, which brought the atomic bomb into existence— and his grad student Hartland Snyder proposed what they thought was an intriguing idea. They thought it would be diverting and valuable to calculate what might happen when a star like our own sun ran out of fuel, which of course would happen eventually. Billions of years in the future, the massive gravity of

J. Robert Oppenheimer, pictured with General Leslie R. Groves in September 1945. They have come to the Trinity Test site in New Mexico to examine the devastation wrought by the atomic bombs Oppenheimer helped create in the Manhattan Project. The high temperature of the blasts melted the sand, creating a substance that came to be called "trinitite," which figures in Chapter Eighteen.

our sun would cause it to be crushed all the way down to the size of Earth. Since one million Earths could fit in the gigantic gas ball that is our sun, the idea of the sun shrinking to our relatively tiny terrestrial size was an arresting concept. But surely it would happen. It would have the same mass as the sun has now, but it would be one million times denser. So while it is now a gigantic flaming ball of gas, Oppenheimer and Snyder calculated that it would at that future point be as dense as iron. This was just where the physics led.

Oppenheimer and Snyder were ahead of their time, but they were not alone in trying to work these things out. Others were calculating along similar lines. For example, what if a star much larger and heavier than our sun—of which there are billions—were to undergo a similar shrinking? And why shouldn't it? It certainly would, and others already had. That larger star's greater mass—and much more powerful gravity—would make it end up far smaller than our Earth. A much bigger star would be crushed all the way down to the difficult-to-conceive diameter of ten miles. Overbye explains that under this unfathomable pressure its very atoms would be crushed, so that only a mass of neutrons remained. The physicists figuring these things out realized they had entered a new reality. Where could it lead? And while they were on the subject, what would happen to the largest stars in the universe? Some have diameters four thousand times larger than our sun. What will happen when they collapse under their inconceivable mass and gravity? Today we know. Their mass will become so unfathomably concentrated that light itself will be unable to escape. It was the English Nobel Laureate mathematical physicist Sir Roger Penrose who explained this in 1965, saying that in the end these massive stars would indeed do the very opposite of what the universe had done at the Big Bang. These monstrous stars would eventually go downward and downward, smaller and smaller, until all physics and all science were crushed out of shape and then into non-existence. They would in fact disappear all the way down to a singularity, when they would effectively put up an "Out to Lunch" sign, except that they would never return, having disappeared altogether. They would take themselves to an unknown realm beyond our ability to investigate or understand. They would scientifically be observed to go beyond science, disappearing into themselves, like a Fakir making himself vanish, like a snake swallowing its own tail.

Here again—apart from the Big Bang—was another case of science leading beyond science. And like the Big Bang, it was undeniable. It was as though science were a ladder leading to a hole in the sky, but when you followed it up into the hole, the ladder vanished behind you. *Poof!* No more science. At a conference in New York in 1967, the Princeton physicist John Wheeler gave these inconceivable horrors a name: he called them black holes.

Overbye ruminates on these singularities:

> What were they? They were at once liberation from the gray law and enforcers of the ultimate unknowable law of laws, tangible evidence of a mystery more powerful than anything we could think of, a truth that would fry your brain or blind you if you saw it—like the face of God, waiting there at the end of time.... They were magic. The idea that the laws of physics—gray sober relativity—should predict the existence of singularities was astounding. The singularity theorems, to me, were like evidence of a miracle, of a magic outside of physics itself. I wanted to know...if such miracles, such singular terrible transformations, were real. If we couldn't see God, would we at least know God was there, even if sulking in a black hole or at the end of time?[1]

The Game Is Over

Despite the conclusions of such as Einstein, Friedmann, Lemaître, and Hubble, many continued to be so irritated by the idea of a Big Bang that they continued to refuse to accept it and spent their careers wriggling away from it, keeping hope alive that they would be able to once again return to the status quo of a universe without a beginning. For them the expanding universe theory was a fad, and they would show it to be so. They called their idea of a static and eternal universe the "Steady State Theory." Chief among its proponents was Fred Hoyle, who was so disdainful of the idea that the universe had exploded into being that in a 1949 BBC interview he sneeringly described this

---

[1] Dennis Overbye, *Lonely Hearts of the Cosmos: The Story of the Scientific Quest for the Secret of the Universe* (New York: Back Bay Books, 1999), 123–24.

A staunch proponent of the "Steady State" model, Sir Fred Hoyle inadvertently coined the term "Big Bang," and later teamed with Chandra Wickramsinghe (center) in proposing the so-called Panspermia theory. They are pictured here with Dr. Lee Spetner (right) in denouncing the Archaeopteryx fossil as a forgery.

ridiculous idea as "the Big Bang." But this blown raspberry backfired quite badly, and anyone referencing the unpalatable theory from that day forward referred to it as "the Big Bang," thereby taping this phrase—like some everlasting "kick me" sign—to poor Hoyle's back.

By the mid-sixties, however, all wiggle room on the issue would vanish. The end of the controversy began when a Princeton physicist named Bob Dicke got to thinking that perhaps there was actual evidence of the Big Bang that could be discovered and shown as incontrovertible proof that it had happened. He knew that extremely early on—very soon after the Big Bang itself—the universe had been an expanding fireball of inconceivable heat. So the question was: To where had all that heat escaped? Of course it had dissipated, but it could only have dissipated as far as the universe extended, which the Big Bang model said was certainly not forever. If our universe really were a finite, closed system, all that heat would still be around, trapped. And if it had dissipated evenly, it should be measurable, even if the level of heat was now exceedingly small. Dicke calculated that the very early universe must have been about a billion degrees, which would have produced high-energy gamma rays. If that were true, these gamma rays would still exist all these billions of years later, probably now as radio waves. It stood to reason.

But could they be detected? Could that heat from the Big Bang fireball—now literally scattered across the entire universe—somehow be measured? If those billion degrees of heat were once contained in a universe that was extremely small, but were now scattered throughout our impossibly large universe, they wouldn't be much, but they wouldn't be nothing. Could we find them?

Dicke spoke about the possibility of detecting this remaining "background radiation" to two of his graduate students, who promptly built an apparatus to do just that. But rather bizarrely, just a few miles away at Bell Labs in Holmdel, New Jersey, another pair of radio astronomers had already detected what Dicke's graduate students were looking for, only they didn't know it. Their names were Arno Penzias and Robert Wilson, and all they knew was that there was always an annoying and mysterious hiss coming from the radio antenna they were calibrating for their own research. They desperately wanted to get rid of it and were having conniptions trying to discover its source. It was present every minute both day and night and was absolutely everywhere they pointed their antenna. Other folks at Bell Labs had been having this same hissing problem for years. It was a gremlin in the system they had learned to ignore. But for the work these two young men were doing, it had to be eliminated.

So first they completely disassembled and reassembled the electronics of their antenna. But the hissing was still there. Could it be pigeons? They shoveled away the pigeon droppings that had aggregated on their equipment and shooed away the birds. But the hissing remained. Then they taped over some loose rivets that might be causing the problem. But the infernal hissing kept on hissing. There was no getting rid of it.

These two young men eventually read the paper postulating the existence of the background radiation and realized that what they were trying to get rid of was that background radiation—exactly what Dicke's grad students were looking for. They knew it was coming from beyond our galaxy, but not from any particular source. Because it was coming from everywhere. Literally. It was those billion degrees of heat dissipated over 13.8 billion years, so that it now measured just 2.7

degrees Kelvin. And since Penzias and Wilson hadn't been able to get rid of it—and never would be—they were happily able to parlay their discovery of it into a Nobel Prize. Because they had done it: they had discovered actual proof of the Big Bang. After this, anyone clinging to the idea that the universe had no beginning was instantly transformed into a dinosaur. There was no way around it, and no going back: The Big Bang happened. The subject—and the universe—was closed.

Once the consensus had shifted, those who couldn't believe the universe had a beginning found it virtually impossible to explain themselves, and most except for Fred Hoyle ceased trying. But the picture would get worse still. In the 1990s, NASA's COBE satellite detected this "microwave background radiation" with such extraordinary precision that we were finally able to see that the explosion from the Big Bang was not perfectly uniform, but contained just enough "lumpiness"—for lack of a better word—to create aggregates of matter in the form of stars and planets and other objects in outer space. It was a stunning confirmation not merely of the background radiation, but of how exactly we could understand it and the early universe after the Big Bang. The work was sufficient to get the team who worked on it—George Smoot and John Mather—their own Nobel Prize. After that, any chumps still holding a torch for Miss Steady State Universe generally kept it to themselves.

So the strange story is that physics eventually proved that the laws of physics had not always existed, nor had the universe in which they manifested themselves. Evidently there really was a point—literally—beyond which science could not go. For materialists for whom science was everything, it seemed a cruel and quirky betrayal. Science, and the universe science existed to measure and observe, could themselves be observed at that curious and mystifying point 13.8 billion years ago to disappear. At the beginning of time. And space. In the beginning.

As for Allan Sandage, he was never tempted toward materialism and its scientistic constrictions.[2] He was open to whatever was true, to wherever the

---

[2] The term "scientism" refers to the materialist philosophy that says that outside science, there can be no knowledge.

facts led, even if it was beyond his scientific system, which is to say he was a true scientist, unafraid of following where science might lead, even if that was beyond itself. If there were truths beyond his telescope's reach, what of it?

But what had become the biggest question for Sandage was not whether the universe had begun with a bang. He knew that it had. And he knew exactly where it had come from: nowhere. And he knew how it had gotten here—which was somewhere—from there, which was not. The question for him now was simply: Where was it going? Now that it had expanded from nothing to what it is presently, would it keep expanding forever into the infinite future? Or would it at some future moment cease expanding and then fall backward into itself, like a ball that is thrown high but eventually slows to an instant of stasis where gravity overtakes its upward momentum, and then falls back down the way it came, decreasing in size and eventually collapsing into the greatest black hole imaginable? And if that, then what?

Sandage wasn't sure what he would find, but he had no dog in the fight, so to speak. He was simply scientifically curious and fascinated to know what could be known. But he sensed God in the details of it all, just as he did in other marvels. In a conversation in the mid-seventies he said:

> To think the universe happened only once. That makes it even
> more mysterious, in a sense. [What happened before the first
> microsecond...is outside the realm of science.]... But it is no more
> mysterious than noting the tremendous complexity of the comical
> balance of the human body. You cut yourself—and why is it the
> white corpuscles know exactly where to go to close the wound?
> That's a miracle. And I don't believe that's due to progressive selec-
> tion of the fittest. It's just too fine a mechanism. I don't know what
> I'm saying now, I don't know what the next sentence is.... I don't
> mean that points to the existence of God, whatever that means.
> Newton's laws are God, in a sense. But I find it all so rational and
> so amazingly beautiful and so mysterious.[3]

---

[3] Overbye, *Lonely Hearts of the Cosmos*, 185.

Overbye's book makes clear that Sandage was one of those rare figures self-confident enough to be open-minded, not to cling to any preconceived notions concerning the nature of reality, or even the limits of science. He was what we must call a genuinely free thinker, with enough stature in the scientific community not to fear what others might think. Overbye says Sandage thought about these things without worrying whether his thoughts were scientific or philosophical or theological. He was a scientist unconstrained by the restrictions of what had become a kind of scientific dogma, although that dogma was not at all scientific, but was rather simply philosophical bias. Sandage felt that "the world was too magical to be an accident, although in his milder moments he admitted that he didn't know enough about evolution to be shooting his mouth off." Actually, he did. But he was too humble to provoke those on the other side of this divide, and not willing to spend much time arguing about it either. He had other fish to fry. But he couldn't stop his mind—and sometimes his mouth—from going whither it listed. That was the joy of thinking, wasn't it, and wasn't that connected to the deepest ideas of science and life? Why should anyone constrict that?

Overbye remembers a lunch in 1975, when Sandage was ruminating on the possibility of God. A nearby couple asked if they might join the conversation. The man was a minister and thought Sandage must be, too. Sandage was thrilled. Two years later he said:

> I don't know what I would call myself. If you believe anything of the hard science of cosmology, there was an event that happened that can be age-dated back in the past.... Just the very fact that science [can make] that statement, that cosmology can understand the universe at a much earlier state and it did emerge from a state that was fundamentally different. Now that's an act of creation. Within the realm of science one cannot say any more detail about that creation than the First Book of Genesis.[4]

---

4 Ibid.

Clearly his mind was groping its way forward at that time. "I think that the whole rationality of the universe is a mystery," he said. "The fact that Newton's and Einstein's equations work is one of the world's great mysteries. And in that sense I'm very religious."[5]

But around 1980 Sandage seems to have been sufficiently persuaded by what he understood to become a Christian, though not quite publicly. But he was obviously fed up with the academic posturing, and with the affectation that had become common in his field in which scientists drifted beyond the clouds to a vaunted realm in which only they knew what they were saying as they discussed their arcane, *entres nous* theories on the nature of the universe and reality while seeming to have forgotten the simple childlike questions many scientists had started with in the first place.

In a conversation with Overbye, Sandage mocked some of the trendy theories and terminology in vogue at the time, which to him made no real sense and had no purchase in reality.

> "What is a superstring?" [he asked.] "... what is the nature of nothing? Does that statement [make] any sense, or is it gobbledy-gook? The nature of nothing. What they say seems to be absolutely nonsense. They say the universe could create itself out of nothing, a self-causing entity, because they say you could do it with zero energy.... Well, that's just using words to convince themselves they can earn a living...."[6]

Then with typical graciousness he said that statement was unfair—but of course it certainly wasn't unfair, even slightly. It was a legitimate question. "I can talk the same language but I don't understand the words, and the more I read [the journal] *Nature* and these popular books and [attend certain] conferences, I can talk the language better year by year. But I understand less and less of the thing. It's fascinating, but I don't think it gets down to the nub. I

---

[5] Ibid.

[6] Ibid.

think it's a philosophical leap that can't be made, that there's an edge to science beyond which the questions of *why* are outside the realm of science." He continued in the same vein, asking Overbye:

> Do you believe in grand unification theories? Why? Because everyone you respect tells you to. You are seduced by its beauty. And because it is so beautiful, it has to be true.... Why do you believe that's true any more than the existence of God, which is also a beautiful theory and also explains a great deal? It's a hypothesis that is checkable in its consequences.... Yet you would reject that beautiful hypothesis.[7]

As we said earlier, it was at that 1985 conference that this grand old man of astronomy and the heir to the great Edwin Hubble would come out of the closet as that rarest of rare creatures: the top scientist in his field who was willing to acknowledge publicly his belief in God—and not merely in God, but in the God of the Bible.

Although Stephen Meyer was then just a young geophysicist working for an oil company, the conference and Sandage so affected him that he was never the same, afterward going to Cambridge to study philosophy and the history of science, and then going on to write numerous books on the very questions Sandage raised that day. In *Return of the God Hypothesis*, Meyer recalls goggling at the scientific luminaries assembled. The philosopher Antony Flew, then arguably the world's most prominent atheist, was there, as were other atheists and agnostics. Also there were the Harvard astrophysicist Owen Gingerich, who was openly a Christian, as was the biophysicist Dean Kenyon. Donald Goldsmith was there, the man who had served Carl Sagan as principal science adviser on the *Cosmos* TV series in which a materialistic worldview had been declared and popularized to Western culture.

The young Meyer remembers his astonishment at seeing Hubble's heir publicly acknowledging that his science had carried him beyond the atheism and agnosticism of many of his peers. Meyer also recalls that in his talk on the

---

[7] Ibid.

Big Bang, Sandage "shocked many of his colleagues by announcing a recent religious conversion and then explaining how the scientific evidence of a 'creation event' had contributed to a profound change in his worldview."

Meyer remembers that Sandage looked at the audience intensely as he spoke. "What has happened in the last fifty years," he said, "is a remarkable event within astronomy and astrophysics. By looking up at the sky, some astronomers have come to the belief that there is evidence for a 'creation event.'" Meyer was impressed with Sandage's candor and took furious notes of what he said, including the following:

Dr. Stephen C. Meyer

Courtesy of Stephen C. Meyer

> I now have to go from a stance as a complete materialistic rational scientist and say this super natural event, to me, gives at least some credence to my belief that there is some design put in the universe.... I am convinced that there is some order in the universe. I think all scientists, at the deepest level, are so startled by what they see in the miraculousness of the inner connection of things in their field ... that they at least have wondered why it is this way.[8]

Sandage was careful to say there were still questions and that of course science could not "prove" God, but he hardly shrank from the clear implications of what science had learned from the skies and was quite willing to side with the God whose handiwork he saw in them, and perhaps had seen with greater intensity—and magnification—than anyone in the world.

Robert Jastrow of the Goddard Institute was on the stage that day too, and although an agnostic Jew, he did not lean away from the clear implications of what he was watching. In the famous conclusion to his book *God and the*

---

[8] Stephen Meyer, *Return of the God Hypothesis* (San Francisco, California: HarperOne, 2021), 108.

Astronomers, Jastrow puts it memorably well, so much so that what he said may serve as a fitting end to our discussion.

> [The discovery of a definite cosmic beginning] is an exceedingly strange development, unexpected by all but the theologians. They have always accepted the word of the Bible: In the beginning God created heaven and earth.... It is unexpected because science has had such extraordinary success in trying the chain of cause and effect backward in time. For the scientist who has lived by his faith in the power of reason, the story ends like a bad dream. He has scaled the mountains of ignorance; he is about to conquer the highest peak; as he pulls himself over the final rock, he is greeted by a band of theologians who have been sitting there for centuries.[9]

---

[9] Robert Jastrow, *God and the Astronomers* (London, United Kingdom: Readers Library, 2017).

CHAPTER THREE

The Fine-Tuned Planet

The most famous atheist in the world was riding in the back of a car. Suddenly, someone from the front seat put a camera in his face and asked him which argument was the best from the "other" side—meaning the side that argued *for* the existence of God.

In the course of his fortune-gathering series of "debates" with rabbis, priests, ministers, lay believers, and imams, Christopher Hitchens had heard them all. So what *was* the best argument from the other side? Would he say? Could he admit there was any argument on that side worth dignifying? Hitchens was very rarely anything other than a forensics bully, never conceding a grain to the other side of the scale, even when he knew the truth was otherwise. For him the affair was less about finding the truth than humiliating his opponent at any cost, evidently believing the audience wouldn't know the difference.

But it so happened in this unique case—for reasons we may never know—that he answered quickly and honestly. "It is the fine-tuned argument," he said. "The fine-tuning, that one degree, well, one degree, one hair [of difference]...even though it doesn't prove design, doesn't prove a Designer.... You have to spend time thinking about it, working on it. It's not a trivial [argument]. We all say that."

This was a rather dramatic concession from the self-styled *enfant terrible*-turned-snarly-curmudgeon who generally conceded nothing, lest it give comfort to the scoundrels who dared take the other side of the debate over whether God exists. When he said "We all say that," Hitchens meant the three others—Richard Dawkins, Daniel Dennett, and Sam Harris—who had come to be known as "The Four Horsemen of the New Atheism" for their bitter spate of angry books and appearances in which they savaged religious people of all kinds, never bothering to distinguish between Torquemada and the 9/11 hijackers on the one hand and Saint Francis and Dietrich Bonhoeffer on the other. These celebrated proponents of the "New Atheism" had heard many arguments against their view, but Hitchens said it was this one—the argument of a "fine-tuned" universe—that they all thought the best.

Hitchens was adamantly opposed to those backward religionists he loved to demonize as the embodiment of evil—although ostensibly he didn't believe in evil. No matter. It suited him at the moment. But for some reason he seemed to have let this cat out of the bag. The fact that he said his colleagues also felt this way is still more significant, because many of them have publicly averred the opposite, denouncing the argument as idiocy. But here on camera Hitchens made plain that all of them felt as he did. And how could they not? Anyone hearing the argument for the first time is knocked backwards by it, usually wondering how it could be that they hadn't heard it before.

But what exactly is the fine-tuned argument?

It is simply that there are certain things about our universe—and about our planet—that seem to be so extremely perfectly calibrated that they can hardly be coincidental. If these things were even slightly different, life would not even be possible. One classic example has to do with the size of Earth, which just happens to be exactly what it needs to be in order for life to exist here. Of course most of us cannot imagine that the size of our planet would have any bearing on whether life could exist here, but as it happens, we are perfectly mistaken. One rarely hears about this, but it is established fact: If our planet were smaller or larger by even the smallest of margins, life here could not exist. When we see how many things must be just *so*—and then just *happen* to be just so—we cannot help but wonder if perhaps mere coincidence isn't enough to account for it.

Most of this fine-tuning also involves what is described as the "Goldilocks Principle," meaning that there are actually two directions in which things can go wrong—or they can be "just right," as Goldilocks deemed the bed and chair and bowl of porridge she settled on after rejecting the other choices. As with the story of the Three Bears, we find that on Earth and in this universe, things could be too this or too that—too hard or too soft, too big or too small, too hot or too cold—but in every case it just so happens that they are "just right" for life. The size of our Earth is but one of innumerable—and ever-increasing—examples.

That is what is especially remarkable about the "fine-tuning argument": the more time passes, the stronger it gets, because science discovers more and more examples of it. So it is one thing to say, as the scientist Carl Sagan did, that there are two parameters necessary for life, and Earth just happens to meet both of them. It would be the same if there were five necessary parameters or ten. We still might be able to see Earth's having met these parameters as a matter of simple good luck. But as the decades have passed and science has uncovered scores and scores and then hundreds of such examples of perfect fine-tuning, the odds become far too astronomical to dismiss as luck or coincidence. The overwhelming impression is that the burgeoning welter of perfect coincidences has mounted to a level impossibly beyond anything we can put down to coincidence, so that even the most hostile atheist must at least wonder whether it is all precisely as it is precisely because it was intentionally designed to be that way.

Why Haven't We Heard This Before?

Most people have never heard about any of this. There are two main reasons for that. The first is that it cuts against the narrative that the

Darwin four years before *On the Origin of Species*.

scientific establishment has been pushing with all its might and main roughly since Darwin. The fine-tuning argument is that the universe and the planet on which we all live did not come into existence by accident but were deliberately and intentionally created. This idea, like the discomfiting idea of a universe with a beginning, is very embarrassing to anyone wed to a strictly materialistic account of things. And as we say, it is the more embarrassing because the constant stream of scientific discoveries makes it stronger over time. That science is the principal engine driving this can come across as a particularly stinging irony for anyone wedded to that old atheistic narrative.

And what a strange reversal of fortune it seems. Far from the idea that science and faith are enemies, or that science is increasingly pushing back any need we have for God, we discover that the forward march of science is instead pushing back the argument *against* God. It is an upending of the idea that people of faith worship a "God-of-the-gaps" who is increasingly irrelevant as science fills in those gaps. On the contrary, as science progresses we see that the God-of-the-gaps is actually a creation of the atheists, and the Creator God of the Bible is a God whose existence is increasingly bolstered by science. The idea that people of faith cling to God to avoid science has been replaced with the idea that atheists cling to their invented God-of-the-gaps idea to avoid the real God who created the universe that science is discovering, and whose existence is increasingly undeniable because of those very discoveries. In a way it seems that in flaunting this invented God-of-the-gaps, atheists have projected their own insecurities onto people of faith and have used their God-of-the-gaps idea as a crutch for themselves, who were too insecure—and perhaps too prideful—to accommodate the possibility of a real God whose existence is revealed by scientific discoveries.

But another reason most of us have not heard the fine-tuned argument is simply that evidence for it has been piling up incrementally over the decades, and there was never any single moment when it was suddenly known. The strength of it has grown quietly. But it has piled up so much in the last decades that now some atheists have felt the need to address it, albeit without very much gusto, so that simply avoiding it is usually the preferred tack.

So What Is the "Fine-Tuning" Argument?

Once upon a time it was possible to believe that life could exist anywhere in the universe, and we assumed that life probably existed on many planets. That's because we believed that the conditions for life were not difficult to meet. And since there were so many stars and planets, it only followed logically that there must be plenty of life out there. In fact, in the year *Time* published its famous cover story, the astronomer Carl Sagan said there were only two criteria required for life to exist on any given planet. One was having a star something like our sun, and the other was being the right distance from that star. Since those two conditions were so easy to meet, there must be literally billions of planets in the universe that could support life. Given this now very primitive understanding of how easily life could emerge from non-life in such places, Sagan confidently calculated that there should be innumerable planets with life. This kind of thinking—coupled with *Star Trek* on TV every week—led to the widespread idea that a colorful variety of life existed throughout the universe. And it was only a matter of time before we found it. Or it us.

NASA/JPL

Carl Sagan

Not long after Sagan made his bold pronouncement, however, subsequent scientific discoveries made it increasingly untrue. The more science learned about the conditions necessary for life, the more it found new criteria that were just as vital as the two Sagan had mentioned. Eventually there were dozens, and the more science learned the more there were. So of course the probability of life in the universe plummeted drastically from billions of planets "probably" having life down to millions and then to thousands. Every time another condition was discovered that was necessary for life, it mathematically reduced the number of planets down until the conditions mounted so high that the number of planets that might support life was winnowed to almost nothing. Eventually, the conditions science reckoned necessary for life had risen so high that the idea that life existed anywhere at all—as it obviously did on our planet—seemed more and more miraculous, and then even outlandish. It didn't make sense that we existed. And yet here we are. What to make of it? It seemed that the only rational answer for our existence was that everything in the universe had been intentionally designed so that life here could exist.

So that was the fine-tuned argument, and whenever folks like Hitchens bumped into it, they knew there was little they had to say against it. So they began to migrate toward far-fetched scenarios, like the existence of an infinity of universes—despite there being no evidence for that—and saying that one of them probably just happened to have all the right conditions for life. And of course by further happy coincidence we happened to be living in that universe. Lucky we! The unscientific nature of this idea seemed no barrier to embracing it, because the idea of a world fine-tuned by some Creator was simply too unpleasant to consider, so that the New Atheists had fled into that realm of pseudo-philosophy we call wishful thinking.

As we have mentioned, evidence for extreme fine-tuning increases as science advances. The "Fine-Tuning Argument" is also often called "The Anthropic Principle," because *anthropos* is the Greek word for "human being," and these strangely perfect calibrations create the perfect environment for human life.

As we talk about fine-tuning, we should clarify that there are two principal ways in which things appear to be fine-tuned. The first concerns the universe itself, meaning that vast everything that emerged from nothing into something 13.8 billion years ago. The second concerns our planet specifically, which came into being roughly 4.5 billion years ago.

The Size of Earth

We've all grown up being exposed endlessly to science fiction TV programs and movies assuming that life exists throughout the universe on all kinds of planets. So it would never dawn on us that the size of our planet could have anything to do with whether life could exist. We might accept that a planet's size could affect what kind of life emerged, but how could it affect the existence of life itself? As I mentioned earlier, in the 1960s (and then through the ensuing decades, through the magic of reruns), the actors William Shatner and Leonard Nimoy—in their guises as Captain James Tiberius Kirk and Mr. Spock—rocketed through the universe to a new planet each week, encountering varying types of life, although most of them were curiously anthropomorphic. But the idea of life everywhere in the universe has been part of the zeitgeist of our time. Based on this idea the Search for Extraterrestrial Intelligence (SETI) project was launched, scanning the universe for radio messages from distant civilizations. Nothing was ever found, but scientists kept trying. Of course we now know that the premise was extremely optimistic, and as time passes such efforts come across as willful naivete, because we can now see that far too many things need to be "just so" for any planetary environment to be friendly to life.

One of the simplest examples of this has to do with the size of our planet. We now know if our own Earth were any bigger or smaller, life here could not exist. This is only one of the parameters we have discovered as necessary for life, but it's a good place to begin.

The first question must be why the size of a planet would have anything to do with whether life could flourish, and the first and simplest

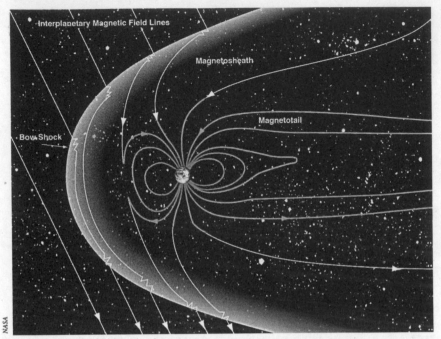

Structure of the Earth's magnetosphere.

answer has to do with our magnetic field. Who ever thinks about Earth's magnetic field? But it happens nonetheless to be magnificently important in many ways. If Earth were any smaller, our magnetic field would be weaker, and what we call the "solar wind" would quickly strip our atmosphere down to almost nothing, so that we would end up like Mars, which is of course a lifeless world. And who thinks about the solar wind? But if we did, we would realize that it is a stream of charged particles—"ion gas" or plasma—made up of electrons, protons, and some alpha rays blasted toward us every moment from the sun. But because of the size of our planet, our "magnetosphere" is just powerful enough to protect us from that radiation. The magnetospheres of the gigantic planets Jupiter and Saturn are also very powerful. And just as happens here on Earth, their magnetospheres deflect the solar wind so that it travels mostly around them instead of to their surfaces. Here on Earth, the solar winds would have long ago stripped away our hydrogen and oxygen, which of course make up water, which could hardly be more important. Mars is not much smaller than Earth, but it is just small enough that its magnetosphere cannot protect it, and as we have said, most of its atmosphere was stripped away eons ago. This is just one aspect of the fine-tuning of Earth's environment, illustrating how little it would take for life here to be impossible. But it's a fact that if Earth were slightly smaller, there could be no life here.

But if Earth were any larger, we would have other life-killing problems. In their book *The Privileged Planet*, authors Guillermo Gonzalez and Jay Richards explain that a larger Earth would have more powerful gravity, so that no water or methane or carbon dioxide could escape our atmosphere, which would be so thick we couldn't breathe. Our air would be more "viscous." According to Gonzalez and Richards: "Earth may be almost as big as a terrestrial planet can get." Again, who would ever think that the size of our planet would be so precisely and perfectly calibrated for life? That if it were even slightly smaller or larger there could be no life whatsoever? But the more science learns, the more we see that the science fiction scenarios we have grown up with are hopelessly out of date and have confused us into believing that the conditions for life on any given planet can vary dramatically. But now we know that they cannot.

Running Asteroid Interference

We venture into the sublime madness of water in a subsequent chapter, and if ever there were something we took for granted, that would be it. But before that, let's simply acknowledge the uncontroversial fact that water is inescapably central to life on Earth. But because of this, several things must also be very precisely just so. For example, if we were even slightly closer to the sun, most of our water would have evaporated, and life couldn't exist. By the same token, if we were slightly farther away, all water would have frozen, also making life untenable. As we have said, even Carl Sagan in 1966 knew our distance from the sun was dispositive. It is one of the easier things for us to understand about fine-tuning.

But whoever would have dreamt that the presence in our solar system of the so-called "gas giants," Jupiter and Saturn, was just as crucial? After all, why should these colossally large and very distant planets have any bearing on whether life here could exist? And yet we now know that is the case, and it's one more thing we didn't know back when Carl Sagan was making his overconfident predictions. It turns out that Jupiter and Saturn—like planetary linebackers—run interference for us. In other words, if they weren't where they are, our planet would endlessly be pelted with meteorites and asteroids. Perhaps a thousand times as many would make it to our surface. Can any of us imagine spending our lives gazing upward in fear? Actually, we wouldn't ever have come into being, so it's a moot point. But now we know that it's only the tremendous mass and gravity of these two monstrously large planets that protects us, because they pull most of these speeding objects away from us—either by simply deflecting them into outer space or actually absorbing them into themselves. So life on Earth without them simply would not even be possible. Have you ever heard this before? And now that we know this is what science has taught us, we must wonder: Is it merely a happy coincidence that they are there? Or is it possible that our existence here was intended all along, and these titanic planets were intentionally put where they are?

In case anyone is not convinced that endless flights of asteroidal missiles hitting Earth would affect the conditions needed for life, we should recall the asteroid that hit Earth sixty-six million years ago, kicking up so much dust that our atmosphere didn't let light in for the longest time, killing off much plant life, not to mention 75 percent of all animal life on the planet, including all the dinosaurs. But imagine: That single asteroid was just seven miles in diameter, and Earth is eight thousand miles in diameter. It's hard to think something so comparatively small could have such a far-reaching effect. But of course it did. So we can also imagine that if something like this were happening more often, life here would never have had any real chance of beginning at all. We didn't understand until 1980 that it was that asteroid that killed off the dinosaurs, but once again, the more science reveals, the more extraordinary our existence seems.

Since we are on the subject, we should mention the 1908 Tunguska event, when an asteroid only three hundred feet in diameter—inexpressibly tiny in comparison to our planet—exploded above an uninhabited region in Siberia. When it did, it instantly flattened *eighty million trees* and caused so much atmospheric disturbance that the effects were noticed as far as London. Can we imagine if such things happened constantly? We should try, because without Jupiter and Saturn, we know now that it would be happening. So it's a fact: If Jupiter and Saturn weren't there, we wouldn't be here.

The Moon

Most of us don't think much about what the Moon is doing where it is, or whether it might have any serious effect on life here. In fact, if there were a list of things we take mostly for granted—like the blue color of the sky or the air we breathe or the ubiquity of water—the moon would have to be near the top. After all, there it is and always has been, quietly reflecting the sun's light, and waxing and waning so wonderfully calendrically that we have used it to mark time forever, just as we have used our own orbit around the sun and have used Earth's own revolution around its axis to do the same. The Bible poetically calls the moon "the silent witness in the sky." There it is and always has been.

But who among us knows its presence is crucial to life on Earth, or knows how it got there? Science only recently came to where it finally understands how the moon came into being, and to see that the details of its size and proximity to Earth are inescapably central to our existence. For example, we now know that if the moon were slightly smaller or larger, life here couldn't exist. But before we go into that and other things, let's look into how our moon came into being.

How the Moon Was Formed

When I was growing up, no one knew how the moon had come into being. There were theories, but not until the six Apollo missions from

1969 through 1972 did we have enough facts to begin to grope our way toward an answer. Well into the 1980s and beyond, most of us had heard that the moon came to us from another distant galaxy, that as it swept close to us the gravity of Earth ensnared it—and it's been with us ever since. Another theory was that it was created when Earth was created. But neither is the case. What actually happened—which we only know because of recent science—is undeniably more interesting and far more amazing than any previous theory.

First of all, about 4.5 billion years ago the planet that eventually became Earth was very different from what it is now. To be accurate, it wasn't yet Earth. Most of us haven't heard about this because it was only recently understood. But the planet that became Earth was actually smaller than Earth. So it was a kind of proto-Earth that scientists usually refer to as Theia. But one day a few million years after the formation of this proto-Earth, something happened: A Mars-sized object just *happened* to hit Theia at *just* the perfect angle and at *just* the perfect speed. The object that collided with the proto-Earth also had precisely the right composition. This all happened very shortly after the formation of our solar system, and shortly after the formation of the proto-Earth as part of the solar system. But we know that if it had not happened—and happened precisely as it happened in every detail—we would not be here. It is another inescapably amazing "coincidence" to consider.

So what happened? As we have said it was the mysteriously perfect collision of two planet-sized spheres hurtling through infinity for millions and millions of years. Space is unimaginably vast, and the spaces between planets and stars are much greater than we can imagine. So it's not as if collisions between monumentally huge objects happen often. To say they do not is an astronomical understatement. Planets and stars are usually so far away from each other that whole galaxies can pass through each other with no collisions. So what happened when this Mars-sized sphere hit the proto-Earth was an exceedingly rare event. But more importantly, it was so precisely perfect in every way that the planet that emerged from the collision was extremely different from what it had been before as the smaller proto-Earth called Theia. And after the collision it just happened to have everything necessary to support life. So we know that if the angle of the collision had been different, or if the speed of the collision had been different, we would not be here. We also know that if the planet-sized object that collided with the planet that became Earth had been different in size or composition, we would not be here.

This is not science fiction. It is what science has rather recently come to understand. It seems miraculous, no matter what one's view of the situation is. But science is not in the business of proclaiming anything miraculous, even if something seems miraculous. Science is simply in the business of finding out what happened. But science now knows enough to say that if any details of what happened had been even slightly different, we could not be here now. So what *did* happen? Many things.

First, as a result of this inconceivably powerful collision, the super thick atmosphere of the proto-Earth—Theia—exploded off into outer space, never to return. So the new planet—what we today call home—suddenly had a much, much thinner atmosphere. We know that the atmosphere on the proto-Earth was forty to a hundred times denser than the atmosphere afterward, and breathing it would have been like trying to breathe sand. So because of this extremely perfect collision, our planet instantly had a new atmosphere, one thin enough for sunlight to penetrate so that plants could grow, and thin enough for us to breathe as we are doing this very second. It is hard not to think that the whole thing was pre-planned, because it is so strangely perfect, but all science can tell us is that it happened.

As a result of this perfect collision, another entirely necessary thing happened. The Mars-sized object hit the proto-Earth so hard that most of the Mars-sized object actually became part of the proto-Earth, increasing that proto-Earth to the size of Earth today. But science now knows that the mass that was added in this collision was absolutely crucial. For example, as we have said, we were previously too small to have a magnetic field able to protect our atmosphere from the solar wind.

The part of the Mars-sized object that did not become part of the new object we now call Earth exploded away into outer space, and then congealed to form the moon. We can think of it as something like an unimaginably perfect billiard shot executed on a table light-years in length. And the shot itself was so inconceivably powerful that the two similarly sized balls did not bounce off each other but rather became part of each other, instantly creating a single larger ball—and ejecting enough mass to form a second ball about a quarter the size of the other. The large one was of course Earth and the smaller one our moon. What could be stranger? Yet if it had not happened *precisely* as it did, science tells us that we would not be here.

There's more that resulted from this collision that is also centrally important to the possibility of life on Earth. For example, the moon that emerged from this collision was precisely the size necessary for life to emerge and flourish on the newly formed Earth. To be clear, the size of our moon is outrageously large when compared to other moons in our solar system. But anything at all smaller would not have been sufficient to stabilize the wobble of our axis, as it has done ever since and is doing now. But science tells us that the moon's stabilization of our axis is another unavoidable prerequisite for an environment where life could exist. For example, it enables us to have just the right seasonal variation, with seasons mild enough that the temperature does not fluctuate wildly, which would make life impossible. So this perfect collision just happened to happen, and the size of Earth and the size of the moon and the atmosphere and the axis of Earth were all magically and perfectly and suddenly established, so that we could eventually live here as we now do.

But because it is only recently that science has settled on all of this, most of us simply haven't heard about it. Now that we do know it, however, we can add this breathtakingly perfect collision to the list of what appear to be outrageous coincidences. It is all really far too baffling to understate or to fully understand, but this is what science has come to know.

A Moon among Moons

Now that we know how it was created, we can focus on the moon itself and the crucial role it plays in enabling life on Earth. Let's first rehearse some basic lunar facts. For starters, our moon is extremely large compared to other moons in our solar system. Our moon is 27 percent the size of the Earth, which is dramatically greater than the relative size of any other moons in our whole solar system. And precisely because of its size, as we have said, it has a vital steadying effect on our planet, making us wobble very little on our axis, and giving us vitally stable climates. But our moon is so large that it also has enough gravity to cause our oceans' tides, which are also crucial to the ecosystems of our coasts, which are themselves vital to the rest of life on the planet. This is only the science of the matter, but we cannot be blamed for being astonished, for who among us has ever dreamt that the details of our moon could be absolutely crucial to life on Earth?

To appreciate just how odd our moon is, we have to take a look at the other planets. But even before we talk about its size, the simple fact that we have only one moon is another striking anomaly. Again, this is likely something we assume, as though it's merely normal, but it is very far from normal. Earth is the only planet in our entire solar system with one moon, and no other planet has one that can compare to the huge size of ours, relatively speaking. There is nothing in our solar system to compare with it.

For example, Mercury and Venus have no moons at all, and Mars has two, although they are so comically tiny it almost seems wrong to call them moons. Our moon's diameter is two thousand miles, while Mars's two "moons" are fourteen and eight miles across respectively. Then we come to the gigantic planets of Jupiter and Saturn, which have so many moons that we literally can no longer count them. Jupiter has roughly seventy-nine moons in a tremendously wide variety of sizes, and at some point they are so small we can't really classify them as moons, so we stop counting. But even the largest of these, Ganymede, is extremely tiny when compared to Jupiter. Jupiter's diameter is eleven times that of Earth—so roughly ninety thousand miles across—but Ganymede is just three thousand miles across. So compared to even the largest moons in our solar system, ours is dramatically large. After Jupiter there is ringed Saturn, with roughly eighty-two moons; and then Uranus, with twenty-seven; and then Neptune, with fourteen. Now is not the time to argue whether the next planet is a planet, but whatever Pluto is, we can settle on the fact that it has five moons. So once again, nothing in our solar system can compare to our moon in its being singularly huge—and also in being singularly single, the only moon in Earth's orbit, which is of course why we simply call it "the moon."

Right on the Eclipses

Like many things we are discussing, most of us haven't given eclipses very much thought. They happen. What of it? Previous generations did not take them so much for granted. Perhaps you've read the novels by Mark Twain or H. Rider Haggard in which the sophisticated protagonist in a hostile land uses an almanac to predict an eclipse to astonish the natives, who had been threatening violence. Perhaps you saw an episode of *Gilligan's Island* with the same plot. But did you know that these fictional versions took the idea from an actual event in 1504?

Christopher Columbus was that year stranded on the island we now call Jamaica. The natives were gracious hosts, feeding Columbus and his crew. But six months discovered the limit of their hospitality. They would no longer part with their own food to help these strangers. Columbus realized his men would die of starvation. That's when the resourceful Genoan consulted an almanac, observing that a dramatic lunar eclipse would soon take place. So he warned the natives that if they stopped feeding his starving men, the moon would show its great anger with them. Of course the lunar eclipse took place exactly as predicted, and Columbus's crew got their food and lived to tell the story.

But as we have said, most of us either take eclipses mostly for granted, or at least are not appropriately stunned at how strange it is that they occur as they do. I'm speaking especially of what we call "total eclipses," in which the moon comes between the sun and Earth, or Earth comes between the sun and the moon. These events are dramatically more amazing than most of us realize. As ever, one must know the facts for proper context and appreciation, so here they are.

The distance from Earth to the sun is roughly 93 million miles, and the distance from Earth to the moon is roughly 240,000 miles. Therefore the distance from Earth to the sun is almost exactly 400 times the distance from Earth to the moon. You can do the math and see. But here is where it gets genuinely mystifying. The diameter of the sun is 865,370 miles, and the diameter of the moon is 2,159 miles. If you do the math, you will see this means the diameter of the sun is almost exactly 400 times the diameter of the moon. Is that a mere coincidence? Because if this is true—and of course it is—it means that these two heavenly bodies will look *precisely the same size* to us here on Earth. Despite the staggering difference in their sizes, from the vantage point of Earth, the sun and moon appear to be the exact same size. Again, this is so anomalous that it cannot be underscored enough, and yet most of us haven't given it a thought. We probably think: *Of course they look the same size. They're the sun and moon. What other sizes should they be?* They are all we have ever known, so we may be forgiven for not having noticed this astonishing phenomenon. But once you think about it, you realize it is impossibly strange that something so absolutely perfect would simply happen.

But there's more to it. Only because of this extremely striking astronomical "coincidence" do we have total eclipses on Earth, in which the disc of one covers the other nearly perfectly. Again, once one sees this, it's challenging not to scratch one's head. How is it that the sun and moon happen to fit over each other so very precisely during these eclipses? Why do they match up as though they were made to do that? When one knows the circumstances and details of all the other planets in our solar system, the whole thing seems even stranger. Nothing close to this happens on any other planet. So if one aspires to be a dedicatedly rational person, one can't help suspect that perhaps this isn't mere coincidence. It just seems too perfect and too strange. But there it is. Who can help but wonder whether these things are not accidental or coincidental? Can it be that this outlandish and happy oddity was actually intended—and just for us?

Still, we might wonder: What exactly is the point of this celestial legerdemain? It seems there are a few reasons. For one thing, without eclipses, we could never know many of the things we do. Eclipses have made it possible to measure and understand things that would have been impossible to discover any other way. In *The Privileged Planet*, Guillermo Gonzalez and Jay Richards say that perfect solar eclipses "are optimal for measuring a range of important phenomena, such as the solar flash spectrum, prominences, starlight deflection, and Earth's rotation." Perhaps the most important thing about them is that they have made it possible for us to know many things about our sun. Because it is so bright, we on Earth cannot see its edge—or corona (Latin for "crown")—at all clearly, except during a solar eclipse. So during eclipses we have learned innumerable things, including how and when the sun throws up solar flares, which can change what is called "space weather" and can affect our satellite transmissions, which we obviously rely on more and more. Even more dramatic are what is called Coronal Mass Ejections (CME), which are so powerful they can blow out transformers right here on Earth. Without total solar eclipses, we could not have discovered them when we did.

In 1868, while observing a solar eclipse in India, a French astronomer and an English physicist even discovered a new element. They saw it in the sun's spectrum during the eclipse and named it helium, after "Helios," the Greek name for the sun. It was not until 1895 that helium was discovered here on Earth. But the most famous example of an experiment involving an eclipse is when in 1919 Sir Arthur Eddington observed that the light from the sun was affected by gravity—just as Einstein predicted in his Theory of Relativity. This suddenly proved with direct observation what had previously been an extremely challenging and much-doubted mathematical theory. But because of an eclipse, Einstein's theory was shown to be correct.

But the relative sizes of the sun and moon as seen by us on Earth touch on the issue of symmetry and beauty. Just as with many things in nature—the aforementioned blue of the sky and the staggering panoply of creation, for example—certain phenomena seem to affect us in a way that points beyond the simple scientific facts. The existence of the sun and moon seems to point to something ineffable, even before we know how extraordinary it is that they appear the same size to us. What is it in each of us that finds them beautiful, and what exactly is beauty? Can it be that they were put there in part for us to marvel at, to draw us out of ourselves as we gaze at them and contemplate our lives and our place in the universe? But that is another story.

Where We Are in the Universe

Before we move from this chapter on the fine-tuning of Earth to our next chapter on the fine-tuning of the entire universe, we should touch on what lies between them. Because the very placement of Earth *within* the universe is an example of fine-tuning. This is probably even harder for us to comprehend than the idea that Jupiter's and Saturn's existence is crucial to our existence. But even the position of our solar system within our galaxy—the Milky Way—is vital to the existence of life here on Earth.

Our solar system is located on the inner edge of the Orion Arm of our galaxy, about twenty-six thousand light-years from the center. Science now understands that this is crucial to life on Earth in several ways. If we were closer to the galaxy's center, the radiation hitting us would be far greater, because there are many more stars in the galaxy's center than out here on the spiral arms where we exist. So at the center there are more "active galactic nucleus outbursts" (AGNs), as well as more supernovae and more gamma ray bursts. That would make life here impossible. We would also be far more likely to be hit by comets, which are more numerous. Gonzalez and Richards call where we are in our solar system the "Galactic Habitable Zone," meaning that it is the ideal location for a planet like ours to form and support life.

But if we were farther out from the center, there would be other problems. Stars farther out are orbited by planets significantly smaller than Earth, so as we have said, that would mean no atmosphere capable of supporting life. Neither would they be able to sustain plate tectonics, which is another element absolutely crucial to life as we know it that we will touch on in Chapter Five. The authors even say that our galaxy is better suited for life than 98 percent of the other galaxies near us. For one thing, it is shaped like a spiral. Stars in elliptical galaxies have less-ordered orbits, like bees flying around a hive, so they are more likely to visit their galaxy's dangerous central regions. They're also more likely to pass through interstellar clouds at disastrously high speeds. So in many ways our galaxy—a late-type, metal-rich, spiral galaxy with orderly orbits and comparatively little danger between spiral arms—just happens to be that rare galaxy perfectly suited for life, and our placement within that galaxy also happens to be perfectly suited for life.

What shall we make of any of this? Science now tells us that all of these varied parameters are not merely helpful for life on Earth, but are inescapably necessary for it? Can we face that our existence looks like nothing less than a mathematical impossibility? It is as though the more clearly we see these things, the more difficult they are to take in.

CHAPTER FOUR

The Fine-Tuned Universe

We have already talked about some of the fine-tuning on Earth, and in our next chapter we continue that conversation. But for now, let's look at the fine-tuning of the universe as a whole. Many of us would never think about such a thing because our universe in its impossible vastness doesn't immediately seem to have any bearing on whether there would be life on our planet. But in keeping with our larger theme, the more science has discovered about the formation of our universe, the more we have come to see that it appears to exhibit design in a host of ways. In fact, the universe as a whole bears evidence of fine tuning that makes the fine-tuning of Earth seem small in comparison.

The conclusion is increasingly strong—and now essentially unavoidable—that if the universe were not precisely as it now is, life on Earth would not exist. In a 2007 *New York Times* op-ed, the popular English physicist Paul Davies wrote:

> Scientists are slowly waking up to an inconvenient truth—the universe looks suspiciously like a fix. The issue concerns the very laws of nature themselves. For 40 years, physicists and

cosmologists have been quietly collecting examples of all too convenient "coincidences" and special features in the underlying laws of the universe that seem to be necessary in order for life, and hence conscious beings, to exist. Change any one of them and the consequences would be lethal.

Paul Davies is not a man of faith, but he is a true scientist, meaning someone who is unafraid to deal with the facts on the table, whether he likes them or doesn't. Scientists have been seeing what Davies writes about for decades, but only the securest among them have been honest enough to say so publicly. Just as anyone is disinclined to advertise unpleasant evidence against their position, scientists predisposed against the implications of fine-tuning have tended to keep quiet. But at diverse times and in diverse places—as with Christopher Hitchens in the back of the car—they sometimes let on that they know all about this, and about how devastating the facts are.

For example, in his widely unread 1988 bestseller *A Brief History of Time*, Stephen Hawking wrote:

> If the overall density of the universe were changed by even 0.0000000000001 percent, no stars or galaxies could be formed. If the rate of expansion one second after the Big Bang had been smaller by even one part in a hundred thousand million million, the universe would have recollapsed before it reached its present size.[1]

Those are insane figures and scorchingly tall odds, but there they are, and from the mind of Stephen Hawking, no less. He certainly was not one who liked the idea of a universe fine-tuned to such a heart-stopping level, but he nonetheless sometimes expressed what the immutable facts revealed. In that same book he said, "It would be very difficult to explain why the universe

---

[1] Stephen Hawking, *A Brief History of Time* (New York: Bantam Books, 1988), 126.

would have begun in just this way, except as the act of a God who intended to create beings like us." Again, considering the source, this is an astounding admission, especially because in decades after he tried to wriggle away from this conclusion any way he could, often manufacturing solutions to the universe's beginning that seemed intentionally difficult to comprehend by anyone clinging to the rules of common sense. Nonetheless, in his famous book, he was indisputably frank about what he saw and what the obvious conclusions seemed to be.

The astrophysicist Fred Hoyle was also candid about the universe's fine-tuning, despite being a long-time and dedicated atheist. In fact, as we have said, he led the charge in wrinkling his nose at the repulsive idea of a universe with a beginning, and inadvertently coined the term "Big Bang." But in 1959, a decade after this, he was giving a lecture on how stars in their interiors created every naturally occurring element in the universe and was explaining that they do this with the simplest element: hydrogen. "If this were a purely scientific question and not one that touched on the religious problem," he said, "I do not believe that any scientist who has examined the evidence would fail to draw the inference that the laws of nuclear physics have been deliberately designed with regard to the consequences they produce inside the stars." It seemed obvious to him, and he even had the guts to say those who did not agree were bothered by this on "religious" grounds. But to him it was clear, however little he liked it. He said that if one did not think a designer had done this, "then we are back again to a monstrous sequence of accidents." And he liked that conclusion even less because he knew it to be laughably far-fetched.

Two decades later, Hoyle went even further, writing in the Caltech alumni magazine:

> Would you not say to yourself, "Some super calculating intellect must have designed the properties of the carbon atom, otherwise the chance of my finding such an atom through the blind forces of nature would be utterly minuscule." Of course you would.... A common-sense interpretation of the facts suggests that a super intellect has monkeyed with physics, as well as with chemistry and

biology, and that there are no blind forces worth speaking about in nature. The number one calculates from the facts seem to me so overwhelming as to put this conclusion almost beyond question.[2]

Hoyle is typical of those brave souls who refused to twist the science to fit his worldview, nor to twist the conclusions away from where the science pointed—even if it was to an "intelligent designer" of some kind. But neither would he accept the God of the Bible as a solution to that designer's identity. That was a bridge too far, nor did it seem to him necessary. Surely one could be true to one's scientific understanding by talking about a designer without leaping to embrace the God who had parted the Red Sea. But just as Hoyle reluctantly came to see that science showed the universe was not eternal, but had a beginning in the Big Bang, he also saw the design in the universe from the science, even though—like Melville's Bartleby—he would have preferred not to. From the point of view of science, Hoyle's laudable honesty concerning things he was disinclined to accept is actually inspiring. "[I]f one proceeds directly and straightforwardly in this matter," he said,

> without being deflected by a fear of incurring the wrath of scientific opinion, one arrives at the conclusion that biomaterials with their amazing measure of order must be the outcome of intelligent design. No other possibility I have been able to think of in pondering this issue over quite a long time seems to me to have anything like as high a possibility of being true.[3]

The Mass of the Universe

To get specific about what details of the universe point to design, we can start with the biggest picture of them all: the mass of the universe, which is

---

[2] Fred Hoyle, "The Universe: Past and Present Reflections," *Engineering and Science*, November 1981, 8–12.

[3] Ibid.

one of the most startling examples of so-called fine-tuning. Just as we can grasp the concept of Earth's needing to be exactly the size that it is, we must wrestle with the idea that the universe must be roughly the size that it is, too. But as you will soon see, the fine-tuning of the mass of the universe cannot really be described with the adverb "roughly." It is a level of exactness that is essentially impossible to comprehend.

First of all, the mass of the universe is not something we knew until rather recently, and the very idea of what such a thing even could be is itself difficult to envision. But again, science eventually got to where it can tell us, and with an almost blood-curdling specificity. We may as well cut to the chase and say that the mass of the observable universe, measured in kilograms, is 1.5 times 10 to the 53rd power. That is only the observable universe, and it is a small fraction of the mass comprised of dark matter and dark energy, but we have enough to worry about without getting into that subject.

To talk about the mass of the universe another way, we can simply state the number of atoms in the universe, which is about 10 to the 80th power—so a one followed by eighty zeroes. It's of course amazing that we know that, but we do. Still, these are just numbers. Another way to think of the size of the universe is to say that it contains 2 trillion galaxies, each of which contains 100 billion stars, most of which are comparable to our own sun, whose diameter is 865,000 miles across. But there are not just stars in the universe. There is also a near infinity of other objects such as planets, moons, asteroids, comets, nebulae, and so on. So these are some ways in which we can get some idea of our universe's mass.

But what is truly hard to comprehend—and this is putting it mildly—is that science has determined that the mass of the universe is fine-tuned to a level that is, as we say, essentially incomprehensible. Nonetheless, according to what the physicists tell us, the mass of the entire universe is exactly what it must be for life to exist on Earth. Before we go into what we mean by "exactly," we can dilate for a moment on why scientists believe this. For example, scientists say that if the universe's mass were the tiniest bit smaller, the elements necessary for life—nitrogen, oxygen, and carbon, for starters—would never have come into being. This is related to the second reason, which ends up being much more interesting, and has to do with gravity.

We have said that the more mass something has the more gravitational pull it exerts. So we now understand that if there were *any* more mass in the universe—and we will say what "any" means in a moment—the gravity would be too much and would not have allowed the universe to expand from the Big Bang to where it is now. At some point the gravity—if it were even the tiniest bit greater—would have overtaken that expansion, would have put the brakes on it, so to speak. It would have eventually pulled everything back down into objects much larger than our sun, which would have ended up as black holes and neutron stars, which are so dense that atoms themselves would be crushed. So of course the aforementioned elements necessary for life would never have been created, since life could never exist on neutron stars or in black holes. But on the other side of things, if there were any less mass in the universe, then its expansion would have been too fast. So gravity would not have had the chance to create the stars that exist now, nor the planets, and so the universe would just be an endless scattering of gas and dust.

But where this gets interesting to the point of maddening is when we talk about just how fine-tuned the mass of the universe is. In his book *Why the Universe Is the Way It Is*, Caltech astrophysicist Hugh Ross gives us the frightening details:

> At certain early epochs in cosmic history, [the universe's] mass density must have been as finely tuned as one part in 10 to the 60th power to allow for the possible existence of physical life at any time or place within the entirety of the universe. This degree of fine-tuning is so great that it's as if right after the universe beginning someone could have destroyed the possibility of life within it by subtracting a single dime's mass from the whole of the observable universe or adding a single dime's mass to it.[4]

A single dime's mass. Everyone knows that the mass of a dime is almost nothing. Yet Hugh Ross declares that is the amount of mass that

---

[4] Hugh Ross, *Why the Universe Is the Way It Is (Reasons to Believe)* (Grand Rapids, Michigan: Baker Books, 2008), 35.

would have caused the universe not to come into being. Are we supposed to take this seriously? That the mass of a dime is what could have made the difference between our existence and non-existence? How can we rationally process something so outrageous? And yet science has progressed to the point where it can tell us this as a fact. Still, the notion that the entire mass of the universe could not deviate by the mass of a single dime has to be among the most preposterous statements anyone has ever made in the history of language. But again, there is a monumental difficulty, because this is not the hare-brained conjecture of some madman, but the bloodless scientific consensus. It isn't something that science can explain, of course, and it makes many scientists deeply uncomfortable. But there it is: an incomprehensibly outrageous scientific fact that stymies any thinking person into silence. What is there to say?

But why should we jump into the deep end of the pool so soon? The mass of the universe is only one element of fine-tuning, and yes, it is frightening to any sensitive thinking person. But there are dozens and even now scores and hundreds of variables that are fine-tuned, albeit not quite to that disturbing level. For example, let's talk for a moment about the four fundamental forces in the universe.

The Four Fundamental Forces

Most of us who aren't physicists don't know about the four fundamental forces, but they are as important as anything we can imagine, since they hold the universe together, down to holding together every single atom in the universe. For clarity, these forces are 1) gravity, 2) the electromagnetic force, 3) the weak nuclear force, and 4) the strong nuclear force.

Paul Davies has touched on the fine-tuning of these specifically:

> It is hard to resist the impression that the present structure of the universe, apparently so sensitive to minor alterations in the numbers, has been rather carefully thought out. The seemingly miraculous concurrence of numerical values that nature has assigned to

her fundamental constants must remain the most compelling evidence for an element of cosmic design.[5]

Of course "nature" doesn't typically assign numerical values to things, much less to things established less than one-millionth of a second before nature herself exploded into being from nothingness. That's the point. Nature has no intelligence capable of working such things out, nor any will or intention to create anything. And yet each one of these four fundamental forces has a fixed value so precisely calibrated for the universe to come into being that we can hardly resist assuming someone was behind this, someone with infinite intelligence and a preexisting desire to create the universe in its limitless vastness and variety. One thing we seem to know with dead certainty is this: It could not have happened "randomly." No one who understands what is involved dreams it "just happened" any more than the plays of Shakespeare "just happened," or the Parthenon or the Colosseum or the Great Wall of China or the pyramids "just happened." Some things don't just happen; the universe is one of them.

As for these fundamental forces, the only one of the four that everyone understands and experiences is gravity. We have an innate sense of its value, since we know that if it were twice what it is we would feel twice as heavy as we now do. It's not hard for us to see that gravity has a specific value that could be stronger or weaker. We experience it constantly. The other three fundamental forces are much less easy to fathom, but what all four of them have in common is that their value was determined less than one millionth of a second after the Big Bang and has not changed one iota in almost fourteen billion years. But the larger point with regard to fine-tuning is that each of these four forces must be precisely what it is—or the universe would not be able to support life.

Let's start with the *strong nuclear force*. This is what keeps protons and neutrons together. You'll remember that protons and neutrons form the nucleus of every atom, and that electrons orbit that nucleus. But if the force

---

[5] Paul Davies, *God and the New Physics* (New York: Simon & Schuster, 1983), 189.

magically keeping protons and neutrons together were just 2 percent weaker than it is, it wouldn't be strong enough to hold the protons and neutrons together at all, and they would drift apart, giving us an entire universe consisting only of hydrogen—whose nucleus has only one proton and no neutrons. A universe consisting only of hydrogen would not allow for life to exist. But in case that's not impressive enough, we should say if that same strong nuclear force were just 0.3 percent *stronger* than it is, it would also be disastrous. It would cause protons and neutrons to attract each other too much, so that they would pile up and create only large nuclei, such as are found in heavier elements. So there would be no hydrogen at all, and any universe without hydrogen is just as useless as a universe with only hydrogen. No life could exist.

Again, this is what science now tells us. But once we accept this, the real question is how can we not wonder how that exceedingly precise value was established in the first place? It happened almost fourteen billion years ago, in the first millionth of a second after the Big Bang. It's never deviated since, and if it were not precisely what it is life would not exist. Is that not at least curious? Why did it just happen to be exactly right immediately, so that the universe could come into being as it has, eventually supporting life on our planet?

Turning to the *electromagnetic force*, we remind ourselves that for life to be possible, we need a whole raft of elements —not just hydrogen, oxygen, iron, helium, nitrogen, and carbon. At a bare minimum, human beings require about twenty-two different elements. We may remember from chemistry class that the way atoms join to form molecules has to do with electrons leaping from their orbits in one atom over to the orbit of another atom. It is the electromagnetic force that keeps the electrons in orbit around their nuclei. So science tells us that if this force were slightly weaker, electrons would leave their orbits too easily. But if it were slightly stronger, they would never budge from their original orbits. In either case, for enough elements to exist, this force needs to be perfectly calibrated. And yes, it just happens to be perfectly calibrated. And here we are.

But more impressive by far than the calibration of each of the four forces is the perfect calibration of the ratios between them. For example, Paul Davies has calculated that if the ratio between the strong nuclear force and the electromagnetic force were different by one part in ten to the sixteenth power, life could not exist. This is another inconceivable level of calibration, but this figure is given to us by an agnostic who is one of the top physicists in the world. According to Davies, if this ratio were different by that infinitesimally tiny amount, the universe as we know it would not exist. Why haven't we heard of all this before?

Let's look at one more ratio between two of these forces, the gravitational and the electromagnetic. We know that a universe that did not contain enough large stars and small stars would not permit life. Large stars are necessary because in their interiors life-essential elements like iron are produced, without which life could not exist. Iron is required to make hemoglobin, which delivers oxygen from our lungs to the rest of our body and delivers carbon dioxide from our body's tissues to our lungs. Iron is also required for innumerable other things. But iron is only produced in stars called supergiants, meaning they are anywhere from ten to seventy times the size of our sun. Eventually—after literally billions of years—they explode into supernovae, releasing all their iron and other things into the universe, which is how all the iron in our bodies and on our planet got here. Although that was of course a long, long time ago.

But we also need small stars, like our sun, which is able to burn steadily for billions of years, and we need stars smaller than our sun, too. But for such a variety of stars to exist depends on the ratio between the gravitational force and the electromagnetic force. As you may have guessed, this just happens to be perfectly fine-tuned. The ratio between them must be exact, down to one part in ten to the fortieth power. One followed by forty zeroes is a painfully large number. If we said the ratio couldn't be different by one in a million—ten to the sixth power—anyone would understand that this ratio was astronomically fine-tuned. A million or billion are numbers we can begin to understand, or at least fool ourselves into thinking we can understand. But one followed by forty zeroes? Yet that's what the physicists insist is required for small stars and large stars to exist so that our lives could be possible.

Hugh Ross gives an illustration that might help us appreciate what one in ten to the fortieth means. He tells us to imagine covering the contiguous United States and Alaska with dimes. When you're done, cover Canada in dimes too. Both American dimes and Canadian dimes work equally well. Then cover Mexico and half of Central America, just to be safe. Now repeat the process until the dimes are piled so high that Mount McKinley is not visible. (That's roughly twenty thousand feet high.) Then continue this process until the dimes are twelve times higher than Mount McKinley—which is to say about 240,000 feet high. Okay, now continue this process until the dimes are five thousand times higher than that. That should make them 240,000 miles high, at which point they will be bumping into the moon, but don't worry about it, because no one lives there.

Once this is completed, do the same thing with a billion other continents the size of North America, piling the dimes 240,000 miles high on each one. If you can't find any continents exactly the size of North America, join the club. You should now have a billion areas the equivalent of North America covered with dimes to an altitude of 240,000 miles. If you've missed any of the billion continents, now is the time to go back and make sure you've covered all billion. Once you're sure you have, tell a friend that among the dimes covering these billion continents to the height of the moon there is— somewhere—a single red dime. It could be on any of the billion continents, and any level within the moon-high piles. Refuse to tell your friend the answer, no matter how close you are. So if you can imagine that single red dime somewhere in those moon-high piles covering a billion continents the size of North America, you have a solid idea of what the maximum amount of deviation can be in the ratio between the gravitational and electromagnetic forces in order for life to exist.

Many other fine-tuned variables are nearly as crazy, or worse. And we have to remind ourselves that if any one of these variables is wrong, the whole universe would vanish along with life. This is what science has determined. Every one of these variables must be precisely calibrated. We might finally mention that if the value of the gravitational force were different by one part in ten to the thirty-fourth power, the universe wouldn't have any planets capable of sustaining life. All of these levels of fine-tuning are what science insists are absolutely necessary for life to exist on our planet, however preposterous it might sound. But there is one more level of fine-tuning we should mention.

The American Nobel Prize–winning physicist Steven Weinberg is an atheist with a particular disdain for religion. Before he was able to accept the Big Bang, he admitted that the Steady State theory was "philosophically the most attractive theory because it least resembles the account given in Genesis." But Weinberg nonetheless admits that life "as we know it would be impossible if any one of several physical quantities had slightly different values," as we have been saying. But nothing we have mentioned can compare to the number Weinberg has determined to be the most fine-tuned constant yet discovered. In talking about the energy density of the universe—what is often referred to as the "cosmological constant"—he gives us the most extravagantly grotesque number of them all, in the most confounding example of fine-tuning. Weinberg says that if the value of this cosmological constant were different by just one part in 10 to the 120th power, life could not exist.

But what are we to make of a one followed by 120 zeroes? One part in a million would get the point across, but a million is only a one followed by six zeroes. A trillion is a one followed by twelve zeroes. A quadrillion is a one followed by fifteen zeroes, and a quintillion is a one followed by eighteen zeroes. From there we go to sextillion (one followed by twenty-one zeroes) and septillion (one followed by twenty-four zeroes) and octillion (one followed by twenty-seven zeroes). Who has use for such numbers? Since we had some ink to spare, we can spell it out. We are talking about a deviation of one part in 1,000,000,000,000,000,000,000,000,000,000,000,000,000, 000,000,000,000,000,000,000,000,000,000,000,000,000,000,000,000,00 0,000,000,000,000,000,000,000,000,000. Can there be any real point to such a surfeit of zeroes? The number of atoms in the universe is ten to the eightieth power. Our universe is ninety-three billion light-years in diameter. One light-year is about six trillion miles. Our minds cannot begin to fathom

these things. But these are simply what science—advanced as it now is—
requires that we accept.[6]

So at what point do we see that our existence—logically speaking—cannot
be anything close to a random occurrence? We have not mentioned that each
of these outlandish numbers must be multiplied by all the others to get the
full picture. We get a number so impossibly large that there can be no way to
imagine that our universe and our planet—and we ourselves—are simply here.
But science says that changing any one of the parameters mentioned even
slightly would destroy the ability for life to exist. So simply to shrug and say
this all simply happened "by chance" seems beyond the pale. Saying that would
be infinitely dumber than what Jim Carrey's character in *Dumb and Dumber*
says, after being told by the pretty girl that the chances of her dating him are
one in a million: "So you're telling me there's a chance!?"

No. Not really. No.

---

[6] Somehow Weinberg doesn't believe in God. But paraphrasing Lady Bracknell in Oscar Wilde's
The Importance of Being Earnest, we might say that Weinberg's inability to fathom that whoever
did this fine-tuning might be God may be regarded as unfortunate. But that he would publicly
admit this must be regarded as carelessness.

CHAPTER FIVE

More Planetary Fine-Tuning: Water and Sunlight

Until writing this book I was blissfully ignorant of the superlative strangeness of water, so I imagine that the reader confronted with this startling idea may be put off, wondering whether he wishes to wade into what might be a murky chapter full of strained points on a subject too strange to be serious. After all, it's water. How weird can it possibly be?

Having discovered its strangeness only recently, as I say, I am sympathetic to this view. Who among us would ever imagine water could be anything but extremely normal in every way? In this it is very much like air, being everywhere, so that we take it for granted. Like air too, in its purest form it is perfectly clear and essentially odorless and tasteless. What is there to say about it? Is it not the unavoidable standard by which we measure every other liquid? And what does it do other than what we might expect it to do? What curious properties might it have of which we are unaware? We all know that sometimes it evaporates into clouds which eventually rain down on us, and sometimes it freezes into snow or ice, which can melt again and create streams and rivers which run to the sea. It can be very picturesque and comforting, but how in the world can anyone think of the substance as anything more than perfectly ordinary?

Just as most of us have not goggled at the seemingly identical sizes of the sun and moon in the sky, nor have gushed with gratitude that Jupiter and Saturn pull giant flying objects away from our heads, we would hardly imagine there is any reason to think much about water. Its centrality to our lives is such a given that it is inevitably and not inappropriately mostly ignored. After all, 71 percent of Earth's surface is covered with water, and 65 percent of our bodies are water. Our brains and hearts are 73 percent water. If "absence makes the heart grow fonder" and "familiarity breeds contempt," it seems only natural that we should take it for granted. In the spoiled modernity of the West, few of us have ever been thirsty for long, nor gone without a shower or bath for very long. We are otherwise generally unappreciative of water and indifferent to it. And why shouldn't we be?

The Wildness of Water, or H2Whoa!

If you come across *The Wonder of Water*, by the British Australian biochemist Michael Denton, you will discover things you cannot have imagined, and will almost certainly be shocked into acknowledging how bizarre water is, and how taking it for granted is simply a mistake born of ignorance. And after understanding these things about it, you will likely recognize its existence and abundance on Earth as yet one more suitcase of evidence that the way things are is so dramatically improbable that we must at least wonder—if we are to be intellectually honest—how it can all be possible, and whether a God of infinite intelligence may have made things this way intentionally, perhaps even with an eye simply toward freaking us out when we had enough scientific knowledge to understand such things. If, on the other hand, we could forget we ever had encountered water, and could come upon it as for the first time, we could not avoid being astonished by it.

In one episode of *The Simpsons*, the family visits a water park where one of the scarier rides is called "H2Whoa!" I think that as we consider the startling idea that water is deeply strange on a host of levels, calling it "H2Whoa!" might be particularly apposite. For example, let's start with asking why ice floats.

Why Does Ice Float?

We know that when water moves from a liquid to a solid, it turns into ice, which floats. Who can imagine anything else? But it's only because we are so accustomed to water and floating ice that we regard it as somehow normal.

But it is not. Nearly every substance in creation gets denser as it cools, and therefore gets heavier. So by the time it gets cold enough to become a solid, it is always denser and heavier than the liquid form of the substance, and therefore sinks. What could be more logical? But in this regard, water happens not to go with the flow, so to speak. On the contrary, water is actually 9 percent *less* dense when it freezes into ice, and is therefore lighter than liquid water. This is the first strange thing about it. And it is precisely because of this and many of water's other strange properties that life exists on our planet, as we shall explain.

But the idea that water floats is even stranger than we might first think. That's because water does get heavier and denser as it gets colder, just as most substances do. But when it cools to 39 degrees Fahrenheit, that process suddenly reverses, after which it gets lighter and less dense. So yes, water that is 70 degrees Fahrenheit is lighter and less dense than water that is 50 degrees Fahrenheit. But for some perplexing reason water ceases to become denser and heavier the moment it hits 39 degrees. From that point down to its freezing point of 32 degrees, it changes direction, becoming less dense and heavy. By the time it hits 32 degrees and turns to ice, it is 9 percent less dense than the water around it, as we have said, and it floats.

Substances that float in their frozen or solid form are extremely rare. Melt chocolate and you'll see. Melt butter. Or wax. The solid part is denser than the liquid part and sinks. But not with water. But as we have said, this is not merely a random, strange property. Like most of the oddities already mentioned, this property of water happens to be crucial to the existence of life on Earth.

For example, if ice did not float, lakes and other bodies of water would freeze from the bottom up, completely destroying their ecosystems—or never developing them in the first place. But because ice floats, it forms on the surfaces of lakes and ponds and rivers and arctic oceans. If it froze from the bottom up it would cause a runaway freezing of all the water above it. And because it floats on the top, it even creates an insulation barrier for the water beneath it, protecting it from the cold above the ice, and allowing the life beneath to survive. But this is one of water's least bizarre qualities.

For example, from a chemist's point of view, the freezing and boiling points of water are entirely out of line with what we should expect. The Nobel Prize–winning Hungarian biochemist Albert Szent-Györgyi wrote: "The extraordinary nature of water is borne out by the two constants used most frequently for the characterization of substances: melting and boiling points."[1] We can rather accurately guess the freezing points and boiling points of substances by the sizes of their molecules. But not in the curious case of water, which dramatically defies our expectations. Szent-Györgyi says that for a molecule its size, water should boil at 32 degrees Fahrenheit. Not freeze at 32 degrees, but *boil*. Of course water doesn't boil until it reaches 212 degrees Fahrenheit. Szent-Györgyi also says that according to the size of the water molecule, it ought not to freeze until it reaches the incredibly cold temperature of -148 degrees. The presence of liquid water in most regions of the planet is absolutely *de rigueur* for life. So if our planet were farther from the sun or closer, or if water froze and evaporated at different temperatures, life here would not be possible.

Water's freezing point is also crucial when we travel straight up in our atmosphere. That's because its very low freezing point is what prevents it from evaporating into outer space. At an altitude of six miles, where jets fly, the temperature is usually something like 70 degrees below zero. At that very cold temperature hydrogen, nitrogen, and oxygen still remain gaseous. But of course water—though made of oxygen and hydrogen—freezes long before it gets that cold. So by the time any water vapor gets that high up—in

---

[1] Albert Szent-Györgyi, *The Living State: With Observations on Cancer* (New York: Academic Press, 1972), 9.

what is called the troposphere—it promptly freezes and drops back down to Earth's surface. If it didn't, it would continue to rise further until the ultraviolet rays in that part of the atmosphere broke it apart into its components of oxy-

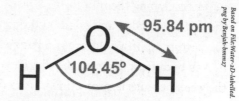

Water molecule with bond lengths and angles.

Based on File:Water-2D-labelled. png by Benjah-bmm27

gen and hydrogen. The super-light hydrogen would swiftly escape the atmosphere, never to return, and Earth would be quickly depleted of water. In fact, it would have been depleted of water eons ago, and life here would never have come to exist. We believe this is what happened on Venus, since it is so close to the sun and doesn't have a cold troposphere.

The reason for most of water's strange properties is the very strong hydrogen bond in the H_2O molecule. This is one reason for water's high viscosity and high surface tension, as well as its high polarity, each of which plays a role in making life possible, and all three of which often work together to enable water to do things we likely never consider. The extremely high surface tension of water is superseded only by that of mercury. We can observe this property when a water strider manages to "walk" across the surface of a pond, or when we pour water a bit higher than the rim of a glass and it manages to hold together without flowing over. Its high surface tension also makes it form into drops much more easily than liquids with lower surface tension.

Denton explains that water's high viscosity is particularly important. But who ever thinks about water's viscosity? Nonetheless it is because water has just the right viscosity that it is able to erode rocks, which turns out to be utterly central to life on Earth, something else most of us likely have never thought about. Who would think erosion could be in any sense positive, much less central to the flourishing of life on Earth? But it is, and dramatically so. Water flows much faster than something more viscous, like olive oil, and as it flows it picks up bits of stone and sand, which act like a kind of sandpaper on whatever the water flows over, aiding in the process of erosion. And by eroding the rocks over which it flows, the water continues to carry the rock particulate and minerals and metals along, distributing them wherever it goes. This is crucial, because these vital minerals and metals become part of the soil wherever the water takes them—and all the places in between—and the plants that drink that water get the nitrates, magnesium, and other minerals they need to survive. And the animals that drink the water and eat the plants get these vital minerals and metals too. On and on it goes. But who would ever think water's viscosity and ability to erode rocks was intrinsically important to plant and animal life far from where that water had originally come?

Water also has a singularly unmatched ability to dissolve nearly anything it comes in contact with. It is therefore called the "universal solvent," and this property has to do with the water molecule's high polarity. So as water erodes the rocks and soil over which it flows, much that it carries along from those rocks and soil eventually dissolves to become an invisible part of the water, enabling the water to carry it much further than it could carry larger bits of rock or grains of sand. Denton writes: "It is hard to conceive of a more ideal agent than water for dissolving the vital minerals in the Earth's crust." So water carries both dissolved and undissolved minerals and metals everywhere it flows, feeding innumerable life forms that, if not for the water, would have no way of getting those vital ingredients. Even water's strange property of increasing in volume when it freezes helps erode rocks, because water drawn into the fissure of a rock sometimes freezes, and the expanding ice causes the rock eventually to break apart.

But Michael Denton says the power of water to erode rock is so powerful that it ought to have eroded every mountain down to nothing, and to have destroyed all life on the planet millions of years ago. For some idea of water's extraordinary powers of erosion, we may consider the dramatic example of Niagara Falls, where the rushing water over the ages has eroded the solid rock so much that the falls are now seven miles farther back than they were merely twelve thousand years ago. This is a dramatic example, but over hundreds of millions of years, even the mildest erosion becomes dramatic.

Denton says the level of erosion in many places is two to ten millimeters per year, so in ten million years, that would erode twenty to a hundred thousand meters. Mount Everest is less than ten thousand meters high.

But if this is the case, how have the mountains of the world managed to avoid being ground down into the oceans many times over? How has life existed on land for four hundred million years and in the oceans for four billion? The answer is something we knew almost nothing about until the 1960s, and another example of how things work together to create an environment that seems curiously—if not spookily—calibrated to support life. We are talking about plate tectonics. Water erodes rocks, but the moving continental plates work in the opposite direction, continually creating new mountains, for example. We now know that the process of plate tectonics gives our planet its variety of climates and altitudes, and most crucially, ensures a constant recycling of all the minerals and metals in our rocks and soils. Denton writes that plate tectonics explain

> why the continents exist and persist, why mountains are never finally ground to sea level, why the hydrological cycle can replenish the essential mineral content of the terrestrial hydrosphere endlessly over billions of years, ensuring the continuance of life on land, and why the seas have never been depleted of their dissolved salt and mineral content.

We've mentioned that the strange composition of the water molecule—with its very strong hydrogen bond and its high polarity—is at the center of most of water's strange properties. But it is also because of this strong hydrogen bond that water does not compress easily, which also happens to be crucially important. Medical science says that because of this quality, blood can be pushed through our veins effectively, as blood is comprised of 80 percent water. In fact water's molecular properties make it so especially difficult to compress that even at the depth of a mile under the ocean's surface, its volume is only compressed by 1 percent. We can hardly imagine the pressure underneath more than five thousand feet of liquid water. After all, it's heavy stuff: a single gallon weighs over eight pounds.

As we said, the high surface tension, high viscosity, and high tensile strength of water enable it to do many crucial things. Because of all three, trees are able to pull water all the way up into their highest branches through the exceedingly tiny capillary pathways, all the way up to the leaves that drink in the sunlight. Via photosynthesis the sunlight that hits the leaves activates the chlorophyll in them so that the water breaks apart into hydrogen and oxygen. The oxygen is released into the atmosphere—so that we can breathe it, among other things—and the carbon dioxide absorbed by the leaves combines with the hydrogen left behind to create sugars and other carbohydrates that feed the tree. As a result of water's particular viscosity and high surface tension, water is perfectly suited to sink down into various soils while not sinking so quickly that it does not also stay available to the roots of plants for the necessary time.

There is an inconceivable amount of water on our planet—326 quintillion gallons at last count[2]—which helps keep Earth's air temperatures stable. That's because water retains heat extraordinarily well—or doesn't conduct it well—and remains the same temperature for a considerable time, despite the vagaries of the temperature in the air above it. So it acts as a coolant when all else around it gets hot and as a heating element when all around it gets cold.

Is Sunlight a Happy Coincidence?

Andrew Parker is a visiting research fellow at Oxford's Green Templeton College, where he heads up the research team on photonics structures and eyes. So he knows something about sunlight. In *The Genesis Enigma*, Parker cites a coincidence so bizarre that to him it hardly seems possible, and yet there is no question that it is not only possible, but also has been a fact of life on our planet for nearly four billion years. The "coincidence" he has discovered—but

---

[2] Not including the fountains at Caesars Palace in Las Vegas.

cannot get over—has to do with "the sun's output and the transparency of seawater." We will describe this in more detail shortly, but to sum things up, Parker says the sun

> has a peak in its energy output—in its electromagnetic spectrum—and seawater has a peak in its ability to transmit this electromagnetic spectrum. Strangely enough, *and there is no scientific reason for this* [Parker's emphasis], the two peaks converge on the same narrow window of wavelengths—the visible light range. Considering the vast range of wavelengths in the sun's output, it is indeed a mighty coincidence that this minuscule region is also that which travels best through seawater.[3]

To explain this more clearly, we have to go back to when life appeared on our planet, roughly 3.9 billion years ago. The first life was in the form of single-celled organisms. (How they came into being from non-life is something we examine in the next chapter, but let's put that question aside for the moment and simply think about life suddenly existing and then reproducing and reproducing.) But science tells us that a serious problem reared its head immediately, because the energy—or food—on our planet was limited. This meant that in time—some scores of millions of years, perhaps—it would all be used up, and that would be that. Life would die out. Since life has now been here for nearly four billion years, we see that this problem was somehow overcome. But how did this happen, given the very real issue of a limited supply of energy? How did the life that emerged nearly four billion years ago continue to exist through the vast eons all the way until the present time? What did it eat? If the energy on Earth was fixed and finite, what happened?

Obviously, the single-celled creatures did not care one way or the other about solving this problem. They were unaware of their own existence and did not trouble themselves about how they might sustain their

---

[3] Andrew Parker, *The Genesis Enigma: Why the First Book of the Bible Is Scientifically Accurate* (New York: Dutton, 2009), 61.

species—or any life—into the distant future. Nonetheless something happened so that life did not run out of fuel and managed to continue through the nearly four billion years until the present. But what?

According to Parker, not very long after the first life appeared on Earth a second kind of life appeared called cyanobacteria, which is just the fancy name for "blue-green algae." Cyanobacteria are exceedingly tiny single-celled creatures that possess a strange ability that the previous single-celled creatures did not possess. Cyanobacteria are able to extract energy from beyond our planet. So the finite amount of energy on this planet was suddenly no longer a problem, and life could continue here indefinitely. But how did these single-celled creatures perform this extraordinary trick? Through an ability called photosynthesis, they were able to magically tap into an extraterrestrial energy source. In other words, they were able to use the sunlight shining into the water to feed themselves. It is almost as if they had ninety-three million-mile-long straws and could drink energy directly from the sun. Of course that wasn't necessary, because these cyanobacteria could simply float along in the water and let the sunlight come to them. And that sunlight via photosynthesis was turned into food, and the problem was solved.

But this is where we bump into the bizarre "coincidence" that knocked Parker for a loop and that he sees as so bizarre that it cannot be a coincidence. That's because what these cyanobacteria were able to do four billion years ago, and still do, is only possible because of two simultaneous—and totally unrelated—outrageous "coincidences." Each of these "coincidences" is too much to take in, but the two of them together are simply stupefying and force us to wonder if something else is at work. So let's talk about each of the two "coincidences."

The first has to do with sunlight. Parker and Denton both explain that the sun emits an impossibly vast variety of electromagnetic energy. We are familiar with sunlight, but that is a very, very tiny part of the electromagnetic energy coming from the sun. That electromagnetic energy ranges from infrared radiation, microwave radiation, and radio waves, which have long wavelengths, to ultraviolet radiation, X-rays, and gamma rays, which have shorter wavelengths. The spectrum of electromagnetic energy emitted by the sun is actually so vast that to appreciate it, we may imagine a deck of playing cards that stretches beyond our atmosphere and all the way to the next galaxy, called the Andromeda Galaxy. That's essentially the range of the EM (electromagnetic) spectrum emitted by our sun. And then we learn that visible light—meaning sunlight—is a very, very, very tiny part of that spectrum. To imagine how tiny, we should think about two or three of the cards in the middle of that deck. Remember that the deck of cards representing all the energy coming from the sun is so tall it would stretch beyond the Milky Way to the next galaxy. And the sunlight part of that spectrum is the equivalent of a couple of cards.

But this is where it gets dramatically stranger. Seventy percent of all the electromagnetic energy coming from the sun just happens to fall within that impossibly narrow range, represented by two cards in that nearly infinite deck. It is within that tiniest of ranges within that outrageously vast spectrum that the sun puts out 70 percent of all its energy. Of course this is amazing and strange, but far more amazing and strange is the fact that there is no understandable scientific reason for this to be so. It *just so happens* to be the case, and *just so happens* to be extremely lucky from the perspective of life on Earth.

But as we have said, there is a second and similarly bizarre coincidence, totally unrelated to the first one. It has to do with seawater. Once again, for no scientific reason whatever, the seawater on the surface of our planet just happens to be able to transmit sunlight's visible energy dramatically better than any other of the vast varieties of energy it emits. We don't understand why this is. It's just a strange but true property of seawater that scientists have observed. But to make this point more clearly, we have discovered that seawater absorbs almost all the energy that comes from the sun in every part of the vast spectrum of electromagnetic energy. So all the energy in the electromagnetic spectrum— energy with long wavelengths such as infrared radiation, microwave radiation, and radio waves, and energy with short wavelengths such as ultraviolet radiation, X-rays, and gamma rays—is absorbed by seawater. Except for sunlight. For some reason, seawater does not absorb sunlight, but instead strangely allows sunlight to pass *through* it. We cannot understand why this is so. But when we couple this entirely shocking coincidence with the previous entirely shocking coincidence about sunlight, we may be permitted to wonder what sort of madness we have encountered. What in the world is going on? Like Andrew Parker, Michael Denton repeats the facts simply, so we cannot miss it:

> Water strongly absorbs electromagnetic radiation in every region of the spectrum except for the visible region, the only region in the entire spectrum useful for photobiology. Water, in one of the most staggeringly fortuitous coincidences in all of nature, lets through only the right light in an infinitesimally tiny region of the [electromagnetic] spectrum....[4]

So seawater absorbs almost all of the energy from the sun, except for that impossibly tiny part of the spectrum we call sunlight. That it lets pass through. And that sunlight hits the cyanobacteria in the water, and those cyanobacteria just happen to be able to convert that sunlight via photosynthesis into food. What both Denton and Parker marvel at more than they can properly express, however, is that these two bizarre "peaks" in sunlight and seawater have no scientific reason whatsoever to match up. They have nothing to do with each other. They are each absurdly small points in the spectrum—tinier than we can possibly imagine—and yet for no reason at all that makes the slightest sense, they happen to coincide perfectly. And only because they do was life possible nearly four billion years ago and is life possible today. Only because of this most bizarre of all coincidences can cyanobacteria draw limitless energy from the impossibly distant sun. And because of the unfathomable convergence of two seeming impossibilities does life on Earth have a limitless source of energy.

Of course this outrageously strange phenomenon in our seawater lies at the heart of almost everything else in the life cycle of the planet. The ability

---

[4] Michael Denton, *The Wonder of Water: Water's Profound Fitness for Life on Earth and Mankind* (Seattle, Washington: Discovery Institute Press, 2017), 113.

of cyanobacteria to take in sunlight through the water isn't isolated. It is connected to all the life on our planet and formed the foundation of all life that has followed ever since. Parker explains that

> the cyanobacteria extracted not only water from their environment, but also carbon dioxide. In return [the cyanobacteria] gave the atmosphere oxygen. An oxygenated atmosphere is far more conducive to life, and the protective ozone layer that formed [in our atmosphere] guarded the Earth's surface from the sun's high-energy ultraviolet rays, which destroy biological material.

Not to drop one's jaw at such things seems at least inappropriate, if not downright rude. Can we not admit that on some occasions pure and unbridled astonishment is the only fitting response? This is what science now tells us is the state of these things. But what are we to make of it? How is it that these things *happen* to seem so perfectly designed and fine-tuned for life? In many respects it all seems rather humbling. But what makes it all the more strange is that it is only because of recent advances in science that we can understand these things. As science progresses, more and more such elements of fine-tuning are being discovered, to where they have become such a veritable mountain we can hardly help seeing it, even if we might for one reason or another much prefer not to. Again, the irony of the situation can hardly be avoided: Scientific advances have made it increasingly impossible to be an intellectually fulfilled atheist. What to do?

We know that sunlight and seawater did not calibrate themselves, nor that natural selection had anything to do with their having these strange properties, nor helped these bizarre properties in each of them to match up so perfectly, like two bullets striking each other with such precision that they both cease moving forward and together drop vertically. The precision of this is like the precision of the collision in which the moon was formed. If either that event or this coincidence had happened in any way ever so slightly differently, life on Earth would not exist. Can we stare at these things long enough to appreciate their miraculousness? Or shall we look away and pretend we've never seen any of it? At what point does a thinking person simply say "Uncle" and move on?

CHAPTER SIX

How Did Life Originate? or "You Can't Get Here

from There"

Have you ever considered the stunning flora and fauna on our planet? The panoply of terrestrial life is almost too vast to imagine. There are 900,000 different species of insects alone. There are 400,000 species of plants, including mimosa plants that immediately fold up their leaves when touched, and carnivorous plants that eat flesh, and monstrous eight-foot-tall plants that bloom once every 40 years and have a fragrance that mimics the stench of rotting corpses. There is a plant existing only in the harsh desert of Namibia that can live 1,500 years, and in California there is a tree called the General Sherman that sprouted from the forest floor when Aristotle was a boy. It now stands 275 feet tall, with a trunk whose circumference is 113 feet.

The variety of animals is equally astonishing. Among the birds on our planet are ostriches that stand nine feet tall and weigh three hundred pounds, as well as bee hummingbirds, which weigh two grams—the equivalent of a dime. The largest mammal is the blue whale, which reaches nearly one hundred feet in length and weighs up to four hundred thousand pounds. Can we imagine a single animal tipping the scales at nearly half a *million* pounds?

At the other end of the mammalian scale is the Etruscan pygmy shrew, which weighs 1.8 grams—less than the bee hummingbird—and averages 1.6 inches in length. The range of marine animals beggars description too, ranging from giant squids 45 feet in length to marine viruses just 40 nanometers long.[1] A few years ago scientists discovered a translucent fish living 5 miles (26,000 feet) deep in the Mariana Trench, where it withstands water pressure amounting to the weight of 1,600 elephants, give or take. Speaking of whom, elephants can weigh 14,000 pounds and stand 13 feet high *at the shoulder.*

Finally, a word about speed. The fastest human beings in the world have reached 29 miles per hour for a few seconds. Cheetahs can hit 70 miles per hour. Some birds can fly over 100 miles per hour, and peregrine falcons can dive vertically at nearly 250 miles per hour.

Two Unavoidable Questions

But this dazzling juggernaut of life leads us to two supremely important questions. One gets a lot of attention, while the other essentially gets none. The first has to do with how this indescribable variety of life came to be, and usually involves what we call "evolution." How did we go from invisible single-celled life to hippopotami and butterflies, for example? An infinity of conversations, articles, books, symposia, conferences, television programs, and films have been devoted to this subject. Though there is much to talk about, we will not talk about any of it in this book, because we must talk about the second question, which is never mentioned, much less discussed. But before we tackle the second question, let's at least sum up the answer to the first one, which we can do in a single sentence: Some people believe God was involved in how all life forms came into being, that he intended to create all life, including

---

[1] A nanometer is a billionth of a meter.

us humans, and did; while others believe there is no God, so everything happened by accident, randomly evolving from a single cell all the way up to all the life that now exists. That's about it. But the second question is what will concern us here.

So what is it?

The Second Question

The second question is simply this: *What happened to bring life into existence in the first place*? How did the first life on Earth come into being *out of non-life*? Life has been around for about four billion years and has taken a staggering variety of forms, as we have mentioned. But how did the first life of single-celled organisms come into being—from non-life? What does science have to say about that? Or has the scientific establishment been avoiding the subject for some reason, such that we never seem to hear this question asked, much less answered?

As we say, once upon a time there was no life on Earth. But then— suddenly—we made the infinite leap to what we call "life." It was a grand leap, like Evel Knievel jumping the fountains at Caesars Palace in Vegas, minus the broken bones. Science says that the first life was a tiny organism comprised of just one cell. But it was life, just as much as we are life. It was alive. But the components that comprised it were *not* life, just as much as plastic or a stone or a silver coin is *not life*. So exactly how did non-life make that dazzling leap? How did we jump from some non-living chemicals—like nitrogen, oxygen, ammonia, hydrogen, and methane, all of which obviously have zero properties of what we call "life"—to the astounding miracle of life itself, which has the magical ability to replicate itself and eat and excrete and do all the things that living beings do? And again, how in the world can it be that we never seem to ask this extremely important question? Why don't we?

The Miller–Urey Experiment

When we ask this question, some bright souls may vaguely recall something from their high school science books that they believe settled this question. It was on the test, remember? We are referring to the famous 1952 Miller–Urey experiment, where a couple of University of Chicago scientists ran an electrical current through a glass flask containing four of the most basic chemicals—water, methane, ammonia, and hydrogen—which were assumed to be what was around on Earth *before life came into being*. They called it the *prebiotic* (before life) *soup*, which they assumed covered the surface of our planet four billion years ago. Stanley Miller and Harold Urey theorized that because lightning struck the water frequently at that time in Earth's earliest stage, the electricity probably had the effect of "catalyzing" the simple chemicals in that prebiotic soup into something more complex. So they did their experiment with an electrical current simulating the lightning—and *voila!* They eventually managed to get some amino acids out of it all, and that was that. It was settled.

Of course it was not settled. Far from it. It was only the first baby step that gave everyone the idea that non-life might be able to begin the process of toddling *toward* life. Amino acids themselves are certainly not anywhere close to life. But it was assumed that whatever else was supposed to happen after that first step would happen, and eventually things would keep combining together in the direction of life. So the amino acids were assumed to somehow magically combine into proteins, which is extremely complicated. And those proteins—and other crucial components like carbohydrates—were assumed to somehow "combine themselves" into the impossibly complex organic confections known as "living cells." But this was a little bit like saying that because you had once glimpsed a baseball in an open magazine across the garage you could probably pitch a perfect game in the World Series. In fact what the scientists were saying was a much greater stretch.

But from 1952 onward, this was the general idea. Those four simple chemicals were believed to have existed on the early Earth and so, over eons of time—with a little nudge from electricity via lightning—they combined to create several amino acids, and the infinitely complicated remainder of the process was just *assumed* to have happened. And it was also assumed that we would be able to recreate the many intervening steps in the lab *eventually*, just as Miller and Urey had created amino acids. So the question of life's origin seemed effectively to be settled, which is why we never hear about it anymore. The Miller–Urey experiment led us to believe that science had essentially answered this question. And perhaps because most of us are too embarrassed to admit that we don't remember much about the Miller–Urey experiment, we join the quietly assuming throngs in never bringing it up, and go on assuming right along with everyone else.

It's interesting—and sometimes embarrassing—to observe how consensus forms. The Miller–Urey experiment was such a loudly broadcast triumph for science that no one seemed to feel the need to follow up to see what happened afterward. And the fact is that almost nothing happened, despite heroic efforts from scientists. The fact is that we never really got much past Miller–Urey and the amino acids. Yet we have been pushing this theoretical Rube Goldberg concept forward nonetheless, as though we were making progress. So when it comes to this question of how life came into being, the scientific community has been skating onto increasingly thin ice.

So yes, scientists have been trying to show what happened after the amino acids, but in seventy years they have failed to move the ball forward. The scientific establishment isn't anxious to admit failure. After all, they've been out on this limb for such a long time now that it would be tremendously embarrassing to crawl back. So they have essentially said nothing much, hoping that someone eventually would be able to demonstrate something. But it's a fact that we are hardly any further along than we were in 1952. In some ways we are actually further back than we were then.

The problem is that seven decades of trying with no results is such a disaster that no one wants to talk about it. Worse yet, the ongoing failures undermine the perceived importance of the 1952 experiment. So who will be the one to finally address this problem head on? Who will make the big, depressing announcement? Who will say that all that money spent over seventy years did not do what everyone assumed it would? Who will say that perhaps it's time to admit we've been barking up the wrong tree? As it happens there is one scientist who will say these things, and who has begun saying them. But first let's look at the bigger picture.

This Is Embarrassing

The Miller–Urey experiment happened during the Truman administration, five years before the Soviets launched Sputnik. In the now impossibly distant post-WWII environment, it made huge international news and was victoriously hailed as scientific proof that life could be shown to arise out of non-life randomly—and without God, although that wasn't very often brought up at the time, since it was less culturally acceptable. But scientists did not miss that point, and atheist scientists were much less quiet about that aspect of it.

But one thing that has happened since then is that some people have come to see that those initial giddy assumptions were so premature as to be irresponsible, and wrong. Even the Miller–Urey experiment was fundamentally flawed. For one thing, the "prebiotic" soup where life was thought to first come into existence was probably not much at all like what Miller and Urey assumed. We also know that the conditions on the planet were wild, and as far from the carefully controlled laboratory conditions of that experiment as anyone could imagine. But why quibble? Everyone figured that the larger point was made; and that "given enough time" something like what the Miller–Urey experiment showed had happened, and the stuff *after* the experiment had certainly happened. The main point was what the experiment *implied*: randomness over time could do anything. God was not necessary for life. Life could arise out of non-life by natural processes. The scientific establishment already believed they understood what happened *after* the first life came into existence. Darwin's 1859 theory told us that natural selection would take care of the rest. Once you had the simplest life it was only a matter of time before it evolved ever-upward and ever-outward into everything that now exists. So yes, that super simple single-celled organism would eventually split into two cells which would split into four, and in a couple billion years you'd have fish leaping and eventually some of them would crawl out of the water, and the next thing you know you'd have dinosaurs—and then no dinosaurs—and then all kinds of mammals, and then a variety of ape-like creatures, some of which got smart enough to read and write books discussing this very subject.

So for all these years we have continued to behave as though the fundamental problem was solved and all that remained was working out the rest of the details. Except that we didn't. Despite the billions of dollars in research money spent on this and the years that have passed since 1952, the more disturbing and unavoidable the problem has become. Isn't it time we stopped, took a breath, and sorted this all out? Or do we think perhaps no one will be rude enough to circle back and ask us this dreaded and unpleasant question? If you're familiar with the TV detective Columbo, played by the genius Peter Falk, you must imagine him leaving the room, as though he is through questioning the people in it. They breathe a sigh of relief.

But then he suddenly reappears, evidently having just thought of something. "I'm sorry to bother you again," he says, "but I'm afraid there's just one thing that I still don't have straight." (This is when you know it's going to be good, if you've ever watched *Columbo*.) One can't help imagining how he would proceed: "Am I right to assume that you never really explained how life *itself* came into being? Because here we've just been assuming that we knew enough to know it happened—and then we were off to the races, talking about evolution and the whole nine yards. But what about before that? Because ever since that Miller–Urey thing you'd think we would have gotten someplace a little further down the line. I mean, that was a helluva beginning! But we've been taking whacks at this thing for seventy years! Or did we figure this out and I just missed it? Because I can be very forgetful. Just yesterday my wife asked me to get a couple of cans

Courtesy of Jeff Fitlow/Rice University

Rice University's Dr. James Tour.

of what you call it...chili con carne! And what d'you think? Exactly. I forgot all about it! So what the hell, we went out for Chinese. But back to this abiogenesis issue: Is it really true that we don't know how we got from there to there, the first *there* being an amino acid and the second *there* being a single-celled creature with a nucleus and membranes that somehow ingeniously determine what can go in and out and organelles—now that's a piece of work, an organelle! But if I'm not mistaken there are a helluva lot of steps between an amino acid and a cell, and I really wouldn't want to take anything for granted..."

So yes, it's long past time for us to stop churning forward and take stock. What can we say now, seventy years after that intoxicatingly hopeful experiment? In *The Mystery of Life's Origin*, Rice University's James Tour lays out the problem as clearly and patiently as he can, so that anyone in the world of chemistry can understand it. Tour is the world's premier nanoscientist, and likely knows as much about the art of creating molecules as anyone, and he rather bravely is willing to say that the Emperor has no clothes. He flatly states that what Miller and Urey suggested in 1952 didn't solve anything. In fact, he says it's far worse than that. It's not just that we haven't moved the ball forward since 1952, but in the seven decades since we have not only *not* drawn closer to understanding what happened, but have actually moved much further away. The more we have learned about this subject, the more we have actually been able to see that what looked so easy and so tantalizingly close in 1952 is in fact far beyond anything we ever dreamt. It's as if we were aiming at a target in 1952, assuming we would over time get better at aiming, but as we have been focused on aiming, the target has been moving further and further away. By now it is on the other side of the universe, and the idea of hitting it is simply no longer conceivable, even to the most dedicated marksman. What we have learned in these seven decades is that what we have been trying to do is almost certainly much harder than we originally thought.

But who wants to talk about this? How can we admit defeat when we crowed so loudly about having a solution in 1952? The news of Miller and Urey's experiment was earth-shaking, albeit premature. But at the time it was as though we had done what Dr. Frankenstein had done in Mary Shelley's 1818 novel, as though we had discovered the very secret of life itself. We had through science built a tower reaching into the very heavens, and in so doing we had killed any reason to require a deity. We could get there without his help.

Tour explains that two problems in particular have become intractable since the Miller–Urey experiment. One is that the single-celled organism—the earliest and simplest form of life—is now known to be inconceivably more complex than we thought in 1952. The second is that the one thing we thought made the idea of life's emerging via random processes a slam dunk—namely lots and lots of time—is something we now know to be the enemy, because organic molecules degrade rapidly, often under the same conditions in which they were formed. Some of them, like RNA, degrade in hours at room temperature, and need to be stored at -80 degrees Centigrade (112 degrees Fahrenheit), in carefully balanced buffers and metal chelating agents, just to last months. Let's look at the first problem first.

CHAPTER SEVEN

Life Is Far More Complex Than We Thought

When Darwin and others in the nineteenth and early twentieth centuries talked about cells, all they knew was that cells were exceedingly tiny things containing something called "protoplasm," which was a nonsense placeholder word for what they didn't know, much as "ether" was postulated as being a substance everywhere in outer space, although now we know there is no such thing. So it was with "protoplasm." It was just a term to denote an idea. Words have power, and speaking with confidence of "protoplasm" made everyone comfortable, until with powerful microscopes we eventually saw there was no such thing, and that the innards of a cell were actually breathtakingly complicated.

What we once thought was a simple membrane surrounding some gooey "protoplasm" was now seen to contain an astonishing universe within itself, a staggering agglomeration of intertwined parts performing stunningly complex functions. Even the membrane was outrageously sophisticated, being perfectly "water-tight" until it somehow "chose" to allow something in or out, and then did so. The more science learned, the more clear it became that a single cell was anything but simple, and the more it became obvious that something so impossibly sophisticated did not appear to have come into existence by chance. Already in 1978, the evolutionist and Cambridge zoologist W. H. Thorpe said that even the "most elementary type of cell constitutes a 'mechanism' unimaginably more complex than any machine yet thought up, let alone constructed, by man."[1]

Exactly how complex is hard to comprehend. The information in the DNA of a single bacterium alone is equivalent to the millions of words in a shelf of twenty books. The building blocks of DNA and RNA are called nucleotides, which are each involved in signaling, metabolism, and enzyme reactions. Each nucleotide consists of three parts: a phosphate group, a five-carbon sugar, and a nitrogenous base. The smallest bacterium in existence has 5,375 nucleotides. Other bacteria have three million. So how can we really comprehend the complexity of even the simplest cell, which we once thought simply to be a membrane surrounding some jelly-like "protoplasm"? And how is it exactly that these endless numbers of nucleotides are themselves "programmed" to do the complex things they do? We know that they are somehow "programmed"—but how? And can we dare to imagine that cells of such inestimable complexity just happened to show up through the random sloshing of waters on the surface of the early Earth? Because that is precisely what has continuously been proposed over the decades, albeit with increasingly less *joie de vivre*.

In *The Cosmic Blueprint*, the physicist Paul Davies says it "is possible to perform rough calculations of the probability that the endless breakup and reforming of the soup's complex molecules would lead to a small virus after a billion years." He then tells us what those calculations lead to. He says they work out at one chance in over ten to the two millionth power, a "mind-numbing" number, which put more simply would be harder to achieve than just happening to flip "heads on a coin six million times in a row." For anyone who has flipped heads on a coin ten times in a row (try it), you get the idea.

---

[1] Quoted by Michael Denton in *Evolution: A Theory in Crisis* (Burnett Books, 1985), https://www.goodreads.com/book/show/633004.Evolution?from_search=true&from_srp=true&qid=A2rkjnnwi9&rank=1.

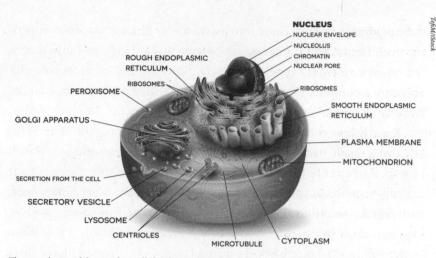

NUCLEUS
NUCLEAR ENVELOPE
NUCLEOLUS
CHROMATIN
NUCLEAR PORE

ROUGH ENDOPLASMIC
RETICULUM

RIBOSOMES

PEROXISOME

RIBOSOMES

SMOOTH ENDOPLASMIC
RETICULUM

GOLGI APPARATUS

PLASMA MEMBRANE

MITOCHONDRION

SECRETION FROM THE CELL

SECRETORY VESICLE

LYSOSOME

CENTRIOLES

MICROTUBULE   CYTOPLASM

The complexity of the simplest cells lies beyond anything science can yet fully comprehend.

Davies concludes by saying "the spontaneous generation of life by random molecular shuffling is a ludicrously improbable event."[2]

But since Davies made these observations, the time in which we know life to have come into being has shrunk tenfold, from roughly a billion years down to a hundred million. So whatever difficulty he is talking about must now be multiplied by ten. Once again, the more time passes and the more science discovers, the worse the problem gets.

There is a Franz Kafka short story titled "Before the Law" in which a man tries for many years to gain entry to "the Law," presumably to speak with a judge. It is classic Kafka, and if you know Kafka, you can imagine how it goes. First of all the guard at the door says the man cannot go in. Then the fearsome guard explains that even if this man were somehow able to sneak past him and this door, there are many doors beyond this through which he must pass, and each of them is guarded by a guard much more powerful than the previous. So the guard explains that the man may not pass—of course without giving any reason—but says that the man may wait if he likes, and indicates a stool where the man may sit. And so the man sits and waits. And waits. But he is never granted entry past this first guard. Eventually years pass (remember, this is Kafka), and as they do the man's chances to get to the judge seem

[2] Paul Davies, *The Cosmic Blueprint* (Philadelphia, Pennsylvania: Simon & Schuster, 1988), 118.

to dwindle. This is what we have come to call a Kafkaesque experience. Finally, when the man is very old and still sitting there waiting to be permitted entry, he finds himself pleading with the fleas in the guard's fur collar, hoping that perhaps they can help him. And then, of course, he dies. Depending on the mood of the reader the story can be either depressing or hilariously funny, because in its two short pages it sums up the experience most of us have had with one thing or another. It also describes exactly where science now stands regarding its long-assumed theories of how life began.

How then did life come into being? No one suggests it was always here, as they used to suggest that the universe was always here. Everyone agrees that there was a time when it did not exist at all, and then suddenly it did. What happened?

The Impossible Complexity of Cells

While we are pondering this most important of all questions, let's return to the outrageous complexity of the simplest life. The geneticist Michael Denton writes:

> Although the tiniest bacterial cells are incredibly small, weighing less than [0.000000000001 grams], each is in effect a veritable micro-miniaturized factory containing thousands of exquisitely designed pieces of intricate molecular machinery, made up of [one hundred billion] atoms, far more complicated than any machinery built by man and absolutely without parallel in the non-living world.[3]

Many scientists have come to the conclusion that what the Miller–Urey experiment suggested cannot be how life first arose. The Nobel-winning Belgian biochemist Christian de Duve, who specialized in origin-of-life research,

---

[3] Chuck Missler and Stephen Meyer, *In the Beginning There Was…Information* (Couer d'Alene, Idaho: Koinonia House, 2020), https://books.apple.com/us/audiobook/in-the-beginning-there-was-information/id1520171524.

discovered might give the wrong impression (of design) and swiftly directed his fellow biologists to vigilantly "keep in mind that what [you] see was not designed, but rather evolved." *It's not what it looks like! I can explain, I tell you!*

But as Meyer explains in his book, it is profoundly ironic because it is precisely due to what Watson and Crick discovered that "the materialist understanding of life has begun to unravel." Meyer calculates the odds of a single functional protein—or a single functional gene—coming into existence via random processes based "upon recent experiments in molecular biology establishing the extreme rarity of functional proteins in relation to the total number of possible arrangements of amino acids corresponding to a protein of a given length." And what did he find? Essentially that the odds of this ever having occurred are so astronomically high we can once and for all be certain that it never happened. To put it in his own words, "the probability of producing even a single functional protein of modest length (150 amino acids) by chance alone in a prebiotic environment stands at no better than a 'vanishingly small' [one] chance in ten to the 164th power."[5] That is, of course, one chance in one followed by 164 zeroes. In other words: it didn't happen.

Of course Meyer was only calculating what it would take for one single functioning protein to come into being. But the simplest living cell contains hundreds of specialized proteins, all performing their own tasks. How can all that have come into being from random molecules bouncing around? And how did they all fall into line to perform that staggering variety of tasks? The more you know about what goes on in a cell, the more you goggle. It gets increasingly absurd.

Dr. James Tour, Nanoscientist

As we mentioned, Rice University's James Tour is widely regarded as the greatest nanochemist on the planet. His awards and credentials bear this out. In 2009 he was named one of the top ten chemists in the

---

5 Stephen Meyer, *Return of the God Hypothesis* (San Francisco, California: HarperOne, 2021), 175.

rejected the chance hypothesis precisely because he judged the necessary fortuitous convergence of events implausible in the extreme. In *A Meaningful World*, Benjamin Wiker and Jonathan Witt say that a cell of the most minimal function "would contain at least 250 genes and their corresponding proteins. The odds of a primordial soup randomly burping up a concoction even half its length are vastly lower than one chance in 10 to the 150th power."[4]

James Watson and Francis Crick.

These numbers are so outrageous that—again—they can seem comedic. We have to be able to laugh, because nothing else will really suffice in facing the hopelessness of scaling a sheer cliff reaching to what amounts to infinity. But many scientists even now remain unwilling to concede the reality of the situation. They seem philosophically unable to accept the idea that life didn't create itself out of nothing, despite the mountainous evidence. The most well-known living atheist, Richard Dawkins, has often been quoted as saying that biology is "the study of complicated things that give the appearance of having been designed for a purpose." Of course, this too can sound unintentionally funny, as when Chico Marx asks the pearl-wearing dowager Margaret Dumont: "Well, who you gonna believe, me or your own eyes?"

What is it about the often seemingly self-explanatory and obvious appearance of design that must not be believed, no matter what? Can Dawkins and others make the case? They have certainly tried. And a half-century before Dawkins there were James Watson and Francis Crick, who in 1953 discovered the magnificently complex and beautiful spiral of the DNA molecule. It was a milestone moment in the triumphal march of science, but Crick was obviously deeply concerned that what he had

---

[4] Benjamin Wiker and Jonathan Witt, *A Meaningful World: How the Arts and Sciences Reveal the Genius of Nature* (Downers Grove, Illinois: IVP Academic, 2006), 18–19.

world for the previous decade, and in 2013 *R&D Magazine* named him "Top Scientist of the Year." He holds joint appointments in the departments of chemistry, computer science, materials science, and nanoengineering, and he has more than 700 research publications and over 140 patents. It is hard to overstate his stature in the field of nanoscience, which includes nanobiology, nanochemistry, and nanoengineering.

Tour is Jewish, born in Manhattan and grew up in the New York area, so when he visited New York City, we met at the Second Avenue Deli in Manhattan.[6] Just before our matzo ball soup arrived he thrust his phone at me unannounced and clicked on the unappetizing video of a white rat whose spinal column had been purposely "severed at the C5 vertebrae" so that it was paralyzed from the neck down. He explained to me that using graphene "nanotubes"—bisected lengthwise into what look like noodles, albeit on an impossibly microscopic scale—he has created tiny "bridges" over which nerves can and actually do regrow. As I watched the video I soon saw the same rat utterly restored. Tour explained that in less than two weeks the nerves from opposite sides of the severed vertebrae grew over the graphene and linked, enabling the rodent to control its limbs again. It seemed a miracle, but Tour said similar technology will make it possible to reconnect severed optic nerves too, so in lectures he says he is enabling the lame to walk and the blind to see, and even though this gets a laugh, he's not kidding.

A list of Tour's other projects—one may consult Wikipedia—is impossibly long and impressive. It includes creating "nanocars," each of which is comprised of a single molecule. His 2005 article about this—titled "Directional Control in Thermally Driven Single-Molecule Nanocars"—was ranked the Most Accessed Journal Article by the American Chemical Society. These are molecules he creates in the lab that are essentially tiny cars with independently moving axles, wheels, and a chassis. And each of them has a "motor" fueled by light. This is not science fiction, but science. Tour explains that if thirty thousand or so of these molecular "cars" were parked side by side, they would take up the width of a human hair.

---

[6] The Second Avenue Deli is no longer located on Second Avenue. This has nothing to do with plate tectonics, and everything to do with brand management.

Tour knows better than most that manipulating literal atoms to build molecules is almost inconceivably labor-intensive, requiring innumerable protocols and careful steps. So he speaks with great authority on this subject, and on the question of whether life emerged "randomly" four billion years ago. He says emphatically that based on what we now know—and on what he knows better than almost anyone—the idea is undeniably preposterous. Tour was the one who first explained to me what we have been saying, that in the seven decades since the Miller–Urey experiment we have not moved one angstrom closer to understanding how life emerged from non-life. Thanks to the work of many scientists over these decades, we have come to see the profoundly humbling reality of the situation and have come to see how deeply ignorant we really are about what happened when life leapt into being from the infinite abyss of non-life. Tour makes clear that only by knowing as much as we now do—having tried and failed and tried and failed over these seventy years—can we truly fathom our ignorance on the subject. In 1952 we could imagine that we were very far along in figuring this out. But now we know far too much to think that. We now know enough to know how truly ignorant we are.

But Tour says the real problem is that scientists are mostly too stubborn to admit this. They so want to believe the thesis and paradigm put forward by Miller and Urey that they ignore the obvious conclusions of their experiments and keep approaching the problem the same way, pretending that very soon we will finally see what we want to see. But Tour knows too much to be taken in; he knows that what they are purporting to be so close to showing actually can never be shown.

"[It] cannot ever happen," he says. "They're fudging it. But I know that they're . . . fudging it and most people and even most scientists don't know enough to argue with them. But I do. And I'm calling them out on it. I'm fed up. We should defund all further research in this direction because we know now for sure that it's like looking for a pot of gold at the end of each rainbow. It's demonstrably a fool's errand, and now it's a gigantic waste of money that could be put to better use."

Of course the decades of failure are part of the scientific process, too. We often learn that our assumptions were wrong, and we have to regroup and make a paradigm shift. But philosophical biases are often at odds with what the science shows us. Many who learned Aristotle's view of the universe refused to accept Copernicus's, many Newtonian physicists bristled at Einstein's theories, and most recently many Steady State proponents were loath to accept the idea of the Big Bang. This is human nature: for some reason the force of ideological inertia often seems to be approaching infinity.

The Unbridgeable Chasm between Life and Non-Life

Nonetheless, Dr. Tour knows too much to be very patient with any foot-dragging on this score. He knows precisely how impossible it is to "create" life from inorganic chemicals and can get specific. In a recent speech, he said:

> First of all, we don't know how to build...the four classes of molecules that are needed for [life. And even] if we had those four classes of molecules, we don't know how to assemble them even into the simplest of bacterium. We don't know how to do that.... Anyone who would say something contrary does not know what they are talking about. Show me the demonstration. Nobody has ever done it and it's not because of a lack of effort; it's not because of a lack of will. First of all they haven't been able to get the molecules to do this and if they could make the molecules—even if we were to give them the molecules—they wouldn't have the information. There would be no inherent information in the DNA. But even if we gave them the DNA in the structure that they wanted, they wouldn't know how to put all the components together because of the sophistication within a cell. The interactomes—meaning the interacting connectivity between the molecules, the Van der Waals interactions—all of these have to be in the right place and in the right order for a cell to function. We don't

even know how to define life, let alone know how to spark it to begin.[7]

The more one talks about this subject, the stranger and more confusing things become. What Dr. Tour says is quite true: we cannot even define life, much less know how it was created four billion years ago or begin to create it ourselves. The more we know how complex even the simplest life is, the less we can even say what life is. This too has over time become an increasingly mystifying mystery.

What Is Life?

In a way, trying to define life is something like when Supreme Court Justice Potter Stewart in 1964 had to determine whether a certain film was "pornography." This required defining what pornography was in the first place, to which he famously said: "I shall not today attempt further to define the kinds of material I understand to be embraced within that shorthand description and perhaps I could never succeed in intelligibly doing so. But I know it when I see it...." Beyond that, he could not say very much.

Isn't that how many of us might define life? Beyond that description, even the greatest biologists are stymied to a sheer standstill. When exactly does a human being cease to be alive? In one moment there is life and in another death. What is it precisely that changes from the one moment to the next? And on the other end of the life spectrum, where we are talking about the simplest life forms, single-celled organisms, how do we define them?

The science writer John Casti in his book *Paradigms Lost* probably put it as succinctly and clearly as possible. "By more or less general consensus nowadays," he writes, "an entity is considered to be 'alive' if it has the capacity to carry out three basic functional activities: metabolism,

---

[7] Discovery Science, "James Tour: The Origin of Life Has Not Been Explained," YouTube, July 5, 2019, https://www.youtube.com/watch?v=r4sP1E1Jd_Y.

self-repair, and replication."[8] It's easy enough to understand what "self-repair" and "replication" mean. Yet the level of complexity involved in these concepts is almost inconceivable. And yet who can easily define "metabolism"? One dictionary says it is "the sum of the physical and chemical processes in an organism by which its material substance is produced, maintained, and destroyed, and by which energy is made available." The simple fact is that we are talking about the most staggeringly complex things, and the more science has learned over the decades, the more complexity we see.

So when we come to the subject of how the first life came into being from non-life, we are talking about something that once seemed easy to postulate, but that has become over time essentially inconceivable, even to the greatest minds of science. Is it any wonder no one has ever been able to show how it happened? In 1977 in *Physics Today*, Ilya Prigogine, who won the Nobel Prize in Chemistry, said: "The probability that at ordinary temperatures a macroscopic number of molecules is assembled to give rise to the coordinated functions characterizing living organisms is vanishingly small. The idea of the spontaneous genesis of life in its present form is therefore improbable, even on the scale of billions of years...."[9]

Time Is the Enemy

Some people argue that there's a chance these things could happen in hundreds of millions of years, but Tour explains that time can be the enemy when it comes to organic synthesis. Many of the chemicals needed are kinetic products, meaning they are not thermodynamically stable. For example, carbohydrates—the main class of compounds—are the units that hook together DNA. These are the units that have identifying aspects on cell structure; these are the units that the cell is going to need

[8] John L. Casti, *Paradigms Lost* (New York: Harper Perennial, 1990), https://www.amazon.com/Paradigms-Lost-John-L.-Casti/dp/0380711656/ref=sr_1_7?dchild=1&keywords=JOHN+CASTI&qid=1623529746&s=books&sr=1-7.

[9] Quoted by Gerald L. Schroeder in *The Science of God: The Convergence of Scientific and Biblical Wisdom* (New York: Free Press, 1997), 118.

for the energy of life. But once they form they begin to decompose. Tour says "unless somebody is there... to fish them out, to stop the process, and put them in a bottle under inert conditions in a freezer," they go away as quickly as they came into being.

Tour explains there are many other similar problems. For example, if random processes somehow succeeded in miraculously creating a carbohydrate or another necessary compound, the random processes don't know how to do it again. They have no capacity to "learn." If they happen to hit it just right by accident, they have no ability to say, "Let's try that again!" Tour says:

> Say it took you four hundred million years to get to a certain point on a synthesis, [but] now you have to go back and make more. But how do you go back and make more? Nature never kept a laboratory notebook.... So even if it could make more, it doesn't know how to, so it's got to start all over again. But it doesn't know how to. [It] doesn't know why to start over again because it doesn't know what it's going toward.[10]

In other words, we now know that because there is zero intentionality in random processes happening over time, the assumptions we have made aren't reasonable. In fact they are fanciful and wildly unrealistic, but they suited the narrative that these things happened without a divine hand guiding them. But Tour has no qualms about saying that the science is now very clear that this cannot have been what happened. And it's time to stop pretending.

Stop the Research!

Dr. Tour underscores the lack of progress in "Origin of Life" research since 1952 by talking about the stunning progress we have accomplished in other fields in that time. "We've had human spaceflight," he says. "We've had

---

[10] Discovery Science, "James Tour: The Origin of Life Has Not Been Explained."

satellite connectivity. We have the internet. We have the entire Silicon era of microchips and computer technology. We have all of this in the same two-thirds of a century, [but on Origin of Life research] we are still exactly where Miller and Urey were." Scientists working on this have succeeded in making some of the chemicals but are "nowhere close to even knowing how to…hook them together…in the proper order. We are clueless on this. Clueless. Because time doesn't solve this, even with all our ingenuity."

In explaining why the current research has not solved the problem—and cannot solve the problem—he reiterates the idea that the eons of time we believed were the reason we could trust this direction in abiogenesis research has been shown to be the very reason we no longer can trust this direction. Again, time only exacerbates our problems.

> Time is not going to solve the problem. You let these chemicals that have been made…sit around, even for months, and you can [see that]—even in the origin of life researchers themselves, when they've let these go for weeks—they show the degradation of these in a period of weeks. Weeks is the twinkling of an eye when it comes to prebiotic timescales.[11]

So the notion that this sort of thing might have happened out in the wild of the oceans billions of years ago becomes even more ridiculous. He goes on:

> The chemicals decompose…. The ammonia environment and cell itself is quite basic. You're going to have extended Aldol reactions coming on. So to think that the molecules could be made and sit there waiting for other molecules to come in, it doesn't happen. Organic chemistry doesn't work that way. Any student that is lazy enough to set up reactions and likes to go home for the weekend without working them up pays the price for that. With a depressed yield, generally…. As soon as the reactions are done or as soon as

---

11 Ibid.

what you want is the optimized yield, you have to stop that reaction and get it away from the starting materials or else what happens is it goes on to polymerize product. Especially when you're making kinetic products, which is not the thermodynamically most stable product, which is exactly what you get in many of the chemicals that are needed for life. So time is actually the enemy.[12]

But then Dr. Tour circles back to another even more frightening problem, which we have touched on already, which has to do with the absolutely absurd complexity of what we are trying to achieve. He says the protein interactions alone that take place in a yeast cell are impossible to comprehend. Words really cannot do justice to the astronomical odds. The numbers involved can only be found deep in the territory of madness. "Remember," he says, "that just the protein interactions in a single yeast cell are 10 to the 79 billion combinations." In case we are not clear on what he just said, he reminds us that the number of "elemental particles in the universe is 10 to the 90th... that's a 1 with 90 zeros after it. But the combinations of just protein-protein [interactions] in a single yeast cell is 10 to the 79 billion. That's not a 1 with 90 zeros after it, but a 1 with 79 billion zeros after it. These are the types of numbers we're talking about."

And in case we are not yet convinced, he reminds us that the thousands of proteins that need to be just right are just the beginning of what we face:

[In] addition to just those three thousand proteins... in that single yeast cell, you still need all the DNA, all the RNA. You need to have all the carbohydrates... remember the carbohydrates have all their own definition ordered by the way they're hooked up.... You can put more information in the carbohydrates that are on a cell surface than you store in DNA and RNA combined. And that information has to come from an original DNA template, plus a series of other enzyme cascades.

---

[12] Ibid.

All of this is in that cell in addition to those interactomes. It's very complex.[13]

So it would seem.

---

[13] Ibid.

CHAPTER EIGHT

More on Origins of Life: Now What?

After facing this ocean of information against the idea that life might "just have happened," most people would conclude that the only reasonable conclusion is that an incomprehensible Intelligence was behind it—a Designer or Creator of some kind. Some of us might not like to draw that conclusion, but should we not follow the logic, nonetheless? If science and mathematics have led us inexorably more and more to this conclusion, why should we shrink from it? Are we not secure enough in the objectivity of science and mathematics to let them speak for themselves? But many in the atheist camp have been less concerned with following the science than with avoiding any conclusion pointing to God, even if it makes them reach beyond science in other directions.

For example, Francis Crick, the very man who discovered DNA's double helix, was only too happy to offer a theory on how he thought life had first appeared on our planet. Writing in the unintentionally tragicomically titled astronomy journal *Icarus* in 1973, Crick theorized that perhaps aliens brought life to Earth. He would not say whether they had traveled earthward on waxen wings, and did not footnote Erich von Däniken. If anyone was tempted to think he must be joking, he crowned his "theory" with the laurel wreath of an honorable "scientific" name: "Directed Panspermia."

But even if Crick's crackpot theory were somehow true, what would it have solved beyond kicking the can of this vital question down the road—and beyond our solar system? If aliens had brought life here, or had "created" life and brought it here, the question would remain: *How had they created life?* That was the question on the table. And would it be too much to ask who it was that had created the brilliant aliens? Or had they created themselves? If any of us had created life in a lab and then carried it down the hall to our supervisor, the question would never be what path had we taken from the lab to the supervisor's office—"tell us whether via elevator or stairs!"—nor what sort of shoes we were wearing as we hustled our newly created "life" along the hallways. The question would simply be *How have you created life? The claim is astonishing. Please tell us how? How?!* There is no other question. How had you done the thing no one ever has done or begun to begin to do or know how to begin to do in a way that gives us clues to how life could arise from non-life? How did you get life from non-life? *There is no other question.* And please show us your work. Holding bacteria in a test tube as you huff and puff from your journey to make the claim does not quite answer the question. So yes, we will need to see your work, and alas, if you cannot show your work, you will of course be suspected of fraud and probably lose your job and reputation forever. Indeed, even if you can show your work, there exists a custom in the scientific community in which one is obliged to repeat one's experiment numerous times to see whether the results can be duplicated.

We know that Francis Crick must have known something about the Scientific Method, having won a Nobel Prize in science sixteen years earlier, but it is never ill-advised to say what everyone is presumed to know, just so there is no embarrassing misunderstanding. But in retrospect we must assume that Crick's noodlings in *Icarus* were a psychedelic-era hallucination only permitted to appear in the august pages of that journal because Crick by dint of his worldwide fame and Nobel had earned the right to sound preposterous and was accorded more latitude than non-Nobelists. But as we say, what he dared to suggest in his sunward flight of science-free fancy did not carry the question closer to any answer, but merely caused our hero to plummet embarrassingly into the Aegean, from which his aforementioned reputation would eventually fish him out. But such speculations are themselves evidence of how high atheists will fly to avoid the horror of the science on the ground if its implications are unpalatable. So we must see irresponsible non-answers like "Directed Panspermia" as the obfuscating ink squirted by an escaping cephalopod in his furious undulation to safety from such vexing questions. Somewhat happily, Crick was eight years later rather more sober-minded than he had been in *Icarus*. "An honest man," he wrote in 1981, "armed with all the knowledge available to us now, could only state that in some sense, the origin of life appears at the moment to be almost a miracle, so many are the conditions which would have had to have been satisfied to get it going."[1]

Lost in Space

In the three decades following Crick's late but nonetheless welcome admission, the evidence that the origin of life was a miracle and not possible in any other way had increased exponentially, as we have said. But this did not prevent the hopeful Richard Dawkins from circling back to the sunny skies over the Aegean. During an interview for the 2008 film *Expelled*, he allowed that yes, the astonishing and baroque complexity of DNA might indicate "a signature of some kind of designer," which initially sounded like the loud thunderclap of a concession. After all, had not he and many others insisted that we must never confuse "the appearance of design" with actual design? He said biology is "the study of complicated things that give the appearance of having been designed for a purpose." So for him to talk about "some kind of designer" in a public interview was shocking. Was he at last

---

[1] Francis Crick, *Life Itself: Its Origin and Nature* (New York: Simon & Schuster, 1981).

Jacob Peter Gowy's *The Fall of Icarus*, circa 1636.

open to discussing these things openly, unshackled from strict atheist dogma? Alas, not. For Dawkins then qualified his statement into smithereens by stating that this "designer" could never be a "divine" designer. He did not say why that precise distinction must be made—nor what, by his standards, constituted divinity. But when pressed to say more about what sort of designer he had in mind, Dawkins reached backward to the groovy solution proposed thirty-five years earlier in *Icarus*, saying that perhaps it was extra-terrestrial creatures who had done the designing. We are left to gather that unfortunately they had deposited their little designs here on Earth anony-mously, like some untethered dog in the neighborhood. The idea of invented aliens giving us the gift of life from the heavens presented, he said, an "intriguing possibility."

That the world's most famous atheist would invent his own creation myth, rather than accept the evidence of science, bespeaks a faith in something far beyond science, and must be seen as an unmistakable betrayal of the science and reason whose praises he had so loudly sung. But his statements went quite unchallenged by the atheist scientists who looked to him as a leader.

Philosophical Paradigm Murders Science

We conclude this chapter on a strange but telling note. It seems that scientists have again succumbed to the temptation to think unscientifically in what they believe is the service of science, although it is actually in the service not of science, but of a philosophical ideology that is the enemy of science. Materialism—or the idea that nothing beyond the material universe exists—implies that God does not exist. And Darwinian evolution has come to be a powerful idea for those ensorcelled by the siren song of materialism, because it puts forth a way of explaining how the variety of life on our planet can be explained with a naturalistic mechanism of self-selection, meaning without a Creator God. But the idea of evolution has become so powerful that it has begun creeping backward into the world before life existed.

When we talk of "origin of life" theories we often use the term "abiogenesis." The terms are used interchangeably and mean the same thing: the process by which elements of non-life somehow randomly come together to produce a living single-celled organism. But a surprising and strange thing occurs when we look up "abiogenesis" in various dictionaries. For example, the Oxford Dictionary defines abiogenesis as "the original evolution of life or living organisms from inorganic or inanimate substances." Evolution? Weren't we talking about a world before life existed? Of course we were. That's the point. Abiogenesis is supposed to be what happens before life, as non-life comes together to form life. But the term "evolution" has somehow been slipped in. How did that happen? How can we talk of "evolution" before we have life? Merriam-Webster, too, says abiogenesis is "a theory in the evolution of early life on earth: organic molecules and subsequent simple life forms first originated from inorganic substances." Again, we are talking of evolution before life. How can we pretend that is possible? It is like talking of gestation before conception. Wikipedia is as well guilty of this shamefully disingenuous sleight of hand. "While the details of this process are still unknown," it says, in great understatement, "the prevailing scientific hypothesis is that the transition from non-living to living entities was not a single event, but *an evolutionary process* of increasing complexity that involved molecular self-replication, self-assembly, autocatalysis, and the emergence of cell membranes."

But again, how can we possibly talk of an "evolutionary process" before there was life on the planet? Apparently, some people are so enamored of the idea of "evolution" they have forgotten what it means. So they have tried to slip it into discussions where it has no business, as though talking of flatulence in the Van Allen Belt. How could someone bring the term *evolution* into the discussion of a process where—by definition—there is no life and there can be no mechanism for evolution?

As we recall, the mechanism behind Darwinian theory is natural selection, or "survival of the fittest." The idea is that as living organisms reproduce, those possessing some advantage will survive. Their genes get passed on, while the genes of those organisms that don't do so well do not. So everyone understands that the theory of evolution by definition presupposes living organisms. As they reproduce through generations we can see change via the "natural selection" of genes. That is the mechanism of evolution, and reproduction is crucial, and there can be no reproduction without life.

It is one thing to discuss Darwin's theory and to believe that life forms can over time alter slightly via mutation or other means—and that those with advantages would "self-select" and survive beyond those without advantages. We have all heard tales or read in textbooks about how a certain animal better fitted to survive would survive, and it seemed self-explanatory. If animals with longer necks could more easily reach the leaves they ate, then in time the course of nature would favor those animals who would bear young with longer necks, and this process would continue, always favoring those with the longest necks, until eventually over the course of millennia we would have giraffes. Even if you don't agree that this is what happened, you can certainly grasp the idea and understand why most of the scientific establishment saw the theory as satisfactory for explaining many things. We can argue about evolution all day long, but before we can ever get to talking about what happened after the first life arose on our planet, we have to figure out how that life arose to begin with. And we know that if it happened, it cannot have had anything to do with "evolution." So how do these three dictionary definitions of "abiogenesis" possibly excuse tossing that term into the mix?

Can it be that everyone has been trained to nod in agreement at the concept of evolution, so that if we sneak it into this conversation on abiogenesis we can pretend that evolution extends everywhere, including into the world before life? The term "evolution" is often used sloppily, as when someone talks of the universe "evolving," as though the lifeless rocks and balls of flaming gas and galaxies were somehow alive. But most people know the term "evolving universe" is meant metaphorically. But anyone using the word "evolution" in defining "abiogenesis" is certainly *not* being metaphorical. On the contrary, they are deftly—and it appears dishonestly—implying that whatever magical process happens *after* we have life can somehow happen *before* we have life too, as though there is some innate universal principle at work. There's only one problem: we have left the realm of science. So again: Why would anyone use the term "evolution" in a definition of abiogenesis, except because their materialist ideology is more important than truth and clarity? Were they hoping to sneak something past their readers? Or did they really believe you could have evolution before life? Which is worse?

In the strange and inaccurate use of this word in these definitions, the term "evolution" has moved beyond the idea of living creatures changing over time to become an entire paradigm, so that like a miasma it flowed in every direction and settled over everything, as though unconstrained by the laws of science. Suddenly everything that changed over time could be spoken of as having "evolved," even though this is obviously not true. But it seems that the giddiness over the concept of "evolution" overtook rationality and crept backward into the world before living organisms, and then hid there, hoping we wouldn't notice.

We don't know why the first living cells split in two and reproduced, but we may agree that they did, and that reproduction was central to what we call life. It is what made it continue forward in time ad infinitum. But because of scientific progress we know that nitrogen and hydrogen and silver and ammonia do not reproduce. Neither do amino acids or carbohydrates. Nor do any of these things eat or excrete or metabolize in any way. Only life does that. So how can non-life be said to "evolve"? It cannot. Unless one is being unintentionally sloppy in the service of a philosophical paradigm one thinks more important than actual science.

PART II

"The Stones Will Cry Out"

CHAPTER NINE

The Evidence of Archaeology

It may be stated categorically that no archaeological discovery has ever controverted a biblical reference.

—Rabbi Dr. Nelson Glueck

The man who delivered the above statement was among the most respected of his century. He was close to many Israeli statesmen, including David Ben-Gurion, Golda Meir, and Abba Eban, and for twenty-four years he was president of Hebrew Union College. In 1961 he delivered the benediction at President John F. Kennedy's inauguration, and in 1963 he was featured on the cover of *Time*. But Rabbi Glueck was most famous for his pioneering work in the field of biblical archaeology.

When one considers that he was more on the theologically liberal end of the spectrum, his statement is the more remarkable. It continued: "Scores of archaeological findings have been made which confirm in clear outline or in exact detail historical statements in the Bible." When someone like Glueck says something as strong as "it may be stated categorically that no archaeological discovery"—ever—has pointed away from the veracity of the Bible, it's hard not to take notice. It's also hard not to wonder whether the book that some think of as a cobbled-together compendium of ancient folktales—most of which are half-remembered and get many details wrong, even if there is some fundamental truth to them—is in fact the inerrant Word of God. How else can we understand Glueck's fantastic assertion that all of the archaeological discoveries confirm what the ancient scriptures say? First of all, is that true? And if so, is it still true today?

We should be clear that biblical archaeology is a relatively new field that only began in the last half of the nineteenth century. Yet within a few decades the number of finds confirming the biblical accounts was overwhelming and flew in the face of the biblical skepticism popular at that time. By the early twentieth century so many finds continued to bear out the biblical account that "The Bible is confirmed by every turn of the spade" became a popular catchphrase. And this trend continued, as illustrated by Glueck's statement from the middle of the century. The track record of biblical archaeology baffled—and continues to baffle—those convinced that archaeology must eventually contradict the biblical accounts.

One of these is James Agresti, an aerospace engineer who in his book *Rational Conclusions* describes being a twenty-five-year-old atheist determined to study the Bible to document its errors. But what he encountered surprised him, and by the time he was finished, he was instead persuaded of its truth. But one of the main reasons for his about-face was what he learned about the archaeological record. Echoing Rabbi Glueck, Agresti concluded: "I have yet to encounter archaeological evidence that shows any part of the Bible to be inaccurate."

My own story is the reverse. I had found faith before I ever considered whether the Bible could be corroborated via the archaeological record. I did not have much hope that it could. I had become accustomed to a cultural narrative that tugged consistently toward a secular and skeptical assessment of such things, and I assumed some things were simply too distant to have much hope of retrieving them via archaeology. I also assumed the staunch hostility in academic circles toward the historicity of the Bible would quash any encouraging chirrups along such lines.

But on Washington's birthday in 1990, I was reading the *New York Times* when to my great surprise I read a headline on page eight: "Believers Score in

Battle over the Battle of Jericho."[1] The article said recent discoveries at Jericho had upended previous conclusions about the biblical account. The dating of recently discovered pottery showed that the fabled walls of Jericho had indeed fallen at the time of Joshua, just as the Bible said, about forty years after the purported Exodus of the Jews from Egypt. It said they had fallen inward, too, so that the Israelites could climb up and over them to take the city, as the Bible said they had. The archaeologist Kathleen Kenyon in the 1950s said the opposite, but these new finds contradicted her data and conclusions.

The article was by John Noble Wilford, as respected a journalist as existed, having two Pulitzers, along with the insuperable accomplishment of having written the *Times*'s epochal "Men Land on Moon" story on July 21, 1969.[2] So I was amazed to read in the notably secular *Times* a straightforward report confirming the biblical account of something that had happened shortly after the death of Moses.

Three years later it happened again. Another *Times* article, this one on the front page, said Israeli archaeologists had discovered a stele bearing the first reference outside the Bible to King David and the dynasty he founded, "the House of David." The article was again by John Noble Wilford, obviously the man to whom such stories were assigned. But the discovery of archaeological evidence for the Bible's King David was genuinely earth-shaking news, since many scholars thought King David was a mythic figure like King Arthur. But here was evidence in stone that David—the giant-killing shepherd boy who became king—had been real, and that his dynasty in the tenth century BC was every bit as historical as that of King Tutankhamen in the fourteenth century BC or Henry VIII in the sixteenth century AD. It was a truly stunning discovery, and as I remembered the article about biblical Jericho from a few

---

[1] John Noble Wilford, "Believers Score in the Battle over the Battle of Jericho," *New York Times*, February 22, 1990, https://www.nytimes.com/1990/02/22/world/believers-score-in-battle-over-the-battle-of-jericho.html.

[2] His name was the only byline on that now-historic front page, whose famous headline marked the first time in the paper's century-long history that it felt justified in employing the monumental ninety-six-point type size.

years earlier I began wondering what else might be discovered. How much of what many of us had presumed was mythical or lost forever was not only historical, but might still be revealed?

Is Archaeology Leading Us to God?

In the decades since, I have read of many more such things and have come to wonder whether the spades and pickaxes of the archaeologists have been doing what the telescopes and microscopes of the scientists have been doing. It seems that slowly but surely, they have been pointing unavoidably to the paradigm-shifting idea that the God of the Bible is real. And as with the case from science, the archaeological trend seems not only to continue, but over time to strengthen. Some of the most astounding discoveries have been made extremely recently—as we shall see in subsequent chapters—including some so astounding that they are a challenge to believe, until one examines the evidence and the context, at which point one wonders less about whether these things are real than about how it is possible discoveries this extraordinary could have been kept so quiet that most people are unaware of them.

Some of the most stupefying in recent years include the identification a decade ago of the biblical city of Sodom, complete with evidence of the details of its incomparably dramatic destruction; and much more recently the confirmation of several discoveries more bewildering still, such as Jesus's childhood home in Nazareth and the very pavement upon which Jesus, wearing his crown of thorns, stood at his trial before Pilate during what is surely one of the most famous scenes in world history. The silent stones of that pavement and many other stones too bear witness to what must have been taken on faith a few years or decades before. To biblical skeptics, the whole thing must seem like some irritating conspiracy.

Beginning of Biblical Archaeology

What we now call archaeology began in the nineteenth century but did not become a serious discipline until the latter part of that century.

To understand why it emerged, we must look back to the Renaissance, which among other things signaled a nostalgia for classical antiquity. People began to look backward—beyond the Gothic landscape of the Middle Ages—to the Roman and Hellenic civilizations before them. A renewed interest in the distant past had bloomed. There always had been travelers who wrote of their adventures, and who reported on strange sights, but now as the English and other colonialist empires expanded into the distant places where the civilizations of antiquity had existed, the desire to bring home treasures from these distant lands grew. Two early and famous examples of this were the 1799 discovery of the Rosetta Stone and in 1801 the grotesque removal from the Parthenon of the so-called Elgin Marbles. Suddenly, the past was returning, and interest in finding more of it grew apace.

Something that helped kick off the field of biblical archaeology was the visit to Palestine in 1838 of an American biblical scholar named Dr. Edward Robinson. He actually made two trips, traveling exhaustively and identifying innumerable biblical sites. Using his exhaustive knowledge of the Bible and history—and of many writers from antiquity—he succeeded in separating much legendary fiction from fact. For example, he agreed that the "Cave of the Patriarchs" in Hebron, where Abraham and Sarah were said to be buried, was indeed authentic while other places—such as "Samson's Well," where the famous strong man was supposed to have quenched his thirst after slaying a thousand Philistines—were not. His most significant accomplishment during this time was his confirmation that the gigantic arch (henceforth named Robinson's Arch) that was once attached to what had been a monumental staircase leading up to the Temple Mount was not a more recent Roman or Muslim construction, but was in fact from the first century BC. This meant that the colossally large walls to which it was attached were from the time of the Second Temple in the sixth century BC. Suddenly there was a tangible, visible link to the great history of the Jews, as well as to the New Testament. These gigantic walls and the arch were something Jesus himself knew. He had almost certainly climbed the stairs the arch had supported.

Josephus in the first century wrote of the arch, which was an architectural wonder of its day. But it was not until Robinson's visit in 1838 that Josephus's description could be identified as the arch still visible to all who visited Jerusalem. Suddenly the world from two millennia past reached into the present, where one could literally touch it. Three years later Robinson published his landmark book on his findings, *Biblical Researches in Palestine*, spurring greater interest in the field, and leading to a spate of finds in the decades ahead, each of which surprised the world by confirming the historicity of the Old and New Testaments.

But the discovery we will discuss first is of no single artifact, but rather of a forgotten people, and of a vast empire as powerful and long-lived as any that ever existed in human history. And if not for the words about them in the Hebrew Scriptures, they almost certainly would be forgotten still.

Who Were the Hittites?

The story of the discovery of the Hittites is the classic example of how the historicity of the Bible was not taken seriously when the nineteenth century began but was taken very seriously by the time it ended. As early-nineteenth-century scholars began to make their case against the historical accuracy of the Bible, the non-existence of the Hittites came to be Exhibit A. There was at least some evidence for nearly every other major people and every other empire, from the Babylonians to the Persians. The writers of antiquity had accounted for them all, and for many other peoples too. But why was there no extra-biblical evidence for the Hittites, who are mentioned in the Bible forty-six times? Why did none of the ancient writers—such as Thucydides or Strabo or Herodotus or Pliny—ever mention them? Historical evidence painted them as demographic phantoms, no less unaccounted for than the Nephilim. What sense did it make that these "Hittites" should exist only in the pages of an ancient document filled with invented stories of angels and demons?

It is interesting that "Hittites" appear throughout the Bible, bespeaking a far-flung existence in time and geographical space too. The first mention comes in Genesis 23, when Abraham purchased what is known as the Cave of the Patriarchs from a Hittite named Ephron. There, in the old city of Hebron on what is today Israel's West Bank, Abraham buried his wife, Sarah, and years later joined her. Apart from the Temple Mount, it is the most sacred site in Judaism. The Bible also says the grandson of Abraham and Sarah, Esau, married two pagan Hittite women, despite the strong disapproval of his parents, Isaac and Rebekah. A few centuries later, in the pages of Deuteronomy, Moses includes them in the list of those occupying the Land of Canaan: "the Hittite and the Amorite and the Canaanite and the Perizzite and the Hivite and the Jebusite...."

In the account of the Syrians' siege of Samaria in 2 Kings, we read that they suddenly retreated when they heard the "noise of a great army." "Look," the Syrians declared, "the king of Israel has hired against us the kings of the Hittites and the kings of the Egyptians to attack us!" We encounter the most famous Hittite in the story of King David's adultery with Bathsheba, who was then married to one of his officers, known only as "Uriah the Hittite." David's son Solomon himself had a number of Hittite wives. The Bible portrayed the Hittites as a vast empire with tremendous power, stretching through the centuries. But where had they gone to? Why was there no trace of them anywhere, even in the ancient literature? Their non-existence was so complete that in 1861, the *Encyclopedia Britannica* devoted a scant eight and a half lines to them, and this was only a polite summary of what the Bible said about them.

For the extraordinary story of their rediscovery and resurrection into history, we must retreat to the first years of the century, where we meet a decidedly eccentric Swiss "explorer and Orientalist" named Johann Ludwig Burckhardt.

Burckhardt was born at Lausanne and studied at Göttingen and Leipzig, afterward traveling to England to work for a British club called the Association for Promoting the Discovery of the Interior Parts of Africa, which is the organization that began the era of British exploration into the interior of the "Dark Continent." To prepare himself for what could be a dangerous trip to Cairo and then to the Niger in West Africa, Burckhardt decided in 1807 to study Arabic and medicine at Cambridge. Already by this time he had enthusiastically "adopted the Arabian costume," cutting a colorful figure on campus. When in 1809 he traveled to Syria, he had so perfected his disguise that he took the name Sheikh Ibrahim Ibn Abdallah and successfully passed himself off as a Mohammedan, although he wrote all his letters in French and signed them "Louis."

In 1812, Burckhardt made a detour through Jordan to look for the lost German explorer Ulrich Jasper Seetzen, who had been traveling in that area looking for the fabled lost city of Petra. Outdoing even Burckhardt in his immersion and assimilation into Arab culture, Seetzen had by then converted to Islam and styled himself "Hag Moses." He went so far as to assume the disguise of a beggar, but fell afoul of some low characters and was subsequently murdered. While on Seetzen's trail, Burckhardt himself happened to discover the extraordinary ancient Nabatean city of Petra, for which he is now most famous.

But it was before this, while traveling through northern Syria, that Burckhardt found himself passing through the city of Hamath, where he spotted some black basalt stones of great antiquity in the foundation of a building. On them was an inscription in a strange-looking language. Burckhardt did not mention what he saw before he died in 1817. But he kept a detailed journal that was published in 1822 as *Travels in Syria and the Holy Land*. It was then that the world first read of the strange inscriptions: "In the corner of a house in the Bazar (sic) is a stone with a number of small figures and signs which appears to be a kind of hieroglyphic writing, though it does not resemble that of Egypt." Looking at these hieroglyphics today, we might well think of Keith Haring pictographs, so we only can imagine how confusing it must have looked to Burckhardt two centuries ago. It resembled nothing anyone in Europe had ever seen. Like the strange cuneiform writing first being seen around that time, it was perfectly opaque. Nor would anyone see these stones again for fifty years, so the mystery deepened.

Meanwhile, something else was happening. In 1834 the French explorer Charles Texier was wandering northward through Turkey looking for the

ruins of a lost Roman city called
Tavium. When Texier and his
men came to the village of
Boghaz Köy he inquired of the
locals whether they knew of any
ancient ruins, whereupon they
led him to some hills overlooking
the village. There Texier was
astounded to behold the rem-
nants of a civilization that did not
look Roman at all but seemed
much older. There were several
colossal fortification walls in the
Cyclopean style at that time
being discovered in Greece. The
size of the stones was extraordinary. Who had put them there?

Swiss explorer Johann Ludwig Burckhardt (1784–1817)

The locals led him further, where he saw another monumental wall.
It too seemed built by giants and was extremely long. Texier walked along
it for what he estimated to be a mile. Then he found still more wall
stretching beyond his sight. What thousands of workers had built this
monstrous barrier and when? Texier eventually came to a monumental
gate on which he saw the larger-than-life bas relief of a helmeted figure
holding an axe. About a mile on he found a similar gate flanked with
huge stone lions. His guide led him further still, until he stood before
yet another site, where he took in another bas relief that depicted a haunting procession of godlike figures bearing some resemblance to the one
he had seen before holding the ax. All of them wore peaked hats and were
unlike anything he had ever seen.

Then he saw a kind of writing that was something like hieroglyphic
pictographs, though he knew it was not Egyptian. Texier walked the
entire perimeter of the great wall, which he reckoned to be about three
miles. What city had it once contained? It would have been even larger

than ancient Athens. The city seemed once upon a time to have been tremendously significant, almost certainly the seat of a great empire. But now it was utterly lost to history.[3]

How could a civilization so obviously magnificent and powerful have died so completely that even those living in its shadow hadn't the dimmest idea what it was? It's almost impossible not to think of Percy Bysshe Shelley's 1818 poem "Ozymandias,"[4] which speaks of the profoundly humbling idea that a world of breathtaking grandeur and majesty—along with those once attached to its unparalleled power—might be forever forgotten, marked only by some inscrutable carvings. Texier knew someone had once lived and ruled here, but who? In any case, he did not publish his account and illustrations until 1862, nearly three decades later.

But one year after Texier's discovery, the British diplomat and antiquarian William Richard Hamilton stepped into the story. Hamilton had entered the lapidary annals of archaeology three decades before. It was Hamilton who personally recovered the fabled Rosetta Stone from a French ship on the verge of spiriting the fabulous object away, in contravention of the treaty

---

[3] David Down, "The Hittites: A Civilisation Lost and Found," *Archaeological Diggings*, July 15, 2016, https://www.hopechannel.com/au/read/the-hittites-a-civilisation-lost-and-found.

[4] I met a traveller from an antique land,
Who said—"two vast and trunkless legs of stone
Stand in the desert... near them, on the sand,
Half sunk a shattered visage lies, whose frown,
And wrinkled lips, and sneer of cold command,
Tell that its sculptor well those passions read
Which yet survive, stamped on these lifeless things,
The hand that mocked them, and the heart that fed;
And on the pedestal these words appear:
My name is Ozymandias, King of Kings,
Look on my Works ye Mighty, and despair!
Nothing beside remains. Round the decay
Of that colossal Wreck, boundless and bare.

signed after that nation's defeat at
Alexandria.[5] Astonishingly, Hamilton was also personally involved in
the second aforementioned story,
regrettably overseeing the uncon-
scionable removal from the Acropo-
lis of the infamously named Elgin
Marbles, an act of cultural barba-
rism without equal even in those
culturally barbarous times, violently
wresting them from their intended
site atop the Parthenon's pediment
and taking them to the British
Museum, too, where they and the
Rosetta Stone can still be seen today.

William Richard Hamilton (1777–1859)

But in 1835, Hamilton was traveling through Turkey when he visited
the same site Texier had stumbled upon. Twelve miles north, in a place
the Turks called Alacahöyük, Hamilton came upon a second ancient site,
this one with a great sphinx figure carved upon a buried city gate. He
didn't publish his account of this until 1842, and as we have said, Texier's
account did not appear until 1862.

But when Texier's account finally was published, the French archaeologist Georges Perrot took note and traveled to Turkey to investigate the spots
Texier and Hamilton had seen and written about. But Perrot found something astonishing that both Texier and Hamilton somehow had missed. It
was a tremendously long inscription—stretching twenty-five feet across—
carved onto a rock face. The local Turks called it Nishan Tash, but even to
them it was as inscrutable as bird song.

Eight years after this—in 1870—our story returns to the city of Hamath
in northern Syria, where Burkhardt in 1812 had seen the strange hieroglyphics
on the basalt foundation stones of some houses. Now it was two Americans

---

[5] It had been discovered by Napoleon's soldiers, but the English claimed it for themselves after
their victory. So Hamilton commandeered a boat to the ship and oversaw the object's removal and
subsequent long journey to the British Museum.

who saw them: one was the Honorable J. Augustus Johnson, then consul-general in Beirut; the other his friend, the Reverend Samuel Jessup, an American missionary in Syria. They found themselves passing through Hamath and like Burckhardt, noticed the stones with their curious symbols.

Their eyes fell upon three further stones nearby, all similarly inscribed in those exotic hieroglyphs. They knew what they were seeing was of great antiquity, unknown to the wider world. So Johnson and Jessup decided they must use a technology that had been unknown when Burckhardt had been there six decades before. They would make papier-mâché impressions of what they saw, wanting a record to share these mysteries upon their return home. But while endeavoring to do this, they discovered that the locals had an outsized attachment to these stones and did not trust these strangers to molest them. It later came out that they believed the stones possessed magical healing properties—or at least they could make good money from those who believed this.

But Johnson and Jessup meant no harm; they only wanted to make what were then called "squeezes" of the inscriptions. These were all the rage in the nineteenth century and involved applying a thoroughly soaked sheet of chemists' filter paper to the intended inscription, beating it with a brush to squeeze out any air bubbles, and then allowing it to dry. When peeled away it gave a very accurate—albeit backwards—facsimile of the inscription.

But the locals were not persuaded that this was harmless, screaming and interfering with Johnson and Jessup. "Fanatical Moslems crowded upon us when we began to work upon the stones," Johnson wrote. So the copies they managed to get were far from ideal. Nonetheless he published the findings, however imperfect, in *First Quarterly Statement of the American Palestine Exploration Society*, which attracted renewed attention to the growing hieroglyphic puzzle.

Shortly thereafter, a hundred miles north in Aleppo, another stone was found with characters in what appeared to be the same lost language.

When Johnson returned to Beirut, he showed the published images to Professor E. H. Palmer, a British explorer. Palmer was making a survey of the Sinai and was intrigued by the inscriptions, as well as by Johnson's story of being unable to get accurate squeezes. Palmer had an idea. He had been accompanied in many of his travels by a younger partner named Charles F. Tyrwhitt Drake, who possessed a remarkable facility for gaining the trust of the locals. (In their travels, Drake and Palmer had desperately hoped to discover another Moabite Stone, which we will discuss shortly.) So Palmer persuaded the Committee of the Palestine Exploration Fund to send Drake to Hamath, thinking he might wheedle the obstinate locals into permitting him

Charles Francis Tyrwhitt Drake, 1877

accurate squeezes of the precious inscriptions. Drake made the trip in June 1871, and although not entirely successful, made passable squeezes of the most important inscriptions. Even better, he brought another technology to bear upon the situation and took some excellent photographs.

Drake and Palmer had traveled extensively with the colorful and fabled explorer Sir Richard Burton—then British consul in Damascus—and Burton co-authored his two-volume *Unexplored Syria* with Drake in 1872. In this they included copies of the Hamath inscriptions, provoking still further interest. But Burton had followed the disastrous horror surrounding the discovery of the Moabite Stone [see Chapter Ten] and knew that a firm hand must be brought to bear, lest everything be lost. He sternly suggested an attempt be made to purchase at least two of the stones outright, "by means of a Vizieral order, intended to be obeyed."

In 1873 Burton published an article in the *Journal of the Royal Anthropological Institute of Great Britain and Ireland* telling of his own subsequent visit to the town, and in detail described the stones and their locations, and even speculated on the hieroglyphic puzzle. Burton was a linguistic savant who spoke twenty-six languages, not including many dialects. In his article he quoted Johnson and Jessup, who believed that the inscriptions were likely a transitional form—a syllabic language—between hieroglyphic pictographs and alphabetic letters. By this time, however, this strange language had been seen in other inscriptions in a number of the farthest-flung locations: some as far west as Smyrna in Asia Minor—today Izmir in Turkey—and some as far southeast as Aleppo. How could any language or culture extend eight hundred miles across—at a time when eight hundred miles was roughly the compass of the known world—and yet somehow be altogether vanished, as though absentmindedly mislaid by history herself?

At this point, an Irish missionary named William Wright enters the story. He had been persuaded by Charles Haddon Spurgeon—the Victorian "Prince of Preachers"—to spend his life on the mission field, and eventually settled in Damascus, Syria, where he began taking a serious interest in the mystery of these much-discussed finds. After studying the evidence for some time, he arrived at a novel conclusion. This is because there was one ancient document in which Wright was an expert, and which had been ignored by those involved in this mystery. Wright believed the document he knew so well held the answer to this confounding puzzle: It was the Hittites!

Wright saw that what the Bible said about the people called Hittites matched the evidence of these far-flung hieroglyphic inscriptions and magnificent ruins, and he said so. But who could know if he was correct?

Another figure now entered the picture too. His name was Archibald Henry Sayce. Like Burton he was a linguistic savant, reading Latin and ancient Greek before he was ten, and eventually reading and writing twenty modern and ancient languages. Although famous as a pioneer in deciphering Assyrian cuneiform, Sayce around this time had taken a particular interest in the Indo-European tongues, which ultimately evolved into all the languages of Europe. As he puzzled over the curious inscriptions, he came to a conclusion similar to Wright's: they were evidence of the long-lost empire of the Hittites. Even so, it must wait until 1880—at a

London meeting of the Society for Biblical Archaeology—for Sayce boldly to lay his cards on the table. In that now-famous meeting, he declared the shocking news: the unknown language written all the way from the Turkish Mediterranean to the Syrian desert was not related to Assyrian or to Egyptian, both of which had become known to linguists by this time, but was instead a completely unrelated hieroglyphic language in the Indo-European family, and was a "syllabic language." Sayce had by then done enough work to puzzle out some of what the otherwise opaque symbols said, and announced that the "people of Hattusa"—to whom some of the inscriptions he had translated referred—were none other than the Hittites mentioned in the Bible.

It was a startling claim, and as always happens in such cases, as we have seen, Wright and Sayce were both roundly attacked by scholars, not least because their claim leaned so heavily on what the Bible had to say. But Wright and Sayce stuck to their guns, and in time more pieces of evidence for their thesis emerged and are emerging still. But it is only thanks to that ancient document known as the Bible that history ever had the honor of discovering the Hittites.

In 1887, for example, 1,200 miles away in Egypt, several clay tablets with Assyrian cuneiform writing were found, addressed to Pharaoh Akhenaten, the father of Tutankhamun. By this time, thanks in part to Sayce, Assyrian cuneiform had been largely deciphered. One of these letters was from a king named Suppiluliumas. And two of these letters had next to the Assyrian cuneiform another language, which was thought to be the same as the mysterious inscriptions. Three years later—in 1890 at Bogazkale—a startlingly impressive hoard of tablets was discovered near the ruins Burckhardt had stumbled upon in 1812. This trove contained what

George McCready Price

Archibald Henry Sayce (1845–1933)

proved to be ten thousand tablets covered in cuneiform. Some of it was Akkadian cuneiform, the diplomatic *lingua franca* of that day, and some was in a hitherto unknown cuneiform. It would be another sixteen years before these tablets would meet the man who could decipher them and solve the puzzle once and forever.

Hugo Winckler was a famously irascible German philologist. The archaeologist David Down described him as having "an unfortunate personality," as someone "who made an instant enemy of anyone he met." But Winckler also "could read the Assyrian cuneiform like [the] morning newspaper." It was this unpleasant genius who eventually deciphered the second cuneiform language on these tablets, identifying it as what we now call "Luwian"—the language of the ancient Hittites. This effectively marked the end of the question whether the Hittites existed and who they were. The Bible was not only soundly and decisively vindicated, but as we have said, it was the Hebrew Scriptures alone that guided Sayce and Wright in untangling the conundrum.

Details about the extent of the Hittites' centuries-long empire now place their beginnings in the twentieth century BC and track their seven-centuries-long rise to tremendous prominence and power under Suppiluliumas, who built the great capital Hattusa, which is the walled city whose ruins Burkhardt found in 1812. At its height it boasted a population of fifty thousand, and we now know that the monumental inscription called Nishan Tash is a list of Hittite kings, the last of whom was Suppiluliumas himself, who had the inscription made, and who led the Hittites in the fourteenth century BC.

The vast scope of their treaties and trade touched virtually every empire and people for the better part of the entire second millennium BC, including the Egyptians, the Mycenaean Greeks, the Assyrians, the Babylonians, and even the tribe of Judah, which is of course how we came to be introduced to them in the first place. We also now know that King Tutankhamun's mother—after the death of her young son and then the death of her husband Akhenaten—wrote to King Suppiluliumas at Hattusa, asking that he send one of his own sons whom she could herself marry in

order to keep her dynasty alive. It would have
been an historic union between Egypt and
the Hittites, the two great empires of that day.
But before this could happen, Suppiluliumas's
enemies murdered his son en route. Nonetheless we know now that the Hittite empire
rivaled the other superpowers of that time,
the Assyrians and the Egyptians, and that
its influence and language continued far
beyond the decline of its empire in the
twelfth century BC.

Hugo Winckler, irascible German
philologist.

It was not until 1953 that the strange pic-
tograph scripts in the foundations of the
houses in Hamath were deciphered and dis-
covered to be the same "Luwian" Hittite language as the cuneiform inscriptions deciphered by Hugo Winckler, albeit in a syllabic hieroglyphic form.
Just the previous year, in 1952, the linguist Michael Ventris had broken the
Linear B code discovered on a trove of baked clay tablets at Knossos in Crete
by Sir Arthur Evans in 1900, showing it to be an earlier syllabic (Iron Age
Mycenaean) form of Greek, later expressed in the Greek alphabet. So the
Hittite language too had been expressed in both a syllabic hieroglyphic form
and a cuneiform. Both the Greek and the Luwian had first been expressed
in the syllabic hieroglyphic form. The Linear B syllabic Greek language of
the Minoans and Mycenaeans preceded the Greek alphabetic language, but
it seems that the Luwian syllabic hieroglyphics—which have been found as
early as 2000 BC—were replaced by the cuneiform version for a time. But
this Luwian cuneiform disappeared after the twelfth-century collapse of the
Hittite empire and was replaced by the older syllabic hieroglyphic form of
the language first seen on the stones in the foundations of the buildings in
Hamath, which attest to the Hittite culture's influence centuries after the
glory days of Hattusa and Suppiluliumas. We also know that Sayce was correct when he determined in 1880 that the Hittite language was a very early
Indo-European tongue, dating back, as we have said, to 2000 BC.

Sabena Jane Blackbird/Alamy Stock Photo

Hittite hieroglyphic script written in the Luwian language.

So we know that the Hittites existed, and in such height and breadth as the greatest of any civilizations. But the Bible alone held their name aloft through the darkness of three millennia, until at long last the new fields of archaeology and philology could catch up with it. Those who clung to the Bible as a source of inerrant truth in all matters—whether geographical or historical or other—had in the story of the Hittites been vindicated once more.

The story of the discovery of the Hittites spans the great distance from the time before archaeology all the way into the mid-twentieth century, but now we go backward to the beginning of the story, to 1846, when archaeology was not quite yet a field, but was just coming to be one. It was that year when Sir Austen Henry Layard unearthed something that for the first time would link the world inside the Bible to the world outside it, and begin the process that continues to this day, in which the events and details in the Bible have been corroborated.

CHAPTER TEN

The Black Obelisk That Became a Golden Spike

Sir Austen Henry Layard can hardly be called an archaeologist, since his excavations—in what was once ancient Assyria and is today northern Iraq—were done before the field of archaeology existed. Most of the men of his day, even if they were careful in how they excavated and were genuinely interested in the ancient history of a place, were nonetheless more treasure hunters than anything else. In some cases—the most grievous of which being the aforementioned case of Lord Elgin—they were the literal grasping arms of the British Empire, seeking to spirit homeward any great treasures of antiquity they could somehow legalistically place just beyond the damning category of "plunder."

Layard was certainly not in this unfortunate category. Nonetheless in December 1846, he was excavating south of Nimrud—what is today Mosul—when his workmen asked him to shut things down. The bitter cold and hard ground made digging the huge trenches increasingly difficult. Layard persuaded his team to dig one more day, but no sooner had they returned to their work after this discussion than a workman's tool struck something hard. A few minutes' digging showed it to be an astounding black limestone stele in the form of an obelisk, topped with the form of a ziggurat and decorated on

The Black Obelisk was hailed as "the most notable trophy in the world."

its four sides with five registers of astonishingly well-preserved bas relief sculptures. It hailed from the ninth century BC, and pictured the Assyrian King Shalmaneser III, who reigned from 858 to 824 BC.

In the images he was shown to be receiving tribute from a number of his defeated subjects, beneath which there was Akkadian cuneiform writing. But in 1846 cuneiform was only just beginning to be deciphered by a tiny handful of scholars, so no one on the site had any idea what it said. But the spectacular images told the story well enough, showing two kings prostrating themselves before Shalmaneser, along with retinues carrying gold and other valuables. Notable among the gifts were a series of exotic animals, among which Layard and his men made out a water buffalo, some two-humped camels, an antelope, elephants, monkeys, and apes. There was even that rarest of almost unknown creatures—a rhinoceros.

Layard knew the stele was a particularly impressive treasure, and very soon he sent the extraordinary object on its way to London, at that time an impossibly arduous journey via river rafts and sailing ships. Merely getting these heavy objects to the river was a challenge. In his 1849 book *Nineveh and Its Remains*, Layard says, "I was again obliged to have recourse to the buffalo-carts of the Pasha," which he describes as "rotten and unwieldy vehicles" that would nonetheless succeed in hauling this and some other heavy treasures toward the Tigris. "On Christmas Day," he continued, "I had the satisfaction of seeing a raft, bearing twenty-three cases, in one of which was the obelisk, floating down the river." The obelisk first made its way very slowly three hundred miles along the twisting and turning Tigris, until it at last came to Baghdad.

As it happened, Henry Rawlinson was stationed there at that time. He would eventually be known as Sir Henry Creswicke Rawlinson, First Baronet, GCB, FRS, KLS, and would be regarded as the "Father of Assyriology." He would even be made a Fellow of the Royal Society for being "The Discoverer of the Key to the Ancient Persian, Babylonian, and Assyrian Inscriptions in the Cuneiform Character." Already in 1847 he led the way in deciphering cuneiform, while the field was in its infancy. So no sooner did the obelisk arrive than he fell on it with eagerness, soon making a translation of the cuneiform and writing a report to send back to the British Museum, which would not receive the actual treasure for some time. Rawlinson's translation referred to a certain "Yahua, son of Hubiri." He said this "Yahua" was "a prince of whom there is no mention in the annals, and of whose native country, therefore, I am ignorant." The report and translation were dispatched to London, where excitement mounted at the eventual arrival of the unprecedented find.

But it would be nearly two more years before anyone in London could see the obelisk. From Baghdad it continued its journey several hundreds of miles more along the languorously twisting Tigris, until that ancient river spent itself into the great Euphrates, which bore the object the remainder of its journey to the sea. Here it was loaded aboard a ship and carried across the Persian Gulf and into the Gulf of Oman before plying its way *eastward* to Bombay. From there it would eventually begin the nearly nine-thousand-mile journey of about six months, traveling around the treacherous horn of Africa and then north to England. So it was not until the fall of 1848 that this treasure arrived in London, by which time the Trustees of the British Museum greeted it with great ceremony, giving it a place of greatest honor on the museum's first floor, in their "Nimrud Central Saloon Gallery." It instantly eclipsed all the other Assyrian antiquities around it, and in the press was pelted with every superlative available, even being hailed as the "most notable trophy in the world."

The obelisk so electrified early Victorian society that it became a necessary pilgrimage for anyone of distinction. Everyone marveled at its antiquity and extraordinarily unmarred images, despite a three-millennia-long interment beneath the sands of what had been ancient Assyria; its second life in the British Museum was a bright feather in the cap of the broadening Empire.

But strangely enough, the obelisk stood in its place of honor and was seen by nearly everyone for two years before the most significant discovery about it was made. This happened in August 1851, when a certain Edward Hincks, an Irish clergyman and Assyriologist of top rank, visited the museum to see the trophy for himself. He stood there among the crowds and read the Akkadian cuneiform very carefully, taking in the notable first extant reference to the Persians—"Parsu"—and continued to make out the characters.

But when his eyes lit on the sentence below the king in the stele's second register, Hincks stopped. Four years before, in Baghdad, Rawlinson had translated this sentence as, "I received the tribute of Iaua (Yahua) son of (the people of the land of) Hubiri: silver, gold, a golden bowl, a golden vase with pointed bottom, golden tumblers, golden buckets, a tiny staff for a king [and] spears," and lamented that there was no record of this unknown figure, as we have noted.

But Hincks had another idea, and we can imagine how his breast must have swelled there amidst the crowds, none of whom could read a stroke of Akkadian cuneiform. For he observed as he read the aforementioned sentence that it read neither "Yahua" nor "Hubiri," but rather significantly read, "Jehu" and "Omri." Since this was true, Hincks understood that the monarch bowing as he proffered tribute to Shalmaneser was none other than the Hebrew king Jehu of the Bible. His identity lay hidden beneath the sands for three millennia and was still hidden even now. But not much longer. For Hincks would soon tell the world the astonishing news. This figure in front of his eyes was the first archaeological confirmation that the Bible's King Jehu was a real king who could be placed in history, apart from the pages of Scripture. He knew that this figure marked the first time that anything outside the Bible could be shown to agree with what lay within it. It was a shattering realignment in the world of scholarship, and while he stood there, no one in the world knew it but Hincks.

Word of this unprecedented find soon exploded in every direction, and the numbers flocking to see this object ballooned yet again, for what stood there in the middle of London was unique and perfectly without antecedent in history. Just as the golden spike on the American continent would eighteen years later link the eastern and western railroads and change the world forever, so this black obelisk once and forevermore like a spike linked the world of the Bible with the world beyond it. And there would be no going back. It was an epochal moment in the history of history.

This 1851 discovery of a biblical king in an Assyrian stele from the ninth century BC struck a thunderous blow against all those inclined to dismiss the Bible as ahistorical and mythical, as no different than the fanciful Epic of Gilgamesh or Homer's accounts of the Cyclops and the Sirens. And because this astounding discovery was made at the very dawn of archaeology as a field of study, it instantly caused everyone to wonder what might yet lie beneath the sands of those endless ancient deserts. Interest in the field predictably skyrocketed, causing something like a gold rush toward the Middle East. Sure enough, over the next decades innumerable similar finds would be hailed as literally solid proof that the Bible was true, and that for historians willing to accept it as such, it could serve as a peerless guide to the past.

The Moabite Stone

Just as it is impossible to overstate the hubbub caused by the identification of Jehu on the Black Obelisk in 1851, so it is impossible to exaggerate the pandemonium in 1868 over what is called the Moabite Stone, or the Mesha Stele. Its discovery and the subsequent corroboration of what it said in paleo-Hebrew with a specific passage from the Bible was perfectly astonishing and unprecedented, and further confirmed that what the Bible said in every detail was true, and could even perhaps be shown to be true. The tumult surrounding its discovery sent fresh crowds wildly scrambling throughout the ancient deserts, hoping to find more of the same.

But as we explain why the Moabite Stone caused such a flutterment of excitement, we must tell the wild story of its initial discovery, and its subsequent horrifying destruction, and finally, its extraordinary and happy reconstitution, all of which illustrate the inestimable value such treasures had among the European powers of the nineteenth century.

The queer tale begins with the figure of Frederick Augustus Klein, an Alsatian-born Anglican medical missionary who had settled in Jerusalem sometime in the mid-nineteenth century. In his efforts to bring physical and spiritual healing to all he encountered, this dedicated man of God sometimes traveled eastward into the dangerous area of Jordan. But Klein had learned Arabic and eventually gained the trust and favor of the Bedouin tribes who lived there, far from the world of contemporary Western medicine. In all the centuries since the Crusades, almost no Europeans had dared to travel through these areas, principally because of the fierce hostility of these tribes.

In the summer of 1868 Klein journeyed on horseback across the Jordan River and then south along the eastern shore of the Dead Sea, finally turning eastward into what had once been Moabite territory. He was accompanied by the son of one of his close friends, Fendi Al-Fayez, who was among the most powerful Bedouin sheiks in the area. On August 19, Klein and his companion were visiting the Bani Hamada Bedouins in what had been the ancient city of Dhiban, which three thousand years before had been the capital of ancient Moab. During this visit, these locals told Klein and his companion of a remarkable and ancient stone, and then happily led them to see it for themselves. It was a black basalt stele about three feet high and two feet wide, with a rounded top, obviously of remarkable antiquity, and most astounding of all, it bore thirty-four lines of what looked much like Hebrew, although Klein could not read it. But seeing this antique object with Hebrew writing on it must have set his heart to racing.

He did not lose the opportunity to make a sketch of it and copy some of the characters. If the writing really was some form of ancient Hebrew, Klein knew he might well be looking at an inestimable treasure.

So on the spot he dared to negotiate with his Bedouin hosts to purchase it. Sure enough they agreed on the sum of one hundred Napoleons, which was something like four hundred dollars, a grand figure for that time. Klein would return to Jerusalem to find the money, which being a missionary he certainly did not have, but he knew German government officials would be beside themselves to claim this prize, as they were anxious to best the other European powers in scrounging historical treasures related to the Bible. The competition between the French, English, and Germans for such things had already been going on for some time.

In Jerusalem ten days later, Klein informed J. Heinrich Petermann, the Prussian consul, of his find; and Petermann, seeing that the writing Klein had copied was indeed Hebraic, lost no time in dispatching a letter to the Berlin museum. On September 15 they telegraphed approval to acquire the object without delay. But somehow things now went awry. Quite inexplicably, the Bedouins had caught wind of the heightened interest in the stone. Had the French or English somehow heard about it and then tried to cut the Germans out of the picture with a higher offer? It seems so.

There is no doubt today that the inscription on the stone makes it among the most valuable objects in the world. But we have no idea which of the three parties knew what at this point. But even if they only had some clues as to what it said, there was enough interest for representatives from three of the world's most powerful empires to trip over themselves and each other to claim this object. So we must skip ahead and tell the reader what we know of the stone today, at least partially to explain the escalating madness among those pursuing it.

As we know now, the writing was Canaanite paleo-Hebrew from the ninth century BC. But infinitely more important even than this, it actually recounted events from a passage in the third chapter of the biblical Book of 2 Kings. This was unavoidably intoxicating, and any-one with the slightest idea along these lines would have been willing to do nearly anything to claim it for their nation. The specific biblical verse reads: "Now Mesha king of Moab raised sheep, and he had to pay the king of Israel a tribute of a hundred thousand lambs and the wool of a hundred thousand rams." And this secret stone hidden among the Bedouins for three thousand years spoke of this very event, and even included such details as "Mesha" being both king and sheep herder. The Black Obelisk of Shalmaneser III hardly came close to this level of specificity and detail, nor did it recount anything from a specific passage in Scripture.

But there was more. The inscription referred specifically to "Yahweh," the God of the Bible, and to the kingdom of Israel itself: "the House of Omri." This was as spectacular as anything anyone might have hoped. We cannot know how much of this anyone knew at the time. It's possible Klein and Petermann knew about one or both of these two amazing references but didn't know about that part of the inscription that recounted the event from the passage in 2 Kings.

Whatever they knew—and whatever the English and French knew—they all knew it was enough to warrant doing anything and everything to get their hands on that stone. But unfortunately, somehow—somehow—the Bedouins knew this too, for Klein and Petermann now learned that the canny tribesmen had upped their asking price tenfold, to one thousand Napoleons. This was an impossible sum, simply out of the question for anyone to pay.

Klein knew that he had to be extremely careful how he proceeded now. He did not return to the tribe himself, but dispatched another Arab friend from Jerusalem, who traveled to Dhiban to see what might be done. It took several months, but he was eventually able to drag the Bedouins back to Earth, and they settled on a price of 120 Napoleons. But by then another neighboring tribe had learned of the imminent removal of this object, and for some reason refused to allow the stone to pass through its territory, so that again things ground to a standstill.

Out of some diplomatic deference—or perhaps because he knew that getting the object out of the Bedouins' territory was paramount—the English figure in this story, Captain Charles Warren, did not interfere, knowing his interest could scotch the Prussians' ticklish negotiations and perhaps ensure that none of the Europeans succeeded. But a Frenchman at the Jerusalem consulate was not so diplomatic. This was an amateur archaeologist named Charles Clermont-Ganneau, who rather recklessly dispatched an Arab friend to see the stone and bring back more information.

Charles Clermont-Ganneau, 1880

The Arab returned with seven lines he had copied from the inscription, which demonstrated the great significance of the stone to Ganneau. Perhaps this was the first time the inscription's meaning was finally known, or some part of it was finally known. Ganneau may alone have understood something of the real value of this object, so he promptly sent another Arab envoy, one Karavaca, to the site. Karavaca was to make a paper "squeeze" impression of the entire inscription and had been deputized to offer a sum far higher than the 120 Napoleons that the Prussians had negotiated, underscoring the theory that Ganneau knew more of what the inscription said.

The Bedouins allowed Karavaca to begin to make his squeeze, but before it had dried, violence exploded. What happened is unclear, but Karavaca may have suffered a spear wound to his face, and one of his two horsemen certainly suffered another to the leg. Reckoning survival the better part of such cultural appropriation, Karavaca's unwounded companion managed to pull the still-wet squeeze from the inscription—unfortunately tearing it into seven pieces, which he shoved into his robe—and the three of them galloped away with the squeeze in shreds but their lives intact.

When he learned of these events, the Prussian Petermann knew he could not return to the Bedouins. It was far too dangerous. But he thought he might now appeal to the Turks, whose Ottoman Empire theoretically extended to the Bedouin territory in question. But by November 1869, when the Turks were ready to dispatch soldiers to seize the stone by force, the Bedouins had already decided on its fate, and would play to the hilt what looked like the role of dog in the manger. That's because the Bani Hamada tribe despised the Turks deeply, having previously been attacked by them. So before the stele could be taken by anyone—much less by their sworn enemies—they peevishly kindled a roaring bonfire around it and brought the priceless treasure to such a temperature that when they poured cold water on it, it did what they expected, cracking in several places until—in a process they helped along by using large stones to smash it apart—the object lay in approximately one hundred pieces of various sizes. Exactly why they did this we can never know for sure. One theory held that they believed there was gold inside, explaining the price the Europeans had been willing to pay, for how could nomadic tribesmen begin to guess what the historical value of an object confirming the events of the Bible might mean to these oddnick foreigners? Another theory suggests they thought they could get more money for the individual pieces.

Whatever they believed, the Europeans' fierce interest in this superlative treasure had at last resulted in its total destruction by the maniacal Bedouins. When the Prussians learned of this unforgivable evil, they dropped their interest in the whole thing completely. For them, the sordid and sad matter was now closed. But not for Ganneau. If he understood anything of what we now do about the inscription, he knew that even in its shattered and scattered form, the object was still worth fighting for. He alone had the copy of the inscription made from the squeeze, albeit in seven shredded pieces, so surely he knew more than anyone what it said. And because he had the squeeze, he could conceivably use it as a key to reassemble the shattered pieces.

So Ganneau regrouped and then through bravery and extraordinary diligence he returned to the Bedouins and incredibly managed to locate and purchase thirty-eight of the roughly one hundred fragments, some large and some small, all of which by then had found their way into the hands of various families among the tribe that destroyed it. The Englishman Warren was eventually also persuaded of the value of the remaining fragments and managed to purchase seventeen small ones himself, while a German scholar who came into the picture was able to purchase one.

In the end, Ganneau's audaciously ambitious efforts bore fruit. First, his thirty-eight fragments were eventually put in the Louvre, after which Warren and the German scholar generously contributed their fragments too. Then, using the fragments of his torn squeeze, along with the fifty-six actual fragments in the Louvre's possession, Ganneau reconstructed the missing portion of the inscription. He then recreated a facsimile of the missing parts and restored the stone so that it could be seen in the Louvre essentially as it was before the Bedouins had destroyed it. It can still be seen there today, where it remains the longest inscription referring to the kingdom of Israel ever discovered.

And so the wild goose chase for this extra-biblical pearl of great price ended surprisingly well. Far more even than the Black Obelisk, it presented the world with spectacular proof that what was found in the Bible could be confirmed beyond it, spurring a spate of renewed interest from all quarters in what was by that time the suddenly burgeoning field of biblical archaeology.

After the landmark discoveries of the Black Obelisk and the Moabite Stone, anything seemed possible. If we could know that in the distant ninth century BC the Moabites and Assyrians each had recorded their dealings with Israel, who knew how far back records of the Israelites might extend, or what still lay buried in the sands of the past, waiting to be revealed? It was only a matter of continuing to dig, and of course the digging did continue, which brings us to the story of the Merneptah Stele.

The Merneptah Stele

In his time, Sir William Matthew Flinders Petrie, FRS, FBA, was renowned beyond anyone in the field of archaeology. He is widely considered to be "the Father of Egyptology" and the list of his discoveries and achievements is nearly endless, including his tutelage of Howard Carter, who would go on to discover King Tut's tomb. But it is for one object that Petrie will always be best remembered, which he realized almost immediately upon laying eyes on it that day in Egypt in 1896.

Flinders—as he was generally known—was possessed of a staggering intellect, which evidently ran in his family. His grandfather Matthew Flinders was a navigator and cartographer who first circumnavigated a certain southern continent, then coined the term "Australia" and lobbied for its acceptance, it seems successfully. Petrie's father was an electrical genius who developed carbon arc lighting, and Petrie's only child John was a mathematical savant who discovered what later became known as the "Petrie polygon." Petrie himself had such astounding mental capacity that he could in his head picture whatever part of a slide rule was necessary to solve a particular math problem, and solve the problem mentally.

Flinders Petrie, circa 1865

But in his autobiography, Petrie recalls that at age eight—in 1861—he already seemed destined for a life in archaeology. When hearing at that age of the careless excavation of a Roman villa on the Isle of Wight, he remonstrated boldly, insisting anything of such antiquity should be excavated with great care. "The earth ought to be pared away inch by inch," the boy had said, "to see all that was in it and how it lay." Appropriately enough, he grew up to be the great pioneer of this very method of "stratigraphic archaeology," which has been used ever since.

In 1896, Petrie was in Thebes—modern day Luxor—when after discovering a statue of the rather obscure Egyptian Pharaoh Merneptah he uncovered a monumental black granite stele, dating from about 1200 BC. It was an astonishing ten feet in height, being the largest stele ever discovered. When the tremendously heavy object was turned over, Petrie saw that it bore a long inscription. Happily along that day was the brilliant twenty-five-year-old German Jewish philologist Wilhelm Spiegelberg, and the two of them read the inscription together. As such steles usually did, it detailed the military victories of the ruler who had commissioned it—in this case Merneptah, whom we believe to be the thirteenth son of his father, Ramesses the Great.[1]

Most of the writing on the stele dealt with Egypt's victories over the Libyans and the "Sea Peoples." But in the last lines of the long inscription Petrie and Spiegelberg read something amazing: "Canaan is despoiled, with every evil [treatment]. ..." No mention of the Canaanites had ever been seen outside the Bible, yet here was evidence of them on a thirteenth-century BC Egyptian stele, corroborating the biblical account. Still, this proved to be small beer when compared with what followed.

The inscription went on to say: "Ashkelon has been captured, Gezer has been taken, Yanoam has been destroyed. ..." Then in the line following the two men read a curious word: "I.si.ri.ar." Spiegelberg, the linguistic genius, was stymied. The whole sentence read "I.si.ri.ar is wasted; its seed is naught." Whatever "I.si.ri.ar" referred to, it was obviously another tribe defeated by the Egyptians under Merneptah during their Canaan campaign.

But as they stared at the cryptic word, Petrie's mind leapt to a solution. "Israel!" he exclaimed. Spiegelberg knew instantly that Petrie was correct, and said as much. Petrie could hardly take in what he now realized. He

---

[1] This pharaoh, also called Ramesses II, lived and ruled into his nineties, being the oldest pharaoh in history.

The Petrie Museum of Egyptian Archaeology

Flinders Petrie, 1903

saw with his own eyes mention of Israel on an Egyptian stele—and from as impossibly far back as 1200 BC. He knew it was a find of unparalleled significance, and as they stood there, he joked: "Won't the reverends be pleased?" Petrie knew what he found that day was so important it would eclipse everything he had ever done, and that night he said as much to those with him at table. News of his unprecedented discovery soon reached London and circled the globe. The existence of ancient Israel could thenceforward be spoken of all the way back to the thirteenth century BC reign of Pharaoh Merneptah, pushing the existence of the people of Israel almost three centuries earlier than the Moabite Stone. It was truly extraordinary, taking archaeological evidence of their existence nearly back to the time of Joshua.

But it was significant for another major reason: it established that the Exodus of the Bible could not have happened later than that date, since the people of Israel were obviously already on their own in Canaan. Many scholars skeptical of the biblical account held to later dates, but one monumental stone buried for three millennia settled the question and forever buried the skeptics' views.

CHAPTER ELEVEN

More Biblical Archaeology: Three Misbehaving Boys Who Changed History

The story of how archaeology continues to confirm the Bible itself contains three stories that beg to be told. In their own way, each illuminates the Old Testament as a faithful and scrupulous account of history. Each also takes place in or very near Jerusalem. But without doubt the most peculiar—if not downright ludicrous—parallel among them is that each of these three stories spanning ninety-nine years (one from 1880, one from 1947, and one from 1979) has at its very center as principal actor a misbehaving young man between the ages of twelve and fifteen. We will present the stories in the order of how badly behaved the young men were, beginning with the least misbehaved.

1. The Dead Sea Scrolls

To introduce the story of what may be the greatest archaeological discovery of all time, we should clarify that when we think of archaeological discoveries, we typically think of stones. Yet this discovery was not of stones, but of manuscripts. The principal difference between them is that stones do not decay over time, while manuscripts do—except perhaps in this story, which is the first reason that the discovery of the Dead Sea Scrolls is so spectacular.

Because manuscripts deteriorate rather quickly, the knowledge we have of ancient history is overwhelmingly from rather recent manuscripts, meaning copies of manuscripts from centuries earlier. For example, Julius Caesar wrote a chronicle of his military successes in ancient Gaul, titled *The Gallic Wars*, during the first century BC, but the oldest surviving copy is a manuscript from the eighth century AD, some nine hundred years later. What manuscripts we have from the Greek historian Herodotus are still further removed from the originals. Herodotus lived and wrote in the fifth century BC, but our oldest manuscripts of his writings are from the tenth through the fourteenth centuries AD, somewhere between 1,300 to 1,700 years later. No one doubts their authenticity, despite the eons of time since the original words were written, mainly because there are innumerable ways of corroborating information from various sources to determine if what we have is reliable and accurate. Of course calculating such things is the important work of historians.

But when we are dealing with the Bible, one finds a predictably high level of skepticism, especially among those who don't take the text very seriously. Thus many have claimed the Bible texts were "changed" in the course of their being copied over the centuries by the monks of the Middle Ages. Skeptics suggest the monks—in league with "the all-powerful Church"—transformed them into what the Church wanted, rather than what they originally were. Though oft repeated, no evidence has ever been shown of this, and many reasons argue decisively against it. Evidence against this thinking emerges constantly, but the events of the story following defenestrated the theory once and for all. At first blush, this tale of a boy discovering inconceivably valuable treasure in a hidden cave seems to have been torn from a book of fairy tales. But it actually happened in 1947.

The Return of Israel

The year 1947 marked the birth of the modern state of Israel, an event that almost seems to have come from a book of fairy tales itself. Here was an ancient nation that had not existed for two thousand years suddenly born anew. How could such a thing happen? It was a reversal of—dare we say it?—biblical proportions, and a turning of history's tables as dramatic as anything. It is especially remarkable when we consider the dramatic end of Israel in 70 AD.

That apocalyptic nightmare happened less than forty years after Jesus's striking prophecy, in which he declared that Herod's Temple—that impossibly magnificent wonder of the ancient world—would be destroyed, such that not one stone would lie on top of another. And so it happened: The brutal Romans burned the Temple to the ground and murdered a million Jews in what must be among the most terrible events in human history, gruesomely enough detailed for us by the historian Josephus. The Jewish people were scattered to the four winds throughout the Roman Empire and wandered the world for almost two millennia, suffering pogroms and persecutions until the most ghastly and unthinkable nightmare in history befell them in the Holocaust, in which six million of them were murdered with a meticulousness so chilling that it must forever stand as one of the most perfect examples of evil.

But then, in some incomprehensible way, as a result of this foulest evil, the world gasped in collective horror and discovered the impetus necessary for what so many had dreamt for so long: the people of Israel would be returned to their ancient homeland. And then almost overnight, it happened. The nation of Israel was resurrected into the present time, leaping from the world of hopes and dreams into modern geography and history.

It was an event so staggering that for many it alone was proof of the God of Israel. In fact three hundred years earlier, when France's King Louis XIV asked the Christian mathematical genius Blaise Pascal for proof of God, Pascal answered easily in two words. "The Jews!"[1] For many, the mere continued existence of the Jewish people, scattered and perse-

---

[1] This exchange is also sometimes attributed to a conversation between Frederick the Great and his advisor.

cuted through the millennia, was enough to prove that the God of the Jews was real and acted in history. But when they returned to the land from which they had been scattered two millennia earlier, no one could avoid the earth-shattering nature of the news, and many couldn't help seeing the hand of God in it. What could it be but a miracle?

The Scrolls Discovered

But that same year something else occurred, with similarly astounding ramifications. It happened east of Jerusalem, along the cliffs overlooking that watery wasteland called the Dead Sea. This superlatively saline body of water is ten times as salty as the world's oceans, and at 1,400 feet below sea level, marks the lowest point on our planet.[2] Along the western shore of this fishless body of water are many cliffs, riddled with caves.

One day early in 1947 a twelve-year-old Bedouin shepherd boy was watching his flocks in this area when—in what sounds like a reprise of Jesus's parable about the lost sheep—he noticed one goat missing and left the rest of his flock to retrieve it. He found himself climbing the cliffs of this area, and in one remote crevice happened upon a very deep cave. Perhaps wondering whether his goat had wandered into its interior, but more likely simply behaving as twelve-year-old boys do, he flung a stone into its black depths. But the sound that followed was not rock striking rock, nor bleating goat. Instead, the boy heard the report of smashed pottery. So he did something else we imagine his parents would earnestly have remonstrated against, had they the opportunity: he ventured into the cave's depths to see what his stone had hit. Another shepherd boy's stone was said to have killed a certain Philistine not many miles from this spot. What had this one done? In its own way it would change history, because as he crept into the darkness, the boy discovered that his missile had hit a large jar. He saw an entire cache of them, standing just as they must have been since someone placed them there long ago.

---

[2] That is five times the depth of Death Valley, the lowest point in North America, and fifteen times lower than Europe's lowest point along the Caspian Sea.

Most were empty, but some still had their lids on. How could he resist? When he removed the lid and looked inside, he was amazed to see what appeared to be old scrolls, covered with linen and black with age.

We now know that in chasing after his wandering property, this shepherd boy had unwittingly stumbled upon one of the most astonishing discoveries of any century, for these scrolls were only the first of what was later discovered to be an almost limitless bounty of them, all in similar jars in ten nearby caves. These jars and the scrolls within them had been untouched for two thousand years. Eventually the scrolls were found to number nearly a thousand, and the writing on them varied, ranging from pseudepigraphical and other extra-biblical documents to the writings of the Essenes, a religious sect from that area and time. But without question the single most significant aspect of this find was that among these scrolls were a number of miraculously well-preserved manuscripts of Old Testament books. In fact it was eventually determined that no less than thirty-seven of the Old Testament's thirty-nine books were represented. Who could have dreamt of such a thing? This alone would have made this archaeological discovery the most important of all time.

As a result of this dramatically unexpected boon, scholars suddenly might answer the question they had been wondering about forever, one they assumed would never be answered: Had the original biblical documents been tampered with over the centuries? And if so, how much? To what extent, if any, had the oft-cited "monks in the Middle Ages" been guilty of working with church authorities to alter the texts to better suit the theological narrative they wished to promote? Scholars had forever wished they might have copies of such texts from two millennia earlier, but knowing how manuscripts deteriorate, they knew this was essentially impossible. So the discovery of these scrolls—intact and legible, hidden in this cave for twenty centuries—was not merely stunning, but seemed providential to the point of miraculous. That they had not deteriorated significantly in all this time was impossible to fathom—and yet there they were.

An astonishing combination of wildly anomalous conditions all had to converge for such fragile and ancient objects to escape their fate, but as we now know, that is precisely what happened. To begin with, the location of these caves was far below sea level, as we have mentioned, in a place of near-perfect aridity. Next, the scrolls were for unknown reasons made of sheepskins, but without the slightest trace of tanning materials, which accelerate the deterioration of parchments. Third, the ink used on the scrolls happened to be made of soot or lampblack, which is inert and therefore extremely long-lasting. And finally, the caves in which these scrolls were stored provided an environment of remarkably stable temperature and virtually no airflow. In other words, no better environment could be imagined. In fact, once the scrolls were examined, it was nearly impossible even for man-made technology to recreate an environment as perfect as the one in which they were discovered. So amidst these unrivaled circumstances, in the silent and dark stillness, these scrolls waited through the silent hours and days of twenty centuries. In that time many empires rose and fell. Haley's comet came and went twenty-seven times. And then one day in 1947, as if in the fullness of time, a straying goat caused a door to be opened to the past.

So what did these ancient manuscripts reveal? Indeed, it was an outrageous amount of information. So much, in fact, that the small-minded scholars who got their hands on them greedily hoarded them and proved slower than glaciers in letting other scholars get a peek at them, marking a truly shameful but unfortunately not atypical act of academic pettiness. So it was nearly fifty years before these windows to another world could be looked through by a greater number of scholars. Surely the largest jewels in this dazzling treasury were the two-thousand-year-old copies of the thirty-seven books of the Bible, which showed that what we possess today as our own Bible is precisely the same as what existed then. Never in human history has an observed absence of change so instantly and dramatically changed everything.

This discovery within the larger discovery was the earth-shaking bombshell of the whole affair. Despite the unfounded but stubborn rumors that the Bible "had been changed" over the centuries, this unexpected evidence at last proved the opposite. As anyone could see—and as clearly as anyone might have hoped— the ancient Hebrew Scriptures had been copied with a perfectly extraordinary faithfulness over the centuries. This illustrated that the reverence the monks and Jewish scribes were believed to have toward their Scriptures was no mere pious tale, but was simply true. It was manifestly proven by these ancient scrolls. In a way, it conjured the idea of the very opposite of a game of telephone, in which time degrades a message into near nonsense, for the message and the words on these scrolls were exactly as they had always been. And apart from the wild happenstance of that shepherd boy's discovery, no one ever would have known.

Among the very oldest of the scrolls were copies of the Book of Isaiah, dating to the fourth century BC, meaning they were only two to three centuries removed from Isaiah himself, an unprecedentedly short period in the world of ancient manuscripts. And as we have said, those who examined it found the text identical to what we have now, twenty-six centuries after Isaiah.

Those who valued the Hebrew Scriptures as sacred always knew they must be unchanged, for changing the very Word of God would be a monstrous blasphemy. The Jewish and Christian scribes entrusted with copying these texts took almost unimaginably stringent measures to copy things so perfectly that not only was no word changed, but not even the letters themselves. In Judaism, each letter was thought sacred. Many had the tiniest but nonetheless deeply significant markings attached to them, which Jesus in the King James translation of the Bible refers to as a "jot"[3] or "tittle"[4]—which he says "will never pass away" or be changed. According to him—and to rabbis and Christian scholars forever—these markings were part of the Word of God, and will therefore remain for eternity. All who understood this knew that the charges that the Scriptures had cavalierly been changed could be made only by those ignorant of how these documents were transmitted over the centuries. But now there existed the most unexpected proof that indeed, literally nothing had changed.

But those biblical skeptics who argued that the documents were altered also held that because of this, the Old Testament prophecies predicting the future did nothing of the kind. For them all such prophecies were invented—by an

---

[3] This is the English word for the smallest Greek letter—"iota"—written as a lowercase "i" without the dot. In English we often use the word "iota" to mean the smallest part of something.

[4] The word "tittle" is etymologically related to the word "title," meaning something inscribed over something else, and in this case refers to a diacritical mark over a letter. It is also related to the Spanish pronunciation mark tilde, which is expressed ~.

"all-powerful Church" in order to control the ignorant faithful—and all examples were a simple case of later scribes inserting whatever they wished, centuries after the fact. But the scrolls' discovery meant such accusations must be set aside, and the bizarre parallels between what had been said and that centuries later seemed to have really happened must be dealt with seriously.

One dramatic example of how the Old Testament was thought to prophesy the future is found in Psalm 22, written a thousand years before Jesus's day but which very much seems to describe a Roman crucifixion, and including details from Jesus's own execution. The psalm even begins with the very words Jesus is said to have spoken on the cross at the point of his greatest suffering.

> My God, my God, why hast thou forsaken me?...
> All who see me mock me;
> they hurl insults, shaking their heads.
> "He trusts in the Lord," they say,
> "let the Lord rescue him.
> Let him deliver him,
> since he delights in him."...
> I am poured out like water,
> and all my bones are out of joint....
> My mouth is dried up like a potsherd,
> and my tongue sticks to the roof of my mouth....
> you lay me in the dust of death.
> they pierce my hands and my feet.
> All my bones are on display;
> people stare and gloat over me.
> They divide my clothes among them
> and cast lots for my garment.

Unless these ancient words really were somehow prophetic, how could this be? Of course skeptics may now believe the New Testament writers inserted these details into their own writings to show Jesus fulfilling the Old Testament scriptures. Nonetheless, these newly discovered scrolls—untouched since before the time of Christ—were shown to be unchanged, and people at last could judge for themselves.

2. Hezekiah's Tunnel

The Book of 2 Kings in the Bible is filled with one after the other of wicked kings "doing evil in the Lord's sight." Over and over we read how the people of Israel and Judah suffered as a result, usually being captured and oppressed by their enemies. So against this murderer's row of monarchs, the benevolent reign of King Hezekiah stands in dramatic contrast. According to the Bible, Hezekiah "did what was pleasing in the Lord's sight, just as his ancestor David had done. He removed the pagan shrines, smashed the sacred pillars, and knocked down the Asherah poles." It even says that Hezekiah broke up the bronze snake that Moses had set up in the wilderness centuries before because the people of God burned incense to it as though it were a pagan idol.

In the last few years, archaeological evidence for Hezekiah has been mounting dramatically. In 2015 a "bulla" seal from around 700 BC was discovered in Jerusalem, bearing the inscription "Belonging to Hezekiah, son of Ahaz, King of Judah." Dr. Eilat Mazar, who discovered it, said it was "the closest we ever can get to something that was held by King Hezekiah himself."

But ample archaeological evidence for Hezekiah had already been discovered in the nineteenth century. In fact, evidence of him was first discovered in the city of Nineveh in 1830 by Colonel Robert Taylor. The "Taylor Prism," as it has come to be known, is a hexagonal object of red baked clay fifteen inches high and five-and-a-half inches in diameter that is covered with cuneiform writing. Two virtually identical objects called "The Sennacherib Prism" and the "Oriental Institute Prism" turned up in the decades following. But when Taylor found it, no one could yet read cuneiform, and he had no idea what he had found. The object languished as many archaeological treasures do while in that strange limbo between what we may call its first and second discoveries, the former being the unearthing of an object, and the latter that time when someone realizes

The Taylor Prism.

its true significance. For the Taylor Prism, this second discovery did not happen until three decades later, at which point it was determined that one cuneiform passage actually referred to Sennacherib's military campaign against Judah's king Hezekiah, linking it to the events in the Bible—just as the Black Obelisk had done in 1851 and the Moabite Stone would do so spectacularly in 1868.

The translated cuneiform passage from the Taylor Prism reads:

As for the king of Judah, Hezekiah, who had not submitted to my authority, I besieged and captured forty-six of his fortified cities, along with many smaller towns, taken in battle with my battering rams.... I took as plunder 200,150 people, both small and great, male and female, along with a great number of animals including horses, mules, donkeys, camels, oxen, and sheep. As for Hezekiah, I shut him up like a caged bird in his royal city of Jerusalem. I then constructed a series of fortresses around him, and I did not allow anyone to come out of the city gates. His towns which I captured I gave to the kings of Ashdod, Ekron, and Gaza.

It's typical of such things that the writer boasts of his victories, but as we see he does not mention actually taking the city of Jerusalem, only of besieging it, so we may assume the siege was unsuccessful. But it was not until two teenagers were playing hooky from school in 1880 that we would know the precise reason and dimensions of Hezekiah's success in defending Jerusalem.

During Hezekiah's time, the principal source of water for Jerusalem was the Gihon Spring. In fact, this spring and the six hundred thousand cubic meters of water that flow from it annually seem to have been the very reason human beings settled in this spot in the fourth millennium BC, making it one of the world's oldest cities. The spring is still today considered one of the major "intermittent springs" in the world. By the time of King Hezekiah, it not only provided all the drinking water for the city's inhabitants, but also was sufficient to irrigate the Kidron Valley beyond the city walls, where many in Jerusalem grew their crops. When Hezekiah discovered that a siege by Assyria's fearsome King Sennacherib was imminent, it was precisely this ample overflow beyond Jerusalem's walls that concerned him. Hezekiah knew that because of this, Sennacherib's men would have all the water they needed, enabling them to remain there for many months, continuing their siege.

In preparation for the coming siege, King Hezekiah strengthened the city's fortifications. But he had another idea too, one that was exceedingly clever and far more ambitious. He would cut off the water supply flowing into the Kidron Valley and deprive Sennacherib of this advantage during his siege. In the Scriptures we read that Hezekiah diverted the water so that it remained inside Jerusalem. Second Kings 20:20 says:

> Now the rest of the acts of Hezekiah—all his might, and how he made a pool and a tunnel and brought water into the city— are they not written in the book of the chronicles of the kings of Judah?

Second Chronicles 32:2–4 also mentions this:

> And when Hezekiah saw that Sennacherib had come, and that his purpose was to make war against Jerusalem, he consulted

with his leaders and commanders to stop the water from the springs which were outside the city; and they helped him. Thus many people gathered together who stopped all the springs and the brook that ran through the land, saying, "Why should the kings of Assyria come and find much water?"

But as we mentioned, it was not until 1880 that we had confirmation of exactly how Hezekiah had done this. This was when a truant teenager unwittingly stumbled—literally and figuratively—upon the inscription that identified the tunnel beneath Jerusalem as "Hezekiah's Tunnel." It was only then that the world learned that those few brief lines in the Scriptures referred to an engineering project of the most ambitious kind.

As a result of that discovery, we now understand that Hezekiah's ingenious plan for keeping the waters of the Gihon Spring within the walls of Jerusalem involved digging a tunnel through the living rock beneath the city. There were already some natural—or so-called "karstic"—pathways here and there in the subterranean spaces beneath the city, but most of the

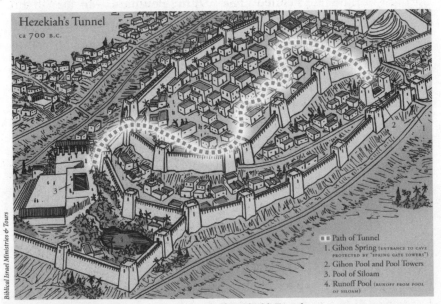

A cut-away of the City of David revealing the path of Hezekiah's Tunnel.

planned tunnel would need to be laboriously carved with chisels and pickaxes. For reasons still unknown the tunnel would take a sinuous path rather than a straight line, and eventually measured nearly six hundred yards. The descent of this tunnel—from the Gihon Spring to the Pool of Siloam—was as gradual as can be, differing only a single foot in its third-of-a-mile journey, just enough for what its engineers had in mind.

Of course the "first" discovery of the tunnel predated its "second" discovery in 1880, when the inscription was found. Its first discovery in "recent" centuries comes to us from the writer Franciscus Quaresmius in 1625. He writes of his friend, a certain "Vinhouen," whose attempt to clamber through the length of the subterranean passage was unsuccessful, but records the successful attempt of a priest, "Pater Julias," a few years earlier. So there were some who knew of the tunnel, but no one knew of its extraordinary provenance from the reign of Hezekiah. After this early-seventeenth-century mention, however, the historical record goes silent, although some visitors to the Holy Land do write about the mysterious flow of waters that seem to travel all the way from the Gihon Spring—in those days called "The Virgin's Fountain"—to the Siloam Pool, wondering whether the flow from the one to the other may be facilitated by "underground pipes," and wondering in which direction the waters traveled.

But then in 1838, the great Sir Edward Robinson galloped on to the scene. This is the renowned American Bible scholar who discovered "Robinson's Arch," which was connected to the supporting wall of the Second Temple, and whose encyclopedic knowledge of the Scriptures and indefatigable spirit in roaming across every inch of the then-unmapped Holy Land enabled him to make what

Edward Robinson (1794–1863)

amounted to a roaring cataract of identifications during his time there, such that his subsequent book—*Biblical Researches in Palestine, Mount Sinai, and Arabia Petraea: A Journal of Travels in the Year 1838*—would become a handbook for travelers for the century following and which, published in 1841, became the magnum opus of the man soon heralded as "the Father of Biblical Geography." The German theologian Albrecht Echt noted that Robinson "was able definitively to disprove a large part of what his predecessors had thought and had written," laying once and for all a firm and trustworthy foundation in the field—one that has been built upon ever since.

In the manner that would vault him to the fore of the field, Robinson minutely notes all those who had written of this passage before, and says that many of the locals whom he and his companion, Eli Smith (also a biblical scholar from Connecticut), spoke with had heard of the existence of a passageway all the way from the Gihon Spring to the Siloam Pool, but they were also united in the widespread belief that the interior of the serpentine cave harbored a dragon—or was otherwise haunted by a jinn or daemon—which accounts for their failure to have explored it themselves. It is worth noting too that Nehemiah in the Scriptures refers to a "Dragon's Well" during his own explorations of the city's walls, and the local memory of this seems to have informed the situation over the centuries. Robinson records every mention in the written records from Jerome in the late fourth century through various crusaders to his own time. So Robinson and Smith vowed to explore what they could of this purported tunnel when the opportunity presented itself.

On April 27, they found themselves measuring and exploring the Pool of Siloam and, seeing they were alone and the level of the water quite low, calculated it to be as good a time as any to begin. And so, carrying lighted candles and a measuring tape, they ventured forward into the unknown fissure. They observed that the passage—never more than two feet wide— had indeed been carved through the living rock, and that, while it for the first forty yards had a comfortable height of fifteen or twenty feet, it began to decrease gradually for the next hundred feet until the ceiling had descended to four feet, after which their progress became increasingly difficult. Still, they kept on. Robinson writes:

> At the end of 800 feet it became so low that we could advance no further without crawling on all fours and bringing our bodies close to the water. As we were not prepared for this, we thought it better to retreat and try again another day from the other end. Tracing therefore upon the roof with the smoke of our candles the initials of our names and the figure 800 as a mark of our progress on this side we returned with our clothes somewhat wet and soiled.[5]

Three days later they would explore the tunnel from the opposite end, at what was then called "The Virgin's Fountain" and is now called the Gihon Spring. If their above-ground measurements were correct, they optimistically put that portion of the tunnel remaining for them to explore to be in the neighborhood of about three hundred feet, never guessing that the inexplicable curvature and zigzagging of the tunnel put the true distance remaining at much closer to three times that long. Nonetheless, the doughty explorers were not easily discouraged:

> ...having clothed (or unclothed) ourselves simply in a pair of white Arab drawers we entered and crawled on, hoping soon to arrive at the point which we had reached from the other fountain. The passage here is in general much lower than at the other end; most of the way we could indeed advance upon our hands and knees; yet at several places we could only get forward by lying at full length and dragging ourselves along on our elbows.[6]

---

[5] Eli Smith, *Biblical Researches in Palestine, Mount Sinai, and Arabia Petraea: A Journal of Travels in the Year 1838*, Vol. 2 (Boston, Massachusetts: Crocker & Brewster, 1841).

[6] Ibid.

The two of them found themselves like eels exploring the long mistakes painstakingly carved by the workmen from another age, only having to turn back when they realized these were false leads culminating in dead ends, like the appendices of some antediluvian monster. Nonetheless they traversed each of these, examining them minutely, and each time backtracked to what they gathered must be the correct way forward:

> The way seemed interminably long and we for a time were suspicious that we had fallen on a passage different from that which we had before entered. But at length, after having measured 950 feet, we arrived at our former mark of 800 feet, traced with smoke upon the ceiling.[7]

After this they continued on, predictably emerging at Siloam's Pool where they had entered three days earlier. Robinson says in a footnote that Quaresmius's correspondent Vinhouen had published an account of his own efforts which they now recognized as remarkably similar to their own, although he had not been as successful:

> He entered at the upper end [Gihon], creeping on his hands and knees and sometimes at full length; until in a low spot his candle went out and he could neither strike a light nor turn round without great difficulty. At length he extricated himself and returned, *"licet bene madidus et sordibus plenus."*[8]

The following day Vinhouen did the opposite of what they had, entering at the lower (Siloam) end, but did not make it all the way through.

Robinson deduced that the tunnel had been dug from both ends simultaneously, and even more brilliantly surmised that when it was

---

[7] Ibid.

[8] "Although well-soaked and full of dirt."

created, both ends of the tunnel must have been inside the walls of Jerusalem. He writes that it appears "as if the advantage of a fortified city had been taken into account; and as if it had been important to carry this water from one point to the other in such a way that it could not be cut off by a besieging army." Robinson comes so close to cracking the code of this venerable mystery that it seems even more remarkable—given his superlative knowledge of the Bible—that he did not. Taking into account how much Robinson contributed to biblical archaeology and geography, it seems fitting that the honor of linking this literal passage linking Gihon to Siloam to the literary passage in the Scriptures should fall to another.

The next candidate accidentally to try his luck was the celebrated Sir Charles Warren,[9] a much-decorated British officer chosen by Queen Victoria to lead the Palestine Exploration Fund, of which she was patron. He unwittingly entered the lists of this competition when he began the first extensive archaeological exploration of the Temple Mount in 1867, inaugurating the excavations that have continued ever since. During this time he discovered what is today known as "Warren's Shaft," a natural "karstic" vertical shaft forty-five feet tall that is connected to the Gihon Spring, and explored various parts of the water system beneath Jerusalem, at some point entering parts of the tunnel Robinson had traversed and describing all of his efforts and discoveries in his 1871 opus, *The Recovery of Jerusalem: A Narrative of Exploration and Discovery in the City and the Holy Land*. To his credit, Warren did suggest that the Pool of Siloam may have been dug by Hezekiah, but this was as far as he got in plumbing the depths of our narrow subject.

So it was not until a fifteen-year-old boy decided to play hooky from the English Mission School in 1880 that the author of the tunnel came to light and its "second" and significant discovery was at last made, forevermore linking the daunting passage to the biblical verses concerning Hezekiah. The boy on whose head the laurel of this honor would rest was a Sephardic Jewish teenager

---

[9] Warren is among the more colorful figures from that era, having been the man who surveyed Gibraltar before his time in Jerusalem, and after this time becoming the London police chief who oversaw the investigations into the Jack the Ripper murders. After this he ran for a seat in Parliament and then commanded troops in the Second Boer War.

Charles Warren in the 1890s.

named Jacob Eliahu Spafford, who two years after this triumph was adopted by Horatio Spafford, the Chicago business-man who was a friend of Dwight L. Moody, and who is known for transmuting the bitter heartbreak of a family tragedy into the hymn "It Is Well with My Soul,"[10] and who afterward moved his family to Jerusalem, where they set up an American colony.

In 1950, no less than seventy years after his exploit, Eliahu's surviving sister Bertha wrote a memoir of her life in Jerusalem and told the otherwise unknown story of her brother's adventure. She heard him tell it innumerable times,[11] often to archaeologists interested in the subject, always saying a "schoolboy" had discovered the inscription revealing the historic truth of the tunnel, but never mentioning that he was himself the schoolboy. Bertha wrote that her adopted brother "was above the average in intellect… [speaking] five [languages] fluently, with a partial knowledge of several others." She said that he always recalled that the tunnel was said to be "haunted by a dragon or genie…. Nevertheless, [he] determined to explore the tunnel." She continued:

> Because of its reputation for being haunted, he had some trouble persuading his friend Sampson, a boy about his own age, to explore it with him, but at last he was persuaded. The boys kept their plan a profound secret. They had no idea of the height or width or length of the tunnel, nor how deep the

---

[10] The composition of this hymn followed the drowning death of his four girls while making a transatlantic passage with their mother, who survived. Afterward he and his wife had other children, including the above-mentioned Bertha.

[11] He died in 1927.

water. They prepared floats with candles and matches attached, and tied these around their necks with strings. Jacob started from the Pool of Siloam side, while Sampson entered from the Virgin's Fount. Their plan was to meet in the middle. Jacob found himself in total darkness and muddy water up to his chin. It was cold and drafty in the tunnel, his candle blew out, his float with the matches submerged in the water, and he could not relight the candle. But he kept on, going his way by keeping his hand on the damp stone wall and feeling under his fingertips the mark of the ancient chisels going forward, from right to left.... Jacob, feeling his way, suddenly was conscious that the chisel marks had changed and were now going from left to right.[12]

According to his sister's account seven decades later, Jacob bravely soldiered forward in the perfect darkness of the watery passage, hoping to encounter his friend, but never did. Eventually, he found himself emerging into blinding daylight at the Gihon Spring, shocking some washerwomen who shrieked at him. This was where Sampson supposedly had entered, but even here he was nowhere to be seen. It seems he had quickly lost heart in the frightening tunnel and had simply returned to school.

So Jacob at last returned to the school too, looking notably bedraggled. He confessed the details of his absence to his teacher, who was none other than the German architect and archaeologist Conrad Schick, who must have been amazed to hear of this—and who was more than amazed when in the course of Jacob's confession the boy let slip a detail from the beginning of his journey. It seems that only eighteen feet into the tunnel from the Pool of Siloam, Jacob had slipped and fallen into the water. But upon recovering himself, his eyes lit upon what seemed to be an inscription on the tunnel's limestone wall.[13]

---

[12] Bertha Spafford Vester, *Our Jerusalem: An American Family in the Holy City, 1881–1949* (New York: Doubleday, 1950), 91.

[13] According to Volume 19 of *Biblical World* in 1902.

The German architect and archaeologist Conrad Schick.

If Schick had any plans of disciplining the boy, we imagine it was here that he kicked them aside, instead skedaddling lickety-split to see the extraordinary inscription for himself. To be an archaeologist alive when something like this should be discovered, and for one's own troublemaking pupil to have discovered it! Sure enough, precisely where the boy had said, there it was still—and there for twenty-six centuries it had been in the darkness, as we now know. The inscription was so encrusted with mineral deposits it was hardly surprising it had never been noticed before, especially since it was far enough in the dark tunnel not to be easily seen. Schick could not make out what it said, but knew enough to believe this could be significant and announced it publicly, so that months later it came to the attention of Oxford's premier Assyriologist Dr. Archibald Sayce—mentioned previously as the man who identified the language of the Hittites—who was then in Jerusalem. Sayce investigated the inscription himself, twice wading into the darkened tunnel. The inscription lay just at water level, and each time he had to crouch uncomfortably in the water for an hour while a friend held a candle and Sayce copied what he could make out of the ancient lettering, including the bottom four inches of the inscription, which were perpetually underwater.[14] According to Sayce, it was Paleo-Hebrew—typical of what would have been used during King Hezekiah's time—and despite the rather poor quality of the inscription, his efforts were quite successful. After his visit, hydrochloric acid was used to

---

[14] Palestine Exploration Fund's Quarterly Statement of 1881.

remove some of the mineral deposits so the letters could be seen more clearly, but little was added to what Sayce had already deciphered. And when Sayce learned someone had touched this ancient treasure, he was outraged, fearing it had destroyed the fragile writing, but thankfully it did not.

The inscription proved unlike anything expected and clarified what was necessary to solve the mystery, since the lettering confirmed a date around Hezekiah's reign. It told the tale of two teams working with pickaxes from either

Jacob Spafford, years after his youthful adventure.

end—as the chisel marks confirmed—hoping to meet in the middle. It has been surmised that there was some sort of competition, because as they neared the midpoint each team's forward progress seems to have taken precedence over the tunnel's height. As they finally drew near each other they could hear each other's voices and, in a flurry, they rushed to complete the task. The inscription reads:

> ...and this is the story of the tunnel while...the axes were against each other and while three cubits were left to (cut?)...the voice of a man...called to his counterpart, (for) there was ZADA [unknown word] in the rock, on the right...and on the day of the tunnel (being finished) the stonecutters struck each man towards his counterpart, ax against ax and flowed water from the source to the pool for 1,200 cubits. And 100 cubits was the height over the head of the stonecutters....

3. The Silver Ketef Hinnom Scrolls

Just outside Jerusalem—literally under the old road from Jerusalem to Bethlehem—are a number of rock-hewn burial chambers. Most were looted long ago, but in 1979, Gabriel Barkay—today an archaeologist with Tel Aviv University—thought them worthy of further exploration. But when he and his team investigated them, the pickings were slimmer than hoped. The oldest thing they found was evidence that one of the chambers was used by the Ottoman Turks to hide their rifles two centuries before. Considering what Barkay had envisioned, it was disheartening. One chamber had initially seemed promising.

> [It] had a series of headrests and burial benches [Barkay remembered]. One bench was shaped like a cushion with six head rests. One bead was found that had been part of the burial gifts. Under the bench, we discovered a repository where they buried the bones and I looked into that repository and saw something that looked like a rock floor. I was disappointed.[15]

Most archaeologists struggle to have their investigations funded, and to keep costs down they often call upon university students studying archaeology. At the time of this dig, Barkay was teaching archaeology at Tel Aviv University, but was a young man still six years from getting his Ph.D. Getting funding—much less university students to help—was out of the question. But the Society for the Protection of Nature in Israel offered a very modest budget, as well as some twelve- and thirteen-year-olds belonging to "a local archaeology club." The presence and "help" of these kids was not ideal—"Thirteen is a dangerous age," Barkay remembered—but it was all that was offered, and somewhat reluctantly, he accepted.

As the day of work began, Barkay found one of the kids from this "archaeology club" to be more than merely unhelpful; in fact he was strikingly annoying, pulling at Barkay's shirttails every few minutes and generally being a nuisance. So when Barkay came up with a way to get the boy out from underfoot, he leaped at it. It happened that the promising chamber—Chamber 25—was relatively distant from the rest. It proved to be a disappointment, but would

---

[15] "About the Ketef Hinnom Silver Scrolls," https://ketefhinnomsilverscrolls.github.io/about.html.

nonetheless need to be photographed, and before that would need to be cleaned. Barkay hit on the capital idea of dispatching the irritating twelve-year-old—his name was Nathan—to do the job. He would be out of sight and earshot for a blissful hour or two. Years later, Barkay recalled realizing the boy would require unmistakably firm and clear direction: "I told Nathan the repository had to be as clean as his mother's kitchen—even if he had to lick it." With these marching orders, the boy trundled off to the distant chamber.

But it turned out Nathan could be trouble from a distance, too. For reasons lost to archaeological history, the twelve-year-old snuck a hammer with him into Chamber 25. While taking a break from cleaning—whether out of boredom, an excess of undirected energy, or both—he began to smash the stone floor of the repository under the bench. Had Barkay witnessed this, he would have shrieked at Nathan to stop, but of course Barkay was far away, relishing the peace of the boy's absence.

As the story goes, under this child's inane hammering the solid rock of the chamber's floor revealed itself not to be as solid as thought. The preadolescent's mindless tattoo eventually proved more than it could bear, and a crack revealed itself, encouraging further hammering. Eventually Nathan was elated to see that his surfeit of youthful energy had opened a hidden chamber beneath the floor, so he reached in and immediately put his hand to a pair of intact pottery vessels. As we might imagine, the boy felt that this—rather than cleaning—was why he was here in the first place, and he excitedly fled the chamber to locate Barkay, proudly showing him the two vessels.

Barkay was nonplussed: Why had Nathan returned, and what were these ancient ceramics doing in his hands? When Barkay understood what had happened, he raced to the chamber. It seemed that this memorably pesky kid—by smashing what everyone believed to be a solid stone floor—had magically opened the door to archaeological history.

Of course at the time Barkay had no idea what else might be in the hole Nathan had hammered into the past. Still, it seemed far more promising than what Barkay himself had found. Although he knew the boy had implausibly coaxed fire from the rock, so to speak, he also guessed that the aggravating child had in this violent act probably accomplished his divine purpose, so he now sent Nathan and his young "archaeology club" confederates home.

But the heady promise of this uncannily opened cache suddenly enabled Barkay to recruit actual archaeology students from nearby universities. With their help he could now excavate this new find in earnest. The pastor of St. Andrews, the Scottish church located just above the excavation site, brought down an electrical hook-up, and by lamplight Barkay and his team of students worked around the clock.

Barkay could never quite fathom the screwball madness of how this secret chamber had bloomed to life, but now he and his graduate students busied themselves in unearthing one item after the other, and they were all from before the sixth century BC. There was no getting around it: the strikingly irksome child and his magic hammer had opened the door to an Aladdin's treasure of objects from pre-exilic Israel. It seemed something from a fevered dream; among the findings were "125 objects of silver, 40 iron arrowheads, gold, ivory, glass, bone, and 150 semi-precious stones."[16] There were also skeletal remains.

Of course most of this was under two feet of filth. Barkay remembered:

> There was a lot of dust and a lack of oxygen. It was very hot. We had to change teams every few hours. There was a lady who was in charge of coffee and sandwiches. Everyone was sworn to secrecy—they weren't allowed to tell parents, spouses, or friends. If word got around Jerusalem that there was such a treasure, the California gold rush would be nothing compared to what would happen here.[17]

A young woman named Judy Hadley from Toledo, Ohio, was among those helping. At some point she brought a decidedly strange-looking

---

[16] Ibid.

[17] Ibid.

object to Barkay, which he later described as "purplish-colored" and "looking like a cigarette butt." In fact there were two such objects, both of them tremendously fragile-looking. What in the world were they?

They turned out to be something almost unimaginable: an impossibly tiny pair of scrolls made of purest silver. Who could have dreamed up such a thing? And they were so extremely delicate that Barkay didn't dare try to "unroll" them, knowing they would fracture into pieces. But even in their rolled state, he saw that the writing on them was in ancient Hebrew characters. He recognized the *Yod He Vav He* letters of the "Divine Name"—the Tetragrammaton that we usually write as "Yahweh" or "Jehovah" and which many Bibles translate as "the LORD," in all capitals.

Of course there was more writing inside, but how to read it? This would take no less than three years to figure out and would eventually involve infrared imaging technology. But at last they were able to unroll them safely and decipher what was inscribed. It was a shock. The writing was nothing less than the familiar "priestly blessing," found in the Book of Numbers, chapter six, which reads: "The LORD bless you and keep you. The Lord make His face to shine upon you, and be gracious unto you. The LORD lift up His countenance upon you; and give you peace." It turned out to be the oldest example of writing from the Bible anywhere in the world and still is to this day. This well-known blessing forms a centrally important place in Jewish tradition, being the same words spoken by Moses's brother Aaron over the Hebrew people. It is generally done with both of the priest's hands raised over the assembly in what modern-day audiences would likely recognize as the Vulcan "live long and prosper" hand formation used by Leonard Nimoy's Spock character in the 1960s TV show *Star Trek*.[18]

But there was a further question concerning the scrolls that could not be solved even after they were unrolled in 1982, and this concerned their age.

---

[18] In fact, Leonard Nimoy came up with the single-handed gesture for his character, having remembered seeing it as a child during an Orthodox Jewish service. It was forbidden to look upon the priests' hands, but Nimoy had gazed out from under his father's prayer shawl and noticed it. He remembered it years later and thought it appropriate to use for his character. The series creator Gene Roddenberry agreed.

Answering that conclusively would take another twenty-two years, because it was not until 2004 that there existed computer enhancement and photography techniques advanced enough to properly reexamine the writing, at which time a University of Southern California team did just that. It then became clear to all parties what they had hoped: the writing was in fact Proto-Hebraic lettering dating from the last years of the pre-exilic period (650–587 BC), just before Nebuchadnezzar's destruction of Jerusalem in 586 BC. So it was not until 2004 that it was confirmed beyond question that this prayer—which appears in the Bible—was known during this very early period.

So the diminutive scrolls summoned into the present by young Nathan's unorthodox methods really were the earliest portions of Scripture in the world, decisively pushing back the known existence of biblical text several centuries, and making this particularly unexpected discovery among the most important finds in archaeological history.

Though neither Barkay nor anyone ever learned what happened to him, one hopes Nathan might via this book or other means learn of the starring role he played in this drama, and of how it was his indefatigably annoying behavior that delivered him to the very spot where everyone else ought to have been looking in the first place—and that also seems to have caused the destruction of an ancient stone floor that had been hiding such treasures as none could have imagined.

These, then, are the strange facts: the extraordinary misbehavior of one twelve-year-old in 1979 led to the discovery of the oldest biblical text in existence; the misbehavior of another in 1947 led to the greatest archaeological discovery of all time; and the misbehavior of a fifteen-year-old in 1880 led to the discovery of Hezekiah's tunnel and the corroboration of one of the most dramatic accomplishments of any monarch in the Scriptures. And so the question comes: Why? Why should three boys, all doing things their parents and caretakers would have loudly forbidden, be the ones to open the doors to some of the greatest treasures of the Bible's past?

It is either a coincidence or a conundrum. Or perhaps it is something else altogether, to which we may find a clue in the first-century letter written to Christians living in the city of Corinth:

> But God has chosen the foolish things of the world to put to shame the wise, and God has chosen the weak things of the world to put to shame the things which are mighty; and the base things of the world and the things which are despised God has chosen, and the things which are not, to bring to nothing the things that are, that no flesh should glory in His presence. (1 Corinthians 1:27–29)

CHAPTER TWELVE

More Archaeology: The New Testament Manuscripts

During much of the nineteenth and twentieth centuries, many academics claimed Jesus never existed, and that most of the people, places, and events of the New Testament were invented. But with the tremendous evidence we have today, such dismissiveness seems inconceivable. Nonetheless, during the decades in which such skeptical winds blew, such now-absurd notions blazed enough to blind millions to the truth. Several lamentable theories regarding the resurrection were floated—including the "Swoon Theory," claiming Jesus never died, but only "fainted"—and most of them found some cultural purchase. Of course serious historians always knew Josephus and Tacitus and others had referred to Jesus's existence and crucifixion, and except for those bearing a stubborn animus to the historicity of the New Testament, few could ignore such trustworthy sources. But such hostility exists yet, and there are those in the academy who even today snipe at the most well-established facts. For example, Josephus twice refers to Jesus in his *History of the Jews*, written in the last years of the first century. The Roman senator and historian Tacitus in his *Annals* writes of Jesus and his crucifixion too, and in a letter to the Emperor Trajan the Roman historian Suetonius—who was also the governor of Bithynia and Pontus—discusses what to do with the troublemaking Christians who refused to worship the emperor.

Although all of these long-known sources are unimpeachable, around the aforementioned 1966 *Time* magazine cover story it was still culturally acceptable to pretend that the historicity of Jesus was an open question. Since most cultural elites were secular, they were not eager to counter these unfounded ideas, and skepticism toward Jesus and the Christian faith reached something of a high-water mark in the West around that time. But in keeping with the thesis of this book, since that moment of maximum skepticism the tide has been flowing almost exclusively in the other direction.

The New Testament Documents

Perhaps the most powerful argument for the historicity of the New Testament is made in *The New Testament Documents: Are They Reliable?*, by the Scottish New Testament scholar F. F. Bruce. In that slim book Bruce makes the overwhelming case that not only are the documents of the New Testament historically reliable, but they are the most reliable in the history of all ancient documents, with no close competitors. No ancient documents begin to approach the New Testament manuscripts from an historical perspective. This is because there are two basic criteria by which historians judge a manuscript. The first is the chronological distance between the manuscript in hand and the original manuscript from which it was copied. The second is the number of manuscript copies, which is how we verify the consistency of what has been written and how we can know that it's not a one-off forgery.

As we mentioned in our discussion of the Dead Sea Scrolls, the writings of Julius Caesar were composed in the first century BC and the earliest copies are from approximately 900 AD, so a full millennium yawns between the original and the manuscript copies we now have. And there are ten copies. We only have seven copies of Plato's works, composed about 400 BC, and these copies also date from around 900 AD, giving us a gap of twelve centuries between the originals and the extant copies. Yet, outside the New Testament, these are some of the very best attested documents.

The Greek dramatists Sophocles, Euripides, and Aristophanes, and the great orator Demosthenes, as well as the philosopher Aristotle, and the historians Thucydides and Herodotus, all have gaps of between 1,200 and 1,500 years between their original writings and our most recent copies. And the number of manuscripts of their works is decidedly modest. We have eight from Thucydides and Herodotus, and no more than five of any one work from Aristotle. Still, no serious historian would quibble about their historical reliability. The great distances between originals and extant manuscripts are typical and thought to be quite trustworthy enough, even with so few copies.

But the New Testament documents, composed in the latter half of the first century, offer an unprecedented and enviable level of reliability. The philosopher and theologian J. P. Moreland sums it up:

> Approximately 5,000 Greek manuscripts, containing all or part of the New Testament, exist. There are 8,000 manuscript copies of the Vulgate (a Latin translation of the Bible done by Jerome from 382–405) and more than 350 copies of Syriac (Christian Aramaic) versions of the New Testament (these originated from 150–250; most of the copies are from the 400s). Besides this, virtually the entire New Testament could be reproduced from citations contained in the works of the early church fathers. There are some thirty-two thousand citations in the writings of the Fathers prior to the Council of Nicea (AD 325).[1]

As we can see, the number of manuscript copies is beyond compare. When we consider how many centuries exist between the originals and the

---

[1] J. P. Moreland, *Scaling the Secular City: A Defense of Biblical Christianity* (Grand Rapids, Michigan: Baker Books, 1987), 136.

earliest manuscripts, we are equally astonished. Although there is a great range in the dates of the copies, all the way from early in the second century up till the Reformation, the existence of many at the earlier end of that range is mind-boggling, as is the idea that some are from less than one or two centuries after they were originally composed. Moreland continues:

> Many of the manuscripts are early—for example, the John Rylands manuscript (about 120 AD; it was found in Egypt and contains a few verses from the Gospel of John), the Chester Beatty Papyri (200 AD; it contains major portions of the New Testament), Codex Sinaiticus (350 AD; it contains virtually all of the New Testament), and Codex Vaticanus (325–50 AD; it contains almost the entire Bible).[2]

Some of these are so close to the originals that, compared with other manuscripts from antiquity, it is almost as though we actually did have the originals. The John Ryland manuscript mentioned by Moreland is the most amazing of all, dating from perhaps only thirty years after the death of its author, who is the Apostle John. This is the disciple who famously lay at the breast of Jesus at the Last Supper and is a principal figure in all four of the gospel accounts. The existence of something so close as almost to be touching the originals—and from a figure directly involved in almost all that took place—is a singularly tantalizing example of historical reliability. The Ryland Papyrus was discovered by Bernard Pyne Grenfell, an Oxford papyrologist, who in 1896 began excavation of a spectacular trove of papyrus in the Egyptian city of Oxyrhynchus.

That discovery site was a dump where people had been tossing things for centuries, and the ancient manuscripts discovered there proved to be something from a fevered dream. For example, a lost satyr play from Sophocles was found, along with previously unknown poetry from Sappho. But what eclipsed these other things instantly and forever was the discovery of a credit-card-sized

---

[2] Ibid.

fragment of what was eventually identified as a part of the Gospel of John, and which was dated at between 100 AD and about 175 AD. The idea that this manuscript of New Testament scriptures from what might have been a single decade after it was composed, or eighty years at the most, marked an almost unthinkable proximity to the authors and figures involved. Just as the Dead Sea Scrolls did for the Old Testament, this fragment undergirded the validity of all later copies and instantly pushed back the reliability of these documents by several centuries. And of course because of what they found at Oxyrhynchus, scholars have ever since been wondering what yet remains to be discovered. If a fragment of the Gospel of John, written nearly during the lifetime of John himself has been found—and was somehow preserved for eighteen hundred years—surely there is more still to find. But what?

The Argument from Quirkiness

Before we move on to other archaeological evidence for the New Testament, we turn briefly to what scholars call "internal evidence" for the truth of the accounts in these manuscripts. For those whose objection is that the Bible was written by people with an agenda, and who were molding a narrative to suit their purposes, there are endless examples clearly arguing against that idea. The kinds of evidence vary, but to anyone sensitive to literature and to how things are communicated in different genres, there are many instances in the long career of the Bible that have what is called "the ring of truth," however subjective that concept might be.

One from the New Testament—as recorded near the end of John's gospel—concerns the number of fish caught after Jesus tells the fatigued disciples to throw their nets back into the water. Something similar happened at the very beginning of Jesus's ministry, as recorded in Luke 5. In that earlier instance it was obviously morning, since the disciples were finished fishing and were cleaning their nets. But Jesus, wanting to speak to the large crowd gathered, chose to step into one of the boats and pushed out a bit from shore. We may assume the shore was curved, and this would have improved his ability to communicate, or perhaps the extraordinary stillness of the water at that early hour helped him project his voice. Many of us have heard people in a boat talking out on a lake, oblivious that their voices would carry so far. The passage says:

> When He had stopped speaking, He said to Simon, "Launch out into the deep and let down your nets for a catch."
>
> But Simon answered and said to Him, "Master, we have toiled all night and caught nothing; nevertheless at Your word I will let down the net." And when they had done this, they caught a great number of fish, and their net was breaking. So they signaled to their partners in the other boat to come and help them. And they came and filled both the boats, so that they began to sink. When Simon Peter saw it, he fell down at Jesus' knees, saying, "Depart from me, for I am a sinful man, O Lord!"
>
> For he and all who were with him were astonished at the catch of fish which they had taken; and so also were James and John, the sons of Zebedee, who were partners with Simon. And Jesus said to Simon, "Do not be afraid. From now on you will catch men." So when they had brought their boats to land, they forsook all and followed Him. (Luke 5:4–11)

The initial exasperation of Simon at being told by a non-fisherman to put his net in the water at an hour when fish are known to be scarce—which is the point of fishing for them at night—is obvious. But when Peter obeys Jesus, not only does he catch fish, but he also catches so many he knows it is a wild miracle, and responds by kneeling before Jesus in profound awe of what has occurred. So it is curious that roughly three years later something similar happens.

By now these disciples have seen innumerable miracles, many far more impressive and dramatic, and have perhaps forgotten about this miracle at the beginning of their time with Jesus, which must seem ages before, considering all that had transpired. But now, after his crucifixion and resurrection, the disciples are back doing what they have always done, what they know best. Yet they are having no luck, having fished all night, as was their custom. And then in the morning as they prepare to end their efforts, a stranger on the shore has the temerity to instruct them to cast their net on the right side of the boat, confidently saying they will find some. How would he know? But with nothing to lose they do what he suggests and sure enough, their nets are instantly so filled with fish that they are flabbergasted. It is then that Peter seems to realize this is precisely what happened three years earlier, when Jesus told him to put the net in the water. Instantly he knows who the stranger on the shore is, and when John blurts out: "It is the Lord!" it seems as though Jesus has slyly played a joke on Peter, knowing that in seeing the vast number of fish, he would suddenly understand what had just happened. So in an explosion of joy, Peter forgets about the fish and dives into the water to frantically swim to the one he loves, whom he has missed so terribly, and whom we soon remember he betrayed three times on the eve of his crucifixion. But before Jesus deals with Peter's failing—by forgiving and restoring him—he says something more practical. "Bring some of the fish!" he says. So Peter goes back to the boat and hauls in the net.

And then we read something odd and striking. It says that the number of fish was 153. What could be quirkier? Why does the Bible record that number? Can there be any reason for saying there were 153 fish—other than that there were actually 153 fish? It certainly doesn't seem like any symbolic number, like 144. Nor can we say it was a rough figure, since it is so extremely specific. Many have tried to ferret out some hidden meaning, but if you have to try very hard to figure out the meaning of something, this may be a clue that there is none. Paraphrasing Freud, sometimes a number is just a number.

But there are innumerable cases in the Bible of such curious details, in which the rather clear meaning is simply that something happened, that someone recorded it, and that it does not fit the larger narrative in any especially meaningful, poetic, or symbolic way. It is merely an indicator that those recording the events did so. All writing is editing, to some extent, since writers usually leave out things they might have included and tell things in a certain order. But every now and then in reading the Scriptures we see examples of lumpiness and quirkiness, of things that do nothing more than point to the simple facts and veracity of what we are reading. If the number of fish had been 100 or 150, we would have assumed the number was rounded, because what are the odds that the number would be exactly either of those? But 153? What can it mean, but that there were precisely that many? If there is any meaning at all, it is probably just that anyone familiar with the normal fishing patterns in that area would have been stunned and impressed by the number. They would have known what an unprecedented and stupefying number of fish it was. And that is all. Such an odd specific inevitably bolsters the validity of the rest of the story.

A similar example is found in the record of what took place that Thursday night in the Garden of Gethsemane, when the Roman soldiers and Jerusalem temple guards arrive to arrest Jesus. The tension during this confrontation is extraordinary. It is after midnight, and as these men lay hands on Jesus to arrest him, the ever-impetuous Peter erupts into action, coming down with his sword on the head of the high priest's servant, cutting off the man's ear. The text is so straightforward and simple that we may forget there was probably an explosion of screaming and gushing blood and then the visceral response of the soldiers with their spears and clubs, who easily might have responded in kind, killing Peter instantly along with the rest of those present. But the verse here is as dull and minimalist as if Ernest Hemingway had written it. It says that Jesus stepped forward and miraculously healed the man's ear, and that all of his followers fled instantly. We aren't so surprised that they fled, for they had no idea what was happening, and knew they might be treated extremely harshly for following the man being arrested. But not all of them fled. As the soldiers led Jesus away, the Scriptures say: "And there followed him a certain young man, having a linen cloth cast about his naked body...." We have no idea why there was someone there wearing only a linen cloth—or "sheet"—and no one has in two thousand years been able to make any real sense of it. The Scriptures say that the soldiers "laid hold of him, and he left the linen cloth and fled from them naked" (Mark 14:51–52). What could be stranger? An anonymous young man is in the Garden of Gethsemane after midnight wearing no clothes, inexplicably wrapped in a linen cloth, and he alone remains behind when all those closest to Jesus have fled. Why don't the Scriptures explain this? And what can be the meaning? Or perhaps there is none, as we think of meaning. Perhaps the blank simplicity of the text attests to the fact that this is merely what happened, and no one knew why, nor felt the freedom to embellish the account with possible interpretations. But perhaps in the interests of verisimilitude they felt the need to retain it. In any event, here is another peculiar detail that defies easy explanation, but that in its own presence and nakedness argues for the simple genuineness of the narrative.

There are other details in the Scriptures that seem not merely to make no particular sense or have any reason to be there, but that even seem to undermine the writers' narrative of the events, so that we might expect them to have been edited out. Yet there they are.

For example, the Scriptures say that on Easter morning several women went to the tomb to finish preparing Jesus's body for burial. Because the sun was setting that Friday after his body had been taken down from the cross and brought to the tomb, they could not finish what they had begun. It was impermissible to do anything on the Sabbath, which began at sundown. So they stopped and went home and had to wait all Saturday, until at the very first opportunity—after sunrise on Sunday—they returned to the tomb to complete their work. They knew they would need to find someone to move the giant stone that was rolled in front of the tomb's entrance. But when they arrived the tomb was already opened—and it was empty. An angel told them that Jesus had risen. Of course the women were undone by this news, trembling and stunned, and ran back to tell the disciples what they had discovered.

But if anyone had concocted this narrative, the last thing they would have done would be to make a group of women the first witnesses at what is the most important event in the entire New Testament. In the patriarchal atmosphere of that time, women were not regarded with much credibility. So why would the writers of these gospels make them the ones to see the angel, and the stone rolled away? Anyone wanting to construct a credible narrative would not have told this detail. This leaves us with the idea that they told the story this way because they could not lie about something so important, even if it worked against the credibility of it all. But they were stuck: the God in whom they believed demanded that they not lie, and that they trust him with the results. What else can explain leaving such a striking detail—on which nearly everything hinges—at the center of this most difficult part of the whole story?

There are innumerable similarly strange details in the Old Testament too, which seem to contribute nothing to the story other than to add additional detail and therefore to argue for bare veracity. In 2 Samuel, we read the awful story in which King David's son Amnon rapes his own half-sister Tamar. Tamar's brother Absalom, furious at hearing this, orders his men to kill Amnon. But at 13:30 in the narrative it says that a report reached David that all of his sons had been killed, not just Amnon. Two verses later David's nephew Jonadab arrives and says, "No, not all your sons have been killed! It was only Amnon!" If one were telling an invented story, why include this bizarre misunderstanding that is cleared up almost immediately and has no bearing on the larger story? Isn't that sort of detail the very mark of non-fiction? It seems to be in the story for no other reason than it happened.

Beyond the Manuscripts

Although the evidence for Jesus of Nazareth and many of the people, places, things, and events of the New Testament has grown over time, the level of specificity and detail that has emerged over the last few decades has increased, sometimes to a level that almost seems impossible, as though specifically intended to twit the dourest skeptics.

We discuss two of the most astounding and very recent examples, both of which concern the life of Jesus himself. The first is the extremely recent discovery of Jesus's childhood home in Nazareth, which is as astonishing as anything we could hope to find; the second is the recent discovery of the actual stone pavement mentioned in the New Testament as "Gabbatha"—upon which Jesus stood bleeding with his crown of thorns during the "trial" before Pilate, and not only of this, but of the very "Bema" seat upon which Pilate sat during this trial. Did anyone ever dream such things still existed, much less that we might discover them in recent years? As with the aforementioned identification of biblical Sodom and other amazing finds, the oddest part of the story is sometimes that such discoveries are not immediately trumpeted to the world, and we will touch on that too.

CHAPTER THIRTEEN

More New Testament Archaeology

Before we come to the most dramatic and recent discoveries, we might take a galloping survey of some other notable discoveries. Because archaeology often links the accounts from the Bible with history, it becomes increasingly difficult—and one might argue by now quite impossible—to banish the biblical accounts to some mythical island far from the mainland of history. We will begin with two early discoveries corroborating relatively minor figures, and then move to three of the most important figures in the New Testament.

Sergius Paulus Inscriptions

In the thirteenth chapter of the Book of Acts, we read that Barnabas and Paul arrived in the city of Paphos on Cyprus, where the proconsul Sergius Paulus summoned them, eager to hear what they had to say. One of his attendants, however, was a sorcerer named Elymas, who was obviously bothered that his master should be drawn to the God who would have forbidden Elymas from continuing his practices. And so Elymas tried to turn the proconsul away from the faith that Paul and Barnabas represented. The Scriptures say that Paul understood what was happening and openly rebuked Elymas, saying:

> "And now, indeed, the hand of the Lord is upon you, and you shall be blind, not seeing the sun for a time."
> And immediately a dark mist fell on him, and he went around seeking someone to lead him by the hand. Then the proconsul believed, when he saw what had been done, being astonished at the teaching of the Lord. (Acts 13:11–12)

The drama of this scene aside, it is hard to imagine that the eminently scrupulous Luke could have inaccurately reported such details as the names of those involved. Nonetheless it greatly bolsters the case with skeptics when stones are found to cry out with precisely the same lyrics as the Scriptures. For example, in 1877 a Greek inscription was discovered on the northern coast of Cyprus. It referred to a proconsul named Paulus and was a very early example of an archaeological discovery confirming what we read in the New Testament. A few years later another stone was found, this time in Rome, referring to an "L. Sergius Paullus" as one of the curators of the Tiber River. It was dated to 47 AD, while the previous stone had a date of 54 AD. The New Testament scholar Ben Witherington III concludes:

> The Latin inscription, datable to the 40s, like the text of Acts 13, mentions a prominent Sergius Paulus as a public figure [and] suggests a connection between the two since clearly Paul's visit to Cyprus must also be dated to the reign of Claudius in the later 40s. This would provide one more piece of evidence, though indirect, that Luke is dealing with historical data and situations, not just creating a narrative with historical verisimilitude.[1]

---

[1] Ben Witherington III, *The Acts of the Apostles: A Socio-Rhetorical Commentary* (Grand Rapids, Michigan: William B. Eerdmans Publishing Company, 1998), 400.

The Gallio Inscription, or the Delphi Inscription

Again in Acts, the historian Luke relates an incident from Paul's time in the Greek city of Corinth. Some fellow Jews had had enough of Paul's theological troublemaking and decided to hale him before the Roman authorities:

> When Gallio was proconsul of Achaia, the Jews with one accord rose up against Paul and brought him to the judgment seat, saying, "This fellow persuades men to worship God contrary to the law."
>
> And when Paul was about to open his mouth, Gallio said to the Jews, "If it were a matter of wrongdoing or wicked crimes, O Jews, there would be reason why I should bear with you. But if it is a question of words and names and your own law, look to it yourselves; for I do not want to be a judge of such matters." And he drove them from the judgment seat. Then all the Greeks took Sosthenes, the ruler of the synagogue, and beat him before the judgment seat. But Gallio took no notice of these things. (Acts 18:12–17)

Just as with the passage above mentioning Sergius Paulus, those disinclined to take the Bible seriously pointed to this passage as evidence that the New Testament could not be trusted as actual history. None of the myriad Roman manuscripts mentioned any Gallio as proconsul of Achaea during this time, nor did any inscriptions. Of course one must wonder why Luke would invent a name and use it three times in such a specific context, or be so sloppy that he would get the name wrong, especially when he is everywhere else so scrupulous. Nonetheless, skeptics of the New Testament often insist on a heightened level of confirmation. But now and again such confirmation comes to light.

In 1905 a graduate student was tasked with going through a dauntingly large pile of inscribed shards from the Temple of Apollo in Delphi. In the course of this endless task he came upon what struck him as a novel inscription. It was by the Roman emperor Claudius himself and dated from sometime between January and August of 52 AD. It referenced "Junius Gallio, my friend and proconsul...." Thus was Luke's accuracy confirmed, as it has been again and again in the decades since with similar details.

Most fascinating, however, is the specificity of the inscription's dating, and it is because of this inscription that we possess the most accurately known date in the whole of Paul's life. It has therefore provided a chronological "anchor" enabling scholars to date all of Paul's other travels and activities. This small inscription is the very stuff of which history is made. Also, because the Bible provided historians with the name of the proconsul of Achaea in that year, they were able eventually to identify Gallio as none other than the brother of the writer and philosopher Seneca, and to add this anecdote from Gallio's reign as proconsul at that time.

The Pilate Stone

During an excavation at Caesarea Maritima in 1961, a stone was discovered referring to Pontius Pilate, whom we know as the principal Roman figure in Jerusalem during the trial of Jesus. We assume that Pilate traveled to Jerusalem as required by his duties, and while there he would stay in Herod's vast and extremely ornate palace. But most of his time was spent in another lavish palace at Caesarea Maritima—or Caesarea Palestina on the Mediterranean. The only record of him until this discovery was in the manuscripts of the New Testament, Josephus, and Tacitus—but now in stone, the existence of this central figure could be confirmed.

Evidence of Crucifixion

Because wood rots, and because wood fashioned into a cross for the purpose of executing a man would not have been valued, the archaeological record gave us no evidence of the gruesome practice from Roman times. We knew of it only from the gospel accounts, and from the writings of Seneca and Josephus. But in 1968 in the Jerusalem neighborhood of Givat HaMivtar, building contractors stumbled across a tomb. It was excavated by the Greek archaeologist Vassilios Tzaferis, who discovered an ossuary inscribed with the name Jehohanan ben Ha-galgula. Among the bones in it was a heel bone with an eleven-centimeter-long nail still piercing it, providing the only archaeological evidence of Roman crucifixion.

Caiaphas Ossuary

In 1990 another ossuary from this period was discovered, containing the bones of the man arguably most responsible for Pilate's decision to crucify Jesus. There are few scenes in the Bible that rise to a higher pitch than the late-night confrontation between Jesus and Caiaphas, the high priest of Jerusalem, who along with the chief priests and elders had decided to trap Jesus and have him put to death. The crowds following Jesus had grown tremendously over the course of his ministry, for what poor soul hoping to be healed did not try to have an encounter with this miracle worker? But near the end of Jesus's ministry, after people learned that he had raised his friend Lazarus from the tomb after four days, the size of the crowds grew further still, as did the expectation that he would reveal himself to be the Messiah come to deliver them from their Roman oppressors and restore Jerusalem to its former glory. So the religious leaders feared losing everything they had been working toward in keeping the peace with Rome, and were desperate to end this burgeoning movement before it went any further. As far as they were concerned, the time to act had come.

So one night, having learned from Judas where Jesus and his disciples would be, Caiaphas sent his soldiers to the Garden of Gethsemane, where they arrested and bound Jesus and took him back into the city and to the house of Caiaphas, who was waiting with the other religious leaders.

For a time they tried to entrap Jesus by questioning him, but were unsuccessful until finally Caiaphas, enraged, cut to the heart of the matter:

"I put you under oath by the living God: tell us if you are the Christ, the Son of God!" Jesus's reply to them was shocking: "It is as you said." And then he went further still: "Nevertheless, I say to you, hereafter you will see the Son of Man sitting at the right hand of the Power, and coming on the clouds of heaven" (Matthew 26:62–63).

That this humble figure had dared not only to assent to being the foretold Messiah, but had then dared to claim he would sit on the right hand of God's throne was more than those assembled had thought possible. In a dramatic act, Caiaphas tore his robe in twain—something in those days done to express bitterest grief—and declared: "He has spoken blasphemy! What further need do we have of witnesses? Look, now you have heard his blasphemy. What do you think?" And the gathered priestly assembly replied: "He is deserving of death."

Because of the destruction of Jerusalem by the Romans in AD 70, it is difficult to know whether any of the names used in such scenes are accurate. But again, thanks to Josephus, we know that a man named Caiaphas became chief priest over Jerusalem in 18 AD. This would seem to be all the corroboration necessary. But it's always helpful to find a second piece of evidence, especially from the world of archaeology, which is what happened in November 1990, when land was being cleared for a water park south of the Abu Tor area of Jerusalem. A bulldozer inadvertently uncovered what turned out to be an ancient tomb.

Work was stopped immediately, and the archaeological authorities notified. The tomb was from the first century and was found to contain twelve ossuaries—stone boxes in which the bones of the deceased are kept. We know that for a brief period in the first century Jews adopted this funerary custom. Among these ossuaries beneath the proposed water park was one of particular ornateness, obviously containing the bones of someone important. Its contents were the bones of a sixty-year-old man, and on the outside of the box was an inscription with the name of the man whose remains it held: "Josephus Caiaphas." The New Testament only says Caiaphas, but the historian Josephus records his full name as "Josephus Caiaphas." So we not only have extra-biblical affirmation of the man involved in condemning Jesus to his death—both in the writings of Josephus and on this stone ossuary—but now we have his bones too.

CHAPTER FOURTEEN

Jerusalem in Jesus's Day

To understand Jerusalem and Israel at the time of Jesus—and to under-stand the events of the New Testament—we should give an overview of the history of the Jews until then.

According to the Bible, it was roughly 1500 BC when God spoke to Abraham, telling him that from his yet-to-be-born descendants God would make a great people. Abraham and his wife Sarah—although very advanced in years—had a son named Isaac, from whom the inhabitants of the nation of Israel were descended. Isaac had a son named Jacob; and Jacob had twelve sons, from whom we get the "Twelve Tribes of Israel." The descendants of these twelve tribes came to live in Egypt, where they were eventually enslaved. Around 1300 BC Moses led them out of their captivity in Egypt, into the Promised Land in Canaan. For a few centuries they were ruled by prophets and priests, and they worshiped in a "Tabernacle in the Wilder-ness," which was located at Shiloh. Then, around 1000 BC the people of Israel began clamoring for a king, such as the other nations around them had. So God gave them King Saul, and then King David, whose son King Solomon built the First Temple in Jerusalem.

INTERFOTO/Alamy Stock Photo

Herod I, "the Great," (72–4 BC).

Solomon's Temple was completed in 957 BC and stood until 586 BC, when the Babylonians destroyed it. But the Persian king Cyrus looked favorably on the Jews and enabled them to rebuild their temple, which they began to do in 539 BC, completing it in 516 BC. This Second Temple stood for almost five centuries, until the time of Herod the Great—an extraordinarily evil figure we likely remember from the Nativity story of Jesus, in which Herod feared that the prophesied King of the Jews had been born and would eclipse him, so he ordered the murder of every male child two years old and younger. It was also as a result of his towering insecurity that Herod chose to rebuild Jerusalem to a level worthy of his own image of himself, so he imposed very high taxes on his subjects. No expense was spared in building a Jerusalem more magnificent than any before or since, and at the literal and figurative apex of it all would be the new temple—henceforth known as Herod's Temple—which would occupy the spot of the previous one. This would burnish his image with the more religious Jews in Jerusalem, many of whom despised him, and would be a monument to himself far greater than any Jew had ever built. But he would not only build an outrageously grandiose temple; he would extensively expand the setting upon which it stood, and in an ambitious feat of engineering, would convert the entirety of Mount Moriah into a vast platform of thirty-six acres, doubling its size.

The monumental retaining wall built to shore up one side of this platform stands to this day and is the sacred spot where many Jews go to pray, as it is the only remaining link to the temple of that time. Most of the stones in this wall range from two tons to one hundred tons, although one of them by itself weighs nearly six hundred tons, or over one million pounds.

At that time, the population of Jerusalem was between one hundred thousand and two hundred thousand, but around each of the three holiest days in the year—the festivals of Passover, Pentecost, and Tabernacles—the population of the city would swell to a million, most of those people having come to make a pilgrimage, which culminated in a visit to the temple. In the year 6 AD Jesus—then age twelve—went there with his parents and many other relatives. Like most at that time he and his family would have bathed in the purifying mikvah bath of Siloam's Pool, and then walked up the extraordinary path just then created by Herod, all the way up to the height of the Temple Mount.

The temple complex and the temple itself were the wonder of that age, a crown atop Jerusalem for all the world to see. But the temple was the jewel in the crown, built of white marble with large gold panels, standing atop twelve steps all around. It was 90 feet long and 150 feet wide and had an entrance of monumentally large bronze doors. Josephus claimed they stood a staggering 49 feet high and 24.5 feet wide. The gold and ivory of the building shone so brightly that it was said no one could even look at it at midday. The interior was covered with ornately carved cedar wood panels overlaid with gold; the floor too was overlaid with gold. The expense and splendor of the building were simply unparalleled, such that even the spikes on the roof designed to keep away pigeons were made of gold as well. But the interior of the building was resplendent beyond compare, being overlaid with gold amounting to twenty metric tons, or roughly 44,000 pounds. This is nearly incomprehensible, but Herod cannot be accused of frugality when it concerned the money brought into the treasury via taxation.

It is at least a curious fact of history that Jesus came into the world right around the time of this most glorious moment in Jerusalem's history, at least architecturally speaking. Of course the Jews were under the Roman heel at that time, but architecturally speaking Herod had brought the city to its highest pinnacle and Jews who lived in Jerusalem as well as those who visited from the far corners of the empire could never have been more proud of what they saw.

So we know that Jesus was there at this greatest moment, and that his coming into the world in that place coincided with this architectural and in some ways cultural zenith of Jerusalem and Judaism. Of course he had been there first as a twelve-year-old, teaching in the Temple after his parents had long gone home, and had to circle back to find him again. When they finally did find him, he rather cheekily said: "Didn't you know that I had to be about my father's business?" It's hard for us to know exactly how that came across when he said it. There seems to be wit and profundity in it, which is characteristic of so much he said as an adult. But for him to say such a thing at the age of twelve is evidence that he was hardly an ordinary child.

It seems likely that when he and his family went there they would have gone with the other crowds of pilgrims to the Pool of Siloam to ritualistically purify themselves before walking up the new walkway built by Herod for the pilgrims who came to Jerusalem each year—a walkway which incidentally has only been rediscovered within the last few years, and which has during the writing of this volume been opened to the public, as though the past is returning more quickly than we can imagine. But the Pool of Siloam in which pilgrims would have bathed on their way up to the temple is the same pool where twenty years later Jesus—as we read in John's gospel—healed a blind man, putting mud on the man's eyes and then telling him to wash in the pool. But we would not have the slightest idea about its existence if a sewer main had not broken in 2004.

Pool of Siloam

For many centuries, scholars have puzzled over the reference in John's gospel to the so-called Pool of Siloam. More skeptical scholars— never being able to explain why he would do such a thing—nonetheless claimed John had simply invented the name. But in 2004 the skepticism about this site would be answered when a very large pipe broke that ran beneath the road at the lowest edge of the ancient city. Workmen were summoned to repair it, and as they dug down to find the ruptured pipe, they uncovered what looked like two ancient steps. They immediately alerted the archaeological authorities, who soon discovered a large pool with "three tiers of stone stairs" leading into the water. This freshwater reservoir was fed by the aforementioned "Hezekiah's Tunnel." Scholars identified it as the fabled Pool of Siloam from John's gospel. It was much grander than anyone had imagined, being roughly the size of two Olympic pools. Scholars now believe it was the world's largest mikvah bath, and the innumerable pilgrims who showed up in Jerusalem to ascend to the Temple would first ritually cleanse themselves here.

New Testament scholar James H. Charlesworth of Princeton Theological Seminary says most scholars maintained the Pool of Siloam was a fiction, "and that John [in writing his gospel] was just using a religious conceit." But of course we have uncovered the actual site itself, just where John said it was. According to the Jewish Talmud, this huge pool indeed marked the beginning of the ascent up the Temple Mount for pilgrims, so it makes sense that Jesus would have passed by here, as everyone did. Because four coins were discovered in the plaster of the steps—all from the reign of Jannaeus, the Jewish king over Jerusalem from 103–76 BC—the pool was obviously constructed during or after his reign. In their 70 AD destruction of Jerusalem, the Romans wanted to obliterate this vital part of Jewish life, so they filled it with dirt, succeeding in their goal for two millennia. But thanks to a burst pipe, the site was rediscovered and can be visited today, attesting once more to the detailed historical accuracy of the gospel writers.

Herod's Temple

But as we return to the larger subject of Herod's Temple—toward which those pilgrims wended their way after they had purified themselves at the Pool of Siloam—we must first admit the glorious structure is completely gone, and almost without any trace. Not only did the Romans destroy it utterly in 70 AD, but even after this, in the early part of the second century, the Roman emperor Hadrian built a temple to Jupiter on the spot, wishing to desecrate what had been there before, and to remake the site in his own image. In the seventh century the Muslims who conquered that part of the world did something similar, marking their own victory with a monumental mosque, which stands today. Nonetheless there have been a number of archaeological discoveries that bear mute witness to the place's previous incarnation as the holiest site in Jerusalem.

For example, in 1871 the Frenchman Charles Simon Clermont-Ganneau, who had so recently gone to such heroic lengths to procure the fragments of the destroyed Moabite Stone, was in Jerusalem. Inside a school near the city walls he spotted an ancient-looking stone with an inscription upon it in Greek uncial lettering. Ganneau read it, and anyone like him who was familiar with the writings of Josephus would have known that what it said made it an absolutely extraordinary object.

The inscription read: "No stranger is to enter within the balustrade round the temple and enclosure. Whoever is caught will be himself responsible for his ensuing death." What Ganneau had found was the very stone once posted at the edge of the "Court of the Gentiles" on the Temple Mount, beyond which no Gentile could go. Of course Jesus surely walked past it many times with his disciples and must have laid his eyes on it often. Thanks to Ganneau, eighteen centuries after the Temple had been destroyed, this vibrant piece of that history was identified and recovered.

A century after Ganneau's discovery, the Israeli archaeologist Benjamin Mazar was just beginning his excavations of the area when in 1968 he found a stone bearing an ancient inscription in Hebrew. It lay far below what is the southwestern corner of the Temple Mount, obviously having fallen from that great height long before. Indeed, the shape identified it as a stone that was part of the parapet. This remaining fragment of a larger stone contained the words "to the place of trumpeting...." Josephus describes the very spot from which it seems to have fallen as the precise station where the temple priests would blow a trumpet to signal the beginning of the Sabbath. Twenty-four hours later they would blow the trumpet from there again, signaling the closing of the Sabbath. It is reasonable to assume that Jesus laid eyes on this stone too, or even touched it. While we cannot know for sure whether he could read the Greek of the other inscription, there is little doubt he could read the Hebrew of this one, and almost certainly did.

As we have said, it is a remarkable thing that precisely during the lifetime of Jesus this Temple and all of its breathtakingly impressive environs were completed. It is also extraordinary that they were planned and built by the very man who had attempted to have Jesus murdered immediately after his birth. But what Jesus is reported to have said about this ambitiously impressive Temple and its magnificent surroundings is even more extraordinary.

In the Gospel of Mark, we read the following:

> Then as He went out of the temple, one of His disciples said to Him, "Teacher, see what manner of stones and what build-ings are here!"
>
> And Jesus answered and said to him, "Do you see these great buildings? Not one stone shall be left upon another, that shall not be thrown down." (Mark 13:1–2)

Once we understand the unprecedented majesty of what Jesus referred to, we must be even more dumbfounded than we were before—for how could anyone have said such a thing? And why? How shocking it must have sounded. Jesus did not tell them when it would happen, but as we now know, this prophecy was fulfilled less than forty years after Jesus said it. Some may believe the gospel writers inserted these things after Jerusalem and the Temple had been destroyed in 70 AD, but anyone who has read the gospels realizes that for many reasons they simply cannot have been writ-ten after the Destruction of Jerusalem.

So Jesus's prophecy of the temple's destruction is inescapably extraordinary, but those who would have heard it at the time can only have thought it outra-geous and blasphemous. Surely it went a long way toward confirming the views of the religious leaders that this man was an imminent danger to everything they stood for and meant to preserve.

Another time he made a statement about the Temple that is even more provocative. After Jesus had turned over the tables of the money-changers in the Temple and chased them out with a whip of cords, the Jewish leaders asked him by what authority he dared to say and do these things. The passage in John's gospel reads:

> So the Jews answered and said to Him, "What sign do You show to us, since You do these things?"
> Jesus answered and said to them, "Destroy this temple, and in three days I will raise it up."
> Then the Jews said, "It has taken forty-six years to build this temple, and will You raise it up in three days?" (John 2:18–20)

First of all, the specificity that this temple took that long to build is fascinating, since we know it to be accurate. Herod began building the Temple in the eighteenth year of his reign, which is sixteen years before the birth of Christ, meaning Jesus was about thirty when he made this statement. But what in the world could Jesus have meant to say he could raise the temple in three days? What must those around him have thought of such a statement? Like so much Jesus said it was almost maddeningly profound and yet simultaneously cryptic too. But we can now understand what he meant.

This Temple was supposed to be the very dwelling place of God, but Jesus was prophesying that the dwelling place of God would—through him—be changed forever. The old Temple would be absolutely decimated, but the new one would be of another order entirely. And so on the third day when Jesus miraculously rose from the grave, he created a new way for human beings to worship God. Jesus had come into the world precisely so God could cease dwelling in this temple of stone and could instead dwell within each human heart by faith. After all, "Emmanuel" means "God with us." So we could each be a new "temple of the Holy Spirit," with God living inside us wherever we went. The wealthy religious rulers of that time could not have understood this, nor would Jesus explain it, and so it simply came across as heretical and tremendously provocative. But after his resurrection his disciples would remember what he had said and understand his meaning.

In Jesus's prophecy that the temple would be destroyed, he went so far as to say that "not one stone will be left on another." We know that somehow this is what actually happened. But why? Why would the Romans have destroyed the Temple to that extent?

By way of background, the destruction of Jerusalem during Titus's siege in September of 70 AD is one of the most disturbing events in history. The Roman historian Josephus gives us the gory details, but the inhuman cruelty and sheer pitilessness of the Romans toward their enemies is too much for modern minds to take in. Once they had entered the city, the Roman soldiers with their swords butchered every single Jew they encountered and set fire to any house with people inside it. When it was all over the streets were choked with corpses and blood. By the time the carnage was over more than one million were dead, and nearly one hundred thousand were taken into slavery throughout the empire.

But we should be clear that Emperor Titus never wanted Herod's magnificent temple to be destroyed, for he planned to turn this singular masterpiece into a Roman temple. But in the unchecked fury of battle one of his soldiers climbed atop another soldier and hurled a firebrand through an open window. Suddenly everything went up in flames. Once he saw this, Titus himself made an attempt to have his men extinguish the fire, but in the deafening crush—and mesmerized to see the flames climb higher and higher—his soldiers did not obey, and in no time the growing inferno was beyond help.

The weeping and wailing of those who witnessed the sublime and holy building aflame was unspeakable, for not only was the work of decades being destroyed in a few hours, but what was inside was being destroyed too. These were the greatest treasures we can imagine—holy relics from their deliverance from Egypt fifteen centuries before, including the most precious Ark of the Covenant, containing the very stone tablets upon which God inscribed the Ten Commandments, and the pot of manna they had saved for all this time, as well as Aaron's rod. These were visible links to that time, impossibly valuable and unable to duplicate, living memories from those glorious moments when God did things so miraculous that we still speak of them today. But during and after the Temple's destruction, all these things were lost. Titus managed to rescue some of the more valuable objects as loot, including the golden menorah and the golden table upon which the Shew Bread was placed. He hauled these treasures with him back to Rome, and in his victory parade triumphantly lifted them for the cheering and jeering crowds.

We now know that not only was this grandest of grand temples destroyed, but that the dark coda to Jesus's grim prophecy—that not one stone would be left on another—was also fulfilled. The staggering amount of gold in the Temple provided the impetus. During the monstrous conflagration, as the dry wood burned and burned, the interior may well have gotten hot enough for some of the gold to melt. But even if it never got that hot, there was so much gold to be had that the Roman soldiers must for days afterward have looked in every nook and cranny of the destroyed temple to find it, only too happy to move the giant stones for what might lie beneath them.

CHAPTER FIFTEEN

Two Amazing New Testament Discoveries

By all accounts Jesus spent much of his adult life in the city of Capernaum, which lies on the northern shore of the Sea of Galilee, about thirty miles from Nazareth. In the first century it was a fishing village with around 1,500 people, and the site of many events in the gospels. It is where Jesus spent much of his time after leaving Nazareth to begin his ministry. Peter lived there with his brother Andrew, and it is where Matthew the Tax Collector lived, too. Presumably Jesus stayed with Peter in his home whenever he was in Capernaum. The town was occupied through the eleventh century, but then abandoned, and it was not until 1838 that Edward Robinson—whom we have mentioned earlier—visited there and discovered an ancient synagogue. But it was not until 1864 that Charles William Wilson identified it as Capernaum from the New Testament. Since roughly 1905 it began slowly to be excavated, and in 1968 the Franciscans Stanislao Loffreda and Virgilio Corbo discovered a first-century home that is now understood to be the actual home of Peter. During their excavations, they found fishhooks and weights for fish nets, along with other objects typical to fisherman in that era and place.

It is fascinating to learn that homes like this in Capernaum would have had a roof made with light wooden beams and thatch mixed with mud, which explains the episode in which some men lower their paralyzed friend through a roof and down into the center of the action, where Jesus was ministering. The passage from Mark 2:4 reads: "And when they could not come near Him because of the crowd, they uncovered the roof where He was. So when they had broken through, they let down the bed on which the paralytic was lying."

We know this happened in Capernaum, and the idea of making a hole in a roof of this nature seems plausible enough, especially for young men desperate to help a friend.

But archaeological excavations of this site reveal that not long after Peter's death the house became a sacred gathering place for the first Christians and may well have functioned as the first church on Earth.

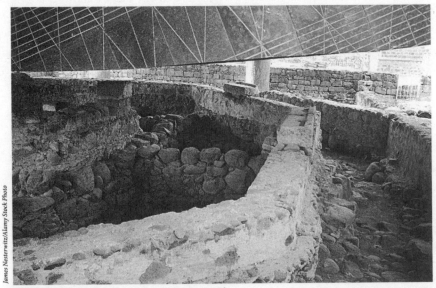

James Nesterwitz/Alamy Stock Photo

Remains of Saint Peter's House in Capernaum, Israel.

Peter's House in Capernaum

In the middle of the first century the home was transformed into what was clearly a communal gathering place. The central room of this rustic home was plastered over—something that was rarely done—and from this period there are different kinds of ceramics than the previous era. At some point the ceramics become large jars used for communal gatherings. And in the decades afterward it actually seems to have been transformed into a small church. *Biblical Archaeology Review* explains that the "room's old stone walls were buttressed by a newly built two-story arch that, in turn, supported a new stone roof. The room was even replastered and painted over with floral and geometric designs of various colors."

The building's key role in understanding how Christianity began was confirmed by more than a hundred graffiti scratched into the church's walls. Most of the inscriptions say things like "Lord Jesus Christ help thy servant" or "Christ have mercy." They are written in Greek, Syriac, or Hebrew and are sometimes accompanied by etchings of small crosses or, in one case, a boat. The excavators claim that the name of Peter is mentioned in several graffiti.

This initial church survived for three centuries, but in the fifth century an octagonal "martyrium" church—typical of those built to mark spots of great historical significance—was built. It is inescapably stirring to think that this was the very home where Jesus, Andrew, Peter, and other disciples met during the three years of Jesus's ministry, and that after those years those who survived met there. It seems impossible that something from so long ago and of such shining importance to the Christian faith really could have survived, and that we today can visit it and see it for ourselves.

And yet what we will now turn to eclipses even the home of Peter in terms of its significance: the discovery of the home of Jesus, Mary, and Joseph in Nazareth.

The Place of Jesus's Trial before Pilate

It is a central moment in the history of the world, when Jesus stood before Pilate. For billions it is an indelible part of the story often called "The Greatest Story Ever Told." According to those of us who assent to this idea, the story is as follows:

We human beings had broken our relationship with God in the Garden of Eden and were banished from it forever. But God had a plan to get us back. Over the centuries he prepared a people—the Jews—for himself, with the intention that from their midst he would bring his Messiah into the world, so that the whole world could come to him. And so he sent his son Jesus to us, and we murdered him. Of course God understood that we would do that, which makes it the ultimate act of sacrificial love, as heartbreaking and beautiful as anything we can imagine. When his fate was in our hands we screamed "Crucify him! Crucify him!" And then later, as he was being crucified, he said, "Father, forgive them, for they know not what they do."

For centuries Christians have claimed they knew where the spot was that Jesus stood before Pilate, where he stood when we screamed for his death. That spot marks the beginning of the Via Dolorosa, from which he carries his cross to the site of execution. But in recent years that location has been shown to be mistaken, and another location has been discovered that much more accurately accords with the accounts we have from the Scriptures.

In his book *The Final Days of Jesus*, the archaeologist Shimon Gibson explains that since medieval times it was thought that the Praetorium referred to in the gospels was near the Antonia Fortress, but for many reasons the consensus is now that it would have been near Herod's palace instead. And so it must be in the vicinity of Herod's palace that Jesus's trial before Pilate would have taken place.

The events leading up to this are well-known. Jesus and his disciples had what we now call the Last Supper in an "Upper Room" in Jerusalem and then went out to the Garden of Gethsemane, where Jesus went off

"Ecce Homo" by Hieronymus Bosch.

alone and prayed with such profound anguish that the Scriptures say blood was seen to drip from his forehead. He knew what horrors lay ahead for him and asked his heavenly father to "take this cup" from him, if it be possible, but concluded by praying: "Nevertheless, thy will be done." We know what was to follow, and Jesus obviously did too, though his disciples seem to have been especially oblivious.

Jesus was then betrayed by Judas and arrested by a contingent of Roman soldiers and Jewish leaders, who led him bound to the home of Annas, the father-in-law of Caiaphas, the high priest. Then he was taken to Caiaphas himself, and finally to Pilate's palace, also called the Praetorium. But Pilate did not know what to do with Jesus. It was the Jews who had a case against him regarding their own faith and their own laws. Pilate was a Roman and did not want to get involved in their affairs. It was hard enough keeping a lid on the tensions in occupied Jerusalem. So to throw the Jewish leaders a bone and end things, Pilate decisively had Jesus taken inside the gate to where the barracks were and had the Roman soldiers brutally flog him. The flagellum they used usually was tipped with bits of lead or bone, so that it tore into the flesh of the victim with each ghastly stroke, often exposing muscles and sinews. After this torture the sadistic soldiers—free to do as they liked with such a prisoner—mocked his "kingship" with a painful crown of thorns. It was a poetic touch of evil that they had no idea would become part of the iconography of a faith they were helping to launch. If this torture had not been enough, they now mocked their victim's status as a prophet by blindfolding him, and each slapped him in the face, taunting him to tell them which one of them had hit him.

After all of this he was brought again to Pilate, who hoped he had assuaged the crowd's bloodlust by the flogging and other quite obvious mistreatment of the bleeding man standing bound before them. Pilate had no reason to do anything worse to Jesus, for Jesus had broken no Roman laws. But the Jewish leaders wanted Jesus dead, and since their own laws did not permit them to do this, they continued to press Pilate, hoping he would use his Roman authority to do what they could not. They knew that Pilate had to yield to them, since he wished to keep peace in Jerusalem. Pilate was desperately uncomfortable. He knew it would not be easy to appease these Jews—who could lead their people in a revolt—and also follow Roman laws. He was in a bind. Here is the famous passage from the nineteenth chapter of John's gospel:

> So then Pilate took Jesus and scourged Him. And the soldiers twisted a crown of thorns and put it on His head, and they put on Him a purple robe. Then they said, "Hail, King of the Jews!" And they struck Him with their hands.
>
> Pilate then went out again, and said to them, "Behold, I am bringing Him out to you, that you may know that I find no fault in Him."

Then Jesus came out, wearing the crown of thorns and the purple robe. And Pilate said to them, "Behold the Man!"

Therefore, when the chief priests and officers saw Him, they cried out, saying, "Crucify Him, crucify Him!"

Pilate said to them, "You take Him and crucify Him, for I find no fault in Him."

The Jews answered him, "We have a law, and according to our law He ought to die, because He made Himself the Son of God."

Therefore, when Pilate heard that saying, he was the more afraid, and went again into the Praetorium, and said to Jesus, "Where are You from?" But Jesus gave him no answer.

Then Pilate said to Him, "Are You not speaking to me? Do You not know that I have power to crucify You, and power to release You?"

Jesus answered, "You could have no power at all against Me unless it had been given you from above. Therefore the one who delivered Me to you has the greater sin."

From then on Pilate sought to release Him, but the Jews cried out, saying, "If you let this Man go, you are not Caesar's friend. Whoever makes himself a king speaks against Caesar."

When Pilate therefore heard that saying, he brought Jesus out and sat down in the judgment seat in a place that is called The Pavement, but in Hebrew, Gabbatha. Now it was the Preparation Day of the Passover, and about the sixth hour. (verses 1–14)

The word *Gabbatha* actually has the connotation of a place of some height, whereas the preceding New Testament Greek term (in English translated as "Stone Pavement") is *Lithostrotos*. *Lithos* is the Greek for "stone" and *strotos* is the word from which we get the English "street" and usually means a mosaic or tessellated surface. So from John's gospel we get the idea that this area actually had two characteristics. Not only was it paved with stones, but it was also up at some height. The passage continues:

> And he said to the Jews, "Behold your King!"
>
> But they cried out, "Away with Him, away with Him! Crucify Him!"
>
> Pilate said to them, "Shall I crucify your King?"
>
> The chief priests answered, "We have no king but Caesar!"
>
> Then he delivered Him to them to be crucified. Then they took Jesus and led Him away. (John 19:14–16)

Roughly since the Middle Ages the area believed to be the site of this trial was thought to be near the Antonia Fortress, and the famous Via Dolorosa has traditionally begun there. But in recent years it has come to light that the pavement in that location, said to be the "Pavement" where Jesus stood, did not exist until a century after his death. It was built by the Emperor Hadrian, after the destruction of Jerusalem in 70 AD. So of course that pavement cannot be the same one upon which Jesus stood, although it is of course possible that this is the spot where those events took place.

But in the 1970s Israeli archaeologist Magen Broshi led an excavation along the western Old City wall of Jerusalem, far from the area of the Antonia Fortress. Among those taking part in the dig was a young man named Shimon Gibson, who has now, many decades later, come to the conclusion that the southwestern corner of the city, where Herod's magnificent palace stood, was the location. And the consensus is that he is correct.

During the excavations in the 1970s the archaeologists discovered "a monumental gateway with the remains of a large courtyard situated between two fortification walls. On the northern side of the courtyard was a rocky outcrop and on top of it was a small rectangular built platform with steps." At the time of this discovery, no one quite knew what to make of it. But decades later Gibson came to the startling conclusion that this gateway was none other than the Gate of the Essenes, which is referred to by the historian Josephus, and which had been misidentified in a few other parts of the city. This alone was important archaeological and historical news.

But far more significantly, Gibson saw that this area accorded perfectly with the description in John's gospel of the place where Jesus's trial was held. Gibson writes: "The gateway complex consists of an inner and outer (Herodian) fortification wall, with respective gates, and a central courtyard open to the sky between the walls. The courtyard (30 by 11 meters) was originally paved on its south side and it had a rocky outcrop on its north."[1] Gibson says that most of what had originally been there was destroyed by the Romans in 70 AD, but what remains now seems to have been built "probably at the time of Herod the Great," in the first century BC.

To have identified the actual spot—and the actual "Pavement" mentioned in the Scriptures—where this famous scene took place is some of the biggest news an archaeologist could hope to find. Most of us have seen images of this great and tragic moment in history. It has been rendered by Rembrandt and by Hieronymus Bosch, and quite famously in the nineteenth century by the Hungarian Mihály Munkácsy and the Swiss French painter Antonio Ciseri. In the last century we have seen it dramatized in many films. Being able to see the very spot doesn't seem to have been something anyone had even dreamt possible. Stranger even than being able to gaze on the pavement is being able to see the very stone "Bema" upon which Pilate sat as he made his judgment.

According to Gibson the courtyard in which this scene played out was just thirty-three feet by ninety feet and was a kind of no-man's land between the Praetorium area and the area outside the city gates. The whole structure of this gate—and this courtyard within the gate structure—had been built so that Pilate could move in and out of the Praetorium to this spot for just such

---

[1] Shimon Gibson, *The Final Days of Jesus: The Archaeological Evidence* (New York: HarperOne, 2009), 98–99.

trials, but still be safely separated from the crowds. So the Jews who had come to watch this scene were not able to get down into the actual courtyard, but merely watched from the surrounding walls. Since it was the day before the Sabbath, they could not have gone inside the Praetorium area anyway, as this would have made them unclean. But from this spot they could have their cake and eat it too. The actual gateway into the Praetorium was itself flanked by a pair of large towers and originally had been created as a private entrance to his palace for Herod, who at previous times had had politically awkward moments, as Gibson relates in his book. After this trial, Jesus would have been taken from this courtyard back inside the Praetorium and would then have been led through the Upper City to Golgotha, bearing his heavy cross upon his shoulders.

It is mind-boggling that after two millennia we have at last found the very place where this most impossibly consequential scene unfolded, and more extraordinary, can still see the very stones upon which the broken and bleeding prisoner stood wearing his crown of thorns. We can see the stone Bema too upon which Pilate sat, as those around shouted, "Crucify him!" We who take the Bible seriously know those crowds were standing in for us, and that the one whom they condemned forgave them, as he does us. But there it happened, and we now can with our own eyes see precisely where his feet stood and where the axis of history—and eternity too—pivoted decisively, just there on those very stones that cry out still.

Now, however, we turn to something perhaps even more astonishing than this.

CHAPTER SIXTEEN

The Nazareth Home of Jesus

"Can anything good come out of Nazareth?" That was the question cynics in Jesus's day sarcastically asked, assuming that a town in the far north could never be the place from which the Messiah would come. Of course it is indeed where Jesus, whom billions call the Messiah, came from. There has never been any question about that, nor about whether his home there once existed. But whether it survived or ever could be discovered never seemed at all very much worth being concerned with.

First of all, on the face of it, the idea that a simple home built over two thousand years ago would survive and eventually be identified as belonging to anyone specifically seems absurd. And in this case, we are talking about a very out-of-the-way village or town called Nazareth, and about an unknown carpenter/builder named Joseph who raised his family of several children there, including his eldest, Jesus. This would have been where his wife, Mary, raised their children and cooked their meals. But this place— both the town and the house itself—would have been distinguished principally by being undistinguished. This was not a palace or any kind of structure that was any different from the innumerable other structures built throughout what we today call the Holy Land. It would have been a very simple home for a working-class family in an obscure village. Why should any such place survive beyond a century or two?

And if for some reason it did survive longer than that—and even survived two thousand years, but was buried beneath the sands of time and the rubble of succeeding structures—how in the world would we ever be able to suspect or reason that it was that abode precisely in which dwelt these now impossibly famous figures: that woman praised above all women who ever lived, and the man whom billions call the Messiah of the world and God incarnate in human form? What human sense could it make that the humble home of figures undistinguished in their lifetimes would survive or ever come to be found?

We have no idea where most of the famous figures from antiquity grew up, unless they were royalty, such as Alexander the Great, in which case we might conceivably be able to discover their palaces. But who can find the childhood homes of the most famous men of ancient Greece—Socrates, Plato, or Aristotle? In more recent centuries, however, when someone becomes famous, we usually do take the trouble to discover in which building they grew up and somehow mark that place. We know precisely where Christopher Columbus was born in Genoa in 1451. The actual house was demolished in the 1680s, but in later years the original was reproduced, and tourists can visit it. The restored home of Shakespeare, built in the 1500s, still stands and can be visited. The six-hundred-year-old home where Joan of Arc was born in 1412 is still standing and can be visited in the village of Domrémy-la-Pucelle. But go back to the 1340s, when Chaucer was supposed to have been born in London, and see what you can find? Absolutely nothing, though he is considered the "father of English literature." The relatively recent cabin in which Abraham Lincoln grew up in Kentucky has vanished, although its sandstone foundation has been preserved.

So two things are at work. On the one hand, the past tends to vanish. Why should anyone remember or preserve the unremarkable home of someone who lived and died many centuries before? And yet we see that as soon as the aforementioned figures became famous, every effort was made to find and preserve their childhood homes. We also know that the figure of Jesus, who grew up in Nazareth and who died by Roman crucifixion in the early thirties AD, may have been an absolutely obscure figure for the first thirty years of his life, but in his final three years he became extremely famous for—among other things—miraculously healing the lame and crippled and bringing sight to eyes blind from birth. He was in those three years followed by vast crowds throughout the countryside and was after the miraculous resurrection of Lazarus more celebrated and sought after still, so that his entrance into Jerusalem was greeted with waved palm branches and with cries of "Hosanna!" and "Blessed is he who comes in the name of the Lord!"

And, of course, shortly after his death many thousands believed he was God incarnate and were so fervent in this belief that many of them went to their deaths before they would renounce it. We also know that those who believed in him did not get wiped out, but continued to grow in number, despite the most brutal persecution imaginable at the hands of the merciless Romans. But we also know that in 313 AD—in the Edict of Milan—Constantine did something so dramatic that it changed the world of his time and ever since. He declared that the Christian religion should be tolerated throughout the Roman Empire. He had himself become a Christian, and suddenly the cruel persecution and murder of Christians ceased. But then he appointed his mother, Helena Augusta Imperatrix, giving her unlimited funds to travel throughout the Holy Land to recover all relics of the Christian faith she could find. Since only 230 years had passed since the Roman destruction of Jerusalem, Helena and many after her were able to identify and uncover many Christian holy sites. For example, the grotto where Jesus supposedly had been born was known by Christians who had worshipped there for decades.

But in 135 AD the Roman emperor Hadrian—as a way of wiping out any trace of this revered site as the birthplace of Jesus—had a Temple to Adonis built over it. Nonetheless the sacred memory of it could not be wiped out, and in 248 AD Origen of Alexandria wrote:

In Bethlehem the cave is pointed out where He was born, and
the manger in the cave where He was wrapped in swaddling
clothes. And the rumor is in those places, and among foreigners of the Faith, that indeed Jesus was born in this cave who
is worshiped and reverenced by the Christians.[1]

By the time Helena got there it was still recognized as the birthplace
of Jesus, so she had the temple torn down and a Christian basilica built
over it. Two hundred years later that was torn down in a Samaritan revolt,
but not long after that the Byzantine emperor Justinian had it rebuilt once
more. And so it went through the centuries, so that today we know exactly
where it is, which is itself both astounding and understandable when one
knows the facts.

Helena also discovered the place on the Mount of Olives where Jesus
was said to have ascended into Heaven and built a Church of Eleona there,
which was eventually destroyed by the Persians in 614 AD, although its
remains have been found. As we see over and over, these sacred places have
been marked over the centuries and millennia, both by their protectors
and detractors.

Although the Romans destroyed Jerusalem in 70 AD, they spent the
next two centuries rebuilding it in their own imperial image. When Helena
arrived, she learned that Hadrian had also desecrated the place of Jesus's
burial by building a Temple to Jupiter above it, just as they had built a
Temple of Adonis over his birthplace in Bethlehem. But Helena had this
temple demolished too, and her son had the Church of the Holy Sepulchre
built there, which was commissioned in 335 AD. So these examples and
many others show that relatively early on many of these holiest of Christian sites were remembered and memorialized—even after some had
been desecrated—and that churches and other memorials were built on
top of them. So the link to the past in many cases has indeed been preserved, and what we still know of these very earliest sacred sites can be
astounding.

---

[1] *Contra Celsum*, Book I, Chapter LI.

Nazareth, where Jesus grew up, was never a traveler's Mecca and was a full hundred miles north of Jerusalem, so we are hardly surprised to learn that Helena never made it there. But we know that in the year 680 AD a Frankish bishop named Arculf visited the Holy Land and Nazareth. On returning home, his ship was wrecked on the coast of Iona in Scotland. The bishop in Iona then was a certain Adomnán, who welcomed Arculf and heard his detailed story of what he had found in the Holy Land, later putting it all in a book titled *De Locis Sanctis* (*On Holy Places*).[2] But what Adomnán wrote thirteen centuries before our time came into play rather recently when some excavations were done in Nazareth, as we shall see.

Twelve centuries passed with no mention of Nazareth germane to our discussion. But in 1881 the French Sisters of Nazareth moved there to build a convent. Not long after they began, they discovered an ancient cistern. Along with the workmen they had employed, and even some children from the school they ran, they began to excavate the area. The Biblical Archaeological Society wrote:

> The [nuns] exposed a complex sequence of unusually well pre-
> served archaeological features, including Crusader-period walls
> and vaults, a Byzantine cave church, Roman-period tombs and
> other rock-cut and built structures. The nuns made a small
> museum of the pottery, coins, glass and other portable artifacts
> that they recovered. Then construction of the new convent build-
> ings revealed the walls of a large Byzantine church with a triple
> apse, polychrome mosaic floors and white marble fittings, rebuilt
> in the Crusader period.[3]

Across the street was the Church of the Annunciation, which was the traditional site of Mary's childhood home, but the large Byzantine church that

---

[2] Adomnán also wrote the definitive biography of his cousin Columba, who brought Christianity to what is today Scotland in the previous century.

[3] Ken Dark, "Has Jesus' Nazareth House Been Found?" *Biblical Archaeology Review* 41, no. 2 (March/April 2015), https://www.baslibrary.org/biblical-archaeology-review/41/2/7.

the nuns discovered was the long-lost Church of the Nutrition—supposedly the site of Jesus's home in Nazareth. It was that place Arculf visited in the late seventh century, as we shall see, for he mentions it as being above Jesus's home. But evidently in 721 AD, Caliph Yazid II had it destroyed, because the next account from a pilgrim to Nazareth comes to us from Saint Willibald in 725 AD, who makes no mention of it.

It seems the sisters had found this church. But neither they nor anyone else had any idea of its extraordinary significance, and although they continued to excavate the site in fits and starts for some time, they never learned the reason this church stood where it did. So another long century would pass before any other serious excavation was done.

In 2006 a full investigation began into this site, under the supervision of Ken Dark of Reading University in England. It was only at this point that the lengthy chronological sequence of well-preserved structures and features began to reveal itself. This included the successive Crusader and Byzantine churches, two Early Roman–period tombs, a phase of small-scale quarrying, and, of the greatest significance of all—and the very reason for all of the other magnificent structures—there was at the bottom of everything a rectilinear structure with partly rock-cut and partly stone-built walls. It finally became clear that exceedingly great pains had been taken through the centuries to mark this structure and to preserve it, precisely as we have observed in other similarly holy sites, such as the supposed sites of Jesus's burial in Jerusalem and his birth in Bethlehem and Peter's home in Capernaum. Dark says:

> …the limestone vessels found at this site indicate that this home was part of a strictly Jewish community, for limestone vessels were not subject to Jewish impurity laws and were therefore very popular during that time among Jews. Many of the surrounding towns show a greater acceptance of Roman culture.[4]

---

[4] Madeline Richards, "Is This House under a Convent in Nazareth the Boyhood Home of Jesus?" CBS News, November 23, 2020, https://www.cbsnews.com/news/jesus-christ-boyhood-home-under-nazareth-convent-israel-archaeologist-says.

Stephen C. Meyer and Eric Metaxas at Socrates in the City in Manhattan. For more information go to socratesinthecity.com. *Socrates in the City*

Christopher Hitchens's perpetual rage at even the gentlest of those professing faith led him to describe the Christian evangelist Billy Graham as "a self-conscious fraud" and "a disgustingly evil man." *Kathy deWitt/Alamy Stock Photo*

Arno Penzias and Robert Wilson (right) at Bell Laboratories, standing by the Horn radio antenna in Holmdel, New Jersey, in 1978. *Science History Images/Alamy Stock Photo*

Richard Dawkins (pictured) has said that atheism cannot lead anyone to violence. Responding to this fatuous claim, the novelist Marilynne Robinson, writing in *Harper's*, said, "The kindest conclusion one can draw is that Dawkins has not acquainted himself with the history of modern authoritarianism."

This illustration shows the approximate sizes of the planets relative to each other. Outward from the sun, the planets are Mercury, Venus, Earth, Mars, Jupiter, Saturn, Uranus, and Neptune, followed by the dwarf planet Pluto. Jupiter's diameter is about eleven times that of Earth's. The planets are not shown at the appropriate distance from the sun. *NASA/Lunar and Planetary Institute*

Merneptah Stele (the "Israel Stele"): the hieroglyphic text of the stele describes the victories of Pharaoh Merneptah. *www.BibleLandPictures.com/Alamy Stock Photo*

Although the Doge of Venice is here pictured peering through Galileo's telescope, there were many recalcitrants who refused to do the same, for fear that their eyes should cause them to stumble beyond Aristotle.

Galileo further scandalized the cognoscenti of his day by painting Earth's moon as seen through his telescope. It seemed no longer to be the opalescent pearl Aristotle had claimed, but was now manifestly a pockmarked, maculate, and even wayward orb.

The KH2 Ketef Hinnom Silver Scroll, the oldest artifact containing text from the Hebrew Bible.

Siloam tunnel, Hezekiah's Tunnel, City of David, Jerusalem. *Siloam tunnel/Alamy Stock Photo*

Holyland Model of Jerusalem. A model of Herod's Temple adjacent to the Shrine of the Book exhibit at the Israel Museum in Jerusalem.

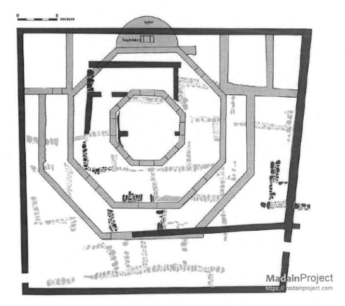

A composite diagram of what was built atop Peter's House in Capernaum. Beneath the Byzantine church (light blue), lay an earlier church structure (dark blue) that had itself been built upon the house (light grey) itself, which was inhabited during the first century AD. *Madain Project [KD1]*

In 2020 archaeologists published findings about this first-century home in Nazareth. To mark and preserve this holiest of sites as the very place where Jesus, Mary, and Joseph lived, two magnificent churches had been built over it during the Crusader and Byzantine eras. The most recent of these was demolished by the Caliph Yazid II in 721 AD, and all traces of this site were lost for twelve centuries.

Dr. Steven Collins pointing to the site of Tall el-Hammam on an aerial photograph displayed on Mount Nebo in 2009. *Leen Ritmeyer*

Photographic reproduction of the Great Isaiah Scroll, the best preserved of the biblical scrolls found at Qumran. *Website of The Israel Museum, Jerusalem. Photographs by Ardon Bar Hama*

But one of the principal reasons Dark believes this first-century home is the very place where Jesus grew up has to do with the workmanship. "Whoever built the house had a very good understanding of stone-working," he says. "That would be consistent with the sort of knowledge we would expect of someone who might be called a *tekton*," the ancient Greek word for "crafts-man" that was used to refer to Joseph. "By itself, that's not got flashing lights saying, 'this is where Jesus lived.'"

But it's underneath a fifth- to seventh-century Byzantine church.

We know now that the church built over this site was enormous, elabo-rately decorated, and probably the Byzantine cathedral of Nazareth. Its loca-tion and grandeur indicate to Dark that "this particular place was considered really important." Its destruction by the Islamic Caliph Yazid in 721 AD almost wiped it from history forever. But twelve centuries later the nuns arrived.

The article continues:

> Just inside the surviving doorway, earlier excavations had revealed part of its original chalk floor. Associated finds, including cooking pottery and a spindle whorl, suggested domestic occupation. Taken together, the walls conformed to the plan of a so-called courtyard house, one of the typical architectural forms of Early Roman period settlements in Galilee. The excellent preservation of this rectilinear structure or house can be explained by its later history. Great efforts had been made to encompass the remains of this building within the vaulted cellars of both the Byzantine and Crusader churches, so that it was thereafter protected.[5]

So just beneath the Sisters of Nazareth convent the evidence of this extraor-dinary Byzantine church was found, along with a spring and two tombs in its crypt, which were certainly built sometime after Jesus's death and resurrection, since no one would have built a home so close to any tombs. The first-century house was probably a courtyard house, and it stands between the two tombs.

---

[5] Dark, "Has Jesus' Nazareth House Been Found?"

Both the tombs and the house were decorated with mosaics in the Byzantine period, suggesting that they were of special importance, possibly venerated.

But what is chilling is to read Adomnán's account of this place from 680 AD. He says clearly that there were two churches there at that time of his visit. One was the Church of the Annunciation, and the other was across the street, being the Church of the Nutrition that we have mentioned. In his account from over thirteen centuries ago, Adomnán—writing down what Arculf himself saw with his own eyes—says that it was between the two tombs beneath the second church precisely that one found the very house where Jesus had been raised by Mary and Joseph.

There can hardly be anything more extraordinary than this discovery, although there is one thing that may come very close, and this is that news of this earth-shaking discovery has been so extremely poorly communicated that it has the misfortune actually of seeming intentional. An article about it appeared in *Biblical Archaeology Review* in 2015, although that itself was oddly tentative. Even so, nothing more was said on the subject since, as though the discovery of the actual home where the Holy Family lived wasn't worth looking into or was a subject too embarrassing for serious archaeologists. Only in late 2020 did Dr. Dark publish the book containing the findings of his continued excavations since 2006, but the book cannot help but strike one as almost calculated to hide the discovered pearl of great price, instead bizarrely focusing on the nesting wooden boxes in which the superlative pearl had been found. The book's title, for example, could not possibly be more underwhelming or beside the point, almost to the point of comedy: *The Sisters of Nazareth Convent: A Roman Period, Byzantine, and Crusader Site in Central Nazareth (The Palestine Exploration Fund Annual).* Could anything be better engineered to bury the lede or to crush out of sight the infinitely important structure for which all of the subsequent structures were built, and which they wished to signify and celebrate and protect? Can we imagine that those who built these structures had any idea that what they built in this most hallowed location would be treated with equal or even more deference than the sacred structure they were so honored and privileged to enshrine? In case anyone could be tempted to buy the drearily titled volume, it was originally listed at $160, just to ensure it is only purchased by a handful of academic libraries and never read (though it's now been marked down to $138). But it is perhaps the publisher's description of the book that most astonishingly and bizarrely suppresses the very thing that ought to be not only its main point, but front-page news in most newspapers. Here it is from Amazon:

> This book transforms archaeological knowledge of Nazareth by publishing over 80 years of archaeological work at the Sisters of Nazareth convent, including a detailed re-investigation in the early twenty-first century under the author's direction. Although one of the world's most famous places and of key importance to understanding early Christianity, Nazareth has attracted little archaeological attention. Following a chance discovery in the 1880s, the site was initially explored by the nuns of the convent themselves—one of the earliest examples of a major programme of excavations initiated and directed by women—and then for decades by Henri Senès, whose excavations (like those of the nuns) have remained almost entirely unpublished. Their work revealed a complex sequence, elucidated and dated by twenty-first century study, beginning with a partly rock-cut Early Roman-period domestic building, followed by Roman-period quarrying and burial, a well-preserved cave-church, and major surface-level Byzantine and Crusader churches. The interpretation and broader implications of each phase of activity are discussed in the context of recent studies of Roman-period, Byzantine, and later archaeology and contemporary archaeological theory, and their relationship to written accounts of Nazareth is also assessed. *The Sisters of Nazareth Convent* provides a crucial archaeological study for those wishing to understand the archaeology of Nazareth and its place in early Christianity and beyond.

This publisher's description does not bother to mention that the "partly rock-cut Early Roman-period domestic building" that it does deign to mention is the only reason for everything that exists around it and is the only reason anyone on Planet Earth is aware of the existence of Nazareth. Nor do they so much as mention Jesus or Mary—or Joseph, who built the home with his own hands—but they do mention what one gathers they see as the most exciting part of the find, saying it is "one of the earliest examples of a major programme of excavations initiated and directed by women." Of course these saintly French women would writhe in horror to think that they had been singled out, but that the one to whom they wed themselves and whose life and person they wished to magnify in all they ever did, including these excavations, was ignored entirely. If ever one needed an example of how the bias against God and the Bible persists in the academic world, surely this example alone would suffice to make the point and close the case.

Ongoing Discoveries

Archaeological discoveries corroborating the biblical accounts have continued steadily since the mid-nineteenth century, but with improving technology—and with the population of Israel growing, which has increased the number of building projects being undertaken—the rate of discoveries seems to be accelerating. Here are a handful of the most recent:

- In 2018 a seal ring was found bearing the name of Pontius Pilate. Given the copper alloy of the ring it is unlikely it was worn by Pilate himself, but rather by someone who represented him and would use it to give his authority to seal documents written in his name. The ring was so corroded over twenty centuries that if not for state-of-the-art photographic imaging technology, the name would have been impossible to read. Also in 2018 a seal was discovered bearing what is almost certainly the name of the prophet Isaiah. Further evidence toward this conclusion is the discovery very nearby three years earlier of a similar seal bearing the name "Hezekiah of Judah." Isaiah and Hezekiah are so closely linked in the Scriptures that they appear together in seventeen verses.

- In 2019 a tiny ceramic pomegranate was found in Shiloh precisely matching the description of those described in Exodus (28:33–35), which God instructed the Israelites to sew into the robes of the High Priest. Also that year, in some dirt near the Temple Mount in Jerusalem, a tiny stone "Beka weight" was discovered. Exodus 38:26 says that such a weight must be used to determine the precise amount of silver required as a donation during the time of the First Temple, built by King Solomon. At that time the Israelites did not have coins, but simply pieces of silver, and this weight of fifty-five grams—or half a shekel—was the precise amount required. If anything ever could confirm this as the actual site of Shiloh, this tiniest of objects would certainly be it.

- In Shiloh, Dr. Scott Stripling of Houston, Texas, continues to direct excavations at what he believes is the very site of the tabernacle in the wilderness, where the Israelites worshiped from the time of Moses until the time of Solomon. The tabernacle was made of animal skins, and of course itself would have decomposed millennia ago, but there have been innumerable smaller discoveries that begin to tilt judgment toward this site. A number of stone altars have been found, along with the aforementioned tiny ceramic pomegranate. God's directions in Exodus 20:25 are that the altar be made of earth, but if of stone then not of stone wrought by anyone, lest it be "polluted." The stone or stones used must be naturally shaped, and Dr. Stripling has found three that seem to fit this description, each with a protruding stone "horn"—for each of the four corners of the altar must have a horn, which signified strength.

- Most recently of all, at Christmas 2020, a building project at the foot of the Mount of Olives was halted when a "mikvah" purification bath was discovered from the time of Jesus. The location is very close to what is believed to be the Garden of Gethsemane. Mikvah baths were often located near places of oil or wine production. A spokesman for the Israel Antiquities Authority explained, "The Jewish laws of purification obliged workers involved in oil and wine production to purify themselves." The Garden of Gethsemane lies at the foot of the Mount of Olives, obviously known for the olive trees that grew there. But the word "Gethsemane" actually means "oil press," and so the discovery of this mikvah bath from that period suggests that this area really was the location of an oil press since ancient times, therefore requiring a purification bath on site. It also lends greater credence to the idea that Jesus—representing Israel, which was always identified with the olive tree—had come here to himself be "crushed," and to endure the agony of accepting his father's will for him.

Conclusions

When archaeological finds in the mid-nineteenth century began to confirm details in the biblical accounts, the heady promise of what might lie ahead was undeniable. But to be fair, no one could then know whether the initial and exciting confirmations of the biblical accounts were anomalies, and whether over time the scales would begin to tip in the opposite direction. That archaeology could show the accuracy of the Bible on historical and other details was then simply a theory. It would take more than a dozen decades and hundreds of excavations before we could see whether this theory was essentially correct or not. So for many decades, that was the question in the air: On which side would the evidence eventually pile up? As the digging and discoveries have continued, however, the welter of evidence has been overwhelming, rarely if even once speaking definitively against the biblical record. So perhaps it is time to call the question. There will and always should be debate about certain individual discoveries, but can we at last agree that the general theory has been affirmed? Even this minute, and at what seems an accelerating pace, new finds illuminate the Bible as something genuinely unique, as an extraordinary window of words through which we can see the distant past. And so perhaps the only real question now is whether those who have been unyielding in their skepticism can find the courage to see that such skepticism has been fairly and slowly but surely weighed in the balance and found wanting. Of course, if history is any guide, we can assume there will always be those for whom the discovery even of a Babylonian wall bearing the words "Mene, Mene, Tekel, Upharsin" would be insufficient. *Quel dommage.*

CHAPTER SEVENTEEN

Ur of the Chaldees Discovered: The Surprising Resilience of the Ancient Past

It seems certain that one of the main reasons some regard the Bible as a book of folktales has to do with the wide circulation of its very earliest stories: of Adam and Eve in the Garden, of Cain and Abel, of Noah's Flood, and of the Tower of Babel. Of course these are the stories most children hear about in Sunday school. But if the standard Bible runs to about 1,235 pages, these earliest stories only make up something like the first nine.

So doesn't it make sense that these very oldest stories—by sheer dint of their great antiquity—would be communicated in a dramatic and poetic way that seems foreign to us? Who would expect them to come to us in the deadeningly dull style of a facts-only textbook? Nonetheless, when many atheists argue against the Bible, they often pick something from one of those nine pages—or even more typically from the first three—figuring that sneering at the cartoonish idea of "a talking snake" will settle the whole matter.

Of course this is not to say that what is found beyond those first nine pages is self-explanatory or presents no difficulties. But it does seem that mocking a talking snake—in what is obviously a poetic retelling of an impossibly ancient and powerful story from a time before time as we know it—looks like someone is simply taking cheap shots for fear of having an actual debate. Might not some atheists set their own standards a bit higher and consider looking at the tenth and subsequent pages of the book with equal scrutiny? It's certainly not the case that there's nothing to mock after the ninth page. For example, already on page ten of most Bibles—in Genesis 12—God speaks aloud to Abraham and tells him to leave his country, and if that's not odd enough, before you know it Abraham is bargaining with God, after which God rains sulfurous hellfire down on Sodom and Gomorrah anyway. So there are plenty of seemingly preposterous events to make fun of, but the further past page nine one wanders, the more there is to talk about—which may perhaps seem too risky for anyone less interested in actually considering the situation than in holding their preconceived notions so tightly as to suggest someone clutching a purse in an iffy part of town.

Abraham and the City of Ur

In any event, it is around page ten or so that the biblical narrative introduces the reader to Abram—later Abraham—who left "Ur of the Chaldees" to go to a place God promised to show him, which one eventually sees is "the Land of Canaan." Of course that is the place Abraham's Jewish descendants have called home for the better part of four millennia. For many, however, the stories of Abraham's divinely inspired wanderings seem little better than what might be called the "founding myth" of the Jews, meaning that it's just a colorful story, much as Rome's founding myth is colorful, featuring abandoned twins named Romulus and Remus, who find nourishment at the swollen teats of a kindly she-wolf in a cave. Everyone understands that's not something that actually took place. But just as we logically dismiss lupine adoption, mustn't we also dismiss the idea of a man led by God through the ancient desert with his vast flocks and family, if only because it hails from a thousand years before the tale of the suckling siblings and their hirsute wet nurse? So as we might expect, from

Discovery of the Ziggurat of Ur (the Great Temple at Mugeyer from the west).

the beginning of the nineteenth century, when such things began to be questioned, the stories of Abraham—and indeed the very existence of Ur of the Chaldees—were read with skepticism.

But as we have seen, what was initially so easily dismissed was often later on not so easily dismissed after all. For example, from at least the seventeenth century onward, a number of European travelers to the part of the world in which Abraham is supposed to have wandered would return with stories of having glimpsed the ancient remains of a vast ziggurat, standing alone in the middle of the blasted wasteland and nothingness of the desert. Whatever it had been and whoever had built it no one knew. But these stories over time continued to return with travelers. Then in 1849, William Kennett Loftus found the site they had mentioned and published a description of the ziggurat. He even found some bricks there—at Tell el-Muqayyar, just south of the Euphrates River in what is today southeastern Iraq—and forwarded them to London, to Sir Henry Rawlinson.[1] Rawlinson examined the bricks and quickly reckoned the site worthy of further excavation.

---

[1] This is the man who happened to be in Baghdad as the Black Obelisk of Shalmaneser III was passing through, and who examined it and made a translation and report of it in advance of its arrival in the British Museum two years later.

So J. P. Taylor, British vice consul at Basra, began excavations at the site in 1853. After he had found a number of inscribed clay cylinders and bricks, he confidently identified the site as the fabled "Ur of the Chaldees," the home of the great patriarch Abraham. And so another fabled world from the ancient Scriptures was pulled from the sand and into the present.

The great site was not thoroughly excavated until 1927, but we now know that this city not only existed at the time of Abraham, but had already been thriving for two thousand years, having been a major city since 3800 BC. And evidence of human settlement there stretches back even further, to the seventh millennium BC. At the time of Abraham, Ur was the largest city in the world, with a population of sixty-five thousand. In Genesis we read that Abraham's father, Terah, took Abraham—and his daughter-in-law Sarah and grandson Lot—out of Ur. They traveled toward Canaan and settled in Haran.

Loftus, who discovered and identified Ur, may also be credited with identifying the city of Shushan—or Susa—which is identified in the Bible as the Persian city where the events in the Book of Esther took place. Shushan is also mentioned in the books of Nehemiah and Daniel. Rawlinson first visited this site in 1836. A. H. Layard visited it some years later. But in 1851 Loftus made some excavations there and soon identified it as none other than Shushan from the biblical texts. The city's discovery, however, is overshadowed by an object uncovered there that ranks among the most significant archaeological discoveries in history, and that further corroborates details from the earliest pages of the Bible.

Hammurabi's Code

In 1901, a Swiss Egyptologist, Gustave Jéquier, had the honor of finding it: an eight-foot-tall stele made of black basalt, covered over nearly every inch with cuneiform writing, and crowned with a bas relief image of a king receiving the law from a god. Once deciphered from the Old Akkadian, it was discovered to be a list of 282 laws, which we now know as the famous "Code of Hammurabi," an unprecedented list of laws laid down by the eponymous Babylonian king. The stele likely stood in Babylon for six centuries, but in the twelfth century BC was taken as plunder by the Elamites, who hauled it back to Susa, where it lay buried until the twentieth century.

This code would have far-reaching historical significance, being ahead of its time in many ways. The preface read: "[The God of the Sky] called by name me, Hammurabi, the exalted prince, who feared God, to bring about the rule of righteousness in the land, to destroy the wicked and the evil-doers; so that the strong should not harm the weak...." But what makes it a uniquely valuable find for those wondering whether the Bible is historically accurate is that this stele presents detailed information about life in that part of the world in the eighteenth century BC. In so doing it further confirms many practices and other specifics from the earliest pages of Genesis.

For example, Genesis tells us that regarding inheritance, Abraham's eldest son, Ishmael—whom he fathered with the slave Hagar—was nonetheless reckoned to be ranked below his younger brother Isaac, whom Abraham fathered with his wife Sarah. Sure enough, Hammurabi's code tells us that, regarding inheritance, the status of the son of the first wife is above that of the son of a slave, even if the son of the slave was born before the son of the first wife.

Later on in Genesis 37:28, Joseph is sold into slavery by his brothers for the sum of twenty shekels; Hammurabi's code puts the price of a slave at twenty shekels. Because of this single object discovered in 1901, it becomes impossible to believe that Genesis could have been composed many centuries later—or over a thousand years later, as some Bible skeptics had been claiming. After all, how could someone know the cost of a slave from a millennium before their time? In his book *Unearthing the Bible*, the archaeologist Titus Kennedy explains that earlier ancient codes set the price lower: For example, the law code of Ur-Nammu from 2050 BC set the price at ten shekels, and the Laws of Eshnunna from 1930 BC set the price at fifteen shekels. The price rose to thirty shekels at Ugarit in the fourteenth century BC and to fifty in Assyria during the eighth century BC. We see that what the Bible tells us is a remarkably accurate figure at the time of the patriarchs. Kennedy also tells us that a trove of tablets found in the ancient Mesopotamian city of Nuzi—first discovered in 1896—similarly refer to many social and cultural customs we find in the patriarchal narratives in Genesis and also are narrowly particular to that part of the world at that time.

It is a curious trend that the more we seem to discover, the more the Bible emerges as an accurate historical record of the events, people, and places it depicts, so that what we once were able to write off as myths and fairy tales we cannot help but fairly observe to be an accurate account of the events, people, and places it depicts. And sometimes it is the specificity and accuracy of certain details that is most impressive.

Jehoiakim's Vermillion Windows

Even by the notably deplorable standards of many of the kings of Judah and Israel, Jehoiakim stands out as a skunk of the first order. He lived in incestuous relationships with his mother, stepmother, and daughter-in-law, and essentially had everyone he disliked murdered. He was also responsible for sending the prophet Daniel to Babylon in order to appease King Nebuchadnezzar, and brutally taxed the people of Jerusalem while he lived in high style. In her book *Etched in Stone*, Lisette Bassett-Brody explains that in condemning Jehoiakim, the prophet Jeremiah specifically mentioned the especially lavish palace he had built for himself:

> Woe to him who builds his house by unrighteousness
> And his chambers by injustice,
> Who uses his neighbor's service without wages
> And gives him nothing for his work,
> Who says, "I will build myself a wide house with
> spacious chambers,
> And cut out windows for it,
> Paneling it with cedar
> And painting it with vermilion...."
> (Jeremiah 22:13–14)

We hardly expect archaeology to corroborate paint colors from the seventh century BC, but when a palace was discovered in 1959, halfway between Bethlehem and the Old City of Jerusalem, it was identified as the one built by Jehoiakim—for it stood inside the fortress he had also rebuilt, just as the Scriptures said. The palace matched Jeremiah's description in even the astonishing detail of windows with "vermillion" painted cedar. Israel's Ministry of Foreign Affairs explains:

> Window balustrades consisting of a row of stone colonnettes, decorated with palmettes and topped with joined capitals in the proto-Aeolic style, were also found. They probably adorned the upper story of the buildings inside the citadel. These decorative architectural elements echo a verse in the book of Jeremiah, which describes the windows in the house of Jehoiakim king of Judah: "And cut out windows for it, paneling it with cedar, and painting it with vermillion...."

Such a level of accuracy underscores the trustworthiness of the biblical accounts. The Bible also says that Jeremiah prophesied that Jehoiakim would be given "the burial of a donkey" and "dragged and dumped beyond the gates of Jerusalem." The fulfillment of this ignominious prophecy is confirmed in the writings of the first-century historian Josephus, who tells us that Nebuchadnezzar had Jehoiakim's corpse flung over Jerusalem's parapet to show the troops below the city that he was dead. The Bible says that after Jehoiakim's death Nebuchadnezzar installed Jehoiakim's son as his vassal, and during the excavation of the palace a seal was discovered bearing the name Eliaquim, whom the Bible mentions as an official to this son. Once again, the smallest and most specific details from the Bible continued to be confirmed.

Of course it is one thing to discover the palace of a king from six or so centuries before the time of Christ, and it is another to speak of that world a thousand years earlier, and even several centuries before the Greek fleet sailed for Troy, making famous the exploits of Achilles and Hector and Odysseus. As we have seen with the discovery of Abraham's

Ur of the Chaldees, perhaps the biblical account of that most distant era is not entirely mythical after all.

But far more mythical sounding than the mere existence of a great city are the events that are supposed to have happened not long after Abraham's journey out of Ur, when his nephew visited the fabled cities of Sodom and Gomorrah. The Bible says these "cities of the plain" were destroyed with the divine fire of judgment, and so very completely and decisively that the mere mention of these places would for many centuries hence fill people with deepest dread and horror. Can there be anything to such a tale? And even if there could, could we ever know about it?

CHAPTER EIGHTEEN

The Discovery
of Biblical Sodom

In 1996, an Albuquerque scientist named Steven Collins was in a modest hotel room in the Israeli city of Arad, on the bleak southwestern side of the Dead Sea. Dr. Collins was a field archaeologist and ceramic typologist who had spent many years studying the millennia-old vessels buried throughout the Middle East. He was also a Christian who believed the Bible was a reliable source of history, and was leading a group on a Bible tour of Israel. But what lay ahead of the group the next day gave him an uneasy feeling. Being a scientist, he was especially careful about making claims, and hated seeing other tour guides say things he knew to be mere speculation.

On the docket the next day were what scholars said were the sites of the biblical cities Sodom and Gomorrah. But Dr. Collins was aware of some of the discrepancies concerning these sites. These things hadn't nagged at him before, but for some reason now they did. So to better prepare himself for the next day, he opened the Book of Genesis and reread the biblical accounts. But reading these words with an actual view of the land to which they referred, he became confused. According to what he was now reading, what everyone had for many decades accepted as the locations for these ancient cities simply couldn't be right. How had he missed this before?

Why certain views harden and become the consensus, never to be questioned, is one of the themes of this book. For Dr. Collins to find himself questioning the consensus about these locations was difficult. Back in the latter part of the nineteenth century most top biblical and archaeological scholars had believed precisely what Collins was at that minute wondering about. As he was now doing, they had read the biblical text and had without any question understood that the location of these fabled cities must be somewhere northeast of the Dead Sea, in what was called the Kikkar Plain, a verdant area surrounding the southernmost part of the Jordan River. That's simply what the text said. There were many other questions to be answered about Sodom and Gomorrah, but their location—along with the other cities of the Kikkar Plain—was not disputed.

But in the twentieth century this changed. That's because a scholar named W. F. Albright—and his protégé G. E. Wright—had confidently and firmly put the location of these cities on the southern edge of the Dead Sea, and perhaps even under the waters of the sea, whose surface level they knew fluctuated over the millennia. Their case for this location was not without its problems, but their influence and stature in the field of biblical archaeology—especially that of the elder Albright—was such that few would dare to question them. Albright had gotten so much right over the decades and had done so much for the field of biblical archaeology that he had earned most scholars' deepest respect, which is often enough to sway people away from the theories of others.

Indeed W. F. Albright was no less than the founder of the biblical archaeology movement; he had magnificently countered the prevailing liberal trend of the previous era toward dismissing the Bible as folklore and had succeeded tremendously in marshaling evidence and arguments against it to show that what the Bible said could not easily be dismissed. So Albright was a great hero to those who took biblical archaeology seriously, and until his death in 1971 he was the field's *éminence grise* without peer.

But very early in his career—in 1924—he had conducted a survey of the Jordan Valley and identified five cities on the southern side of the Dead Sea as the "cities of the plain" described in Genesis. He concluded that the largest, Bad edh-Dhra, was biblical Sodom, and the smaller Numeira was Gomorrah.

So because of his stature, which only grew in subsequent decades, these identifications were hardly challenged. Subsequent excavations even provided good reasons to agree with them. In the 1960s and 1970s, for example, extraordinarily vast cemeteries were uncovered in three of the five cities, with a total of 1.5 million bodies. Surely a tremendous civilization had once lived and breathed there, precisely as one would conclude from the biblical descriptions. Even stronger and more dramatic was the layer of ashy destruction—ranging in depth from four to twenty inches—that had been discovered at Bad edh-Dhra. Part of the evidence too was that the tectonic plates in this region exerted extraordinary pressures upon each other, and over the millennia many earthquakes had occurred. So it was reasonable to speculate that volcanic magma and superheated subterranean gases might have escaped during some of these tectonic cataclysms, which would account for the fiery destruction mentioned in the biblical account. All these things were more than enough to settle the question generally.

But as we have said, there were discrepancies and questions. For example, what appeared to be the fiery destruction of Bad edh-Dhra was believed to have taken place around 2350 BC, five to seven centuries too early for the destruction of biblical Sodom and Gomorrah, which was established at around 1700 BC. Another difficulty was that Numeira's civilization had vanished completely around 2600 BC and had never been recovered. This was nine centuries too early.

How these cities had been destroyed was another question. The biblical account says God "rained down fire and burning sulfur from the sky on Sodom and Gomorrah." It says nothing of an earthquake, although if volcanic ash and lava and scorching gases were vented from within the earth they could certainly be expected to fall down upon the area. The actual text from Genesis 19:25 reads: "He overthrew those cities,

Bizzell Bible Collection, University of Oklahoma Libraries

The Sodomites are struck blind. 1728 illustration.

all the plain, all the inhabitants of the cities, and what grew on the ground." (Other translations say He "demolished," "devastated," "destroyed," and "ended" those cities—describing complete annihilation of their inhabitants and vegetation.) It also says Abraham got up that morning and from his location in Hebron in Canaan more than forty miles away saw smoke rising from the cities "like the smoke of a furnace" (Genesis 19:28). It's hard to imagine what manner of destruction could have done something so devastating that someone forty miles away could see what Abraham saw.

There were other factors against these locations, but as we have said, the way things work in determining the scholarly or popular consensus often has little to do with how such things *should* work. Logic and facts are rarely the only way we process things. So it was mostly Albright's unparalleled authority as the "Father of Biblical Archaeology"—bolstered by the subsequent archaeological excavations following his initial identification—that settled most opinions on this issue, at least among those believing the cities and the story of their destruction was more than folklore and myth.

Military tensions between Jordan and Israel from the 1960s through the late 1990s also made further exploration in this and nearby areas impossible, so the settled opinion had three further decades to ossify. By the time of Dr. Collins's tour in 1996, the identification of Bad edh-Dhra and Numeira with biblical Sodom and Gomorrah was the unquestioned consensus and what brought Dr. Collins and his group to their hotel in Arad that night. So the next morning Dr. Collins had planned to lead his charges to these spots and repeat much of what he and so many others had accepted from Albright and Wright and those following in their footsteps.

Collins was also aware of the theologically liberal scholars who thought the whole thing was simply an ancient fable, and he was aware of others who believed perhaps something had happened here in the mythical past, and the memory of that cataclysm had formed the basis of the biblical stories. Of course the further back in the Bible one went the more tempting it was to see the stories as wholly or at least partly mythical. Many scholars didn't believe the Exodus had ever happened, or that Moses was a real person. Many believed King David was a mythical figure and that the stories of his life were like those of King Arthur and the Knights of the Round Table. Perhaps there had been someone upon whom the story of King Arthur was based, but to take it as seriously as if it had been recorded by Thucydides or another actual historian was ridiculous. Did anyone think there was a real Gilgamesh, or a real Odysseus and Penelope? At what point did mythology and history separate?[1]

---

[1] This issue was never more dramatically explored than when—in the latter part of the nineteenth century—the eccentric German tycoon Heinrich Schliemann decided to "prove" that the civilization of Homer's epics was historically based. The story of the Trojan war and the figures in Homer's *Iliad* and *Odyssey* had long been accepted as mythical, a poetic fiction that Homer had brilliantly woven into the two epics known to every educated person in the Western world. He brought to life a heroic "Golden Age" from the prehistoric mists before the historical era of Greek antiquity, in which we find Pericles and Plato. Anything before the eighth century BC—when the Greek alphabet first appears—was simply mythic prehistory, no more real than the stories of the Cyclops or the Medusa or the Twelve Labors of Hercules. But the brash and brilliant Schliemann had other ideas, and after he had amassed his fortune, he set out in the 1870s to prove via archaeology that the world of Homer was fact and not fiction. He began by traveling to Hissarlik in Turkey to excavate what was said to be the site of Homeric Troy, and he shocked the world in proving that the civilization and figures of Homer's poems—which many utterly dismissed as mythical—had in fact existed. He showed that a great civilization once thought the fanciful fiction of an unknown poet had existed a thousand years earlier, and after uncovering the multi-layered millennia-old civilization of Troy, proceeded to uncover the other fabled places whose leaders had sailed with Agamemnon to Troy: to Pylos which was the home of King Nestor, and to "mighty walled Tiryns," and to King Agamemnon's Mycenae itself, from which we take the name

So apart from Christian scholars like Collins—and before him Albright and others—the idea that these cities and their story of destruction was anything but pure fancy had been dismissed. And even if such places or events like their supposed destruction had occurred, there was no reason to assume we could find them four millennia later. They might now lie in ruins somewhere beneath the Dead Sea, as some maintained.

But Dr. Collins knew that locating Sodom under the Dead Sea was a kind of lazy, unscholarly shrug at the whole affair. It had been established for some time that the water level of the Dead Sea was never lower than in Abraham's day. We even know that it was then at precisely the same level as today. So the theory that Sodom sunk like Atlantis to the bottom of the Dead Sea must be discarded. But as often happens, theories carry on in various circles long after they categorically have been disproved in others. Information and knowledge rarely travel as they should, as we have said.

Dr. Collins knew the biblical accounts were real, and before retiring he read the passages in Genesis. When he noticed the strange discrepancy about the cities' location, he carefully read the whole passage three more times, to be sure he understood it. The text tells us in the first lines of Genesis 13 that Abraham and his nephew Lot left Egypt and traveled north through the Negev desert. They went all the way up to Bethel and pitched their tents between Bethel and Ai, today located in the West Bank, some miles north of Jerusalem. Both men were wealthy, possessing tremendous herds of cattle and many flocks of sheep and goats, along with the many tents to house their herdsmen. In fact, each had so many herds and flocks, requiring considerable lands for pasturing and grazing, that their

---

Mycenaean to describe that civilization which we now know existed from 1600 BC till around 1150 BC, and which dominated that part of the Mediterranean during those centuries. In 1900 Sir Arthur Evans excavated the Palace of Knossos in Crete and uncovered the related civilization of the Minoans, which influenced and preceded the Mycenaean civilization, and there found the mysterious syllabic language called Linear B, which finally in 1952 was deciphered and determined to be an early form of Greek, thereby stretching Greek civilization a full thousand years earlier than previously thought. Strange things do happen, and this is one of the strangest, for it has upended—and continues to upend—so much of what "the scholarly consensus" has already "settled," that if not for a wild figure as brazen and persistent and rich as Schliemann, it all might never have come to light.

herdsmen often quarreled. So Abraham suggested to his nephew Lot that they separate, generously giving his nephew the choice of where to settle. The text says:

> And Lot lifted his eyes and saw all the plain of Jordan, that
> it was well watered everywhere (before the Lord destroyed
> Sodom and Gomorrah) like the garden of the Lord, like the
> land of Egypt as you go toward Zoar. (Genesis 13:10)

The Hebrew term for "fertile plains" is *kikkar*, which means "disk" and also refers to a loaf of bread baked in a circular—or disk—shape.

Collins knew that for Abraham and Lot to see what the text described meant they could not be near the Dead Sea, much less on its southern part. To look toward the Jordan River—which flows southward into the Dead Sea—and toward the fertile plain around it clearly implied they were looking at an area directly north of the Dead Sea, toward the eastern side of the Jordan River. There was no mistaking it from the text. But that location was far from where Collins and his group were in Arad. Again: Why had he not seen this before? And yet who was he to question decades of established consensus?

He knew if he pursued what suddenly seemed so obvious that he would be setting himself against the establishment, who had long ago dismissed the area indicated. Maps showing biblical sites had almost nothing where he believed these five "cities of the plain" were located. But since Collins believed the Bible to be the inspired Word of God, he could hardly slough off what was suddenly so clear. He was unsure what he would tell his group the next day, but more importantly, he was wondering whether he should pursue this further.

In 1996 Dr. Collins was extremely busy with other responsibilities and projects, but he did more research and became increasingly convinced that biblical Sodom and Gomorrah had never been discovered and lay someplace in the Kikkar plain, north of the Dead Sea, probably in Jordan. He knew he must try to find them.

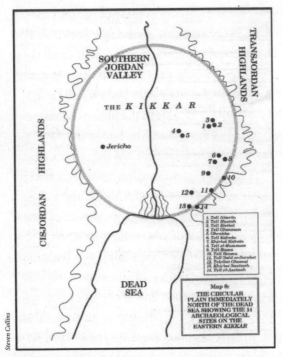

Map image of Kikkar plain.

It wasn't until 2002 that he could plan a trip to Jordan to look into things more closely, but that year he and his wife, Danette, along with some friends went to Israel and then into Amman, Jordan, where they visited the American Center of Oriental Research (ACOR). If anywhere was a good place to start looking into this subject, this was it. When they arrived, they first pored over issue after issue of the *Annual of the Department of Antiquities of Jordan*, looking for clues. But they found nothing. Still, what the Bible said was plain enough. Major cities don't just disappear. Although now and again the depressing thought came into Dr. Collins's head that perhaps that's exactly what they had done. Perhaps the destruction of Sodom and Gomorrah had simply been that devastating, so that no traces existed to be found. The Scriptures didn't talk about some mere earthquake, where everything simply fell where it was. It described an unprecedented conflagration: fire from heaven. Who knew what would remain?

As their research went nowhere, Dr. Collins's traveling companion showed him a book, titled *The Antiquities of the Jordan Rift Valley*, published fifteen years earlier. It was the work of a journalist, R. G. Khouri, with descriptions of every archaeological site in the entire Jordan Valley. And the map in the book—unlike all other maps Dr. Collins consulted—was not blank. It had fourteen black dots, each indicating an archaeological site. He realized two of these dots might hold the answers to this puzzle. Dr. Collins was stunned that in this popular-level book he had found more on potential archaeological sites than in all the scholarly literature. He realized all they needed to do was make a list of the fourteen sites and use the process of elimination to determine which ones fit the criteria for Sodom and Gomorrah. There was information on many of them there in the library. Some were far too early to be considered; others were too late. The Sodom of the Bible had to be a spectacularly thriving center before 1700 BC, the time of Abraham and Lot. And of all the "cities of the plain" mentioned in Genesis, it had to be the largest. The Arabic word for "mount" is *tall*—which we usually anglicize to "tell" or "tel." Each of these tells is typically a great mound of cities built upon cities over the course of centuries or even millennia. Even if not already on a preexisting height, the sheer mass of buildings atop buildings over time can itself rise to a tremendous height.

At the end of their day at ACOR, Dr. Collins and his companions had settled on two large tells that seemed to be the likeliest candidates. One was "Tall Nimrin," which had already been excavated somewhat. It had "monumental Middle Bronze Walls," so the dating was right. Much more intriguingly it had evidence of being abandoned for five hundred years, which would be logical, if one took seriously the horrific destruction described in Genesis. There was pottery up until the Middle Bronze Age, but rather mysteriously none from the Late Bronze Age. The larger candidate was Tall el-Hammam, which somehow had never been excavated.

But before visiting these, they would visit all the less likely spots on the map, just to get a sense of things. They spent the next two days driving all over the great verdant circle of the Jordan Valley, investigating each of the fourteen talls. Dr. Collins, being a world expert in ceramics of this region, picked over the bits of pottery shards that lay everywhere, instantly recognizing the era in which they were made and quickly knowing whether the tall was a candidate for Sodom. It wasn't until the second day that they came to Tall el-Hammam. As they were approaching it in their car, they saw that it was breathtakingly large, far larger than they had dreamt. Dr. Collins said it looked like "a massive ship, riding on a

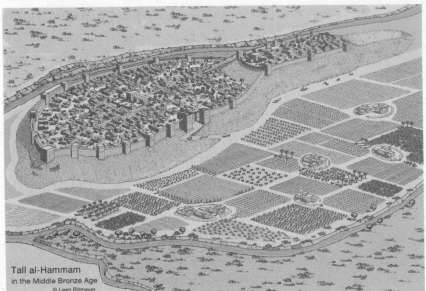

Tall al-Hammam
in the Middle Bronze Age
© Leen Ritmeyer

Steven Collins/TeHEP

Drawing of Tall el-Hammam during the Middle Bronze Age, by Dr. Leen Ritmeyer.

sea of fields." It was stunning, the height of a nine-story building. It also had steep slopes strewn with rocks, which Dr. Collins was tempted to scale, but didn't. Yet he wondered: Why had no one ever excavated this?

The tremendous height made one see its strategic advantage. One could see armies approaching for many miles in every direction. In fact, the Ottomans and Jordanians had used this tell for gun and tank positions, and their treads had dug large trenches like gashes across the landscape. As Dr. Collins scoured this area, he found exactly what he found at Tall Nimrin: a remarkable and confounding absence of any pottery from the Late Bronze Age, as though during that period alone both of these once-great cities were desolate and unoccupied. It was a tremendously hopeful sign. If Sodom and Gomorrah could be found, these two sites were the prime candidates. Their location on the Kikkar plain meshed perfectly with the biblical account, and the odd lacuna where the Late Bronze Age pottery should have been was deeply compelling. At this juncture, Dr. Collins had no further questions. He knew he must dig here.

By 2005 he had finally squared away enough of his other work and raised enough funds to put a spade to the problem, as it were. Over the next several summers that's precisely what he and his team did, being the first to excavate this extremely promising site. The work on Tall el-Hammam was painstaking, so it wasn't until the third season of excavation that they hit what one might well describe as the literal pay dirt for which they had been looking.

They excavated gradually, of course, but Dr. Collins realized that one of the deeper gashes previously made by the Jordanian tanks might help him see more easily what was further down. So he began digging an exploratory shaft in that spot. As they meticulously made their way down, they were racing backward in time, and about nine feet down they came upon a strange "layer of distinct, ash-laden, hard-packed soil." It had not seen the light of day in thirty-seven centuries, and the graduate student digging at that moment, Carroll Kobs, said it still stank of burned ashes. The acrid smell had been preserved for nearly four thousand years.

Obviously, this was tremendously exciting and offered evidence of what could have been a fiery civilization-ending cataclysm around 1700 BC, precisely when the Bible indicated. But perhaps even more exciting was what lay just above this layer from 1700 BC. The layer immediately atop this ash-laden layer was from the tenth century BC. This was the extremely strange evidence for which they had been daring to hope. It seemed that this civilization was thriving for many centuries, but then suddenly, around 1700 BC, the civilization had stopped dead—and then did not start up again for seven centuries. Anyone unfamiliar with the story of Sodom and Gomorrah would have been completely baffled. Why would a piece of the primest real estate for many miles—boasting a commanding view of the area that was unparalleled, and an abundance of water and greenery—be utterly abandoned for seven hundred years? Even if a meteor or volcanic explosion or some other event had devastated this Middle Bronze Age city, why should it lie uninhabited for so long? How had seven centuries of nothingness descended so decisively on a site of such unequivocal value? Even if the city had been destroyed, wouldn't someone have settled on it far sooner than seven hundred long years later?

To understand the great peculiarity of such a long hiatus, we have to consider what Sodom was like in its prime. For one thing, it had been a thriving walled city for 2,500 years *before* its destruction in the seventeenth century BC. In other words, it had been continuously populated from over 6,000 years ago. Such a long stretch of civilization in one spot is nearly impossible to imagine. But it shows us that it was indeed an unprecedentedly spectacular location for a city, situated right in the middle of a major trade route, with inexhaustible sources of water. So before its destruction it had existed for 25 continuous centuries. Real estate was every bit as important then as it is today, and there simply weren't many places to compare with this one. The size of the city was immense too, more than ten times the size of Jerusalem. And its colossal walls and fortifications were so impregnable that as far as we know, no enemy ever managed to breach them. Dr. Collins and his team soon saw the entire city had been surrounded by a rampart consisting of 150–200 *million* mud bricks sloping outward at a 35-degree angle and coated with dried mud so that no one could climb it. Then atop this monumental rampart stood a 12-foot-thick wall three stories high. There was even a second huge wall around the centermost part of the city, providing further protection for the elites living there. But then it all ended so decisively and horribly that no one dared to inhabit it again for seven centuries.

A clue to why it remained barren for so long comes to us in the Egyptian name for the place following its destruction. They called it Abel, "the place of mourning." The Hebrew sense of the word has the strong connotation of "mourning after a calamity." In the book of Numbers the site is called an uninhabited "wasteland," and all throughout the Old Testament it stands as a frightening warning of desolation, a hellish landscape utterly devoid of life. Life went on all around it, and we have the record of many figures in the Bible passing it by, but no one dared scale its haunted heights. Isaiah, Jeremiah, Ezekiel, Amos, Zechariah, Micah, and Zephaniah all refer to it as the ultimate horror, as the nightmare picture of what happens when God's unmitigated judgment descends to wreak its havoc. Jesus too mentions it several times, as do several New Testament writers, though their distance in time from the destruction was seventeen centuries.

So what did happen on that day so long ago? Can we ever know?

In *Discovering the City of Sodom*, the 2013 book that Dr. Collins and his co-writer Dr. Latayne C. Scott eventually wrote to tell this extraordinary story, they explain that the layer of hard-packed ash and "destruction debris" from the terminal Middle Bronze Age stratum is between eighteen inches and six feet deep. "Embedded in those layers," they write, "are broken and tumbled mud bricks, smashed and charred pottery vessels and other day-to-day objects, and human bones—all violently churned into a tell-tale ashy matrix."[2] Whatever happened left behind a wake of destruction unlike anything anyone had ever seen. There was literally nothing to compare with it.

In a more recent report, from 2019, they describe it similarly:

> The matrix had every predictable material in it—pieces of mud-bricks, chunks of charred wood, cobble-sized stones and pebbles, pieces of plaster, pottery shards, and a variety of objects—but the mixed matrix did not have a typical "gravity" order to it. One excavator gave it a descriptive name: "the Cuisinart effect." Indeed, the matrix composition had the look of having been thrown into a blender.[3]

What is even more staggering about the violence is how widespread it is, for this bizarre seven-century gap is not limited to Sodom but extends to all of the surrounding cities and towns in the Kikkar region. Archaeologists in this region call it the "Late Bronze Gap." But Collins

---

[2] Steven Collins and Latayne C. Scott, *Discovering the City of Sodom: The Fascinating, True Account of the Discovery of the Old Testament's Most Infamous City* (Brentwood, Tennessee: Howard Books, 2013), 156.

[3] Steven Collins, Gary A. Byers, Carroll M. Kobs, and Khalid Tarawneh, "The Tall Al-Ḥammām Excavation Project Season Fourteen 2019 Report: Excavation, Interpretations, & Insights," filed with the Department of Antiquities of the Hashemite Kingdom of Jordan, October 2019, p. 24.

explains that this "Bronze Age Gap" only includes the cities and towns in the Kikkar plain. Everywhere else beyond that, civilization continued along, uninterrupted in any way.

One measure of the devastation comes to us from the archaeologists who excavated Tall Nimrin—which Collins now believes is biblical Admah—in the 1980s and 1990s. They found "Middle Bronze wall foundations, the deep-sunk large bases which were intended to anchor the superstructures of buildings, inside the perimeter of the city, but they found no [Middle Bronze] residences, none of the typical eighteen-inch-thick walls of domestic dwellings. They said this was 'highly unusual.'"[4] So what sort of force could possibly tear away walls that thick across an entire city, leaving almost no trace of them, and leaving only the foundations below? What in the world could have happened to cause such sweeping destruction?

Another clue to what happened came to Carroll Kobs the day she was down in the shaft where she discovered the layer of ash. While digging, her trowel hit something hard within the ash. It was a piece of pottery about the size of her palm. But when she turned it over, she and Dr. Collins saw that the other side was covered—or glazed—with a "greenish, glass-like surface." Dr. Collins's heart sank immediately. Being a ceramic typologist, he knew immediately that any glazed pottery like that was Islamic and couldn't be older than the seventh century AD, when this technology came into being. Carroll handed the shard to Dr. Collins, who flipped it over to the unglazed side again. But when he looked at it up close, he had no doubt he was looking at a piece of Middle Bronze Age pottery. In fact, he knew that it was the "shoulder" of a large forty-gallon jar—*pithoi*—used to carry water, olive oil, or wine. Since glass melts at about 1,500 degrees Fahrenheit, the glaze could only mean that the shard had been subjected to heat of that temperature. Dr. Collins had excavated things like that before that had been in a room that caught fire while containing extremely flammable oil or something like that. It was possible.

But when one of the volunteers, Dr. Gene Hall, finally saw it, he had another thought, saying it looked exactly like trinitite. Hall had been in the

---

4 Collins and Scott, *Discovering the City of Sodom*, 165.

military in the 1940s, when—just 120 miles south of where Dr. Collins now lived in Albuquerque—the first nuclear tests were conducted in the desert of New Mexico. The director of the Los Alamos lab was J. Robert Oppenheimer, who gave the first nuclear test the code name "Trinity," so the area was thenceforth called "Trinity Site." The heat from that blast was so intense that it instantly melted the sand, turning it into green glass. Those who later found

Preserved Middle Bronze Age mudbrick walls, Upper City palace complex. All of the thick, palace-complex walls were sheared off at this level by a violent, northeast-moving destruction event.

Smashed grain jars and other vessels suspended in the 1.5-meter-thick Upper City MBA destruction matrix.

Steven Collins/TeHEP

Drone photo of the Middle Bronze Age palace complex excavations as of 2020.

this substance dubbed it "trinitite." Hall's comment got Dr. Collins's attention, because one strange thing about the shard of pottery was that this green glass-like glaze was ultra-thin, and only on one side. It seemed to him that unlike other bits of pottery he had seen that were subjected to intense heat, this had only been subjected to intense heat for the shortest time before it cooled. What could explain that?

When he got back to the States, Collins had the shard tested at the U.S. Geological Survey lab at the New Mexico Institute of Mining and Technology in Socorro. When the geochemist Nelia Dunbar saw it, she immediately said: "Nice piece of trinitite." But when she turned it over, she saw that it was a piece of ancient pottery. So of course it couldn't be trinitite. Twelve hours of tests later they got new information. They could clearly see that the glassy material had not dripped onto the pottery, but was actually the pottery itself, melted. They also saw that part of the interior of the pottery showed signs of exposure to extreme heat. An eighth of an inch from the surface melt—inside the ceramic itself—it had obviously gotten so hot that a zircon crystal—which is a salt crystal—had lost its typical angularity and had in a millisecond melted into an infinitesimally small globule, like a tiny bubble, only visible through the electron microscope they were using. This meant that the *interior* of the ceramic at some point—very briefly—had reached at least 2,000 degrees Fahrenheit. How intense could the heat have been outside the pottery to create this temperature inside the pottery in that briefest fraction of a second? Of course whatever had caused that super intense flash was another, larger question.

The more they talked about what might have caused this, the more they realized every suggestion must be rejected. Except for one. The only one that seemed to fit is what is usually called an intense "airburst event." These have happened on other parts of the globe, where a meteor or astcroid penetrates Earth's atmosphere—but explodes before it makes impact. That is precisely what happened in 1908 on a staggering scale in Tunguska, Siberia. Nearly a thousand square miles of forest—eighty million trees—were incinerated and flattened in an instant by the force of the detonation. People hundreds of miles away were knocked off their feet from the shock waves, and the meteorological disturbance was so great that all across Asia and Europe the night sky was lit up for three days. People in London could read newspapers at midnight. The "impact event" has been estimated to be the equivalent of fifteen megatons of TNT, or a thousand Hiroshima bombs. And yet this inconceivably destructive event would only have required a single small asteroid of about three hundred feet in diameter, exploding five miles above Earth's surface.

Many other "impact events" had happened in pre-history, such as the huge one that led to the extinction of the dinosaurs sixty-six million years ago. We also know that one must have occurred over the Egyptian desert some time before the birth of King Tutankhamun, whose mummy was decorated with a piece of breastplate jewelry featuring just such a piece of exceedingly rare green glass. As we have noted, the Bible says Abraham—who at the time of Sodom's destruction was in Hebron, some forty miles away—could see "the smoke of the land which went up like the smoke of a furnace."

And so the evidence builds with each year that Dr. Collins has indeed found what many thought unfindable, or simply mythical. But since his first discoveries, the excavations and the story have continued. In 2011 Dr. Collins's team for the first time found human remains, and they have found many more since. In 2012, however, they found what for Dr. Collins was a nearly unbelievable dream come true: the city gate of Sodom, the very place where Lot sat thirty-seven centuries ago. Every archaeologist of that Bronze Age is familiar with the huge city gates constructed around many of these cities, and when in 2012 Dr. Collins found this fabled gate, tears came to his eyes. In *Discovering the City of Sodom*, he says that he had visited and measured most of the monumental gates from that time, so he knew exactly what he was looking for. He had seen the gates at Dan, Ashkelon, Gezer, Megiddo, Hazor, Shechem, and Beth Shemesh. And now in this eighth season of excavating Sodom, he had found this holy grail, the very gate of Sodom. It was quite what one would expect for a city of that size in that period. Four gigantic towers and a central opening six feet wide. It would have been the bustling marketplace where innumerable transactions took place, and the very spot where Lot had sat, as described in the pages of Genesis. Very few archaeologists are able to lay claim to discovering anything quite so remarkable, and certainly no archaeologist has ever found anything from the Scriptures older or more famous.

Dr. Collins's book came out in 2013, but the excavation continues. The more time passes the more the consensus has shifted to this site as the only candidate for the ancient city whose destruction is described in Genesis. And as the evidence mounts up, this recent discovery begins to emerge as one of the most astounding archaeological discoveries of all time.

What makes it especially important, though, is that this discovery was the direct result of taking the biblical text seriously. Only the Bible gave a clear location for Sodom and Gomorrah, identifying them as large cities in the "cities of the plain." Only the Bible made it clear Abraham could have seen Sodom burning from over forty miles away. Dr. Collins only searched for these cities where he did because he had a deep confidence in the scriptural account. And the good reason for that confidence has been borne out in his excavations. It was this confidence that the Bible spoke truth—coupled with his knowledge of the scientific and other developments in the story, such as the depth of the Dead Sea at the time of Abraham, and the various problems of the previously and erroneously identified sites to the south of the Dead Sea—that all came together.

In a way, the discovery of this vitally important ancient city and the strange way in which it was dramatically swept from history through a supernatural disaster—of what we might advisedly call "biblical proportions"—is a signal example of what is possible when we value the biblical accounts. What else Dr. Collins will find there is not known, but what he has already found—and what many in the fields of archaeology have assented to and confirmed—is that the Sodom and Gomorrah of the Bible were real. And the destructive event that befell them was real too, as proven with the tools of modern science. Thanks to Dr. Collins's faith in the trustworthiness of the Hebrew Scriptures, both cities and their grim fates have in our time been resurrected from the ash heap of myth and legend into the realm of history and science.

PART III

What Is Truth?

CHAPTER NINETEEN

The Four Horsemen

In answering the question posed by this book's title, one cannot avoid some mention of the so-called "New Atheists," who burst on to the cultural scene some fifteen years ago, but who have lately been mostly quiet. But their rancorous campaign against religion for some years is the most recent expression of atheism in Western culture, such that many who today call themselves atheists have the principal figures of this movement to thank, namely Richard Dawkins, Daniel Dennett, Sam Harris, and the late Christopher Hitchens, who sometimes styled themselves the "Four Horsemen of the New Atheism."

What marked their movement was the exuberance and fury with which they condemned religious faith, for they were not content merely to maintain God's non-existence. On the contrary, they rather energetically denounced all religious expressions as irrational and as somehow "anti-science," and therefore as intolerably vile and eminently dangerous, and in need of forceful eradication by whatever means available—whatever that might mean.

But their arguments have not stood up well, which will perhaps surprise anyone who recalls the showering sparks and billowing smoke that attended their cantankerous eruptions in many books and speeches and debates, through which they glowered steadfastly and unpleasantly, as though smiling might be taken as unseriousness. But how were they so well received by many of the cultural mandarins who gave them the many opportunities to make their case? For a clue we may turn to their books, which were such impressive bestsellers that at the height of their popularity one felt a responsibility to see what all the fuss was about, if only to become familiar with the accusations being put forth. In a world full of people longing for answers to the ultimate questions about meaning and transcendence, those of us who present the God of the Bible as the answer to such questions should certainly try to understand the views of those on the other side of things. And surely those in the culture not having any particular point of view were interested in understanding what these highly educated and mostly well-spoken fellows might be saying, and were therefore only too happy to oblige them and see what they might have to say.

So it was in a similarly well-intentioned effort that I located a copy of the most famous of their books, Hitchens's *God Is Not Great: How Religion Poisons Everything* (Twelve, 2007). Surely, I must learn something from it, even if I disagreed with its premise and thought its title puerile.

As I settled down to read the book, I deliberately ignored the title. Christopher Hitchens was prone to be deliberately provocative, and one assumed the title was an especially pointed example of that, calculated to draw attention. But even as I plunged ahead into the thicket of his sentences, I became very quickly but surely mystified. I found that I couldn't make any real sense of what I was discovering. I don't mean I didn't understand the meaning of the sentences; that I understood all too well. What I couldn't make head or tail of was how such a popular book by someone so previously brilliant could be so aggressively—I thought even ambitiously—awful. I didn't need to wonder too hard how the book could have been popular, because what it did very well—via unconnected anecdotes and mean-spirited hyperbole and witticisms— was confirm and further inflame the deep emotional animus many readers felt toward "religion" of some kind, or of any kind at all. But the book so unconscionably elided the sharp differences between religions that it was eventually embarrassing to read, until I no longer could continue and simply had to look away, as it happened permanently. But how could someone like Hitchens possibly be so confused? It was a conundrum. Nonetheless, for anyone hoping to learn something about the sincere views of these atheists, the book proved not merely to be the proverbial tough sledding, but was really more like trying to sled uphill in August.

I tried and tried to continue, but the more I read the more I became hardened in my conviction that the book was among the most disappointing, least coherent, least logical, and least enticing things I had ever read in my life, and in this I am including L. Ron Hubbard's *Dianetics* and some confusing carp recipes. I realized I was listening to a master rhetorician speaking to an audience he must have regarded as beneath him, and who was obviously taking advantage of this inequity by being so intellectually sloppy and discursive that those of us who knew what he was capable of as a writer and thinker were embarrassed, and not just for him but for his publisher too, and for anyone in the general neighborhood of the factory where the books were printed. Still, what could account for this discursive intellectual slumming, if anything could, and for this unfortunate swan dive gutterward?

Did Hitchens simply find himself needing money, and know that with some Scotch fuel he could easily rant with faux profundity on this subject for pages and pages in that withering tone for which he was famous, like a thundering British admiral dressing down his men, blasting a sitting seabird out of the water with his blunderbuss as he fulminated before finally staggering back to his stateroom for more grog? Or was Hitchens himself so emotional on this issue that he really was unable to see himself, was unable to unflare his nostrils and cool his temper long enough ever to get ahold of himself and say something worth saying? It was baffling. Surely he could make some real points on this worthy subject, instead of taking potshots so wild and cheap that it defied understanding and surely made him plummet in the eyes of not a few previous admirers. How could someone so incisive on other subjects be so patently obtuse on this, unless it was the purest mercenariness imaginable or something else equally awful, like someone whom you can see becoming angrier and angrier as they talk, finally betraying themselves by saying things they no longer have the power not to say, thereby giving the listener a hideous X-ray of their unaccountably wounded psyche? In any case, I must beg the reader's pardon and here confess that after thinking this over for some time I was very sure I had no idea. Evidently some things must simply be kept at arm's length and goggled at, whose greasy clogs refuse to be plumbed.

Anger and Ridicule

As I have already intimated, what struck me especially in Mr. Hitchens's book was the excruciating absence of serious argument and the concomitant tangled bird's nest of various self-contradictions.

What was even less escapable was the corrosive and almost frightening anger that seemed to drive it all. As it happened, it was this anger that most of the "New Atheists" had in common, the smoking thread that seemed sinuously to snake its way through everything, sometimes taking a sinister and dark form, but more often an adolescent one, as though this perpetually seething quartet were each stuck in a take-no-prisoners effort to obliterate someone who had sadistically abused them long before they had the ability to fight back—for what else could explain it? Points were often made with unpleasantly generous portions of swagger and sneer, and sometimes upper-class snobbery too, clearly meant to belittle their less ostentatiously educated opponents. With Hitchens there could be genuine wit, but with many others there were often fatiguing cliches, such as: "Well, you don't believe in Zeus or Osiris or Thor or Ganesh, do you? I just go one god farther than you. I don't believe in your God, the God of the Bible." If they had punctuated these ripostes with an outthrust tongue and the declaration "so there!" it might have nicely underscored the schoolyard effect. When they committed similar sentiments to print, "God" was often spelled with a lowercase *g*, as though this were especially edgy, in the way that "shape poems" were thought to be in the 1960s.

Of course, what went along with this was the noticeable lack of humility or grace toward those with whom they disagreed, and they usually seemed much less interested in actually convincing their opponents than in scoring points with the audience members already on their side. So there was an untoward lack of respect toward those who thought differently, and a generally dehumanizing tone, garnished now and again with moments of outrage. Again, why? Most people interested in the big questions about life and meaning and truth are genuinely interested in hearing arguments they can understand or think about, and perhaps learn from. Any mature adult with a reasonable level of self-esteem should hardly become furious to the point of empurplement over those putting forth different ideas; but somehow the bristling emotion seemed to be the argument, or was meant to be, as though stooping to civility might implicate one in the idiocy of the other side.

All Religions Are Not Equal

The single argument—or thesis, really—that the New Atheists hammered almost to the point of excluding others was that all religions are fundamentally irrational, while "science" and atheism are rational. And since all religions are utterly irrational, all religions are therefore equally evil. But did even they themselves believe what they were saying? Did they mean to put the Christian faith of Dr. King and Mother Teresa equal with the religion of animist cults that sacrificed human beings to appease nature gods and guarantee good crops? Did they believe that William Wilberforce should have kept his religion to himself and not argued for an end to the slave trade in the British Empire? He believed that the Bible was clear that we were all equal in God's eyes and are commanded to do unto others as we would have them do unto us. Did they wish to denounce that, and the abolitionist efforts that sprang therefrom? Or could they really believe that the heroic and brilliant Dietrich Bonhoeffer went to the gallows for nothing, that his speaking up against Hitler and for the Jews of Europe because his faith led him to do this was foolish and impractical and that he should have minded his own business?

Wilberforce and Bonhoeffer and Dr. King and Mother Teresa all come to mind when we think of people of faith led in their courageous efforts by the God they believed had created them. That the "New Atheists" could wave these heroes away just as they would wave away the devotees of a bloodthirsty human-sacrifice cult is obviously absurd. Nonetheless, they did their best to maintain this manifestly irrational posture, all the while shouting that they alone were devoted to rationality, while all religions were inherently irrational. It was lamentably rare that they were called out on this childishness, but while Hitchens was promoting his book on the *Charlie Rose* program on PBS, the host asked about Bonhoeffer, whom most would rightly regard as a great hero of Christian faith in action, at the cost of his life. Hitchens didn't miss a beat, actually claiming that Bonhoeffer was not a Christian at all, but a humanist, whatever that might mean. In any case, it was nonsense, but Charlie Rose did not feel up to countering it, and the bold lie was allowed to stand.

Another word must be said on the New Atheists' insistence that they stand for reason and rationality. To claim one is pro-reason is a nice beginning, but you've only described the system you hope to use going forward. It's like saying you are pro-math, but you never go on to solve any math problems. You just talk *about* math. Being for logic in principle isn't worth much if you cannot be logical in practice, and in their arguments and debates and books they were not. When math and science and rationality put a man on the moon and bring him back to Earth safely, we applaud. These things have done something beyond themselves. But when someone's whole argument is that they are for reason and against those who are against it, they have gotten nowhere. Nor did we ever get to hear what they were promoting as a replacement for what they were insisting must be razed. In the end, they were promoting absolutely nothing—if not actual nothingness itself, or even nihilism.

Questioning Questions and Doubting Doubt

Another argument these "Horsemen" put forward was that religion is evil because all who profess belief in God are strident and unyielding and dogmatic, as though everyone who believed in God were a sword-wielding member of the Taliban, longing for a violent theocracy, and in the meantime vigorously sniffing out other people's sins in order to condemn them and then decapitating or defenestrating or otherwise punishing those who had committed them. Had none of them really ever visited a soup kitchen? The caricatures they painted of faith were not only tremendously and shamefully dishonest, but were ultimately and patently ridiculous to most people. Nonetheless, they kept at it.

It could go without saying, but of course the most profound Christians in history have often had deep questions about the faith they proclaim, and for which many of them died. So the idea that having questions or doubts negates faith in the God of the Bible is hardly logical. One might even say that the closer one comes to knowing God, the more questions one has. Faith and questions are not at all mutually exclusive. And for that matter, don't we all have questions about science? After all, it has failed us so many times. For decades scientists and the scientific establishment insisted on something without giving any quarter to those on the other side, until later we realized their view was quite wrong. But we don't throw science out as a result of these errors. We understand that there can be misunderstandings and that people are often loath to change to a new paradigm, but we have enough faith in the idea of scientific inquiry to stick with it even when it sometimes leads us astray, and even when it is sheer ideology that is merely hiding under the aegis of scientific inquiry. We all live with these tensions.

But the New Atheists were not large enough to contain such multitudes and likely would burst at the seams for trying, so they simply persisted in taking potshots at God and at faith and seemed only to want to confuse their readers and listeners toward assent with their grim conclusions. But they could not do so with real arguments, and instead employed rhetorical techniques. Their persistence in this forensic dishonesty eventually helped many people cease to take them very seriously, because in the end they seemed to have no governing principles and were only taking advantage of those of us who did. If only one player thinks cheating is permissible, the contest will not be very robust. But we should ask ourselves: Why did we ever expect people who genuinely believed in nothing to have governing principles? On what basis would they have them? Of course, they eschewed revealing their revulsion to governing principles and continued to pretend they had them. But they would unhelpfully volunteer that they were adamantly opposed to unreason and irrationality, even as they were themselves being unreasonable and irrational.

Atheists often express a bitterness and an anger that inevitably appears to belie their declared stance of impartial rationality. Many persecuted Christians on the other hand—including many who were martyred—express an indefatigable and seemingly inexplicable joy. Let's start there.

If Life Is Meaningless, Why Rage?

Most of these polemical atheists seem to be bitter at the state of the world—or at the religious believers whom they blame for the state of the world, as though their inane and irrational beliefs were the only thing standing between mankind and utopia. But even if this were true, is it not logical to ask why a true atheist should protest anything at all?

Because if there really is no God, then it surely follows that there is no order or meaning in the universe. We are all accidental excrescences who bear no inherent value and who have no transcendent purpose. If this is true, by what standard could an atheist claim one way of being any better than another? And given the fundamental meaninglessness of life, why bother trying so hard to change things anyway? If all of our lives have no more meaning than the life of a gnat or a blade of desert grass in the middle of a vast wasteland—or a scorpion or a grub under the leaves of a forest floor a thousand miles from any road—what does any of it matter? Certainly they must see that according to their doctrine the length of our lives or the size of our brains does not change the meaninglessness of our existence. And if they protest on this somehow, saying that yes, but we are here now and must make the best of it, we still must ask why? On what basis must we make the best of it? If in a few decades we will all be as nonexistent as the ant that scrambles along my windowsill will be in two years—or in five seconds if I decide to crush him—why should we attend to these lives we are leading now in any way at all? Most of us on the planet feel that we should, of course, but isn't that view in perfect contradiction with the atheist doctrine? Don't the rest of us feel we should because we have a sense that there is more to everything than mere matter? That our lives have inherent purpose and extraordinary value, even if we can't say exactly how or why this is?

The inability of atheists to consistently live out their "views" is the first and most powerful argument against those views. But isn't the essentially universal feeling that we should all "do what we can" to make things better the best evidence that real atheism is a practical impossibility, that it's only something that could have been dreamed up by people whose lives really do have intrinsic meaning, even if they cannot understand how that is? If there is no Creator and our lives are perfectly accidental, why should we logically care about anything any more than a worm does, or a piece of lichen? Hundreds of millions of years pass in which they do not exist, and then at some point they exist, and soon enough they cease to exist, and another several hundreds of millions of years pass in which they do not exist and never again will exist. What of it? Is that not our story, according to the atheist doctrine? But is there a soul on the planet who actually believes that and lives as though that is true?

How then is all the debating and writing these atheists do anything but self-evidently meaningless? And can they not see that all of the debating and writing by those of us who believe our lives do have meaning—and that a God, who is perfect love, created us in his own image and longs for us to exist with him in a state of bliss for eternity—is an effort we understand to be worth making? This alone is the most curious of all questions. To what end precisely did Christopher Hitchens and his fellow atheists rail and rage? It is the ghastly conundrum at the heart of all the atheists say. And they cannot explain their way out of it. So they run away from it via clever rejoinders and sudden shifts to other subjects.

According to his own beliefs, Christopher Hitchens is as nonexistent now as he was before the planets formed. What drove him to bother as he did, to expend himself so mightily, except an internal contradiction that he defiantly refused to acknowledge about what he so histrionically claimed to believe? By his doctrine, putting a bullet in his own head and the heads of anyone he knew to be suffering was by far the more logical way of dealing with the problems of the world. So why didn't he? Is it because there were undeniable things inside him that made him "know" this was wrong, even though he couldn't philosophically support those "knowings," and therefore either assiduously avoided thinking or speaking of them—or else manufactured illogical workarounds, which he assumed those on his own side would support because they didn't see the illogic of them? Did Hitchens refuse to publicly acknowledge these contradictions because he knew that that would end the joy of pretending to fight for something that mattered, that would jerk his fun run to a dead stop at the end of logic's unforgiving and short leash? Why are so many militant atheists unwilling to step back and see the bigger picture, as many agnostics do?

Agnosticism

The reason doctrinaire atheists like Hitchens and Dawkins blurt the word "reason" every twelve syllables may simply be to distract us from the inescapable fact that they are themselves being unreasonable and illogical. They won't acknowledge it, but surely they must know it. After all, one can never logically prove there is nothing beyond the world of matter, but one certainly can say one doesn't know or isn't sure, and is therefore not an atheist, but an agnostic. Agnosticism can be perfectly logical. We can have questions. We can wonder at much of what the Bible says, not understanding it or agreeing with it. But to leap from this to the idea that we can know that there is no God and can say that belief in God and in the Bible is irrational is itself irrational. The only conclusion we can draw from a stance of unyielding atheism is that atheists are so unaccountably tortured by even the possibility that there might be a God that they cannot so much as admit the possibility. And this, of course, is the reason behind their flight from reason and their wild insistence that only they are rational. Because of what we must assume is their anger at God—because that's how it comes across, despite their protestations, or perhaps because of them, and their anger at the loathsome ninnies who believe in God—they must simply insist that he does not exist, even though they must abandon reason to do so. They refuse to be open-minded and genuinely inquisitive, and will belittle and bully their opponents into silence if that is the only way forward in their crusade. And is it not perfectly ironic and curiously fitting that those who denounce people of faith as dogmatic moralists themselves are the fiercest bullies and ideological prigs? Their unwillingness even to tolerate dissent would be almost comical, were it not so genuinely sad, once we leave the heat of the debate and think of their strange and untenable position—and were it not somewhat frightening, too, since we know where such atheist intolerance has often ended, historically speaking.

The Welsh poet Dylan Thomas is a good example of a genuine agnostic. He seemed not to believe there was a God but continually wrestled with all of the evidence that there might be—or even must be. So rather than being insufferably dogmatic, he and his poems come across as genuine and vulnerable and honest. He wrestled with the tension between a world that often seemed bereft of God, and that nonetheless also often seemed somehow, if only obliquely, to point to God. His father was bitterly and vocally atheistic, but his mother was a church-going believer, and Thomas seems in his capacious soul to have had room for elements of both views. The famous villanelle in which he writes of watching his dying father slipping into the darkness of a bleak eternity is probably the best-known of all his poems. "Do not go gentle into that good night," he writes. "Rage, rage against the dying of the light." He seems to say that even if you think you are sliding down, down into nothingness, you ought nonetheless to fight against it all the way with all your might and main. Do not accept it, but "rage" with every last breath and calorie of energy against it. But why?

The only answer must be that Thomas somehow instinctively understood that there was something in our lives that was extraordinarily and inestimably valuable, no matter what evidence there seemed to be to the contrary. He wrote about this contrary evidence too, but in this poem—one of the most touching and famous of the century—he seems to say that there is something of infinite value that we sense is worth fighting for. Our lives could not merely be something temporary to be sloughed off, nor could fatalistically resigning ourselves to the darkness and nothingness be the right way. This instinct on his part toward hope, despite all, was itself a bright blaze on the trail toward meaning and truth, and probably toward God, too. Thomas's was no easy doctrine, and so he brilliantly worked out his struggles on these issues in verse for years, for all the world to see. He could not shrink from the contradictory evidence, but neither was he ever foolish enough to try to build a philosophy out of it—or an anti-religion, either, for somehow he knew that was impossible.

Those like Thomas, for whom faith did not come easily or at all but who dared to face the difficulties of the larger questions, deserve our admiration and gratitude, if only for their honesty. Not everyone has a clear revelation of God and truth sufficient to end their doubts. And so we return to the unhelpful raging against the light itself that we see in Hitchens and his friends. It is simply not logical that any of them could believe what they purport to believe, because to believe it and live out that belief would be a logical absurdity and an impossibility, a snake swallowing its own tail. Any of us who truly wishes to believe that there is no God cannot fully do so. To pretend that we emerged from nothing and go toward nothing is untenable. People who know God exists know that when he created us in his image, he made us long for meaning, and there can be no escaping that, however we wish to try. We may twist away from the truth, but there is a gyroscope in every atom of our being that works against such twisting, that forces us to be righted and to yearn for light and meaning and truth and goodness. And with irony magnificently lost on them, these atheists betray this very fact in the writing of their books and their other advocacy for their position—because as we have said, if there is no God and life is meaningless, why say anything at all? Why bother? Why make the effort to convince anyone of anything if those to whom you are talking are no more than bugs or stones or tumbleweeds?

And yet these atheist authors cannot help themselves. They write and write and try and try to convince others, but according to everything they seem to say in doing so, these very activities are meaningless, are chasing after wind.

CHAPTER TWENTY

Is Atheism Evil?

The New Atheists believe religion is somehow uniquely evil. It seems to them to be the expression in civilization of everything that must be hated. As we have said, this perspective is at least very silly, and more likely a number of far less anodyne things. And once again, the idea that they cannot take the trouble to distinguish between all religions and wish to throw them into the same stew pot only underscores the larger inanity of their fury. It's a strange fact, for example, that they genuinely pretend to be unaware that hospitals and caring for the sick come out of a Christian worldview because Christians invented hospitals. Or that the larger idea that those with wealth and power should care for those who are powerless and poor comes from the Bible. Because of their abysmally bleak world-view in which transcendence and meaning do not exist, atheists have no reason or motivation to care about injustice, and so they often don't. Or if they do, they do so in contradiction of their larger philosophy.

In any event, New Atheists really have accused religion in general of being especially and uniquely evil. This is very difficult to take seriously, especially for anyone with the slightest knowledge of twentieth-century atheist governments. Even more difficult to take seriously is the idea that, having dispensed with God, these men wish to talk of good and evil. Nonetheless, if they do wish to speak of good and evil, we might for a moment aim our spyglass at the proponents of atheism and see what happens when atheism is embraced by those with limitless power over their fellow human beings.

Before 1991, the Oxford mathematician John Lennox traveled innumerable times to the Soviet Union and to Soviet bloc countries. Since the fall of the Soviet Union he has gone back and spoken with those who once believed that communism might be a good thing, who thought that atheism could bring about a better world. "We thought we could get rid of God," they said to him, "and retain a value for human beings. We were wrong. We destroyed both God and man."

Isn't that the story of the twentieth century? Once you get rid of God, you get rid of the idea that human beings have any inherent dignity or worth. It's unavoidable, and what happens in places where those ideas disappeared amounts to perhaps the most monstrous evil in all of human history. Lennox says some of his friends from Poland are amazed that there can be proponents of atheism after its unavoidably gruesome record, but they know that Hitchens and Dawkins built a significant following through their books and speeches. "Dawkins has lost contact with the realities of twentieth-century history," they said. "Let him come here and talk to us, if he is really open to listening to evidence of the link between atheism and atrocity." What happened under atheistic communism is hardly unknown, but the New Atheists seem curiously untroubled by this.

Lennox counters the New Atheists brilliantly in his book *Gunning for God*, as does David Berlinski in his book *The Devil's Delusion*, in which he writes:

> Somewhere in Eastern Europe, an SS officer watched languidly, his machine gun cradled, as an elderly and bearded Hasidic Jew laboriously dug what he knew to be his grave. Standing up straight, he addressed his executioner. "God is

watching what you are doing," he said. And then he was shot
dead.

What Hitler did not believe and what Stalin did not believe,
and what Mao did not believe, and what the SS did not believe,
and what the Gestapo did not believe...and what the commis-
sars, functionaries, swaggering executioners, Nazi doctors,
Communist Party theoreticians, Intellectuals, Brown Shirts,
Blackshirts, Gauleiters, and a thousand party hacks did not
believe was that God was watching what they were doing.

And as far as we can tell, very few of those carrying out
the horrors of the twentieth century worried overmuch that
God was watching what they were doing either. That is, after
all, the meaning of a secular society.[1]

The willful myopia of the New Atheists comes to a sharp point in
Dawkins's claim that atheism cannot lead anyone to violence. Writing
in *Harper's Magazine*, the novelist Marilynne Robinson answers this
manifestly fatuous assertion:

Why would anyone go to war for the sake of an absence of
belief? It is a peculiarity of our language that by war we generally mean a conflict between nations, or at least one in which
both sides are armed. There has been persistent violence against
religion—in the French Revolution, in the Spanish Civil War,
in the Soviet Union, in China. In three of these instances the
extirpation of religion was part of a program to reshape society
by excluding certain forms of thought, by creating an absence
of belief. Neither sanity nor happiness appears to have been
served by the efforts. The kindest conclusion one can draw is

---

[1] David Berlinski, *The Devil's Delusion: Atheism and Its Scientific Pretensions* (New York: Basic
Books, 2008), 26.

that Dawkins has not acquainted himself with the history of modern authoritarianism.[2]

Reviewing Hitchens's book in the *Wall Street Journal*, Peter Berkowitz pointed out that Hitchens was somehow adamantly opposed to making any distinction between "authentic and corrupt and just and unjust religious teachings." Hitchens of course childishly insisted on maintaining his position that all religions are equally wrong and evil, while atheism is of course always right and good, which led Berkowitz to ask "why the twentieth-century embrace of secularism unleashed human depravity of unprecedented proportions."

John Gray, the Professor of European Thought at the London School of Economics, in his book *Black Mass* says:

> The role of the Enlightenment in twentieth-century terror remains a blind spot in Western perception.... Communist regimes were established in pursuit of a utopian ideal whose origins lie in the heart of the Enlightenment.... Pre-modern theocracies used fear to enforce religious orthodoxy, but they did not aim to remodel humanity any more than did traditional tyrannies. Leninism and Nazism aimed to achieve such a transformation.[3]

The German historian Arnold Angenendt, in his internationally praised opus on church history, *Toleranz und Gewalt* (*Tolerance and Violence*), puts it in precise perspective. He says that the Spanish Inquisition (from 1540 into the mid-eighteenth century) executed 827 people, and the Roman Inquisition killed 93. No one facing murder for what they believe or don't believe will be much buoyed by these low numbers, for even a single human being murdered along such lines is one human being too many. Nonetheless, the

---

[2] "Marilynne Robinson's Review of Richard Dawkins' *The God Delusion*," *Harper's Magazine*, October 20, 2006, reposted to MegDoes Blogs, November 8, 2011, http://megdoesblogs.blogspot.com/2011/11/?m=0.

[3] John Gray, *Black Mass: Apocalyptic Religion and the Death of Utopia* (New York: Farrar, Straus and Giroux, 2007), 36–39.

eagerness with which atheists have carried on about the "unparalleled evils" of the historical Church betray the incontrovertible facts of history. Their emotional thunderings against the crimes committed "in the name of religion" are calculated to imply that the numbers murdered "in the name of God" must be limitless.

One wonders whether the atheist apologists are so dramatic in their exaggerations simply because they mean to win an emotional victory and thereby put their opponents on their heels. But facts are facts. So even if the New Atheist apologists ignore them, they exist; and it remains an unendurably horrible fact that dedicatedly atheist regimes in the last century alone tortured and slaughtered multiplied millions, usually for their Jewish or Christian faith. In fact, those executed by the handful of atheist regimes amount to about 150 million. Can anyone begin to fathom such numbers? The disparity between this grimmest of historical realities and the comparatively minuscule numbers of those killed "in God's name" is almost too embarrassing to discuss. So it seems that Hitchens and others have gone out of their way to slap away any mention of the atheistic atrocities—even daring to say that it is that aspect of atheist regimes that alone bears striking resemblance to religion, which itself is an atrocity. It is the sort of diabolical lie to which Stalin aspired, and that can never robustly enough be answered with words.

The special wickedness of atheism in this arena cannot easily be escaped. Again, the historical facts are settled. But whenever it is brought up the Four Horsemen seem with all alacrity to gallop toward the nearest arroyo—there to hide out till the coast is clear. The idea that 150 million human beings were murdered by atheist regimes might be the single most disturbing fact in the history of the human species. And yet, because of the cultural milieu of the West we have somehow been unable to call those guilty of this on the carpet and have handled the devotees of this murderous creed—for such it is—with kid gloves, somehow feeling it would be unseemly to mention these things. But how can we any longer avoid our responsibility in this? We can no longer keep silent.

Perhaps the principal reason we cannot now keep silent is that the devil's head specter of atheistic communism—naively thought gone in 1991—has roared back to power, mostly in China, where the atheistic leaders have sanctioned the torture and murder of Uyghur Muslims with especial impunity, as well as Christians, Buddhists, and numerous others who are unable to toe the atheistic party line. But because of those suffering this moment, it is time we call out whoever would skip gaily past the mass graves. The blood of those murdered in the name of atheistic totalitarianism cries out for justice, and if we cannot at least acknowledge these unavoidable facts, what does that say about us?

We cannot therefore any longer allow militant atheists to accuse Christians—or "the Church"—for every evil under the sun when they cannot honestly address the facts of history. These include the fact that the Crusades were military operations conducted almost exclusively in defense of attacks from the martially inclined Muslims, whom Hitchens throws into the same pile as other "religious" offenders, such as the violent and bloodthirsty Quakers, Shakers, and Millerites. We really must have clarity on these things.

So yes, it is an ironic and nightmarish fact that in the very short time during which atheism was adopted by entire nations, it stands alone in history as guilty of the very things of which the Horsemen accuse the Christian Church. How Hitchens in particular squirmed from under such marmoreally heavy historical realities, like much else in his bag of forensic tricks, is almost humorous in its audacity. Almost. He dared to say that to the extent any atheistic regimes were guilty of such things, they were—are you ready?—behaving in ways remarkably similar to organized religions. In this statement alone he earns his reputation as the hammer-wielding Saint George for whom every problem becomes a fire-breathing religious nail.

More to the point, however, this is a level of sophistry that—even for a man to whom sophistry became a kind of god—cannot seriously be excused by the rest of us. As we say, it is an incontrovertible—and for atheists a damning—fact that murder by militant atheist regimes is a fact of such Himalayan proportions that it tends to block our sight of anything beyond it.

So however such apologists for atheist murders might hope to deflect us, we must press on. The murder's the thing. It is so well documented as to be starkly beyond dispute. There is simply no way to escape this indictment other than to ignore it by shouting anything else as loudly as possible. But if we are interested not merely in facts but in truth, we cannot be distracted. We cannot ignore it. Because these are telling facts, telling of an inhumanity beyond imagining, telling of the sky-scraping evil of a world without God.

Of course numbers like 150 million people are so huge and so abstract that they can be numbing. So let's be more specific. In the year 1937 alone, the dedicatedly atheistic Soviets murdered 106,300 clergymen. They hoped this would help in eradicating the evil of Christian religion. If you ever have been in a stadium capable of holding this many persons you will have some idea of what the most evil regime in the history of the world is capable, and in the space of a single calendar year. And of course this was only the number of clergymen whom the Soviets murdered in that year. It is a level of wickedness that must take the breath of any sensitive human being away but is of course merely a fraction of the far wider evil done in the name of eradicating "religion" by violent means. The Soviets—in the course of their adoption of what they called "scientific atheism"—murdered between twelve and twenty million human beings. Again, the numbers are too much to be borne. Let us say it again: nowhere even among the most egregious examples of religious malfeasance in history do we begin to approach the scale of such atheistic atrocities. It is atheism alone—and especially "scientific atheism," to use the cheerful Soviet parlance—that sought to murder en masse those whom they could not tolerate, and with whom they did not wish to coexist.

While we reel at these horrors, we may well ask: What can account for the disparity between those murdered by atheistic regimes and those murdered by people claiming to murder "in the name of God"? We might consider that those acting in the name of religion at least ostensibly took human life so seriously that they rarely did the worst of what they did in the indiscriminate way that atheists did. Even the most evil actors "in God's name" were somehow restrained. But those acting in the name of "scientific atheism"—or atheism in general—were under no such constraints. For them life really was nothing special, so mistreating or torturing or murdering millions was in no way ideologically different from exterminating vermin. It was simply a practical effort, just as Hitler's murder of millions of Jews was essentially a practical effort. They were too much trouble alive and so, not believing them to be entirely human—or if they were, what of it? Since being human was itself nothing sacred—they should be killed, and killed with as much efficiency as was then possible. Actually, the efficiency of the Nazis in these murders could be praised as extraordinary, were it not for the dizzying evil of what we would find ourselves praising.

It was not, however, merely that outspoken atheists—or less explicit but nonetheless practical atheists like Hitler—felt human life had no particular value. It was also that they feared the mere existence of people of faith, knowing faith and its adherents to be a frustratingly resilient and powerful force against what they claimed was "truth"—even if they believed in no such thing as "truth"—and they feared that unless they wiped it out entirely it would come back to defeat them. And in this they were, of course, quite correct. Thus their brutality against people of sincere faith was especially diabolical. Anyone reading the books of Richard Wurmbrand, for example, such as *Tortured for Christ*, will have some idea of the Tartarean depths to which the atheist state would go in crushing faith in the God of the Bible.

In any event, as we have been saying, any nonsense hailed as evidence against the wickedness of faith cannot hold a candle to the unfathomable abysses of blackest evil perpetrated by those acting against faith. These facts alone are enough to drown out the fiery arguments of Hitchens and his nihilist brethren a thousand times over—which makes us wonder whether their bitter books and acid speeches betray an ignorance of history unequalled among educated persons on their parts, or rather a bottomless cynicism toward their audiences' ignorance of history. Or perhaps they betray some spiritual connection—perhaps felt but of course by definition denied—with the forces whose dark deeds they so assiduously and sinuously strove to avoid mentioning at any and all costs.

Among the cruelest wickednesses perpetrated against persons of faith was their incarceration in mental hospitals by the Soviets. So many books have been written about these evils that one must again marvel at the ability—whether via genuine or willful ignorance, or because they found themselves in some agreement with the perpetrators—of Hitchens, Dawkins, Dennett,

Harris and their less-famous ideological co-travelers in countenancing these exceptional evils. Since they straight-facedly claim to care about human suffering at the hands of ideological actors, you would hope that the crimes done against people of sincere faith by atheists—and in the express cause of enforcing atheism—would be all they would need to change their views. But you would hope in vain. After all, what is hope? Can it be shown to exist by a falsifiable experiment?

One only need skim Aleksandr Solzhenitsyn's *The Gulag Archipelago* to get a taste of what state-powered atheism was capable. But this heroic warrior against Soviet communism who wrote innumerable books detailing the horrors of that ideology did not begin life as any kind of anti-communist. On the contrary, he was himself pro-Soviet and was twice decorated for his actions against the Nazis while serving in the Soviet army. But in a letter to a friend just before the war's end this military hero cracked a joke or two and referred to Stalin as "the man with the mustache." For this mildest epistolary japery he was arrested and swept off to the unimaginable horrors of the Soviet work camps, where for the first time in his life he saw the reality of the regime and ideology for which he had so bravely fought. In time his views changed, as we might well have guessed. As I first learned in reading Charles Colson's spectacular book *Loving God*, Solzhenitsyn eventually returned to the Christian faith of his early youth and spent the rest of his life chronicling the evils of the Soviet atheist regime.

We must return again to the 1966 *Time* magazine cover article from which this book borrows its antithetical thesis. It becomes obvious only in retrospect how willfully naive or ignorant the Western cultural elites were to the systematic torture and murder of anyone daring to question the Soviet doctrine of atheism. Because if they were not naive and ignorant to these things, how could they so blithely and thoughtlessly have asked the question "Is God Dead?"? As the Germans had done during their National Socialist phase—and as all totalitarian societies do, along with China and North Korea in our own day—the Soviets used propaganda to such effect as must at least be embarrassing to those in the West who ever accepted it. Of course, "propaganda" is a fancy word for "systematic state-sponsored lying," which is done by these regimes without embarrassment because those who live in a world without God have moved beyond such bourgeois ideas as good and evil, or lies and truth.

In a world without God—including in the atheist utopias envisioned by Dawkins and Hitchens—such ineffable notions as truth are out of bounds, or at best are seen as the decadent luxuries of deluded persons. Truth cannot be measured with calipers, nor weighed nor photographed. Why pretend it is anything other than a phantasm?

The Soviet leader Joseph Stalin, a dedicated atheist materialist if ever there was one, expressed this general idea when at the Tehran conference with Winston Churchill and Franklin D. Roosevelt he said: "How many divisions does the Pope have?" For this cruelest of world leaders, only military might—which is to say power—is what matters. And moral considerations—such as might be suggested by the Pope in any postwar agreements, which occasioned his question—were by no means anything to be reckoned with. In fact the famous phrase attributed to Stalin is most likely apocryphal, having been simplified from what he actually said when he was informed that the Pope might be present and might have some voice in the postwar agreements between the Soviets, Americans, and British. To this he said: "And how many divisions will the Pope have contributed to victory [over the Germans]?" In either case, Stalin was expressing the atheist idea that the only thing that counts is power.

Pontius Pilate understood this too, and in some generous interpretations of the question "What is truth?" he can at least be seen to have been wondering about it, and possibly asking Jesus at least somewhat seriously for an answer, as though there were still some part of him interested in the subject. But the Soviet monster called "Uncle Joe" was far past such sensitivity and was interested only in pushing the annoying idea of "morality" out of his negotiations.

CHAPTER TWENTY-ONE

Atheists Who Found God: Sartre, Flew, and Camus

Atheism is a long, hard, cruel business.

—Jean-Paul Sartre

There have been many great thinkers and artists for whom a world without God is no happy thing, but rather is simply what they have come to think is likely true, however unpleasant. In other words, they are far too thoughtful to leap for joy like the New Atheists, to whom a godless world seems nothing more than a golden ticket to an amusement park of guilt-free pleasures. Thomas and others seem to be haunted by the greater sadness of the idea, and seem genuinely to long for meaning, but having found none, soldier on in the midst of the bleakness, continuing to look for signs that perhaps they are mistaken.

The great filmmaker Ingmar Bergman was like this. Anyone who has seen his masterpiece, *The Seventh Seal*, knows that it depicts the prospect of a world devoid of God as terrifying. Bergman's questions about God are especially profound in this film, which is set in the Middle Ages during an episode of the Black Death, so that it has a foreboding and apocalyptic feel. Flagellants wander through the streets, hoping to purge themselves of whatever it is that has afflicted everyone, and in one scene an unbalanced young woman accused of witchcraft is taken to her execution at the stake. The film's principal figure is Antonius Block, a knight returned from the

Crusades played by Max von Sydow. The knight is looking for meaning and longs to hear from God. The film's title refers to the passage from the Book of Revelation, which is mentioned at the film's beginning and end: "When He opened the seventh seal, there was silence in heaven for about half an hour."[1] The theme of God's silence is at the center of the film, and the knight encounters various figures, none of whom give him the answers he is looking for. He is also engaged in a chess match with Death, a grim white-faced figure who shadows him throughout the film.

But at one point Block stumbles across a young family and their infant, who treat him to a picnic of wild strawberries and milk. For the knight, this family and this time with them is a powerful antidote to the otherwise howling emptiness of the universe around him. Clearly Bergman too sees in this inno-cent trio something powerful, a clue that there is goodness in the universe, that we are not alone. The knight says as much when he thanks the couple for their kindness to him. "I'll carry this memory between my hands," he tells them, "as if it were a bowl filled to the brim with fresh milk. And it will be an adequate sign—it will be enough for me." Although Bergman has a reputation as someone for whom God is silent, he doesn't give the impression that this is satisfying or preferable to a God whom we know is there. Like Dylan Thomas he seems to believe that God must be there and that there must be goodness in the world, as evidenced by this sweet family.

Although principally known as a comedian, the filmmaker Woody Allen falls into a similar category. He has often spoken of his deep admiration for Bergman and has obviously been influenced by Bergman's work. In numerous interviews he has made perfectly plain that he is an atheist, and that like the French existentialists he realizes this means that life is absurd; but he is mani-festly unhappy about this and says as much. Unlike the New Atheists, he and Bergman recognize the sorrow of a world without God or meaning, and one gets the idea that he thinks those tickled at the idea of such a world as foolish as those who are sure there is a God. Allen doesn't know how to deal with what he feels is the truth of the matter except forgetting about it as best he can in staying busy, or occasionally by dealing with it directly in his art. His 1987 film

---

[1] Revelation 8:1.

Crimes and Misdemeanors more than any other directly addresses the big questions concerning whether there is a God who watches us. Anyone who sees that film can never think of Allen as being among those who hopes there is no God.

In this chapter we will look briefly at three atheist philosophers who—like Thomas, Bergman, and Allen—looked deeply enough at the implications of a world without God to become displeased with it, and who eventually found themselves moving toward the other side of the question. These three philosophers were among the most famous atheists of their time, but each in his own way as a result of probing the question seems eventually to have found his way to genuine belief.[2]

As with much in this book, these stories can be researched and the facts confirmed, but except for the story of Antony Flew, very few have heard them. News of Albert Camus's pilgrimage doesn't seem to have been made public until forty years after his death.

Jean-Paul Sartre

Certainly one of the most famous atheists of the twentieth century—and probably the best-known philosopher—was the existentialist Jean-Paul Sartre. Sartre's best-known books are *Nausea* and *Being and Nothingness*. In the play "No Exit," he famously wrote, "*L'enfer c'est les autres*," which is usually translated as, "Hell is other people." He was a rigorous intellectual who saw through much of modern bourgeois life and condemned the majority of people for living thoughtlessly, for conforming to a way of life that contradicted itself and which he called living

---

[2] A fourth atheist philosopher, Alasdair MacIntyre, bears mention in this grouping too. The *Encyclopedia Britannica* regards MacIntyre as "one of the great moral thinkers of the late 20th and early 21st centuries." Indeed, his 1981 book *After Virtue* is generally considered one of the most important books of moral philosophy of the twentieth century. Early in his career MacIntyre was a committed Marxist and in the 1950s was a member of the Communist Party of Great Britain, and an atheist. But while in his fifties he found himself trying to convince his students that Thomas Aquinas's philosophy—called Thomism—was wrong, but by the end of this process he had himself wended his way to Christianity, to which he converted. He had come to see that the Enlightenment project that attempted to get to morality via pure reason was destined to fail.

Jean-Paul Sartre

in "Bad Faith" (*mauvaise foi*). But what did it mean to live "authentically"? That is what he meant to understand, and it wasn't at all easy, nor did he claim it to be, and he is known to have assuaged his own *weltschmerz* with alcohol and an endless cavalcade of women.

Sartre had an "open" relationship with his fellow existentialist Simone de Beauvoir, whom he met in 1929 and who is most famous for her feminist manifesto, *The Second Sex*. According to the writer Louis Menand, the attraction toward Sartre was not purely physical. Menand unkindly described Sartre as "about five feet tall... he dressed in oversized clothes, with no sense of fashion; his skin and teeth suggested an indifference to hygiene. He had the kind of aggressive male ugliness that can be charismatic...." Sartre and de Beauvoir continued their curious relationship for decades, during which they unsurprisingly slept with innumerable others. Menand says that words "constituted [Sartre's] principal means of seduction: his physical approaches were on the order of groping in restaurants and grabbing kisses in taxis." Together Sartre and de Beauvoir vigorously challenged the norms of bourgeois French society, as though sleeping around were an act of exceptional moral courage.

Both predictably became devoted Marxists, and for a time Sartre was a great defender of Stalin, even after the chilling horrors of the Gulag became known. In the 1960s, Sartre traveled to Cuba to admire Fidel Castro and Che Guevara, the latter of whom he fatuously described as "the most complete human being of our age" and "the era's perfect man." The historian Philip Johnson accused Sartre's works of leading to and inspiring the murderous regime of Pol Pot's Khmer Rouge, a claim that is unfortunately difficult to discount, and impossibly unpleasant to contemplate. But yes, ideas have consequences, and for intellectual titans like Sartre those consequences are often for *les autres* one will never meet.

Sartre took many other radical positions, including in 1964 publishing his autobiography, *The Words*, in which he condemned all literature as simply another bourgeois way of avoiding reality. When that very same year he was—rather awkwardly, one imagines—chosen as the winner of the Nobel Prize in Literature, his embarrassment was pronounced. Of course Sartre pointedly declined to accept the honor, setting the table for Marlon Brando and others to see such awards as opportunities to punish the public with their political views. In 1977 Sartre and de Beauvoir joined other French intellectuals such as Paul-Michel Foucault, Jacques Derrida, Roland Barthes, and Alain Robbe-Grillet in signing an open letter calling for the ending of "Age of Consent Laws," arguing for the "right of twelve-year-olds to have sexual relations with anyone they chose," doubtless giving such as Roman Polanski the idea that in time everyone would see the light and reject the antique taboo against child rape.

And yet there were hints throughout Sartre's life that perhaps he was not quite convinced of what he publicly claimed. Sartre seemed to be too thoughtful and searching to glibly accept atheism as an unbridled good. In an interview with *Il Politecnico* in 1946, he said that atheism was the idea "that man is the creator, and that he's abandoned and alone in the world." He went on to say that this belief was "not a happy optimism, but in its deepest sense, is a desperation."

In *Le Monde* in 1949 his fellow atheist philosopher Albert Camus said that in Sartre there was a great deal of "atavistic antagonism towards god." According to Camus, "Sartre's excessively rabid stand against god is an ontological proof of his deep-down faith in some creator. The man (Sartre) is a closet believer who'll die not as an atheist but as a believer." It was a shocking thing to say at the time, but in time would prove to be shockingly prescient.

It was not only his friend Camus who believed Sartre was somehow haunted by the idea of God. The philosopher and Greek Orthodox theologian Christos Yannaras also thought that Sartre was not the atheist he claimed to be and proclaimed him "the most important theologian of the West's philosophical tradition." Sartre's essential failure to develop a morality apart from God eventually led to despair and anguish. His was a rigorous atheism, so that he felt the burden of a life without God. In his autobiography, he put it bluntly: "Atheism is a long, hard, cruel business."

Sartre continued to try to work out a philosophical system that made sense of the human condition in a world without God, and in 1974 hired a young man named Benny Lévy as his private secretary. But Lévy was an Egyptian Maoist who during those six years with Sartre began to explore his own Judaism, and it seems clear that in their conversations Sartre's thinking about God was reawakened, causing him to rethink many of his earlier views.

In 1980, the last year of Sartre's life, Lévy conducted an interview with him, about which Father Stephen Wang—a Catholic priest and philosophy professor in England—has written:

> In these final philosophical reflections Sartre seems to repudiate much of his life's work and embrace ideas such as the need for an objective morality, the transcendent end of the human person, and a quasi-messianic notion of how society can find perfection. When pressed, he insisted that these conversations did indeed express his opinions, and that they were not foisted upon him by Lévy.[3]

If this wasn't clear enough, Sartre summed it up by saying: "I don't feel I am the product of Chance, a speck of dust in the universe, but someone who was expected, prepared, prefigured. In short, a being that could be here thanks only to a Creator. And this idea about a creator is referring to God."[4] Can we imagine that Jean-Paul Sartre said such things?

---

[3] Father Stephen Wang, "Sartre's Faith," Bridges and Tangents, February 21, 2010, https://bridgesandtangents.wordpress.com/2010/02/21/sartres-faith.

[4] Ibid.

Of course his many friends and devotees were outraged at this news. It seems especially to have set Ms. de Beauvoir's teeth on edge, and she wrote bitterly about what she considered Sartre's personal betrayal of her and all who had followed his work, saying he had fallen "into superstition."

Sartre spent his whole life trying to philosophically work out how it was possible to go on in a world without God. He had never established that there was no God, nor claimed to—which is something no one can do anyway, despite claims to the contrary. But at the end of his life he seemed to have come to the end of his search and was able to accept what he previously could not. But why?

This is of course one of the things about so-called deathbed conversions. As much as they are often discounted as fearful and desperate leapings toward some chimera, they are often the opposite. Dr. Samuel Johnson famously said: "When a man knows he is to be hanged in a fortnight, it concentrates his mind wonderfully." The conversion of someone close to death is often evidence that they at last had the ability to think clearly, with none of the distractions of life, such as having to face friends who disagree with you or having to give up some of the things you fear turning to God might mean giving up.

When one is thinking less of one's position in society and more about what is increasingly unavoidable, one has less to lose in facing some things. It doesn't take the great courage it might have when one was in the swim of adulation for dancing with the Spirit of the Age. One can finally be free to see things as they appear to be. So it was with Sartre, who at the end of his life understood that it was not possible to believe in any kind of morality without God, nor could he any longer believe his existence was the product of blind, random forces.

Nonetheless, de Beauvoir was unable to accept this news and seems to have been personally offended, saying: "How could I explain this senile act of a turncoat?" But there was more to be scandalized about. On Father Wang's blog, a certain M. A. Dean claimed that at the time of Sartre's death, when Wang was a student at Notre Dame, the writer and theologian Father John S. Dunne personally told M. A. Dean that a priest friend of Dunne's "had been called to Sartre's deathbed, where the noted atheist confessed his sins and came into the Church."

Albert Camus

Henri Cartier-Bresson / Magnum Photos

Albert Camus, 1947

The oldest American institution in all of Europe is the American Church in Paris, which stands on the Quai d'Orsay. Howard Mumma, a forty-something Yale-educated minister, had landed the plum position of guest preacher there for several summers in the late 1950s. For the first month of Sundays, though, Mumma had no idea that Albert Camus was in his congregation.

Like Jean-Paul Sartre, Camus was a French existentialist, though he always rejected the term, preferring to style himself as an advocate of "Absurdism"—the idea that life is meaningless. But he believed that there was no excuse for nihilism and tried to find a way forward in a universe bereft of God and meaning. Camus's most famous works are *The Myth of Sisyphus* and *The Stranger*, and he was so celebrated during his short life that he won the Nobel Prize at the age of forty-four in 1957.

For Camus, the central issue of existentialism was what to do about it. And of course the most fundamental question—given what he saw as the utter meaninglessness of life—was whether to commit suicide. To be or not to be. Camus viewed suicide as arising naturally as a possible solution to the absurdity of life. Unlike the cocksure New Atheists, Camus did not shy away from the ramifications and implications of what he had come to believe.

While Sartre was unconscionably pro-communist, Camus despised the Soviets for their cruelty and totalitarianism and fought bravely in the

French resistance during Germany's occupation. Like Sartre, he was dedicated to working out a morality—or the possibility of it—in a world without God and meaning. "Is it possible," Camus wondered, "for humans to act in an ethical and meaningful manner, in a silent universe?" But like Sartre, his intellectual chin-pulling on these grave issues did not prevent him from being a notorious womanizer, and his marriage suffered.

Howard Mumma recalls his own arrival in the vast and well-appointed Paris church that first summer in the mid-1950s. There was a huge crowd, so he was naturally surprised and excited, but soon realized it was the organist they had come to see. Marcel Dupré was a renowned virtuoso of the instrument and would be there three more Sundays. On the fifth Sunday the size of the crowd diminished dramatically, and when the service was over Mumma walked to the church steps to greet the parishioners, as was his habit. This time he observed a group of them surrounding someone, to whom they were extending their bulletins for autographs. It was Albert Camus.

Camus introduced himself to Mumma, confessing that he had come the first four Sundays only to hear Dupré but today he was there for Mumma's sermon, and asked whether they might have lunch the next day. He told Mumma he had come to church "because I am searching for something I do not have, something I cannot even define."

In his book *Albert Camus and the Minister*, Mumma details how over the course of many meals and conversations, Camus made it clear he was not happy believing there was no God and that the universe had no meaning. It seemed utterly unacceptable:

> Something is dreadfully wrong. I am a disillusioned and exhausted man. I have lost faith, lost hope, ever since the rise of Hitler. Is it any wonder that at my age, I am looking for something to believe in? To lose one's life is only a little thing. But, to lose the meaning of life, to see our reasoning disappear, is unbearable. It is impossible to live a life without meaning.[5]

---

[5] Howard E. Mumma, *Albert Camus and the Minister* (Brewster, Massachusetts: Paraclete, 2000), 14.

In contrast to the New Atheists, Camus saw what it meant if the world were devoid of God and meaning, and he was hoping to be wrong.

In another conversation he told Mumma of his friendship with the French philosopher and mystic Simone Weil, whom he met in 1939, and how her own faith journey from atheism had influenced him. "I wish I could find whatever it was that moved her thinking," Camus said. He went on to say that his well-known belief in a meaningless universe was no longer certain, in part because of his friendship with Weil. He confided in his friend:

> I have made a great deal of money because I have been some-
> how able to articulate man's disillusionment...I have written
> things that have meant a great deal to many people.... I
> touched something in them because they identified in my writ-
> ings the anguish and despair that they all felt. I spoke to the
> meaninglessness and uncertainty, the basic tenets of which I
> am uncertain I still believe.[6]

Camus felt a responsibility to these readers and fans. He could no longer stand behind what he had written, but he did not know exactly what to say or to believe either. He was clearly on a serious search.

When Mumma learned that the only Bible Camus owned was a Latin Vulgate, which he had been given as a child by his mother and the parish priest, Mumma made a point of tracking down a Bible in French and gave it to him. Camus leapt in and began reading the Pentateuch, which they discussed.

At the end of the summer, just before Mumma was to return to the United States, Camus said: "I am not a sentimental man, but I want you to know that your sermons and our all too few conversations have meant a great deal to me."

Mumma did not return to Paris and the American Church for a few years, but he and Camus immediately resumed their friendship, dining together and always talking about God. Toward the end of that summer

---

[6] Ibid., 47.

of 1959, Camus suddenly asked whether Mumma performed baptisms. It seems obvious Camus knew his friend would soon be leaving again and wanted to make some kind of commitment. "The reason I have been coming to church is because I am seeking...." he said.

> I'm almost on a pilgrimage—seeking something to fill the void that I am experiencing, and no one else knows. Certainly the public, and the readers of my novels, while they see that void, are not finding the answers in what they are reading. But deep down, you are right. I am searching for something that the world is not giving me....
>
> Since I have been coming to church, I have been thinking a great deal about the idea of a transcendent, something that is other than this world. It is something that you do not hear much about today, but I am finding it. I am hearing about it here, in Paris, within the walls of the American Church.[7]

At some point Mumma learned that Camus had not stopped reading the Bible. Far from it, he said he had read the Old Testament at least three times and had been making notes.

> Since I have been reading the Bible I sense that there is something—I don't know if it is personal or if it is a great idea or powerful influence—but there is something that can bring meaning to my life. I certainly don't have it, but it is there. On Sunday mornings I hear that the answer is God.... You have made it very clear to me on Sunday mornings, Howard, that we are not the only ones in this world. There is something that is invisible. We may not hear the voice, but there is some way in which we can come aware that we are not the only ones in the world and that there is help for all of us.[8]

---

[7] Ibid., 86–87.

[8] Ibid., 87.

As the conversation continued, Camus said he identified strongly with Nicodemus, the Jewish religious leader who came secretly to speak to Jesus at night. Camus said that like Nicodemus he was confused about Christianity and what it meant to be "born again." So Mumma asked him what Jesus's reply to Nicodemus was, and Camus remembered it all, repeating it with enthusiasm.

As a pastor, Howard Mumma could see that his friend was getting serious about all this, so he spoke about what it means to be born again. "It is to wipe the slate clean," Mumma said, "to receive forgiveness. It is to receive forgiveness because you have asked God to forgive you of all past sins, so that the guilt, the concerns, the worries, and the mistakes that we have made in the past are forgiven and the slate is truly wiped clean...."

Mumma went on some more, and then he told Camus: "You are seeking the presence of God himself." Mumma remembers he was himself nervous at that moment. He writes: "Albert looked me squarely in the eye and with tears in his eyes, said, 'Howard, I am ready. I want this. This is what I want to commit my life to.'"

At that point Mumma might easily have led Camus in what is often called "the Sinner's Prayer." But being a rather high-church Methodist, he didn't think along such lines. Instead, the conversation devolved to baptism and whether it was necessary for Camus to be baptized, since he already had been baptized as a child. Mumma thought that first baptism would suffice. But Camus said that hadn't meant anything. Now he understood what was at stake, and he wanted to be baptized. Mumma then began pressing him on whether he was willing to make a public confession of his faith and to join a church. But Camus didn't want to join a church or denomination. He didn't want to attract attention in that way and at that time. He wanted to be baptized by Mumma, but for some reason Mumma demurred, wondering if perhaps Camus was really ready to take such a step. So nothing happened. Camus wished to drive his friend to the airport when it was time to leave, but a special goodbye luncheon at the church had been prepared, and Camus met him at the airport to say goodbye. "My friend, *mon cheri*," Camus said to him, "thank you. I am going to keep striving for the faith."

As it happened, Camus would never be baptized nor have the time to write about what had transpired in his heart and mind, because only a few months later—on January 4, 1960—he was riding in the passenger seat of his publisher's Facel Vega sportscar, speeding toward Paris. Camus had been in his country home in Provence and had sent his two children and his wife of twenty years ahead on the train two days earlier. Though no one knows exactly how, on a long and wide stretch of road the car veered into a plane tree. He was killed instantly, at the age of forty-six.

Perhaps because of his intense privacy regarding such matters, the obituaries written about him did not reflect the journey he had been on to find God. And Mumma did not write of any of it until 2000, when he was himself ninety-two. So until now, most of the world has never heard that one of the world's most public atheists had eventually found his atheism unsatisfactory and had turned toward God.

Antony Flew

Antony Flew was one of the foremost atheists of the twentieth century. He declared himself an atheist at fifteen and went on to a brilliant career in philosophy. While at Oxford in the academic year 1949–50, Flew often attended C. S. Lewis's Socratic Club, and although he thought Lewis "eminently reasonable," was nonetheless unconvinced by his arguments for God. In fact, it was in 1950 that he wrote an essay titled "Theology and Falsification," which ended up becoming the most widely reprinted philosophical publication of the previous fifty years. In 1976, he wrote another landmark work titled *The Presumption of Atheism*. Though often regarded as the leading academic atheist of his time, Flew was never as bitterly polemical as the so-called "New Atheists" who followed him.

Antony Flew

"My whole life," he said, "has been guided by the principle of Plato's *Socrates*: Follow the evidence, wherever it leads."[9] But where it eventually led him, to the shock of many of his followers, was to seriously question atheism and then flatly reject it. It was in 2004 that the most famous academic atheist of the century declared that he had come to believe in God. More specifically, he believed in an intelligent Creator of the universe and was now a Deist. The bitter howls of those feeling betrayed by the atheist genius they had followed were not long in coming. That December he wrote: "I have been denounced by my fellow unbelievers for stupidity, betrayal, senility and everything you can think of and none of them have read a word that I have ever written."[10]

The summer following this I found myself at a C. S. Lewis conference in Oxford, England, where in a forum at St. Aldates Church—just across the street from the famous Christ Church Meadow—I got to meet Flew and hear him talk about his conversion. He recounted his repulsion at the idea of a vengeful God who would cast people into eternal tortures and made clear he could not believe in that God, but affirmed his belief in an intelligent Creator— in "the Aristotelian God," as he put it. For him the facts were clear as a bell, and there was no going back. The advances in science over the previous decades—specifically the arguments for the fine-tuned universe—had rendered atheism logically untenable. The attacks continued, but Flew had been around this block and was not about to take them lying down. When Simon Fraser University's Raymond Bradley published his criticisms of Flew's position in George Soros's *Open Society* journal, Flew wrote a letter to the journal calling the piece "extraordinarily offensive" and put Bradley in the category of "a secularist bigot."

Flew was so convinced of the scientific arguments for design that he even took the step in 2006 of signing his name to a letter advising the British government to be willing to include "Intelligent Design" in school curricula. The following year in an interview with the Christian ethicist Benjamin Wiker,

---

[9] Edward Feser, *The Last Superstition: A Refutation of the New Atheism* (South Bend, Indiana: St. Augustine's Press, 2008), 2–3.

[10] Ibid., 2.

Flew spoke of his "growing empathy with the insight of Einstein and other noted scientists that there had to be an Intelligence behind the integrated complexity of the physical Universe."

In 2007, to make his new stance and arguments unmistakably—almost cheekily—clear, he wrote a book titled *There Is a God*, once more explaining that the new scientific evidence showed there was insufficient time for life to come into being from non-life, as he and so many had believed. Others who had achieved top distinction in the academic world, and who had come to Flew's conclusion decades earlier, knew from personal experience that his book would provoke rage. Dr. Francis Collins, called it "[t]owering and courageous... Flew's colleagues in the church of fundamentalist atheism will be scandalized." Nicholas Wolterstorff, Yale's Noah Porter Professor Emeritus of Philosophical Theology and a Christian, called the book "fascinating" and said it would "come as a most uncomfortable jolt to those who were once his fellow atheists." And Dr. Ian H. Hutchinson, the head of MIT's Department of Nuclear Science and Engineering, said the book would "incense atheists who suppose (erroneously) that science proves there is no God." But Flew didn't care whether his new thinking might upset some people, saying "that's too bad" and again directing them to "follow the evidence," as Socrates had suggested.

"The philosophical question," he said, "that has not been answered in origin-of-life studies, is this: How can a universe of mindless matter produce beings with intrinsic ends, self-replication capabilities, and 'coded chemistry'? Here we are not dealing with biology, but an entirely different category of problem."[11] Flew stands alone in his passage from being one of the most celebrated advocates of atheism to coming to believe in God, daring to say so, and explaining himself publicly.

Because Flew came to faith in God a few years before his death in 2010, and wrote of it, news of his conversion received the attention it deserved. But Camus's and Sartre's conversions were almost entirely unreported. Nonetheless, now we know the whole truth: that these three most famous and most

---

[11] Michael Ebifegha, *The Darwinian Delusion: The Scientific Myth of Evolutionism* (Bloomington, Indiana: AuthorHouse Publishing, 2009), 255.

thoughtful philosophers of the twentieth century all found their way beyond atheism and even beyond agnosticism, all the way to God himself.

CHAPTER TWENTY-TWO

Problems with Atheism: Faith and Science Are BFFs

Anyone who ever got near the writings or perorations of the New Atheists has heard over and over that science and faith are sworn enemies. This is untrue. In fact it is as untrue as any falsehood could be, since the truth of the matter is quite the opposite, as we shall see. But the idea has been in our culture at least since the Scopes Trial in the 1920s, and the New Atheists and their acolytes have shouted it like a marketing slogan, which in some ways it has been. Some of them must have known they were cynically exploiting the general cultural ignorance on this subject. But they also gave the impression of being afraid that if they stopped beating the drum of this idea for a moment some innocent child along the parade route might pipe up that it was a lie and expose the idea for the fig leaf apron that it was. So they haven't.

Since they are not advancing this canard within earshot at present, we should review the facts of the matter and see how badly many of us have been taken in on this subject. To this end, there are four basic points:

The first is that the false idea that faith and science are incompatible stems from a fundamental misunderstanding of both faith and science, both of which need to be properly defined and understood. The second is that the well-known story of Copernicus and Galileo as scientists at war with the Church is false. The third is that many of the greatest scientists in history were deeply committed to the Christian faith, and not only saw their faith as compatible with science, but as inextricably intertwined with it. And fourth—and surely the most distressing to materialist atheists—is the almost unknown fact that science as we today know it arose precisely because of Christian faith—not in spite of it. To those of us raised on the mother's milk of this misunderstanding, this will be difficult to believe, but it is nonetheless perfectly true and must be understood. A corollary to this fourth point is the idea that it is actually atheism—not faith—that is inherently incompatible with science.

Misunderstandings about Faith and Science

To understand why faith and science are not at all incompatible, we must clarify what faith is and what science is. For example, many people mistakenly believe that "faith" means believing in things that are not actually true. They seem to think that faith exists on another plane from all else, and that we can believe things "by faith" that are not rational. This is completely false, but it is another false idea that the New Atheists have exploited. Of course there are many beliefs—including religious beliefs—that are simply wrong, and thinking people are simply obliged to separate them from those that are true. But the New Atheists stubbornly refuse to do this and absurdly lump all religious beliefs together, refusing to look at the facts. Ironically, this puts them in the same category as the enemies of Galileo who refused to look through his telescope, fearing the facts might change their hide-bound opinions. So of course any educated person of faith knows there are elements of any faith that are challenging to believe, but no thinking person would say it doesn't matter whether those things are true. Truth inescapably matters. Some religious beliefs—like the resurrection of Jesus from the dead—are difficult to believe, but no one who is a Christian could say it doesn't matter if it actually happened. But there are other religious beliefs that are difficult to believe because they are actually not true, so we should not believe them.

For example, the New York–based writer Julia Day gives us the following summation of a Norse creation story, which few would think compatible with the scientific and historical accounts of things. No one reading it today could say they believe it.

> There was nothing in the beginning. Not sand, sea, heaven, or earth. But then there was Niflheim—the Mist Home. From the Mist Home came twelve rivers. When the rivers spread north they froze, and everything was ice. From the ice came Ymir, the first frost-giant. Ymir was not a god, and eventually he turned evil.
>
> A cow formed from the ice that created Ymir, and from her teats came enough milk to feed four rivers. Ymir fed on the rivers, and the cow fed on the salt in the ice, and after she licked the ice for three days straight a man named Buri emerged. Buri had a son named Bor, and Bor had three sons. One of his sons was Odin, the most powerful god of all.
>
> Evil Ymir and the three sons of Bor had a showdown, but eventually Odin and his brothers prevailed. Ymir's blood became the sea, which drowned all but one of the frost-giants. Bor's sons dragged Ymir's corpse into the middle of Ginnungagap. His bones became the rocks, his hair became the trees, his skull became the sky, and his brain became the clouds.
>
> Then, Bor's sons turned two logs into a man and a woman, and the man and woman created two children so beautiful that the gods became jealous. They pulled the boy, Moon, and the girl, Sol, up into the sky and enslaved them forever. Sol will forever drive the chariot that carries the sun, and Moon the chariot which carries the moon.[1]

The idea that the New Atheists would throw a story like this in the same category as the entire Bible—which is a vast library of historical chronicles,

---

[1] Julia Day, "4 Beautiful, Bizarre, and Disturbing Earth Origin Stories," All That's Interesting, August 31, 2014, https://allthatsinteresting.com/origin-stories.

parables, narratives, poetry, and pastoral letters, among other things—is both silly and lazy. If atheists are going to cast stones at religion, they should specify which religion and should say which aspects of that particular religion are at issue. If that is too difficult, we may save ourselves the trouble of taking them seriously. Faith should never mean believing in things that are not *actually* true.

As we mentioned, Christians unequivocally believe that Jesus rose from the dead, but they also understand that the resurrection of a human being from bodily death is neither easily understood nor believed. They know that if it happened, it is a miracle. Like the Big Bang, it defies everything we know from science, but there is too much evidence for us to ignore it. Whether it happened matters. If it didn't happen, the entire Christian faith falls apart. Christians cannot simply wave away the issue, or fudge it by saying yes, but it only happened "in the spiritual realm"—or that it happened "metaphorically" or that Jesus "rose in the hearts of his disciples." Any serious Christian knows facts matter, and the fact of the resurrection matters most of all. So whatever miracles we say happened must actually have happened, or we must reject both them and the faith that insists upon them.

If someone said their faith teaches that a giant frog is holding up the earth, we cannot say, "That's fine for you to believe. That's your faith." We must understand that anything that is not true for everyone is not truth at all. Some things might be difficult to believe but are still true. The idea that the universe began in an explosion nearly fourteen billion years ago is one of them. Other things might be difficult to believe and are completely false, like the idea that the moon is made of green cheese. Other things that are easy to believe might also be false, like the idea that George Washington wore wooden teeth. The only vital question in every case is whether these things are genuinely true. Whether or how we can prove it is a secondary issue. So faith is not some vague way of thinking that can assert things that aren't true.

What Is Faith?

A famous passage in the New Testament says: "Now faith is the substance of things hoped for, the evidence of things not seen" (Hebrews 11:1).

This is likely among the most misunderstood sentences ever written. That's because misguided people have used it to justify the erroneous idea that faith is something that may exist apart from evidence or reason, which we have said is untrue. What the statement does mean is that faith engages with another kind of evidence than we usually expect. That other kind of evidence is not apprehensible with our eyes—or for that matter, is often not something we can take in with our other senses, as we can other things. But all of us rely on that other kind of evidence all the time. We do not only interact with the world through our five senses.

For example, when we think of Homer's Penelope waiting for her husband Odysseus for twenty years, we regard her as a model of faithfulness and as a truly good and praiseworthy person. But why? Is it because despite the lack of evidence that her husband is alive and will return to her, she nonetheless believes that he will? Because she does have evidence. It's just the kind of evidence that is beyond our five senses. Part of the evidence she has is her husband's character before he left for Troy. Her evidence is based on the previous life of the man she knew and lived with and loved, but whom she now cannot see or touch. But it is real nonetheless. Her memory of him—and her faithfulness to that memory—cannot be seen or touched or smelled or tasted or heard. But it is inescapably real. And we praise her for her belief that he will return in a way that we wouldn't praise her if she had received word about him. Her faith in him requires something more, and that faith we see as worthy of our admiration and praise. But it is based on something real, otherwise of course it would be sheer foolishness.

Similarly, we read in the gospels of the disciple Thomas wanting to see the nail prints in Jesus's hands and the wound in his side. We understand this and sympathize with him. Nonetheless Jesus says, "Blessed are those who have not seen and yet have believed" (John 20:29). One might get the impression from this that we are not to ask for proof and not to care about evidence, but that is simply not the case. The fact is that Jesus is implying Thomas should have known without seeing hard physical evidence, because he already had enough evidence to believe without seeing and touching. Jesus often expressed his impatience with his disciples and said things like, "How long have I been with you?" In other words, why don't you get this idea yet? How much more do I need to show you? So faith means "understanding something" and seeing what we "should" see, based on what we have already seen. But it's not based on nothing. It is hard evidence, but of another kind.

So the idea that faith is a "leap in the dark" makes faith sound like it is based on nothing and is foolish. But God does not want us to be foolish. We might better say that faith is a leap into the light. It is a leap in the direction of truth and life and light. It is not an idiotic leap away from rationality and good sense and logic and truth. It is a wise leap that includes all these things but that often goes beyond them to where mere rationality and good sense and logic cannot reach.

In other words, faith is usually a leap away from cynicism. We have all met someone who is bitter and who has been burned by life and is so wounded they vow never to be "taken in" again. So they harden themselves to the point of stepping away from the innocence of children. And in dedicating themselves to never be fooled again they can become fools of another kind. If we insist that the only way we can really know anything is via "science," we limit our scope of knowledge severely. Science cannot tell us what wisdom is or what goodness is, but who would suggest that these things are nothing? No culture in human history would think that, but this is what the New Atheists have said many times.

In fact, the Bible itself says that we see clearly how wrong the New Atheists' assertions are concerning faith and science. Writing in the middle of the first century in a letter to the Christians in Rome, the Apostle Paul said, "For since the creation of the world His invisible *attributes* are clearly seen, being understood by the things that are made, *even* His eternal power and Godhead, so that they are without excuse" (Romans 1:20). In other words, not to be able to see beyond the material world to the Author of that world, or to see how that world expressed his character, is simply willful ignorance. It does not take a genius to make this observation, although Paul certainly was one. King David said virtually the same thing a millennium earlier in the first four verses of Psalm 19:

The heavens declare the glory of God;
And the firmament shows His handiwork.
Day unto day utters speech,
And night unto night reveals knowledge.
There is no speech nor language
Where their voice is not heard.
Their line has gone out through all the earth,
And their words to the end of the world.

Both of these biblical writers are saying that God makes an argument for himself through the material world. The material world is evidence for him and for his character and nature, and we may investigate it to discover more about him and about the world beyond the material too. So the New Atheists' unwillingness to see what genuine faith is mostly is a posture. It simply cannot stand up to reason. Their definition of faith is a false definition.

Faith and Reason

Returning to the miracle of Jesus's resurrection, the Apostle Paul makes exceedingly clear that if it actually did not happen, those of us who profess to be Christians are pitiable. He says that we can and must only believe in what is true. Paul says that he previously told them in Corinth that Jesus "was buried" and "rose again the third day." It must have happened—and happened literally—or everything about Christian faith becomes meaningless. Paul goes on to say that Jesus was seen after his resurrection by Peter and other apostles, and then says that Jesus was "seen by over five hundred" Christians at one time. He also says that most of those who witnessed these things are still living and could therefore presumably be questioned about what they saw. He does not hedge his bets. The scientific term for something like the resurrection is usually called a "singularity": We might know it happened, but we do not know enough to explain it exactly, nor can we recreate it as we would an experiment in a lab. Yet we know what we know. And again, if it turns out that this thing we claim happened ever can be shown not to have happened, we must go with the facts. Paul even writes that if the resurrection did not actually happen, Christians "are of all men the most pitiable."[2] The facts and the truth matter to those most serious about faith.

In another letter written to his young charge Timothy, Paul says, "But reject profane and old wives' fables, and exercise yourself toward godliness."[3] Can it be clearer that this historical figure who wrote much of what we today call the New Testament believed that reality and truth and facts mattered and that any sloppiness was not to be tolerated? And can it be far from the truth that the misrepresentations of the New Atheists on this score are themselves closer to "old wives' fables" than to rational arguments, and that the Four Horsemen and their ideological cavalry have spread their stories with the same inattention to consistency that we find in idle and scurrilous town gossips?

It is not merely the supremely educated theological intellectual Paul who insisted on accuracy and eyewitness accounts and facts. The humble and entirely uneducated fisherman Peter also understood and wrote of this same idea. It is simply foundational to the Christian faith. In the late sixties of the first century—as he faced death for what he believed and taught—Peter wrote: "For we have not followed cunningly devised fables, when we made known unto you the power and coming of our Lord Jesus Christ, but were eyewitnesses of his majesty."[4]

He's probably referring specifically to the event that took place on the Mount of Transfiguration, where he and James and John saw Jesus transfigured and temporarily restored to his full glory, accompanied by Moses and Elijah. The apostles were quite aware of the seeming madness of what they were saying to those who did not believe, and they went out of their way to make it as clear as possible that they understood that eyewitness accounts mattered, so that even facing death, Peter wished to be supremely accurate in what he was saying he had witnessed.

---

[2] 1 Corinthians 15:19.

[3] 1 Timothy 4:7.

[4] 2 Peter 1:16.

The Apostle John—who alone among the twelve apostles was not executed at a young age for maintaining his belief in these things, but who lived to a ripe age, finally being exiled as an old man to the island of Patmos—continued to the end of his life to say that what they believed and had been teaching others was not to be taken "on faith," in the sloppy sense of that term which the New Atheists would use, but rather were things that had been encountered with their five senses. "That," John wrote, "which was from the beginning, which we have heard, which we have seen with our eyes, which we have looked upon, and our hands have handled...."[5] He had been there when Jesus was transfigured on the mountain and had been there when Jesus did his innumerable miracles. He had been there when Jesus was crucified, and he was the first disciple to sprint to the tomb and find it empty, with the grave clothes lying in such a way that they could not have been lying unless the body around which they were so carefully wrapped had miraculously escaped them. He knew most people could never believe him, but what choice did he have except to explain as carefully as he could what he had seen and leave it at that?

And, of course, John and the others had seen the resurrected Jesus innumerable times. They had been with him and had spent years with others who had been with him and spoken with him after his resurrection. Why would these men—and innumerable other men and women—go to their deaths for a preposterous lie? But in case anyone doubted how they understood things, they over and over made the claims that they had themselves seen these things with their own eyes, so that those who knew them to be neither mad nor liars would believe what they were saying.

---

[5] 1 John 1:1.

CHAPTER TWENTY-THREE

The Boundaries of Science: More Than Meets the Eye

Have you commanded the morning
since your days began and caused the dawn
to know its place....
Have you entered the springs of the sea
Or have you walked in search of the depths? ...
Where is the way to the dwelling of light?
And darkness, where is its place....
Has the rain a father?

—Job 38:12, 16, 19, 28

Science is not the only path to knowledge or truth. Yet the New Atheists have made this idea the bedrock foundation of all else, so that they are not merely atheists, but are really also strict materialists. Since they know science is limited to what it can tell us about the material world, they have made the irrational leap to say that the material world is all that exists. This is false and reductive, as though someone were to insist that human beings are only the sum of the chemicals that make up our bodies. Most of us know that we are far more, because we know that goodness and truth and beauty and love are real things, even if they can't be isolated in an experiment with glassware or measured with calipers. So to assert that only the material world is real and that the only reality is material reality is a kind of willful madness. But it seems that because materialist atheists cannot prove that the soul exists via scientific means, they skip past vast fields of logic and claim it has been proved the soul does not exist. It has not. Nor can it be.

Of course limiting reality to the material is arbitrary and illogical. In fact it is perfectly unscientific. It is also silly, as though a baker were to announce that anything that cannot be baked is not food. It's utterly subjective, and like all perfect subjectivity, it is meaningless. Even in the world of science we often reason our way toward a conclusion without physical evidence. This involves using our imaginations and is called hypothesizing or theorizing. If scientists didn't do that, we would never have discovered anything. So on this we must be clear: even if we are only talking about matter and science, we are nonetheless at some point forced to go beyond the strangely strict parameters laid down by materialists. The history of science itself is a history of people using imagination and intuition—of theorizing based on what facts and evidence we have thus far. In doing this we are often obliged to use models we cannot see with our eyes or discover with our four other senses, but which we believe must be there based on previous information.

A Brief History of Matter

Even when we talk about matter itself, we eventually may find ourselves drifting beyond the strictly material and the world of our five senses. For example, scientists have theorized about atoms and molecules for millennia before anyone could see them. The ancient Greeks theorized that matter at its foundation was composed of invisibly tiny individual particles, which they called "atoms"—which simply means "not divisible."[1] It wasn't until the late seventeenth century that the Anglo-Irish chemist Robert Boyle and the French chemist Nicolas Lemery came to the idea of what we call "molecules." They thought of what we call atoms as corpuscles and thought that when these united in geometric patterns they made

---

[1] In fact, the modern Greek word for an individual person is *atomo*.

up what we today call molecules. But obviously they were theorizing and could not begin to see what they actually were talking about. Around 1800 the British chemist John Dalton began theorizing about how atoms link up with other atoms to form molecules. He is credited with inventing what we now call "atomic theory," and he worked with indirect evidence. Just as we see the leaves moving on a tree and infer that the wind has moved them—but never see the actual wind, which is invisible—scientists observe things happening and they speculate on how and why these things are happening, hoping to see patterns and make inferences. Sometimes they theorize correctly and sometimes they don't. It is sometimes years or decades before their theories can be confirmed through actual direct observation.

In 1766 the English scientist Henry Cavendish postulated the existence of what we now call hydrogen. He saw that when it combined with what we now call oxygen it created water. So for the first time in human history water was understood not to be a fundamental element—as the ancients believed— but was rather a compound of two more fundamental substances. Fifteen years later he determined that the ratio between hydrogen and oxygen in water was two to one, although this was not confirmed until 1800 when the German scientist Johann Ritter used electricity—in what we call electrolysis—to separate the two elements. In 1811 the Italian Amedeo Avogadro confirmed Ritter's experiment. Avogadro coined the term "molecule," but first used this word to describe both atoms and molecules, and only later understood that molecules were composed of atoms.

But no human being would see a molecule for two centuries. All the science regarding molecules and atoms was done without seeing. Of course some things were seen and observed, but the molecules themselves could not be. Their existence was inferred, but not observed. No one dared to claim that there was anything unscientific going on. In fact this is the very foundation of all of our modern chemistry, so not only was it not unscientific, it was as scientific as science can hope to be. It was the quintessence of science, and yet it did not include what could be seen, either with naked human eyes or aided by optical lenses. In any event, the theorizing continued, and of course it would not have continued if the fundamental ideas behind the theory at the bottom of it all didn't make sense. But this is the essence of much science over the centuries. So the idea that matter is the only thing in existence is not merely absurd, but unscientific. Although it is true that we may not be able to scientifically prove that anything lives beyond the boundaries of our universe, neither can we say we know there is nothing beyond it. That is simple logic. Science has its limits and must accede to the rules of logic and rationality.

Few scientists dispute that all matter in the universe emerged from nothing nearly fourteen billion years ago, in what we call the Big Bang, even though there was no one there to observe it or record it. Science equally maintains that matter and energy cannot be created or destroyed, which is the First Law of Thermodynamics. So science expects us to accept something (the Big Bang) that violates what is an immutable law of matter. But no real scientist has any difficulty in maintaining this awkward tension, because this is simply the strange pass—or impasse—to which logic and the evidence have taken us. Real scientists do not get tangled in these things and know that our imaginations and minds must do their best with what we have at hand.

As we have said, theorizing brings our imagination and our minds into the picture, and without our minds to fill in what we see—or touch or smell or hear or taste—we would know no more about science than a dog or a cat or a mouse, all of whom have the same five senses we do, but lack brains capable of imagining anything at all, including the past, present, or future.

August Kekulé (1829–1896)

While we are on the subject, we might also say that the concept of time itself is similarly dodgy, for who has ever seen it? Or smelled it or tasted it or touched it or heard it? But science has always trafficked in such things, and proudly so. Therefore, any implication that no one should do so is anti-science, as we have said. Though science cannot tell us what time is—nor, for that matter, what energy is—scientists nonetheless have included both these things in their equations, and to rather impressive effect too. So even if we aren't at all sure what time and energy are quite yet, we can certainly work with them as concepts until we do.

A classic example of a scientist using his imagination to great effect concerns one of the greatest of all molecular theorists, August Kekulé. He often told the story of a dream he had in 1862 while dozing in an armchair by a fire in Ghent, Belgium. In the dream he beheld a dancing string of carbon atoms, like a snake taking its own tail in its mouth and creating a circle. When he awoke he realized that this was what benzene must look like—and as it happened, he was right. The idea of course came to him from someplace other than actual experimentation or conscious cogitation. Materialism can only carry us so far. Of course Kekulé never got to see a carbon atom with his own eyes. In fact, it wasn't until 2009 that any human ever saw any molecule. Would it be right to say that we took their existence on faith until then? Yes and no. Anyone who wants to make these issues of faith and science black and white is actually confusing the issue and making everything gray and sloppy. These things are far too important for muddying semantics.

But a stranger question must be raised when we are talking about molecules and atoms. It seems that even when we have recently claimed to see them, we have not seen them, in the strict definition of *seeing*. That's because in order to see them we have had to use various kinds of "imaging." But it is less like taking a photograph than it is like feeling someone's face with one's eyes closed and describing it. This is because light—which is what we use to see and take photographs—has a wavelength that's much too big to illuminate something as small as an atom or molecule. So in the 1920s scientists came up with what we call "electron microscopes," which shoot beams of electrons at whatever we want to "see." Since the wavelengths of electrons can be one hundred thousand times smaller than the wavelengths of light photons, we can magically "see" atoms and molecules. But if we are "seeing" something without light, are we actually "seeing"?

So yes, in recent decades we have created some "images" of molecules and atoms, but we have never photographed them or seen them with our eyes. Actually, it was only in 2018 that we did come close to seeing an atom. This was when a student at Oxford named David Nadlinger managed to take a photograph of a single atom, which marked the first time that human beings could see one, although even so it is such an exquisitely tiny blue dot that one cannot make out any details. Also, it had to be isolated and flooded with laser light, so that one could argue what one saw was actually only the laser light, and that the atom itself was essentially incidental to the photo. But there it was, if one could use one's imagination, the outrageously tiny thing we have been theorizing about for millennia. In fact it was only five years before this that scientists were able to observe molecules doing what we have known they do for 150 years, which is react chemically such that their structures change. But not seeing them do this never prevented us from intuiting and inferring they were doing these things, and then of course from experimenting to see if our intuitions and inferences were correct.

Science Points beyond Science

We have made this point earlier but must underscore it. A terrible thing happened in the lives of strict materialists in the 1960s when it was proved by the discovery of the background radiation in the universe that the universe had a beginning. Previously, one could still say that the universe had always been here, so there was ample time for absolutely anything to happen. Time is, of course, the friend of someone grasping at straws for how things got to be the way they are. But suddenly there was no more infinity of time. Suddenly there was a starting point. But what strict materialists cringed at even more was the idea that time and energy and matter had been created from nothing. Everyone "knew" that this was not possible. And yet there it was. It was embarrassing.

Two thousand years ago Lucretius declared that nothing could come out of nothing—or rather that the only thing that could come out of nothing was nothing. And as we said, the First Law of Thermodynamics says energy and matter cannot be created or destroyed. Energy can change form and become matter, just as matter may change form and become energy. Einstein explained that in his famous formula $E=mc^2$.

But how could they be created as we now know they had been created 13.8 billion years ago? Out of literally nothing burst black empty space and time and every single atom of matter that ever existed. Science essentially says something like that cannot happen, but that it did. What to do? Here was an embarrassing conundrum that could no longer be denied or hidden away in some attic. It was a mystifying Möbius Strip of logic. It was an Escher drawing at the heart of all reality. Science itself leads us outside of science.

The discovery of the background radiation in 1964 cinched the case for a universe with a distinct beginning, one so distinct that there was no possibility ever of transgressing into the world before that beginning—because it is the kind of a beginning without any "before." It is the boundary where space and time cease to exist in a way that so scrambles the human mind that we must simply walk away to gather ourselves. But this ended the idea that the universe had always existed just as a monstrous iron portcullis decisively ends a horse's ability to enter a castle. There is so much about the Big Bang that was discomfiting to strict materialists and atheists. It meant that science had bumped into an impenetrable wall. That wall was infinitely high and infinitely wide. There was no way around it. In other words, science could take us back to the moment of the Big Bang but could not go past it. To many it must have been utterly infuriating. And not only because it suggested a beginning before which science could not go, but it suggested a state of things that was absolutely untenable from a scientific point of view.

It meant that the closer to the Big Bang we went, the smaller the universe got, and the denser and the hotter. Until you arrived at a point smaller than anything physically imaginable, with infinite density, meaning a universe crushed down to where no electron had room to fly around a nucleus. All the space between things had been sucked out as if by a straw. And what in the world is infinite density? Can we imagine it? We cannot. But that's what science had led us to. And it would have had to be infinitely hot too, whatever that can mean. We are of course entirely beyond meaning with such things. We have arrived at a place where any real scientist understands that it is his duty to bow and depart from the room. Science has led us to the end of science. It has led us to the limit of science, to the place where scientists must turn away from science for answers. This is the place where a sign might read: "No Science Past this Point." And a literal point it was too, 13.8 billion years ago. It was all the dimensions of the cosmos contained in one dimension, in a point. How can this be?

The astronomer Joseph Silk said that a "singularity"—which is the official scientific term created to express whatever the "No Entrance" sign meant—"is completely unacceptable as a physical description of the universe...a place where the laws of physics and even space and time break down." This is why when the initial evidence of the expanding universe and the Big Bang appeared to Einstein, it so bothered him that he waved it away as absurd and fudged his equations so that they pointed away from any such thing—later dubbing it the greatest blunder of his life.

And doesn't the Big Bang say even more? If time and space can be shown to have begun at some point in the past, then we know they are not a given, that the idea of something existing outside time and space is possible, and even probable, since the universe had to come from somewhere, even if it's not a physical or material somewhere. By definition time and space came from beyond time and space, from some world where they were created, presumably. Can it be a physical place without time or space? Whatever that place is, it would at least have to have a dramatically different sense of time and of space than we do in our universe. It seems that when we speak of eternity, that's what we are talking about. We are talking about a place that is at once infinitely present and yet also stretching infinitely forward and backward, but that doesn't feel like forever. It is what we may call the "eternal present." We can perhaps imagine this, but it has nothing to do with our five senses. But it really is like a person born blind trying to imagine color. We are in a realm that is not irrational, but that is nonetheless stupefying.

Isn't this roughly what the Bible says about the nature of things? That God, who is outside time and space and who has existed eternally, created this world? Other creation myths simply don't postulate that kind of a God. The Bible says, "In the beginning God created the heavens and the earth."[2] And there are various places in the Bible where God really does seem to be outside

---

[2] Genesis 1:1.

of time. When Moses asks him his name, he says, "I AM" or "I AM WHO I AM,"[3] And Jesus says, "Before Abraham was I AM...."[4] And of course the God of the Bible must be outside of time if he knows the future and tells Moses how the world came into being.

But it is in the poetic drama of the Book of Job that we get the clearest picture of a God outside of time and space. God asks Job a series of breathtaking questions, especially when we consider that it was written centuries before the birth of Christ. God asks, "Where were you when I laid the foundations of the earth?" There is sarcasm in it, of course, so that it is simultaneously glorious and funny. And then he says, "To what were its foundations fastened, or who laid its cornerstone...?" Where in the history of human literature do we have anything else like this? It goes on:

> Who shut in the sea with doors,
> when it burst forth and issued from the womb;
> When I made the clouds its garment....
> Have you commanded the morning since your days began
> And caused the dawn to know its place...?
> Have you entered the springs of the sea
> Or have you walked in search of the depths?

And yet it gets even stranger and more beautiful:

> Where is the way to the dwelling of light?
> And darkness, where is its place
> That you may take it to its territory,
> That you may know the paths to its home?

And then the magnificent: "Has the rain a father?"[5]

---

[3] Exodus 3:14.

[4] John 8:58.

[5] Job 38:1, 6, 8–9, 16, 19, 28.

Clearly the God who is speaking does not exist within this material universe of space and time, and it is clear too that he created this world in which we live. He is not subject to the forces of nature and is not himself a force of nature. He is beyond all these things and behind all these things.

CHAPTER TWENTY-FOUR

The Impossible Bleakness of Materialism

*Religion, by embarrassing contrast [to science], has
contributed literally zero to what we know....*

—Richard Dawkins

There can be discovered no more lamentable illustration of the misunderstanding about faith and science than in the writings of Richard Dawkins. He is himself a scientist, but unlike scientists who understand their discipline, he is also a materialist who believes there can be nothing beyond matter and believes that science alone can give us knowledge. We agree that doing science is scientific, but to unscientifically insist nothing can be known apart from science is to move into scientistic philosophy, which must also mean abandoning logic. But this is the strange devil's bargain Dawkins and some other academics have been willing to make, if only for the thin pottage that is the fleeting admiration of undergraduates.

Dawkins delights, for example, in bringing up the case of Archbishop James Ussher, a seventeenth-century divine who dated the beginning of the universe to the evening of October 22 in the year 4004 BC. Any serious Christian today finds this ridiculous and of course dismisses it for any number of reasons. Yet Mr. Dawkins solemnly beats the drum that accepting Ussher's fanciful conclusion is "typical" of people of faith today. He must assume no one will catch him in this, and so he peacocks ahead proudly, spreading this shimmering fan as often as possible.

It is today unavoidably comical that Archbishop Ussher made his assertion, but for some context about the world in which the archbishop calculated, we may remind ourselves that he entered this world in 1581, the year Sir Francis Drake was knighted by Elizabeth I for circumnavigating the globe. Shakespeare was a teenager. But Dawkins seems to have no ethical problem with performing the calisthenics of reaching backward to the Age of Exploration for "evidence" of how backward faith is. He even says Ussher thundered his pronouncement "with the immense authority of the Church," never telling us which church, since there were many at that time, nor disclosing that most human beings in Christendom never heard of Archbishop Ussher, even during his lifetime. In such assertions, Dawkins has impressively clambered well beyond the tree line, where oxygen becomes scarce.

For further context, we may point out that Johannes Kepler—one of the key figures in the Scientific Revolution and typically held up as a paragon of science—only disagreed with Ussher's chronology by twelve years, putting it at 3992 BC. So obviously believing what the Bible says— and even thinking we can use it to determine the age of the universe, which we cannot—is not an issue of faith versus science, else Kepler would not have taken it seriously.

Kepler wasn't the only undisputed scientific genius who weighed in on Ussher's date. Isaac Newton also took a mathematical whack at the puzzle and settled on 4000 BC, just four years off Ussher's mark. So whatever Dawkins is trying to say in referencing Ussher is such an incontinent mess that we are obliged to look away. It appears he is interested principally in raising his followers' pique against their perceived enemies, and confidently asserts what he likes, as though declaiming *ex cathedra* to the birds and bees from a stump in a sylvan grove. We must not be so rude as to chirrup at him with our facts and logic.

In a 2007 essay titled "The Hubris of Religion," which means to be a full-throated paean to science, Dawkins whips up an intoxicating paella of self-contradiction, ultimately too confusing to digest. But at one juncture he coughs up the entirety of his thinking with the impressive succinctness of an owl pellet:

> Pride can be justified, and science does so in spades. So does Beethoven, so do Shakespeare, Michelangelo, Christopher Wren. So do the engineers who built the giant telescopes in Hawaii and in the Canary Islands, the giant radio telescopes and very large arrays that stare sightless into the southern sky; or the Hubble orbiting telescope and the spacecraft that launched it. The engineering feats deep underground at CERN, combining monumental size with minutely accurate tolerances of measurement, literally moved me to tears when I was shown around. The engineering, the mathematics, the physics, in the Rosetta mission that successfully soft-landed a robot vehicle on the tiny target of a comet also made me proud to be human.

For anyone unaware of what Dawkins has said elsewhere, and what he will say later in the same essay, there would be nothing wrong with these sentiments. But when one reads the paragraph not as he hopes, but as his own materialist philosophy insists, one discovers that—like the proverbial snake swallowing its own tail—it devours itself out of existence, until we stand agog, wondering how he has performed this extraordinary trick.

The first problem arrives in his admiration of the non-scientists in his second sentence. Can the arch-materialist mean to sneak in an appreciation for beauty without our noticing he has done so? He evidently believes praising humans for their accomplishments somehow pits them against the God he claims does not exist. But again, going by the standards Dawkins and the New Atheists insist on, how does he think it is permissible to praise Beethoven, Shakespeare, Michelangelo, and Wren as those in whom we can take pride? According to Dawkins's parochial definitions, what are music or poetry or sculpture or painting or St. Paul's Cathedral that we should so manifestly be assumed to admire them? Anyone with feeling does and should admire them, and we are glad to think that Mr. Dawkins does too, but how can it be that he does so when in his angry pronouncements he has said anything that is not "scientific"—or that is somehow beyond the "material"—is nonsense? To any strict materialist and atheist, all music and art and architecture simply do not fit anywhere, any more than do necromancy or astral projection. For any materialist these things are all equally ineffable and therefore outside the bounds of the material world and science. Most of us know their beauty is transcendent and speaks to our souls, but a strict materialist believes neither in transcendent beauty nor in anything else transcendent. He certainly has no patience for the idea of a "soul." To him music is merely sound waves in certain frequencies detectable to our ears, which have evolved randomly over the eons to hear these frequencies. But in praising Beethoven's music Dawkins's wagon has clattered dramatically far from the ruts of his secularist philosophy, and although we are certainly glad to see it, we desperately wish he might see it too, and explain how he squares this particular circle.

Dawkins must know praising the moving beauty of music is not far from talking about other immaterial things like God, yet he doesn't seem to make the connection or wish to. Can he tell us where and how rationality and "science" come into the picture where Beethoven is concerned? Can he explain why such music might move anyone? One would expect him to say that all of it is nonsense, that blind evolutionary processes have unwittingly bumped us along through the ages to a point where for no particular reason we find certain things "beautiful," sometimes so much that our eyes grow moist. But can he tell us why he himself should be moved by these four geniuses and their art? Is he moved because all of these figures are European white men with whom he finds a primeval and tribal affinity, or does he mean to suggest there is something objective about what he considers beautiful? According to his own severe parameters, he has—alas!—galloped heedlessly into a tar pit, and is descending slowly but surely fossil-ward. He must realize "beauty" and "being moved to tears" can have no part in a life dedicated to a strict materialist atheistic philosophy. And surely he must know that many in England despise St. Paul's and much else that Christopher Wren created precisely because Wren did what he did to glorify the God in whom Dawkins pretends not to believe and whose devotees he curses with such florid expressions of contempt.

It appears he wishes to have things both ways, despite the logical contradiction. In mentioning Beethoven, Shakespeare, Michelangelo, and Wren, he seems to hope some of their cultural and intellectual bona fides might rub off on him, perhaps so that he doesn't come across as a materialist curmudgeon. But isn't it too late for this? Dawkins and Hitchens have been so wildly opposed to anything touching on God or the eternal—and so brutally dogmatic in their pronouncements that the material world is all there is—that to find them praising art or artists is strange and almost reckless, like the thief who almost wishes to be caught and leaves more clues than he should. Or perhaps the whole thing is a deliberate misdirection intended to throw people off the depressing atheist trail, as if to say, "We're not philistines! We can be atheists who appreciate great music and great art!" But on what basis? They have sprinted Wile E. Coyote–like off a cliff, and as they say these things they are absurdly pontificating in mid-air. The uncompromising laws of science know nothing of grace and are already pulling at their legs from the canyon below. Do they not understand that science can only tell them at what speed they will encounter the unyielding planet whose tremendous mass unkindly sucks them toward itself?

In choosing his four examples, it almost seems as though Dawkins wished to undermine his own position. Beethoven composed some of the greatest church music in history, and his "Missa Solemnis"—Latin for "Solemn Mass"—is among his greatest achievements. "My chief aim," he said of it, "was to awaken and permanently instill religious feelings not only into the singers but also into the listeners." Twenty years before, when Beethoven was unable to marry the woman he loved, he dedicated his "Moonlight Sonata" to her and wrote, "I must live by myself alone; but I know well that God is nearer to me than others in my art, so I will walk fearlessly with Him." But what can such a vile religionist possibly have to say to such as Dawkins? Couldn't he rather at least have praised the irksome clatter of Arnold Schoenberg or John Cage?

We must similarly wonder how he believes he can praise Michelangelo, who probably more than any artist of any age expressed the power of Christian faith, and himself evinced it most seriously. His painting of the Sistine Chapel ceiling—among the most religious expressions of any artist—is widely considered among the greatest masterpieces in history and is said to have changed the very course of Western art. On beholding it, Johann Wolfgang von Goethe declared: "Without having seen the Sistine Chapel one can form no appreciable idea of what one man is capable of achieving." And Michelangelo's *Pieta* in cold marble depicting Mary holding the body of her murdered son—is among the most beautiful and moving works ever created. Couldn't Dawkins have praised the hostile horrors of Mark Rothko or Robert Motherwell?

Of the four artists, only Shakespeare is not known especially for his connection to religion, although he is far from secular; but like the other two, Sir Christopher Wren is most famous for his work related to God, for he designed and built the masterpiece of St. Paul's Cathedral in London following the Great Fire of 1666. He was also commissioned to design a further fifty-one churches destroyed in the terrible conflagration, so that his fame rests almost exclusively on his services toward the Establishment Church—which according to Dawkins and his gang of gauche gauchos is the festering nidus of all foulness on our coincidentally inhabitable planet.

If, according to his own system of thinking, Dawkins has no right or reason to take pride in these great artists, one may wonder whether he really is the strict materialist atheist he claims. Perhaps he has softened to the point of common sense. But then one crashes into something so adamantine on this point that any happy hopes are atomized. In praising science, Dawkins says: "Religion, by embarrassing contrast, has contributed literally zero to what we know, combined with huge hubristic confidence in the alleged facts it has simply made up.["] Before we respond more fully, we are obliged at least to ask: Does there exist a sillier sentence in any language? Perhaps it is merely a case of unwitting japery. But alas, the only conclusion to be drawn is that Mr. Dawkins really has no idea that within the confined space of a single essay he has asserted claims that are existential enemies and are holding cocked pistols to each other's temples. Nonetheless it's a confounding puzzlement: Can this man who is a fellow of the Royal Society really be unaware that he has leaned so far out over his skis that he has begun somersaulting?

One may also earnestly wonder if the sentence about religion contributing "literally zero to what we know" was missed by everyone in the various drafts of the editing process. Or perhaps none of the venerable authors' editors had the courage to bring it up. Of course Dawkins has said as much elsewhere, so it does appear he thinks it logical that all "knowledge" comes to us via scientific inquiry, and that apart from science there is no knowledge. But what he doesn't seem to know is that this belief is itself a matter of faith and not science (or that it takes infinitely less faith to believe in the Resurrection, which is at least theoretically possible.) But Dawkins does believe it, and with the sort of frightened and blind faith that spooks at the approaching sound of evidence and logic. Yet this perfectly irrational conviction is at the lifeless heart of the strange and unappealing doctrine called atheist materialism. What view of the world could be more asphyxiating? Perhaps it was in somehow sensing this that he felt the wild instinct to doff his cap to the four great artists mentioned, assuming his readers would miss the contradiction, as he seems to have done.

The only way to make sense of what Dawkins is saying is to assume he honestly cannot see the percussive incongruity at play. On the one hand he says we are essentially robots, amazingly constructed by chance through natural selection. On the other hand we are able to create and appreciate things of ineffable beauty and mystery. But if scientific

---

[1] Christopher Hitchens, Richard Dawkins, Sam Harris, Daniel Dennett, *The Four Horsemen: The Conversation That Sparked an Atheist Revolution* (New York: Random House, 2019), 19.

knowledge is the only kind of knowledge, how are we to appreciate the aforementioned artists? What is art that Dawkins should be mindful of it? And the creators of that art, that he should praise them? And what is Socrates's much-vaunted ideal of "self-knowledge" but unscientific fluff borne to us by Zephyrus from the myth-filled world of pagan antiquity? And what is that invisible thing called "wisdom," hailed by millennia of human beings, if not a mere hardware glitch yet to be naturally selected by some genetic Mengele for death? Shall not such things be reckoned worthless and disposable because they dare to exist beyond the gleaming palisades of "science"?

If we are to take Dawkins at his word, we eventually must put to him the uncomfortable question about where he gets the idea that murdering and raping are in any way "bad" and generally to be eschewed? Is it from scientific experimentations with falsifiable hypotheses that he knows these things? What are the experiments that determined this, and why hasn't someone shared them with the world? Or can we all guess that he and his ideological comrades know these activities are in fact not bad at all, but dare not say so for fear of unpleasant backlash? But isn't it true that according to these doctrines murder and rape are merely activities resulting from the evolutionary process that knows nothing of good or evil, and therefore cannot be condemned? Pray, won't you tell us?

Again, Dawkins and the other glum horsemen cannot have these things both ways. So they must cleverly change horses midstream to suit their argument, hoping those invested in what they are saying won't notice who is on which mount when, or at least won't say anything if they do notice, since it's all in a good cause—not that there is anything intrinsically or objectively or morally good, but perhaps no one will bring that up either.

Still, it is remarkable. In one moment the materialist curmudgeon praises the poetry of Shakespeare and the wordless beauty of the creations of Michelangelo and Beethoven and Wren, and in the next he moralistically denounces anything undiscoverable by science as a wicked stepchild who should be sent into the woods to be eaten by wolves. Surely he knows no computer will ever understand why the Sistine Chapel or St. Paul's Cathedral are unutterably glorious, because to understand that one requires something that cannot be concatenated via natural processes, for it partakes of glory itself. Does Mr. Dawkins not see that such beauty as he has praised points inevitably to things as far beyond "science" as the nebulae are beyond the lighting aisle at Costco?

And what shall we make of his tears at the monstrous particle accelerator beneath the Franco-Swiss border except that Dawkins himself is the creation of a Being who is glorified by these things that peer into the heart of His impossibly great creation? Can Mr. Dawkins never realize that according to his scientific theories, tears and the emotion one feels at anything are just a mysterious quirk of evolution no different than the unfortunate webbing between some people's toes? Perhaps at some point in our prehistoric past when we were sprinting for our lives across the African savannah some of these things had a purpose, or when we were climbing as fish with nubby legs from the water toward our brave terrestrial futures. But does he not realize that according to his philosophy his feelings are just leftovers from some time when they helped, which they now do not? Does he not know that they are phantom limbs, still aching and twinging, though they are not there at all? We are happy to think Dawkins and his equine confreres appreciate things outside science, but how much better it would be if they dared to appreciate the untenable contradiction of their position and made some honest effort to address it.

CHAPTER TWENTY-FIVE

The Founding Myth of Atheism: Galileo, Copernicus, and

the Church

In the beginning of this book we discussed how science is leading us toward faith in God. But what if we discovered that faith in the God of the Bible itself is what has led us to science? As it turns out, we have. Before we explain that, however, we should look at the central and founding myth of secularism and atheism, which is the story of Galileo's battle with the Church.

According to the venerable narrative most of us have heard more times than we could count, Galileo's persecution by the Church was the opening salvo in the war between faith and science, or between religion and "reason." But like so much else we "know" to be true, it is not true at all. There are numerous reasons for the popularity of this deeply misleading narrative, but in my own lifetime it may have been the 1973 BBC mini-series *The Ascent of Man* that played the greatest role in advancing it. Of course by then, seven years after the 1966 *Time* magazine cover, the culture had already generally shifted from the idea of God, so the TV series was only promoting the established trend. But to see how far this false narrative has been pushed in the decades since, we need only mention that when the book version of *The Ascent of Man* was republished in 2011, Richard Dawkins was chosen to write the new foreword. The idea of atheism as marching hand in hand with science and progress—and the idea of faith and religion as being "anti-science"—had become an entirely unchallenged narrative.

Galileo and the Church

The story we have all heard is that in the early seventeenth century authoritarian religious forces crushed the free-thinking scientist named Galileo, and champions of reason and science have been fighting the forces of faith and religion ever since. As we have said, this is not true, but as with many untruths, there is enough truth to make the story plausible. True stories are also usually more complicated than the Bowdlerized fairytale versions, which is one reason we accept the myths and legends as readily as we sometimes do.

To set the record straight, we must first say that Galileo was no enemy of the Church—and far from it. He was a deeply serious Christian who saw no disparity between what the Church taught—or what the Bible said—and what science revealed. Indeed, the very idea was unthinkable to him. And he would be deeply upset to think that his own experiences could have led people through the centuries to think it. Like most scientists throughout history, Galileo knew that no such divide existed, nor even could. The truth of God simply could not contradict the truth of nature, which God himself had created. Truth was truth, however and wherever it manifested itself. In fact, in the late Middle Ages the "Two Books" idea had become popular: one book being the Holy Scriptures, and the other being the "Book of Nature." Galileo even referred to this idea specifically in his famous letter of 1615, in which he laid out his understanding of how faith and science support each other.

As most of us recall, the central issue between Galileo and the religious authorities was whether Earth was the center of the universe or not. The generally accepted "Geocentric" theory held that it was, and that the sun and planets revolved around the earth. The less popular "Heliocentric" theory held that Earth and the planets revolved around the sun. But the Heliocentric theory was nothing new. It had been popularized in the third century BC by Aristarchus, and was put forward in the century before Galileo by Nicolaus Copernicus. So to understand Galileo's story, we must first go back to Copernicus.

Copernicus

Copernicus

Nicolaus Copernicus was born in 1473 in Poland, which was then Royal Prussia. His father was a prosperous merchant, and so, like many in the higher social circles of his day, Copernicus was able to pursue such interests as he wished. In the course of his dramatically eclectic life he was a mathematician, a medical physician, an astronomer, a governor, a diplomat, a classics scholar, and a clergyman. He was also a polyglot and a groundbreaking thinker in the field of economics.[1] But it was for his groundbreaking work in astronomy that Copernicus would become known.

Copernicus, like Galileo, lived at a time when all truth was one. What he learned via science could never compete with the truth of the Scriptures, any more than science could compete with mathematics. For him, God was the God of all truth, whether scientific, philosophical, mathematical, or theological. So to divide faith and science as we often do today was inconceivable, and

---

[1] In 1517 he formulated the "Quantity Theory of Money," which is the idea that the amount of money in circulation in a given economy is directly related to the prices in that economy. In 1519 he formulated a principle that 250 years later came to be called "Gresham's Law."

Copernicus could never have dreamt that his astronomy might be troubling to the Church, which he—being a clergyman—revered.

We should explain that Copernicus decided to delve into whether Earth revolved around the sun or vice versa precisely because the question had never been fully settled. Aristotle in Greece in the fourth century BC and Ptolemy in Egypt in the second century AD believed Earth was at the center of the universe, but as we have said, Aristarchus in the third century BC believed the sun was at the center. By the time of Copernicus, Aristotle's perspectives in many things had gotten the upper hand, but there were a number of astronomical discrepancies with this view. So Copernicus wondered if the Heliocentric model would help clear them up. By 1510 his astronomical observations and calculations led him to conclude that Aristarchus had gotten it right, and that indeed it was the sun at the center, and not Earth.

So the issue was never an issue between the Christian Church and the ancient pagans of Greece and Egypt. In all things the Catholic Church was only too happy to adopt the best of what classical antiquity had to offer, and any truth found in Aristotle and Plato was as valid as the truth in Augustine and Aquinas, for example. As we have said, by Copernicus's time most believed Aristotle was correct. So when Copernicus's efforts caused him to contradict Aristotle, some were scandalized. But their dismay had nothing to do with what the Bible said. It was rather the idea that anyone would dare to contradict Aristotle, whose ideas the Church had so thoroughly imported into its understanding of everything.

Interestingly enough, those theologians most put out by Copernicus's theory were not found in the Catholic Church, but in the new Protestant Church of the Reformation leaders. The only serious Catholic opposed to his theory was a Florentine Dominican, Giovanni Maria Tolosani, and his objections were little read and mostly ignored. So the idea that the Catholic Church of Copernicus's time had theological problems with Earth's not being the center of all things is simply untrue.

Just like Galileo a century later, the popular misconception is that Copernicus's scientific discoveries contradicted what the Church taught. This narrative claims that because Copernicus's science had demoted man from being the center of the universe, the God the Church believed had put man at the center was also discredited. In other words, we who thought we were special in God's eyes had been shown by science not to be so special after all. But this too is erroneous. Nonetheless this false version became so powerful that "the Copernican Revolution" is today widely thought to be a signal event in science's eventual triumph over faith and the Church.

The actual story is quite different. For one thing, there were many significant persons in the Church who were fascinated with Copernicus's discoveries and directly encouraged him in them. And because Copernicus himself had a doctorate in canon law and was a cleric, there can be no question that he was not on the "other" side of any supposed divide between science and the Church. So for a number of years Copernicus freely shared his "heliocentric" thinking with friends both inside and outside the Church, and in time it gained favor in some circles. The Vatican itself never took any official position, and most within the Church assumed the truth would eventually be revealed.

This is not to say there weren't some with strong feelings against the idea, but such feelings did not fall along any theological lines. It is a well-established fact of history that any challenge to a widely held theory will be controversial, no matter who is doing the challenging, nor who is doing the defending. The philosopher Immanuel Kant wrote about this in the eighteenth century, and in the twentieth the philosopher Thomas Kuhn wrote of it. So Copernicus was rightly concerned that in upsetting this particular apple cart he would anger certain devotees of Ptolemy and Aristotle, and he declined to publish his major work on the theory until he was on his deathbed in 1543. But it had nothing to do with the idea of science contradicting Church teaching; it was a simple matter of going against Aristotle. Of course Aristotle had never given a moment's thought to whether his beliefs accorded with the Hebrew Scriptures, of which he was perfectly ignorant. But by the Middle Ages—thanks largely to Thomas Aquinas—many in the Church held Aristotle in as high esteem, or perhaps higher, than the Bible itself.

During Copernicus's lifetime, then, there was no tension between "faith and science," neither on this nor any other issue. Indeed, his model struck many in ecclesiastical circles as an extraordinary solution to the persistent problems with the Geocentric model. In the summer of 1533, Johann Widmanstetter, who was a secretary to Pope Clement VII, explained Copernicus's model to the Pope himself, who was extremely enthused and grateful to hear it. Two cardinals were in attendance too. And three years later the Cardinal Archbishop of Capua wrote Copernicus from Rome:

> Some years ago word reached me concerning your proficiency, of which everybody constantly spoke. At that time I began to have a very high regard for you.... For I had learned that you had not merely mastered the discoveries of the ancient astronomers uncommonly well but had also formulated a new cosmology. In it you maintain that the earth moves; that the sun occupies the lowest, and thus the central, place in the universe.... Therefore with the utmost earnestness I entreat you, most learned sir, unless I inconvenience you, to communicate this discovery of yours to scholars, and at the earliest possible moment to send me your writings on the sphere of the universe together with the tables and whatever else you have that is relevant to this subject....[2]

So the highest figures in the Church were not bothered by Copernicus's theory, but as we mentioned many Protestants took strong exception to it. For example, a certain polemical Dutchman named Wilhelm Gnapheus penned a scathing comedy in which Copernicus was lampooned as "Morosephus" ("Foolish Sage"), an aloof ninny who dabbled in astrology. More serious theological figures weighed in too. Martin Luther's right-hand man Philip Melanchthon wrote:

> Some people believe that it is excellent and correct to work out a thing as absurd as did that [Polish] astronomer who moves the

---

[2] Jerzy Dobrzycki, ed., *Nicholas Copernicus on the Revolutions, Volume 2* (London: Macmillan, 1978), xvii.

earth and stops the sun. Indeed, wise rulers should have curbed such light-mindedness.[3]

And John Calvin in his *Commentary on Genesis* said: "We indeed are not ignorant that the circuit of the heavens is finite, and that the earth, like a little globe, is placed in the center." In his commentary on Psalms 93:1, Calvin wrote:

> The heavens revolve daily, and, immense as is their fabric and inconceivable the rapidity of their revolutions, we experience no concussion.... How could the earth hang suspended in the air were it not upheld by God's hand? By what means could it maintain itself unmoved, while the heavens above are in constant rapid motion, did not its Divine Maker fix and establish it.[4]

Of course, this was precisely the sort of thing that Augustine—eleven centuries earlier—had foreseen as a potential trap for overzealous and intellectually sloppy Christians, and which Galileo would quote in his famous letter many years later, when things on this subject at last came to a head, as we shall see.

After Copernicus's death there was no particular movement in any direction. The great Johannes Kepler was convinced Copernicus was correct and stuck by him, but the Danish astronomer Tycho Brahe[5] and others were bothered by Copernicus's system because it did not accord with Aristotle. Brahe came up with the "geo-heliocentric" theory, in which the moon and the sun circled around Earth, but all of the other planets revolved around the sun.

---

[3] Czesław Miłosz, *The History of Polish Literature* (Berkeley: University of California Press, 1983), 38.

[4] John Calvin, *Commentary on Psalms*, https://www.ccel.org/ccel/calvin/calcom11.ii.i.html.

[5] At age twenty Brahe lost much of his nose in a duel in the dark over who was the superior mathematician with his third cousin Manderup Parsberg, and for the rest of his life he wore a prosthetic brass nose, affixed with paste. On special occasions he wore a silver or gold prosthetic.

Johannes Kepler (1571–1630)

So when Galileo Galilei entered the picture, there was no established thinking on this question, and certainly no strong and united animus against it. Though the preponderance of opinion still remained with Aristotle and Ptolemy, enough had embraced Copernicus's theory to make the question far from settled. Copernicus was of course proven correct in foreseeing a great hue and cry from certain quarters if the issue was pressed openly, which was why the publication of his definitive work on the subject coincided with his own exit from the planet and managed to kick the troubling can down the road for others.

So it was not until the first years of the next century, when Galileo discovered the newly invented telescope, that the story continues. He earnestly believed that the wonders he saw through this device were so overwhelming that others looking through it could not fail to be convinced of what he saw. It was in this spirit that Galileo stooped down to pick up the aforementioned can and the troubles began.

Galileo was a polymath and genius in many fields, including optics. No sooner had the telescope been invented than he set about improving it, and in 1609 the heavens were opened, both to him and to anyone else who wished to see—but as we shall ourselves see, not everyone wished to see. Nonetheless, Galileo continued making more powerful telescopes and marveled at what he saw that had never before been seen by anyone. He saw the rings of Saturn, and the moons around Jupiter—naming some of them for his Medici patrons—and he saw our own moon with such clarity that he observed vast and deep craters on its surface, and tall mountains too. Being a gifted artist too, Galileo made a number of watercolors of what he observed. He must have known that news of the moon's irregular surface would vex Aristotelians across Europe, because Aristotle firmly held that the moon's surface must be perfectly smooth. So even in this simplest of all observations Galileo was thought to be challenging Aristotle, and indirectly the infinity of Aristotelian ideas woven inextricably into the entire scholastic system.

Because of Aristotle—and having nothing to do with anything in the Bible—all planetary orbits were thought to be perfect circles and all heavenly objects to be perfect spheres. But the moon had come to be even more than merely perfectly smooth and spherical. By Galileo's time it had come to represent purity and perfection itself and was even symbolic of the Immaculate Conception of Mary. But now this troublemaker Galileo had showed that it was not a perfect sphere at all, nor was its face pristine. Rather it was badly pockmarked, as though ravaged by scrofula or the pox. For many at the time, it was as though Galileo had via sorcery transformed the opalescent face of the Virgin into some craggy-faced hag, or even a senescent and syphilitic whore. Would no one defend her honor against these telescoping insults? The Aristotelians in the universities were not about to take this lying down, and they began to plot how they might repay this sky-gazing upstart for his insulting affrontery.

We may recall that a central issue for the Vatican in its dealings with Martin Luther had been his bold contempt for Aristotle. So in response to Luther's churlishness, they had in the century before Galileo reaffirmed their devotion to Aristotle, who in their minds had by now swelled to the value of a dozen popes. Many die-hard Aristotelians even refused Galileo's invitations to look through the magical device for themselves, deeming it unnatural to use this "tube" in looking at the heavens, as if the damning evidence of their own eyes would implicate them in Galileo's grave crimes.

Kepler had stood firmly by the Copernican model, and in a letter to him Galileo wrote: "What would you say of the learned here, who, replete with the pertinacity of the asp, have steadfastly refused to cast a glance through the telescope? What shall we make of all this? Shall we laugh or shall we cry?" One of these obstinate professors taught with Galileo at Pisa and Padua. Shortly after refusing Galileo's invitation to squint through the telescope, this aged man passed away, at which Galileo quipped that he hoped this man who had

Galileo's initial CYA epistle to the Grand Duchess was eventually expanded and published as a treatise.

declined to look at the heavenly bodies while on Earth might now take the opportunity to do so while traveling to Heaven.

In 1611 the knives against Galileo were being sharpened, and his Florentine friend Lodovico Cigoli wrote to inform him that "ill-disposed men envious of your virtue and merits met [to discuss]...any means by which they could damage you." But all remained quiet until the end of 1613. That's when the Medici family—Grand Duke Cosimo II and the Grand Duchess Christina—who were Galileo's patrons during this period, invited a former student of Galileo's to dine with them, as well as a professor of philosophy from the University of Pisa named Cosimo Boscaglia. When Galileo came up for discussion, Boscaglia seized the opportunity to pour poison into the duchess's ear, whispering to her that what troubled him about Galileo's ideas was their contradiction of the Holy Scriptures. This mortified the grand duchess, whose faith was deeply important to her, and who raised the subject with the others. Her concerns were assuaged somewhat by Galileo's former student, who leapt to his defense. Nonetheless, when the scene was related to Galileo, he was furious. After all, it was his esteemed patrons who had heard this vile calumny. So he set about writing his now-classic letter to the grand duchess, in which he lay out his thinking on the proper relationship between science and matters of theology. It is extremely clear from this letter, which runs to the length of a treatise—which it indeed became in a subsequent draft—that Galileo took the Scriptures very seriously. In the letter he quotes a passage from Saint Augustine:

> In points that are obscure, or far from clear, if we should read anything in the Bible that may allow of several constructions consistently with the faith to be taught, let us not commit ourselves to any one of them with such precipitous obstinacy that when, perhaps, the truth is more diligently searched into, this may fall to the ground, and we with it. Then we would indeed be seen to have contended not for the sense of divine Scripture, but for our own ideas by wanting something of ours to be the sense of Scripture when we should rather want the meaning of Scripture to be ours.[6]

Galileo understood that for anyone—much less the Church—to force the Bible to appear to say anything it did not clearly say was to do great injury to it, and to the faith of those who would one day see the contradiction revealed, whether via scientific inquiry or otherwise. And of course it would be an affront to God himself. Later in the letter, in his own words, Galileo expanded on his views:

> I think in the first place that it is very pious to say and prudent to affirm that the holy Bible can never speak untruth—whenever its true meaning is understood. But I believe nobody will deny that it is often very abstruse, and may say things which are quite different from what its bare words signify. Hence in expounding the Bible if one were always to confine oneself to the unadorned grammatical meaning, one might fall into error. Not only

---

[6] Galileo Galilei, "Letter to Madame Christina de Lorraine, Grand Duchess of Tuscany," *Interdisciplinary Encyclopedia of Religion & Science*, https://inters.org/Galilei-Madame-Christina-Lorraine.

contradictions and propositions far from true might thus be made to appear in the Bible, but even grave heresies and follies.[7]

In order for us to understand the exegetical twisting some did to support their Aristotelian views, we quote that verse most used to support the "geo-centric" theory. Psalm 104:4 declares that God "set the earth on its foundation; it can never be moved." To insist this be taken literally is absurd, especially since the psalm immediately continues in what is manifestly figurative language: "He makes the clouds his chariot; and rides on the wings of the wind." No one ever believed such verses were meant literally. But to shore up their Aristotelian views, the previous verse about Earth's sitting on a "foundation" from which "it can never be moved" was indeed taken literally—and those who took it that way could never be moved from their position.

The story of how secular academics manipulated figures in the Church to press their overwhelming advantage—and ultimately force Galileo to recant his views—is a deeply shameful episode, but as Giorgio de Santillana magnificently explains in his book *The Crime of Galileo*, it is in no way the story of a battle between a secular scientist and the Christian faith. And the notion that the Vatican figures guilty of this episode can or should stand in for all persons of faith, or even for the Christian faith, is mistaken on several levels, as is the idea that Galileo could be squeezed to conform to the modern caricature of a "free-thinking" scientist battling the Church. As further proof that there was nothing inherently troubling to the Church about the "heliocentric" theory, we recall that no efforts were made against it for a century after Copernicus shared it, and seventy years after he published the opus providing the full details.

So when secularists recast this story, first asserting that "the Copernican Revolution" proved via science that we humans are insignificant—so that we were not created by a loving God but only arose on this planet by accident—they are actually casting Copernicus in their own image, as they do Galileo after him. We now know that Copernicus was bucking theories put forth by

---

7 Ibid.

Ptolemy and Aristotle, neither of whom were Christians, nor ever even read the Hebrew Bible.

In a way, the powerful figures who opposed Galileo—whether secular or clerical—were the members of a ruling elite with great powers at their disposal and with no real fidelity to anything beyond their own power. It is not surprising, but is at least ironic, that in this way Galileo's persecutors resemble today's secular scientific establishment, which inveighs against and perspires over anything challenging the theories they cling to, often as prematurely as some attacked the Heliocentric model in Galileo's time, forgetting that their first fealty must be to the evidence and to science itself, wherever it leads, and not to the paradigm that will guarantee them funding and tenure.

The Copernican Revolution

As we may see from the profound Christian faith of Copernicus and Galileo—as well as Kepler in between them—both the idea that science during this period was advanced by those of a secular bent and against the will of men of faith is a secular fantasy. Newton, too, whose theories finally vindicated what Copernicus began and Galileo furthered, was himself a man of deep Christian faith. For all of these geniuses, the scientific exploration of the natural world was a way to glorify the God who had made it, and in whose service they knew themselves to be working. So it is a profound disservice and injustice to all of them—and to history and science too—to insist that they play these ill-suited roles in our contemporary drama.

Furthermore, the recent secular idea that the Copernican model of the universe was a blow to the Church is simply mistaken. For example, the historian John Herman Randall insists that the Copernican view of things "swept man out of his proud position as the central figure and end of the universe, and made him a tiny speck on a third-rate planet revolving about a tenth-rate sun drifting in an endless cosmic ocean." This is a willful misrepresentation of history and science both, as it was men of faith who advanced these theories, and in so doing showed that there were more things in Heaven and Earth than are dreamt of in Aristotle's philosophy.

Those familiar with the fine-tuning argument discussed earlier in this book must know that where we are physically in the universe is especially irrelevant when compared to the infinite value God has evidently bestowed upon us by creating the vast infinity of the cosmos for what appears to be our sake, so that we could be a jewel of infinite price mounted in the setting that is all else in the impossibly vast creation. So if those enamored of man's "Copernican" fall to the periphery of the universe wish to take their lead from science in reckoning man's value, they must now see that value to be higher than can plausibly be reckoned. One hopes that anyone courageous enough to accept this reevaluation might also take a less dim view of the one who has given us such value.

CHAPTER TWENTY-SIX

Christianity Begat Science

Modern science [is] a legacy, I might even
[say] a child, of Christianity.

—C. F. von Weizsäcker

It is one thing to say that faith and science are compatible; but it is of another order entirely to say that Christian faith itself led to the rise of modern science. This may be the very last thing devoted secularists wish to hear, but from an historical perspective it is quite undeniable, so it is therefore past time that this be clearly understood and made known.

In *The Soul of Science: Christian Faith and Natural Philosophy*, Nancy Pearcey and Charles Thaxton make the case particularly compellingly, explaining that it was the worldview of the Christian faith that uniquely enabled science to emerge and flourish. In other words, science did not come inevitably into human culture, and without Christian theology, it could not have emerged as it did. The science writer Loren Eiseley says that "several great civilizations have arisen and vanished without the benefit of a scientific philosophy." That these many great civilizations did not produce what we think of as "the scientific method" or "the scientific revolution" is a curious historical fact. So when and how and why did science arise? Why did it happen when it did and where it did?

To be clear, science as we know it arose only in Western Christendom in the late Middle Ages and flourished in the early sixteenth and seventeenth centuries in what we now call the Scientific Revolution. Eiseley says science is "an invented cultural institution, an intuition not present in all societies, and not one that may be counted upon to arise from human instinct." He explains that science "demands some kind of unique soil in which to flourish." As Pearcey and Thaxton point out, Eiseley rather reluctantly admits that Christianity itself is at the heart of what gave rise to science. "In one of those strange permutations," he writes, "of which history yields occasional rare examples, it is the Christian world which finally gave birth in a clear, articulate fashion to the experimental method of science itself." Unlike Hitchens and Dawkins, Eiseley prizes truth enough to admit what he sees, whether he likes it or doesn't. But Pearcey and Thaxton make it quite clear that Eiseley is far from alone in seeing this. Innumerable scholars from the widest variety of philosophical viewpoints have acknowledged the same and have admitted "that Christianity provided both intellectual presuppositions and moral sanction for the development of modern science." But in perpetuating the ahistorical myth that science and religion are enemies, the Four Horsemen of the New Atheism pretend to know none of this and gallop along silently.

Pearcey and Thaxton say a number of cultures in antiquity—ranging from the Chinese to the Arabs to the Greeks—produced a level of learning and technology actually higher than that of medieval Europe. Yet none of these cultures ever gave us anything approaching the science that first emerged in late medieval Europe, and that came to fruition during the Scientific Revolution of the sixteenth and seventeenth centuries. Only Western Christendom gave birth to science as a "systematic, self-correcting discipline," and subsequently brought us the spectacular scientific advances we have enjoyed ever since. But why? What did Western Christendom have that was missing from these other extraordinary and otherwise advanced cultures? Was it simply a happy coincidence that things developed this way? Might Western Christendom have led to science not because of—but in spite of—its beliefs?

It seems not. Philosophers of science and historians of many stripes all agree that it was the Christian theology prevalent across Europe during this time that opened the door to the scientific revolution and to the extraordinary discoveries that have followed. For example, the esteemed historian Alfred North Whitehead says the rise of science in Christian civilization was owing to "certain habits of thought, such as the lawfulness of nature." According to him, these habits and ideas came directly from the "Christian doctrine of the world as a divine creation." In other words, Christians believed that the matter in the universe had order and obeyed certain rules because of the God who created them, so it followed that they could understand those rules and that order, which led to science as we know it.

In his book *The Grand Titration*, the biochemist Joseph Needham makes this point, explaining why he believes Chinese culture never gave rise to anything like the Scientific Revolution:

> There was no confidence that the code of Nature's laws could be unveiled and read, because there was no assurance that a divine being, even more rational than ourselves, had ever formulated such a code capable of being read.[1]

The Nobel Prize–winning biochemist Melvin Calvin makes the same point:

> As I try to discern the origin of that conviction [that the universe could be understood rationally], I seem to find it in a basic notion discovered 2,000 or 3,000 years ago, and enunciated first in the Western world by the ancient Hebrews, namely, that the universe is governed by a single God, and is not the product of the whims of many gods, each governing his own province according to his own laws. This monotheistic view seems to be the historical foundation for modern science.[2]

---

[1] Joseph Needham, *The Grand Titration: Science and Society in the East and West* (Oxfordshire, United Kingdom: Routledge, 1969), 327.

[2] Melvin Calvin, *Chemical Evolution* (Oxford: Clarendon Press, 1969), 259.

If is of course undeniable that in the ancient world and in the Eastern religions of Asia the ideas of a single God, and of an ordered universe that this God created, were entirely foreign. The historian Carl Becker says that the Western European Christian idea that "God is goodness and reason" led naturally to the idea that "his creation must somehow be…good and reasonable. Design in nature was thus derived a priori from the character which the Creator was assumed to have."[3] In 1964, the renowned physicist C. F. von Weizsäcker, in *The Relevance of Science*, put it this way:

> Matter in the Platonic sense, which must be "prevailed upon" by reason, will not obey mathematical laws exactly: matter which God has created from nothing may well strictly follow the rules which its Creator has laid down for it. In this sense, I called modern science a legacy, I might even have said a child, of Christianity.[4]

In *Return of the God Hypothesis*, Stephen Meyer makes the most recent case for these ideas, quoting the social philosopher Steve Fuller, who says that science depends on a "natural order [that] is the product of a single intelligence from which our own intelligence descends." Meyer also quotes the philosopher Holmes Rolston III:

> It was monotheism that launched the coming of physical science, for it premised an intelligible world, sacred but disenchanted, a world with a blueprint, which was therefore open to the searches of the scientists. The great pioneers in physics—Newton, Galileo, Kepler, Copernicus—devoutly believed themselves called to find evidences of God in the physical world.[5]

---

[3] Carl Lotus Becker, *The Heavenly City of the Eighteenth-Century Philosophers* (New Haven, Connecticut: *Yale University Press*, 1932), 55.

[4] C. F. von Weizsäcker, *The Relevance of Science* (New York: Collins, 1964), 163.

[5] Stephen Meyer, *Return of the God Hypothesis: Three Scientific Discoveries Revealing the Mind behind the Universe* (New York: HarperOne, 2021), 25.

Another important reason Western Christendom gave rise to science has to do with the value Christian doctrines place on the material world. Pearcey and Thaxton explain that the Bible teaches that nature is real, while Hinduism "teaches that the everyday world of material objects is maya, illusion." Therefore, it is "doubtful whether a philosophy that so denigrates the material world would be capable of inspiring the careful attention to it that is necessary for science."[6] Christians in "the early church defended a high view of the material world" against "the surrounding Greek culture" of that time. Genesis made clear that God had created the world "good," so the Greek idea—which we find in many other religions and philosophies, that the goal of this life is to escape the material, or to escape our bodies—is not a biblical idea, however much some Christian sects have erred in this regard.

The centrality of the human body to the Christian view cannot be clearer than when Jesus, after his resurrection from death, does not appear as a ghost but as a human being in a body with discernible wounds in his hands and feet and side—and with an appetite too, eating "a piece of fish" and honeycomb. If the goal of life were to transcend the corporeal, why would Jesus return in a body that required feeding? So the idea in many religions—and in some bastardized expressions of Christianity—that the body and physical matter are evil and must be escaped, is not found in genuinely biblical faith. Pearcey and Thaxton say that other religions often merged the spiritual with the material, and often worshiped the creation itself. The sun and moon and certain forces of Nature were revered and feared and worshiped, but Christians always understood the material world as a creation of God, over which he had explicitly given them authority. And so not fearing nature, as others often did, they were free to study it.

Stephen Meyer says that both Needham and Marshall Hodgson came to the same conclusion as Whitehead. It was the specifically religious thinking about the doctrine of Creation—"during the Catholic late Middle Ages and Protestant Reformation"—that changed everything, that set the stage for what we now call the Scientific Revolution.

---

[6] Nancy R. Pearcey and Charles B. Thaxton, *The Soul of Science: Christian Faith and Natural Philosophy* (Wheaton, Illinois: Crossway Books, 1994), 22.

The Greeks gave the world Aristotle and Euclid and Pythagoras, not to mention the exquisite Antikythera mechanism, along with countless other inventions and technologies. Nonetheless they were hindered by some deep-seated assumptions foreign to Christendom. What these assumptions are and what they entail is somewhat subtle. For example, the idea that a personal God had created all things was different from the Greek idea that there was an inherent order—a logos—underneath all things. A personal God might choose to do things in a way that was a bit quirkier or more creative and unpredictable than the perfect Platonic idea of a logos. For example, the idea that circles were perfect led the Greeks—Aristotle especially—to be sure that planets must move in circles. But those with a biblical view knew that they must approach creation with humility and were obliged to actually observe how things were, rather than insist what things must be like from some preconceived notions, and of course they discovered that planets orbited in ellipses rather than circles.

In other words, the God of the Bible has personality and was therefore infinitely freer than the Greek idea of the Pure Mind. So discovering what he had created was something like interacting with another person, albeit one who was infinitely intelligent and creative. But he could and did seem to dream up things—creatures and phenomena—that appeared to be far beyond the rather predictable Greek god of the logos, whom Aristotle called "Thought Thinking Thought." What could be more abstract and ethereal—and in its way more dull—than that? Would Aristotle's deity make a giraffe or a whale or a hummingbird? There was an abstract quality to Aristotelian and other Greek philosophy, one that drew them away from the specific and the earthly, and up toward the Platonic forms. There was a dualism at work too that eschewed this world of creation and yearned to transcend it and to achieve the independence from this world that led to "pure thinking"—and to Aristotle's impossibly Apollonian idea of a God that was pure Mind and which they called the Logos.

Of course the God of the Bible is this too, but he is simultaneously also a Person who created the world in all of its stunning and often quirky and imaginative specificity—and who then created human beings in his own image. And then—although he was always separate from his own creation—he nonetheless was involved in it and entered it creatively now and again. So he was not so aloof from us that he did not take a personal interest in us. The Bible depicts a God who created the entire universe and invented atomic structure and subatomic structure and who flung the trillions of galaxies into their courses, but who also wished to create a people for himself. He is obviously a dramatically far cry from the lifeless deity of Aristotle. The biblical God participates in human history, first through Abraham and then Moses and David and others, in order to launch his plan to reach all of the other nations of the world. And of course when the appointed time came, he entered the world himself as a human being, to change the course of eternity too.

This is a wild idea, but the somewhat unpredictable quirkiness of these actions are the actions of the same God, who from his vantage point outside time and space created time and space. This is hardly some Zeus or Ganesh. This is a perfect God outside of time and space who nonetheless deigns to enter the messiness of time and space to create beings in his extraordinary image, who are intended not only for this material world but by faith in him for the world outside time and space in which he dwells.

There is at least one more reason the biblical view of things led the world to science, and this is the idea that humans are fallible and fallen. Fuller says that in the late Middle Ages and through the Protestant Reformation the works of Augustine became popular, and the fourth- and fifth-century genius had brilliantly summed up the Bible's idea of man's twin nature. We were created in God's matchless image, and therefore bore the *Imago Dei*, but because we had also fallen from our perfect state in paradise, we now also bore the *peccatum originis*, or Original Sin. As Meyer explains it, we had the extraordinary rational abilities to investigate and understand the material world around us, but we also "were vulnerable to self-deception, flights of fancy, and prematurely jumping to conclusions." So just as much as we were obliged to be excited about what we might find, we had to be realistic in how we processed what we found. We had to have a system—which came to be called "the Scientific Method"—that allowed us to submit our findings and our theories to an objective and rigorous investigation. We had to humble ourselves as we searched for knowledge by putting our findings and our ideas to the test.

So science was not merely some individualistic Promethean project, but was something that had to be done in common with others. Even if we did not submit our findings to others, we could submit our findings to the rigorous scrutiny of the Scientific Method. We can see how these same biblical ideas led to self-government, too. On the one hand we were free and enabled by God to govern ourselves, but we also needed to make sure there was a way to deal with our temptation to take freedom lightly and to put our self-interest beyond the mutually accepted norms of the common good. So we instituted social contracts and covenants, and created a governmental order with checks and balances. This was the biblical idea of man's twin nature working itself out in history, so that the same Reformation—by returning to these biblical ideas— gave us the Scientific Revolution as well as self-government and the idea of human liberty.

It wasn't until the sixteenth and seventeenth centuries that these ideas were widely accepted, but they first arose in the Middle Ages, especially in the work of the thirteenth-century theologian Robert Grosseteste and his famous student Roger Bacon. The Australian historian of science Alistair C. Crombie has hailed Grosseteste as "the real founder of the tradition of scientific thought in medieval Oxford, and in some ways, of the modern English intellectual tradition." William of Ockham—of "Ockham's Razor" fame—was another thirteenth-century theologian who contributed to moving beyond the ultimately simplistic Greek notions of so-called Aristotelian "substantial forms" and Plato's forms and toward seeing the peculiarities and complexities of the material world. Ockham's emphasis on the need for experimentation was an expression of the biblical idea that "the natural world owes its orderly concourse to the *free* choice of an intelligent creator who could have made nature otherwise."[7]

It becomes unavoidable that Christian theology gave birth to what we presume to call science, so the misleading idea that faith and science—or religion and rationality—are not compatible must be rejected, and this

---

[7] Meyer, *Return of the God Hypothesis*, 28.

tremendously harmful misconception must be publicized. The question is only how so many of us could have been taken in by this silly idea for so long? But it appears that the facts of this matter are so threatening to those in the materialist atheist camp that they have done all they could to keep them hidden. But if the actual facts are that Christian faith is not only compatible with science, but actually led to science as we know it, might it not be possible that what is genuinely incompatible with science is atheism?

Is Atheism Incompatible with Science?

One has often heard that the best defense is a good offense. And knowing what we now know about atheism, it becomes hard not to suspect that atheists have loudly and insistently allied themselves with science and rationality precisely because it turns out to be atheism that is incompatible with these things. As Shakespeare said, "Methinks the lady doth protest too much." In his recent book *2084: Artificial Intelligence and the Future of Humanity*, the Oxford mathematician Dr. John Lennox makes this case:

> Not surprisingly, I reject atheism because I believe Christianity to be true. But that is not my only reason. I also reject it because I am a mathematician interested in science and rational thought. How could I espouse a worldview that arguably abolishes the very rationality I need to do mathematics? By contrast, the biblical worldview that traces the origin of human rationality to the fact that we are created in the image of a rational God makes real sense as an explanation of why we can do science. Science and God mix very well. It is science and atheism that do not mix.[8]

So if science arose directly from the worldview of the Bible, as has been shown, the willful inversion of these facts by the New Atheists is a crime against truth and history worthy of a Joseph Stalin, who of course was an

---

[8] John C. Lennox, *2084: Artificial Design and the Future of Humanity* (Grand Rapids, Michigan: Zondervan, 2020), 114.

atheist himself, but who never felt the need to pretend to be devoted to reason. It seems that the more one knows, the less one sees to excuse the New Atheists and their sour philosophy. The record shows them to be by turns opportunistic, bombastic, and unrigorous on these most fundamental issues, so that taking them at all seriously seems at least a waste of time. They appear not to give a fig for the difficult facts but have shouted themselves hoarse about their ardent dedication to science and rationality, as though nakedly claiming these things is all that is required.

Richard Dawkins may have spent his career doing science, but in talking about what science actually is he has shown himself to be hopelessly confused. We might expect scientists to be able to do science, but we should not expect them to understand the idea of science any more than we can expect a fish to understand how he swims. But as Western culture has become increasingly secular, many of us have looked to scientists to be something like a new priesthood, dispensing wisdom they do not have. So we cannot fault Dawkins for using the bully pulpit he has been given to express his opinions, but we can and must fault him for the wild error in those opinions. He is hardly the first to hurtle heedlessly past the boundaries of his particular field of knowledge, as the enticement to do so is heady. Anyone who has read Sigmund Freud's *Moses and Monotheism* will learn two things Freud did not intend: the first being that Freud's field of expertise was not religion, and the second being that this did not prevent him from thinking it might be.

We have mentioned Carl Sagan, who was the popular voice of science in the 1970s and who was the host of the *Cosmos* TV series of that time. More recently another astrophysicist, Neil deGrasse Tyson, has followed in Sagan's footsteps by hosting a new *Cosmos* TV series. But he has also followed in Sagan's footsteps by putting forward utterly false ideas, and like Sagan, has cheerfully misled millions. For example, Tyson claims it was a falling away from belief in God that enabled Isaac Newton to succeed as a scientist. This is so false that it is staggering, and it is not less than shocking to think that Tyson could have said it, or that the producers of the program could have let it pass. There are mountains of evidence against this and other things Tyson claimed. So how can we doubt that his own bias against faith twisted his ability even to lay out the simplest facts of the story? But then we must also wonder how these self-proclaimed priests of rationality could think that putting forth untruths would serve the purposes of rationality and science.

As recently as 2019, no less a scientific publication than *Scientific American* published an interview with Marcelo Gleiser, a Dartmouth College theoretical physicist, in which he underscored the increasingly less avoidable reality we have been discussing:

> I honestly think atheism is inconsistent with the scientific method. What I mean by that is, what is atheism? It's a statement, a categorical statement that expresses belief in nonbelief. "I don't believe even though I have no evidence for or against, simply I don't believe."
>
> Period. It's a declaration. But in science we don't really do declarations. We say, "Okay, you can have a hypothesis, you have to have some evidence against or for that." And so an agnostic would say, look, I have no evidence for God or any kind of god. (What god, first of all? The Maori gods, or the Jewish or Christian or Muslim God? Which god is that?) But on the other hand, an agnostic would acknowledge no right to make a final statement about something he or she doesn't know about. "The absence of evidence is not evidence of absence," and all that. This positions me very much against all of the "New Atheist" guys—even though I want my message to be respectful of people's beliefs and reasoning, which might be community-based, or dignity-based, and so on…. It's not just me; it's also my colleague the astrophysicist Adam Frank, and a bunch of others, talking more and more about the relation between science and spirituality.[9]

This case has been made many times and cannot be logically refuted. Nevertheless, often playing to audiences ignorant of such things, the New

---

[9] Lee Billings, "Atheism Is Inconsistent with the Scientific Method, Prizewinning Physicist Says," *Scientific American*, March 20, 2019, https://www.scientificamerican.com/article/atheism-is-inconsistent-with-the-scientific-method-prizewinning-physicist-says.

Atheists in their season strutted like popinjays across the cultural stage, drinking in the adulation of those they deceived, and never showing any hints of shame for having done so. What to make of it? One could quote Fielding Mellish and declare it to be "a travesty of a mockery of a sham of a mockery of a travesty of two mockeries of a sham." And isn't it? From what we now know, the books and bitter speeches of these New Atheists appear to be the last gasps of a dead religion. As Gleiser and innumerable other scientists attest, not only are faith and science compatible, but those who try to pervert science into "scientism" and into a preposterous ideology of strict "materialism" are themselves being aggressively unscientific and irrational. It is unavoidable: Atheism is by definition anti-science. These are the strange but true facts, and we must revise our understanding of things to account for them.

CHAPTER TWENTY-SEVEN

Further Problems with Atheism

If we are only matter, nothing matters.

—Eric Metaxas

We've covered the Copernican Principle and how devout atheists have expressed elation at the idea that we on Earth were no longer at the physical center of the universe, as though this somehow demoted human beings and erased the idea of the God who had put them at the center. We've also discussed the idea of the fine-tuned universe and the "Anthropic Principle," which catapults human beings to a level of "special-ness" exponentially beyond merely being at the physical center of the solar system. But before we move on, we might ask why atheists would so revel in dancing on what they obviously believe is the grave of God and the grave of human beings as somehow extraordinary. Why should they seem to leap and twinkle at the idea that we are essentially the equals of eels and cockroaches and bacteria? One may disagree with their logic but must still wonder: Why do they take such inverse pride in denigrating their own species? It seems unavoidably perverse and can seem so dark that it comes across as diabolical, as though in rejecting God they have unwittingly taken on the opinions of God's eternal foe—who himself is not at all confused whether God exists but knows that he does, and despises and

359

wishes to murder him, even at times having assayed to do so, and who uniquely despises those whom God uniquely cherishes.

So the oft-expressed joy at believing we aren't special—even if it isn't true—is curious, nor can it really be called joy. Perhaps the cognate among such persons would be *schadenfreude*. But again, why? Certainly, it cannot be thought normal, natural, or healthy to denigrate oneself, or to hate one's tribe or species. Pride in one's country or hometown is the most normal and natural thing there is and one of the simplest pleasures of life. It is to rejoice in the particulars of our particularity, to say that my school or my team is the best, to say that I love my country and its food and traditions. We all know how that can go wrong, but have we forgotten how its opposite can go wrong? We speak too rarely of how it can be healthy and beautiful, and a way of appreciating something near us that will enable us to appreciate all that is good and true and beautiful beyond it.

We must also ask to what these ideas lead or have led. It is one thing to respect and care for the other species in God's creation, but if we do not ourselves believe we are made in God's image and are not sacred or special in any way, we certainly cannot say that each human life has dignity and inherent value—and then what? If one believes that we are the products of random evolution that blindly selected upward toward, well, us—then we know that by dint of its having happened accidentally it is quite meaningless. We really have no particular value, even if we are smarter than other creatures. So how then can we get away from the logical conclusion that murdering a human being or several human beings is any different than swatting horse flies?

Some atheists such as Peter Singer have openly averred such unpleasant things, which we must applaud for its intellectual honesty. Nonetheless his idea that a newborn baby is no different than a pig or a snake, and may be killed if we choose, doesn't sit well with most people. Is that simply because we are not as enlightened as Mr. Singer? Would it be braver and more honest of us to admit that evolution makes us all equal and that the repulsion at murdering or devouring a child or a neighbor or a parent is only a social construct, one that if we were brave and truly rational we would kick away, with no more difficulty than a child must kick away his aversion to eating the vegetables he dislikes? If a bacterium has no real value and human beings also have no real value, who can stop us from declaring that the laws prohibiting murder should be struck down as vestiges of some ancient irrational order?

Or if we were to assign relative values to all animals—and we could hope to say that we really do have more value and more rights than a beetle or a tadpole—on what basis would we do that? Many like Singer have already done the homework on this for us and have said that our value comes from things other than our common humanity. If we have intelligence and usefulness—and who determines that?—we have more value than someone with less intelligence or usefulness. So bright adults may avoid trouble, but young children may be murdered with no more concern that we would gut a perch or butcher a hog. In fact, the fish and hog have value dead, but the child would not since we still subscribe to the ancient taboos against cannibalism, so we even might wish to argue that killing the child and simply disposing of it would be wasteful. Surely, we could at least make some money from selling its parts and do some good with that.

One problem with this line of thinking is that it is precisely the same as that embraced by the Nazis. There's no way around that. The Nazis cynically gave public lip service to God but were grimly calculating atheists in practice, and the moment they had power they put all the serious Christians in concentration camps or on the front lines of the war, the sooner to die—and then did precisely as they had always wanted to do, without any backward religious people to carp at them. For example, everyone considered mentally ill was thought a drain on the National Socialist state and logically ought not to be fed and cared for with valuable resources that could otherwise be employed in winning the war. Under the gruesome T4 Program, innumerable hospitalized handicapped people were murdered, or rather "euthanized" via injection. Their corpses were delivered to crematoria, and their parents received a package containing their ashes and a letter claiming that they had died of natural causes. They were declared to be "life unworthy of life." The Nazis had the power to say as much and act on it, and did.

It will doubtless upset strict materialists and atheists to be lumped in with Nazis, but taking offense is no argument. And since atheists loudly ally themselves with reason and rationality, how shall we shrink from asking them to defend their positions reasonably and rationally? We must hear how it can be that atheists maintain we are merely material beings with no transcendent value, but blanch and sputter when it is pointed out that this is what Hitler and the National Socialists believed—and carried out with typical and tragic German efficiency. It is what today's Chinese Communist Party leaders believe too, who profit from their convictions by murdering healthy Uyghur Muslims to sell their organs; because wealthy and ailing Saudis fussily reject the organs of non-Muslims and will pay a premium for those of their murdered core-ligionists, the Chinese government is now able to fetch half a million dollars per murder.

The Nazis were similarly logical and rational, and when it came to deliberately murdering millions of men, women, and children, they did not do with the bodies what less calculating murderers would but saw through to the bottom of their philosophy, which declared that not only were these lives not worth keeping alive, but they were valuable for their raw materials when dead, just like an animal's body. The Nazis did not have the technology of today's Chinese Communists, but they did the best they could under the circumstances. Not only were gold teeth removed from the corpses, which any desperate and ordinary grave robber might do, but the Nazis used the hair of their victims and even rendered the fat of their flesh to make soap. And why not? On what grounds would this be in any way objectionable to people who believe we are neither transcendent nor sacred? Aren't our objections just ancient and irrational taboos that we should see through and dispense with? The Nazis even used the skin of their victims to make lampshades and other decorative objects, just as we do with the skin of cows or alligators, so that skin with tattoos was especially prized.

It follows from an atheist worldview that if these human beings have no inherent value, we may well treat them as we would other animals. If we regard them merely as material objects, why shouldn't we who are above them on the evolutionary scale—since having survived them we are by definition fitter—use them for our profit? The Nazis not only accepted Darwin's theory, but were willing to follow its logic to the end. So on what basis do atheists today take issue with these things? And on what basis would the atheists tell the Chinese Communists who are doing similar things today that they should stop? How can we talk about human rights when human beings are randomly selected creatures no different than any others? On what basis could we do that?

Why Such Rage?

So it is interesting to ask what animates atheists—and especially these "New Atheists"—in their scorched-earth campaigns against "religion." Do they themselves know? Why do they exult in the denigration of their own species and why do they boil with fury at those who disagree with them? Their graceless rage at whoever deviates from their subjective orthodoxy has no discernible logic and reminds many of the worst of what one observes in religious zealots. In his book *Gunning for God: Why the New Atheists Are Missing the Target*, the Oxford mathematician John Lennox writes: "Like me there are many scientists and others who think that the New Atheism is a belief system which ironically provides a classic example of the blind faith it so vocally despises in others."[1] Whatever it is that motivates Dawkins and motivated Hitchens to the heights of scorn and invective cannot be rational, despite their irrational claims to rationality. Anyone with the least amount of common sense knows that

[1] John Lennox, *Gunning for God: Why the New Atheists are Missing the Target* (Oxford: Lion Books, 2011), 15.

seeing faults in an idea or philosophy does not necessarily preclude see-ing some good things too. So why can these New Atheists not admit, for example, that not all faiths are equal, or that not all faiths are bad? Why can they not see that many people of faith have even sometimes demon-strated love to their enemies, or have made self-sacrificial efforts to help strangers? But for no reasons that seem clear the New Atheists perversely refuse to concede even these well-documented facts.

Nor would a strictly rational person rage against the idea of faith simply because some people of faith have behaved poorly any more than a rational person would denounce motherhood as a vile lie because there exist some mothers who have not been loving to their children. No one has yet appeared on the lecture circuit to denounce motherhood precisely because we see exceptions for what they are: exceptions. But the New Atheists seem to revel in tossing caution and nuance to the wind. So to search for rhyme or reason in what they say can sometimes be like trying to parse the ravings of a madman. In particularly purple flights they contradict themselves at nearly every turn of phrase, boustrophedoni-cally doubling back on themselves again and again in ways that seem tangential and tangled, and yet the proudly indignant determination with which they speak captivates us and carries us forward until it seems we have entirely forgotten the objection that a moment ago bothered us, for they have moved on and are still moving on and on and on. Part of this may be intentional strategy on their parts, but whether conscious or unconscious—or what part of each—is impossible to say.

Hitchens in particular hardly seemed to care a jot for consistency or truth, but given his anti-creedal creed, why should he have cared? How could he or his compatriots be expected to, for that would require a universal standard, and where could that come from if we and our ideas about such things arose randomly over the eons, like the miasma of a morning fog from the riverbed of our planet's youth? But Hitchens was so good at histrionics—carefully managing his image as the perpetually indignant *enfant terrible*, with his carefully disheveled hair and faux-meaningful gaze of outrage at the stupidities he and his fellow noble atheists had to endure at the hands of unenlightened saps—that he knew like some mountebank or confidence man that by the time you wondered if he had just said something slightly wrong-footed he would charge ahead with another brace or three of witticisms or harrumphs such that you instantly forgot about it. And thus he proceeded through the years into the perfect silence of the grave that he pretended held no meaning or serious questions or fear for him, for it would only hold the quieted and colder form of what he had been all along—an animated and now inanimate animal with no soul or intrinsic value or future of any kind, a pile of nothing much, for we are only matter and more matter, none of which ever mattered one whit, if only we had the honesty and courage to see it.

But again, we ask: If this is true, why thunder as he thundered? What was the point? That question he could never answer seriously or straight-forwardly (and he was smart enough to know it but seems to have kept these questions at bay even from himself via what looked like perpetual forward movement in essays, speeches, books, and debates to the point of haggardness, for to let these important questions linger too long might be the beginning of his undoing, and that would never do). But the larger point is that by insisting on many things that were not true or at least not entirely true, the New Atheists eventually twisted themselves into pretzels of illogic, just as a liar must lie more and more boldly to support the first lie, and wittingly or unwittingly used their emotions—usually passionate anger—as a cover for the logical gaps.

The Brain Is Not a Mind; the Mind Is Not a Brain

We said that atheist materialists assert—with no evidence—that matter is all there is. Since this is not true or certainly cannot be proven to be true, it would lead like all other semi-demi-hemi-truths to cul-de-sacs and trouble. For example, if matter is all that exists anywhere, then although human beings have brains, they do not have minds. This is a crucial dis-tinction. Materialists say there is a squishy wet piece of pink-gray matter inside our skulls and that is who we are. So when you die and it rots, there is no you left. There is no mind or soul apart from that mushy computer in your skull. This is conceivably true, but there is much evidence to the contrary, and it is certain that no one can prove it is true.

Materialists—and of course atheists, who are materialists—know that the concept of Mind contradicts their belief that there is nothing transcendent, nothing beyond the material. So any hint that there is anything beyond our mere organic brains is out of bounds and too hysterical to be countenanced as even conceivably possible. So stories of people leaving their bodies during operations and watching themselves being operated upon—which exist in the multiplied thousands—must be hallucinations, even though these stories often involve the unconscious and anesthetized patient seeing things and knowing things going on during the operation that an unconscious anesthetized patient could not possibly see or know. But these stories must all be rejected, even if they are the stories of brilliant and sober-minded persons, and even if the details of these stories are corroborated by doctors. For the atheist materialist, even to be open to the idea that it is possible some of those stories could be true is asking too much. They must be ruled out by definition.

The idea of consciousness must be waved away too. Somehow—though no one can begin to point to how—our mushy, squishy brains yield something we call "consciousness," where we are aware of ourselves and our surroundings in a way that a robot can never be, despite the fact that he might himself have a complex computer "brain" of circuits which materialists say is in no way any different from our brains, except less spongy and moist. But what is consciousness and how does a mere brain make that leap to consciousness apart from what we call "mind"? No one has any idea. But materialists and atheists assure us that it doesn't matter. As with other impossibly tangled conundrums along such lines they either say A) we don't know yet, but for sure we will find out. We just know we will. And any evidence against our baseless but hopeful attitude is inherently wrong and must be dismissed, and harshly, too, for the sake of humanity. Or B) consciousness is an illusion. So let's forget all about it. There. We're done with the subject.

What would you like for lunch? Not that you really have a choice, since free will and consciousness are an illusion, and you are pre-programmed by your genes to choose some particular thing given the particular circumstances in which you now find yourself. You're what some have called a "meat robot." But don't be depressed about that. It's only depressing if you think about it. Although if your genes have programmed you to think about it you really don't have a choice whether to think about it, do you? Perhaps you're one of those less-fit creatures whose survival ought to be curtailed. Perhaps it's just we who have evolved in the direction of not thinking about the bleak meaninglessness of "life" who should survive and perpetuate the species. But why should "evolution" care about the perpetuation of a species that has no purpose and that cannot face the fact that it has no purpose? Again, we don't know. And if we want to know, it only makes the case that we aren't as fit as those who don't want to know. Get it? Good. Or not necessarily good, since good and evil are immaterial. But something like "good." Or perhaps not. Perhaps even trying to make any sense of this goes against what we are, if we really are only matter that has mindlessly come to produce whatever it is that we are. And if that's true, what is there to say, really? If we are only matter, then nothing matters. Isn't that about the gist of it?

CHAPTER TWENTY-EIGHT

Atheism Unhinged

There are those who take on the moniker "atheist," but wear it lightly, principally because they are unaware of the absurdity such a philosophy expresses, or because they don't have the courage to say otherwise and gingerly accept the label. Such souls are usually more accurately described as agnostics but are often afraid that calling themselves agnostics might show too much sympathy for those they think of as religious fanatics.

Many of these so-called "atheists" prove the weakness of their claim to the title because they say things that sound wonderfully reasonable and therefore betray them as agnostics. For example, the paleontologist and evolutionary advocate Stephen Jay Gould had the wisdom and humility to declare: "Science simply cannot adjudicate the issue of God's possible superintendence of nature." In other words, he saw the logical limits of science and admitted them, knowing that if there actually were a God, science would not be able to tell us much about him.

But those who are militant in their atheism paper over such logical inadequacies. They not only cannot see that science has limits, but preposterously claim that science is our only way of "knowing" anything, and further claim that the material world to which science has access is all that exists. That's like saying that because our eyes cannot smell or taste, there is no such thing as aroma or food. It is of course perfectly circular and silly. They say that science can only access the material world, and yet declare with the impossibility of evidence that the material world is all that has ever existed—or can or will exist.

Hitchens was among the loudest of these and often maintained that the scientific method and "evidence" were the only way to know anything. Hoping to land a wild blow against every "faith" and "religion" at once, he often declared: "What can be asserted without evidence can be dismissed without evidence." This aphorism was repeated so often by his acolytes it came to be known as Hitchens's Razor, catapulting him into the rare shaving orbit of such as William of Ockham. The difficulty with "Hitchens's Razor" is that it unintentionally severs the metaphorical jugular of its eponymous author, since the idea that there is nothing beyond the material world has itself been "asserted without evidence," and can therefore be summarily dismissed.[1]

In the end it seems that the so-called New Atheists and angry and militant atheists have less in common with honest agnostics than with less intellectually respectable groups such as Satanists, who are obviously more animated by a hatred of the God they suspect exists—and the people who claim to follow him—than they are of anything more intellectually robust. They seem to want to pull out all the stops to defeat their theistic enemies and are unmoored by any sense of rationality or logic—or justice or fairness or universal respect for humanity—in how they execute their martial campaigns. So we find them sometimes making statements that reveal as much, as when Hitchens once declared: "I'm not even an atheist, so much as I am an antitheist; I not only maintain that all religions are versions of the same untruth, but I hold that the influence of churches, and the effect of religious belief is positively harmful."[2]

---

[1] I too have an aphorism: "Anything Christopher Hitchens asserts must be spoken aloud in the voice of Fran Drescher. If it does not still seem profound, it isn't." (My acolytes have my permission to call this "Metaxas's Razor.")

[2] Christopher Hitchens, *Letters to a Young Contrarian* (New York: Basic Books, 2001), 55.

He couldn't bother to compare the relative harmfulness of "religion" to that of enforced atheism because this would be inconvenient to his point. It was a kind of game for him, and to someone for whom there is no ultimate reality, what else could it be? He had already told us what we needed to know to see this. The idea of truth was to him beside the point, since he didn't believe in such a thing. That's simply a fact, and while he might not have advertised it, since it would be bad for business, we can't think he was unable to see it. So the rest of this quote, taken from his *Letters to a Young Contrarian*, is enlightening:

> Reviewing the false claims of religion I do not wish, as some sentimental materialists affect to wish, that they were true. I do not envy believers their faith. I am relieved to think that the whole story is a sinister fairy tale; life would be miserable if what the faithful affirmed was actually the case.... There may be people who wish to live their lives under cradle-to-grave divine supervision, a permanent surveillance and monitoring. But I cannot imagine anything more horrible or grotesque.[3]

It seems inconceivable that a man of Hitchens's intellect could miss the implications of his sentences. How he writhes at the idea of God watching him as the most "horrible" and "grotesque" thing his strangely truncated imagination can fathom, and yet blithely blithers and blathers without a nod to the atheist regimes that have always done this and do this today, now even surveilling their subjects and prisoners with fabulous new technology stolen from the West or purchased from immoral Western companies whose names rhyme with Kugel, whom we must imagine would have fought hard to win the lucrative bids on manufacturing the gas chambers and crematoria of the Death Camps. Did Hitchens really imagine that a world devoid of religion would be a utopia, or did the examples from history of atheist regimes simply escape his attention in the moments he was formulating his quotable quotes? That as an adolescent he was taken with Arthur Koestler's *Darkness at Noon* tells us

---

[3] Ibid, 55.

he was never unaware of the satanic horrors of atheist communism, only that at some point he was willing to overlook them.

In case we haven't mentioned it, Hitchens was moving too fast ever to be very consistent, having the rare ability to proceed so hastily— whether in exhaling essays like smoke rings while under the influence of cigarettes and alcohol or in switching topics mid-soliloquy—and keep moving in a way that his audiences could never easily catch him in his self-contradictions or were too amused to care.

His rage at things seems to have also fueled him, as though he were running from something in his subconscious too ghastly to be borne and must keep moving, even at the cost of self-contradiction. In fact, it is his static sense of rage and umbrage and his endlessly affecting this posture that are the only immutable and consistent aspects of his careering persona. Those familiar with his life will see a pattern. When it suited him to be a Labourite he was a Labourite, and when it suited him to declare himself a Trotskyite he did. During this early period he was of course bravely bisexual and courageously and fashionably "anti-Vietnam" and "anti-racist," and then anti-Reagan, but his habit of switching vehicles as often as possible in his escape from whatever was chasing him led him to write screeds against the Clintons and then against (of all people) Mother Teresa, whom he called "the ghoul of Calcutta" for her unpardonable crime of living in poverty and caring for the dying poor among the slums of her adopted city. Hitchens also said that Billy Graham went into the ministry "to make money," as though the man who in his nonstop writing was not beating the bushes for ha'pennies in doing so. After 9/11, he came out as unreservedly supporting the Iraq War, gigging his former leftist friends as he did so, until he finally wriggled from this last cocoon and flew to his grave in the form of an atheist butterfly who denounced all religions equally, which made as much sense as the man who hates all ideas equally. He once said: "I think religion should be treated with ridicule, hatred, and contempt, and I claim that right."[4] One can no longer

---

[4] Barbara Bradley Hagerty, "A Bitter Rift Divides Atheists," National Public Radio, October 19, 2009, https://www.npr.org/templates/story/story.php?storyId=113889251.

ask, "Yes, but what do you mean by religion exactly?" because the man who threw the Wiffle ball of that statement has himself fluttered away to another dimension (although of course he would have argued that he hadn't, since none can be scientifically proven to exist).

While inevitably extremely less entertaining, Hitchens's fellow New Atheists nonetheless offered dramatically similar logic-free bouquets of pique. Richard Dawkins said, "I am utterly fed up with the respect we have been brainwashed into bestowing upon religion."[5] Sam Harris declared his intention to "demolish the intellectual and moral pretensions of Christianity in its most committed forms."[6] Are they unaware that Hitler and Himmler and Stalin and Pol Pot and Mao and Ceaușescu had similar ambitions, or wouldn't that matter?

But the frenzied anger the New Atheists have employed in denouncing those on the other side cannot help but lead to the very real demonization of their enemies—and what could be more logical? Once you have thrown away the very things given to you by the faith you have poured out with the bathwater—things like civility and respecting others and trying to move toward some actual truth—you are yourself at the mercy of the demons you have unleashed, and whether these legions are metaphorical we must leave to the careful reader.

The unbridled fury on display was hardly ever well-disguised as having a larger purpose than to provoke in their audiences a similar fury at their enemies. But such fury in the hands of those who have excommunicated transcendent values has nothing through which to channel the blood of their enemies, which must eventually run. Their ideological forebears are found among the French Revolutionists, who in the name of *liberté*, *égalité*, and *fraternité* slaughtered their opponents like dogs in the street as the mobs roared for more, and who preserved their greatest ire for priests and nuns. Who but the very Devil of Hell could be behind something like that? And if not him, then who? Nominations remain open. But one must wonder: What could cause people to espouse such anodyne values as this French motto

---

[5] Lennox, *Gunning for God*, 217.

[6] Sam Harris, *Letter to a Christian Nation* (New York: Vintage Books, 2006), ix.

publicly and vocally while they butchered innocents? What has history made of that, other than to whitewash it and let it take on newer forms in the Bolshevik Revolution and the Stalinist purges and the Chinese Communist Revolution and the Killing Fields of the Khmer Rouge?

It says much that Hitchens and Dawkins could sufficiently blind themselves to the inevitable course of their calls to arms or would open themselves and their indisputably fine minds to the service of what look like violent spiritual forces. The so-called New Atheists often used the excuse of the 9/11 attacks by Islamic madmen to launch their fusillades against all religions—and therefore sometimes against the very things attacked in those attacks, the religious and moral foundations of a nation "conceived in Liberty, and dedicated to the proposition that all men are created equal." Of course, those are the words from Lincoln's famous Gettysburg Address, and who can imagine what he or Washington might have made of these preening British pamphleteers railing against the God who commanded his followers to "Love your enemies." Lincoln ended his immortal address with the following words:

> It is rather for us to be here dedicated to the great task remaining before us—that from these honored dead we take increased devotion to that cause for which they gave the last full measure of devotion—that we here highly resolve that these dead shall not have died in vain—that this nation, under God, shall have a new birth of freedom—and that government of the people, by the people, for the people, shall not perish from the earth.

It's hard not to see the New Atheists sneering at the humble railsplitter's words, having already established that the God of whom he spoke does not exist. But the idea that they would put faith in Lincoln's God on equal footing with faith in the entity for whom the men flew those planes into buildings is the sort of nonsense that can never be made sense of by anyone wishing to make sense. And of course, quite sadly, it is in their calculated demonization of those with whom they differ that the New Atheists most resemble the 9/11 hijackers and other villains, recent and distant. Hitler's demonization of the Jews could not rest on any substantial intellectual foundations, but it didn't need to. He had enough power to render those with whom he disagreed or merely disliked into soap and ashes, for he never pretended to believe in naive notions such as "the equality of man" or "the dignity of the individual." He would use these ideas when it suited his purposes, would speak of the "nobility of the German worker" as long as it served his ends, and would then send those workers to their deaths with the same indifference that another man tied a shoe. Using human beings as cannon fodder in the services of his greater purposes was consonant with his atheist worldview. There was no transcendence and no good or evil, only power, and he wanted it for himself. Did Hitchens and Dawkins never consider how suspiciously they resembled these villains in their own reckless campaign?

Dawkins himself wrote:

> My last vestige of "hands off religion" respect disappeared in the smoke and choking dust of September 11, 2001, followed by the "National Day of Prayer" when prelates and pastors did their tremulous Martin Luther King impersonation and used people of mutually incompatible faiths to hold hands, united in homage to the very force that caused the problem in the first place.[7]

Where to begin in unscrambling this egg? Dawkins doesn't trouble himself to consider whether those motivated to murder their ideological enemies are in any way different than Jesus, who forgave his murderers. But what is chilling about their cult of nothingness is that they seem to have been willing to say nearly anything in the service of it, to throw those who beheaded Arab Christians in orange jumpsuits by the seashore and those who believe in drowning their enemies in cages and throwing men off roofs in the very same category as

---

[7] Richard Dawkins, *A Devil's Chaplain: Reflections on Hope, Lies, Science, and Love* (Boston: Mariner, 2004), 157.

the Amish who publicly forgave the madman who murdered their girls, and as the African American Christians in Charleston, South Carolina, who publicly forgave the young white man who murdered their friends and family members in a Bible study after they had prayed and shown him kindness. How is it that the dedicatedly persistent sloppiness of this superlatively monstrous position bellowed by these men with innumerable academic degrees and honors can be seen as anything but a kind of madness?

Although one needn't be apoplectic with indignation to spout such sentiments. The musician John Lennon was very far from the venomous hissing of the New Atheists, but the banal lyrics wedded to his movingly melodic song "Imagine" are nonetheless every bit as dull as Hitchens's Razor. Though the song is infinitely more pleasant to hear than the spittle-flecked jeremiads of the New Atheists, the general idea is the same: that if only we could do away with religion our problems would be solved.

But one never gets to ask, "then what?" It is not an unimportant question. Most students of history know that when you destroy something it may be replaced by something considerably worse. Those who got rid of the Tsarist regime had no idea that Lenin and then Stalin would usher in a nightmare that would make the Tsarist world look like very Heaven. It may be that the New Atheists' moment in the sun has so faded in recent years because once they had taken every conceivable potshot at everything they hated several times over, they simply ran out of things to say. They found themselves in the awkward position of the dog who has caught the car, and then slunk away embarrassed, having never formulated any particular plans for the car once he'd caught it.

CHAPTER TWENTY-NINE

Great Scientists Who Were Devout Christians

The sheer number of great scientists in history who were also men of the most profound faith is yet another powerful strike against those who would assert the idea that faith and science could be at odds. For example, was there ever a greater scientist in the history of the world than Isaac Newton? Einstein may have been his equal, or perhaps James Clerk Maxwell, but these two alone mark the extent of serious comparison. So when we learn that this towering genius who discovered gravity and invented calculus was a deeply committed Christian, how can we help but wonder at the sincerity of those claiming faith and science are enemies? The great man who pondered the universe centuries before Maxwell and Einstein wrote: "The most beautiful system of sun, planets, and comets could only proceed from the counsel and dominion of an intelligent and powerful Being."[1] In his 1704 treatise, *Opticks*, Newton said that it was the very business of all science to "deduce causes from effects, till we come to the very first cause, which certainly is not mechanical."

---

[1] Quoted by Tom Bethell in "Don't Fear the Designer," Discovery Institute, December 1, 2005, https://www.discovery.org/a/3074.

Sir Isaac Newton (1643–1727)

When the Enlightenment came along, many atheistically inclined thinkers leapt to use Newton's "mechanistic view" of the universe to push God out of the equation, oddly unaware that they were in direct disagreement with Newton himself. Newton saw that it was God who set the universe tumbling forward into space even before mechanics came into being, or rather that he created the world of mechanics from nothing. And that God, even after setting everything into motion, hardly needed to step away from his Creation. There was no reason for an infinitely intelligent and powerful being outside of time and space to go into retirement and dotage. By Newton's lights, after God created the universe, he was quite capable of staying busy in history, among other things. It is also because of his reverence for the Bible that Newton could intuit that God had existed before the material universe of time and space, and of course Newton did so centuries before science led us to acknowledge the Big Bang that gave us the subsequent world of Newton's mechanics.

But on the towering faith of many of the greatest scientists in the world the New Atheists are quiet as mice. And the list of them is nearly endless. Perhaps the man most responsible for enabling Newton's discoveries was the aforementioned German astronomer and mathematician Johannes Kepler (1571–1630), who wrote: "The chief aim of all investigations of the external world should be to discover the rational order and harmony which has been imposed on it by God and which He revealed to us in the language of mathematics."[2] Robert Boyle (1627–1691) also influenced Newton, and no mention of the world's greatest scientists

[2] Morris Kline, *Mathematics: The Loss of Certainty* (Oxford: Oxford University Press, 1980), 31.

could exclude him who was the first modern chemist, who occupied as central a position in the scientific pantheon as anyone. He founded the entire field of chemistry and was among the very first to employ the scientific method itself. Like both Newton and Kepler, Boyle was a Christian of the most ardent stripe, even writing extensively in theology.

So only having mentioned these three of the greatest scientists who ever lived—and who essentially pioneered modern science itself—we must ask ourselves: Why did it not concern the New Atheists that these giants upon whose shoulders all modern science stands were Christians of the most profound faith, and whose faith did not merely exist alongside their scientific genius, but was by their own understanding at the very heart of that genius? What but the unpleasant awareness of this can account for the New Atheists' so assiduously shrinking from addressing the subject? If they had been jabbering automatons unaware of what they were saying we could excuse the dissonance, but for any of these educated fellows—much less an actual scientist like Richard Dawkins—to insist on the incompatibility of faith and science can hardly be fathomed and only further undermines our ability to take them seriously. Before we skitter from this subject, we must visit one more dizzying genius in the world of science, briefly mentioned a moment ago.

James Clerk Maxwell

James Clerk Maxwell lived two centuries after Kepler, Boyle, and Newton, but his status in the world of science is such that he can only be compared to Newton and Einstein. As a boy of eight he could recite long passages from Milton, and the breathtakingly long 119th psalm,[3] and as an undergraduate at Cambridge, he determined to be as uncompromising in his examination of his Christian faith as in his examination of the natural world. In a letter to his friend Lewis Campbell, who later became a professor of classics at St. Andrews, Maxwell expressed his belief that it was only the Christian faith that invited such total investigation, and that it did not insist

---

[3] William Wilberforce memorized it as an adult and would recite it in the twenty-minute walk from Parliament to his home.

James Clerk Maxwell (1831–1879)

anyone believe what is not true. Maxwell saw that the Bible invites us to explore and investigate the world around us, without prohibiting us from asserting whatever we find, so that science can glorify God—and we need never fear scientific investigation as in any way being a challenge to our faith:

Christianity—that is, the religion of the Bible—is the only scheme or form of belief which disavows any possessions on such a tenure. Here alone all is free. You may fly to the ends of the world and find no God but the Author of Salvation. You may search the Scriptures and not find a text to stop you in your explorations.... Sceptics pretend to have read [the Old Testament and the Mosaic Law], and have found certain witty objections...which too many of the orthodox unread admit, and shut up the subject as haunted. But a Candle is coming to drive out all Ghosts and Bugbears. Let us follow the light.[4]

It is certainly interesting that what Maxwell did in science was to follow the light, perhaps somewhat literally, being the one to show the world that electricity, magnetism, and light were all parts of the same spectrum we now call electromagnetism. All three phenomena travel as waves and move at the speed of light. Maxwell was thus able to predict the existence of radio waves; and perhaps more impressive, as early as 1855 he delivered a paper that set out the three-color process for color photography, and in 1861 produced the first color photograph.

---

[4] Quoted by David Lyth in *The Road to Einstein's Relativity: Following in the Footsteps of Giants* (Boca Raton, Florida: CRC Press, 2019), 105.

But it was in preparing the way for special relativity and quantum mechanics that Maxwell is most highly regarded. Einstein proclaimed Maxwell's discoveries as "the most profound and the most fruitful that physics has experienced since the time of Newton." Indeed, Einstein felt so strongly about what Maxwell had done that in 1922, when he was told that he stood on the shoulders of Newton, Einstein instantly shot back: "No, I don't. I stand on the shoulders of Maxwell."

Probably because of his unparalleled genius as a pure scientist, Maxwell was unafraid to go wherever the science took him, even if it was to the ethereal border of science itself. For example, in an inaugural lecture to a professorship he makes plain that from what he knew of science and the Bible he saw that the universe was not eternal, but had been created; this was in 1860,[5] a half-century before Einstein via his calculations stumbled on the expansion of the universe, and ninety years before Hubble saw it through his telescope:

> ... the mass of each individual molecule, and all its other properties, are absolutely unalterable. In the second place the properties of all molecules of the same kind are absolutely identical.
>
> Let us consider the properties of two kinds of molecules, those of oxygen and those of hydrogen.
>
> [We can procure specimens of each.] Now if, during the whole previous history of either specimen, whether imprisoned in the rocks, flowing in the sea, or careering through unknown regions with the meteorites, any modification of the molecules had taken place, these relations would no longer be preserved.
>
> But we have another and an entirely different method of comparing the properties of molecules. The molecule, though indestructible, is not a hard rigid body, but is capable of internal movements, and when these are excited it emits rays, the

---

[5] They were published as they appear here in 1873.

wave-length of which is a measure of the time of vibration of the molecule.

By means of the spectroscope the wave-lengths of different kinds of light may be compared to within one ten-thousandth part. In this way it has been ascertained, not only that molecules taken from every specimen of hydrogen in our laboratories have the same set of periods of vibration, but that light, having the same set of periods of vibration, is emitted from the sun and from the fixed stars. We are thus assured that molecules of the same nature as those of our hydrogen exist in those distant regions, or at least did exist when the light by which we see them was emitted.

From a comparison of the dimensions of the buildings of the Egyptians with those of the Greeks, it appears that they have a common measure. Hence, even if no ancient author had recorded the fact that the two nations employed the same cubit as a standard of length, we might prove it from the buildings themselves. We should also be justified in asserting that at some time or other a material standard of length must have been carried from one country to the other, or that both countries had obtained their standards from a common source.

But in the heavens we discover by their light, and by their light alone, stars so distant from each other that no material thing can ever have passed from one to another, and yet this light, which is to us the sole evidence of the existence of these distant worlds, tells us also that each of them is built up of molecules of the same kinds as those which we find on earth. A molecule of hydrogen, for example, whether in Sirius or in Arcturus, executes its vibrations in precisely the same time.

Each molecule, therefore, throughout the universe, bears impressed on it the stamp of a metric system as distinctly as does the metre of the Archives at Paris, or the double royal cubit of the Temple of Karnac....

None of the processes of Nature, since the time when Nature began, have produced the slightest difference in the properties of any molecule. We are therefore unable to ascribe either the existence of the molecules or the identity of their properties to the operation of any of the causes which we call natural.

On the other hand, the exact equality of each molecule to all others of the same kind gives it, as Sir John Herschel has well said, the essential character of a manufactured article, and precludes the idea of its being eternal and self-existent.... Thus we have been led, along a strictly scientific path, very near to the point at which Science must stop. Not that Science is debarred from studying the internal mechanism of a molecule which she cannot take to pieces, any more than from investigating an organism which she cannot put together. But in tracing back the history of matter Science is arrested when she assures herself, on the one hand, that the molecule has been made, and on the other that it has not been made by any of the processes we call natural.

Science is incompetent to reason upon the creation of matter itself out of nothing. We have reached the utmost limit of our thinking faculties when we have admitted that because matter cannot be eternal and self-existent it must have been created. It is only when we contemplate, not matter in itself, but the form in which it actually exists, that our mind finds something on which it can lay hold.

That matter, as such, should have certain fundamental properties—that it should exist in space and be capable of motion, that its motion should be persistent, and so on, are truths which may, for anything we know, be of the kind which metaphysicians call necessary. We may use our knowledge of such truths for purposes of deduction but we have no data for speculating as to their origin.

But though in the course of ages catastrophes have occurred and may yet occur in the heavens, though ancient systems may be dissolved and new systems evolved out of their ruins, the molecules out of which these systems are built—the foundation stones of the material universe—remain unbroken and unworn.

They continue this day as they were created, perfect in number and measure and weight, and from the ineffaceable characters impressed on them we may learn that those aspirations after accuracy in measurement, truth in statement, and justice in action, which we reckon among our noblest attributes as men, are ours because they are essential constituents of the image of Him Who in the beginning created, not only the heaven and the earth, but the materials of which heaven and earth consist.

To be clear, Maxwell did not believe in a God who was merely "Aristotle's God" or "Einstein's God," for he was as full-throated in his Christian faith as anyone might be. The minister who visited him as he lay dying wrote:

His illness drew out the whole heart and soul and spirit of the man: his firm and undoubting faith in the Incarnation and all its results; in the full sufficiency of the Atonement; in the work of the Holy Spirit. He had gauged and fathomed all the schemes and systems of philosophy, and had found them utterly empty and unsatisfying—"unworkable" was his own word about them—and he turned with simple faith to the Gospel of the Saviour.[6]

As death approached, Maxwell told a Cambridge colleague:

---

[6] Paulist Fathers, *The Catholic World, Vol. 79: A Monthly Magazine of Literature and Science; April, 1904 to September, 1904* (Forgotten Books, 2018), 493.

I have been thinking how very gently I have always been dealt with. I have never had a violent shove all my life. The only desire which I can have is like David to serve my own generation by the will of God, and then fall asleep.[7]

More Scientists of Christian Faith

For further evidence that science and faith are not merely compatible but inextricably linked we need only glance at the list of leading scientists who were devoutly Christian. The list is so long that we will only add a few to those already mentioned. In the seventeenth century, for example, one finds Blaise Pascal, and in the eighteenth Gottfried Wilhelm Leibniz, Carl Linnaeus, and Antonie van Leeuwenhoek. In the nineteenth are such giants as Joseph Priestley, Charles Babbage, Gregor Mendel, Asa Gray, Michael Faraday, and Samuel Morse—as well as the Four Horsemen of Electricity: Alessandro Volta, André-Marie Ampère, Heinrich Hertz, and James Prescott Joule. In the twentieth century a host of names stand out, including George Washington Carver, Igor Sikorsky, Wernher von Braun, and Werner Heisenberg, who was among the pioneers of quantum physics and was awarded the Nobel Prize "for the creation of quantum mechanics." In a 1973 speech Heisenberg spoke on the very subject we have been discussing in this book:

> As you know, in the development of the sciences, the option has time and again been expressed since the famous trial against Galileo that scientific truth cannot be brought into harmony with the religious interpretation of the world. Although I am convinced of the unassailability of the scientific truth in its own sphere, I have never been able to dismiss the content of religious thinking simply as a state in human consciousness which we have superseded, and as a part which we can dispense with in future. So I have continually been

---

[7] Ibid.

forced during my life to ponder on the relationship between these worlds of the spirit, for I have never been able to doubt the truth of what they are pointing to.[8]

In our own new century, the list is already endless. Through my own Socrates in the City series I have had the honor of meeting and interviewing many of them, including Sir John Polkinghorne, Tel Aviv University's Gerald Schroeder, Lehigh University's Michael Behe, Stanford University's William Hurlbut, Oxford University's Ard Louis and Alister McGrath, Harvard's Armand Nicholi, and MIT's Rosalind Picard. Two more I have had the privilege of hosting are Harvard's Owen Gingerich and National Institutes of Health Director Francis Collins.

Gingerich is the professor emeritus of astronomy and history of science at Harvard and is a senior astronomer emeritus at the Smithsonian Astrophysical Observatory. He is co-author of two successive standard models for the solar atmosphere and is a leading authority on Kepler and Copernicus. He undertook a three-decade-long personal survey of Copernicus's great book *De Revolutionibus*, examining more than 580 sixteenth-century copies in libraries across Europe, North America, Australia, Japan, and China, and

Courtesy of AIP Emilio Segrè Visual Archives, Physics Today Collection

Owen Gingerich

for these efforts was awarded the Polish government's Order of Merit and had an asteroid named in his honor. Gingerich served as vice president of the American Philosophical Society (America's oldest scientific academy), as chairman of the U.S. National Committee of the International Astronomical Union, and as a councilor of the American Astronomical Society. He has also given the George Darwin Lecture (the most prestigious lecture of the Royal Astronomical Society), observed twelve total solar eclipses, and published 600

---

[8] Werner Heisenberg, "Scientific Truth and Religious Truth," *CrossCurrents* 24, no. 4 (1975): 463–73, http://www.jstor.org/stable/24457901.

technical or educational articles and reviews. Upon his retirement in 2000 from Harvard, his course "The Astronomical Perspective" was "the longest-running course under the same management" in the history of America's oldest university.

Many are familiar with Dr. Francis Collins as the scientist given the towering task of heading up the Human Genome Project, one of the greatest scientific achievements of modern times, which is the largest collaborative biological project in the world. It is fitting that among the most well-known and accomplished scientists of our time should not only be a devout Christian, but one who also devotes a considerable amount of time and energy to explaining how his dedication to faith and science are not only compatible, but about how it was science itself that led him to faith, which he does in his powerful book *The Language of God: A Scientist Presents Evidence for Belief.*

CHAPTER THIRTY

Conclusions:
The Meaning of Meaning

Sterling Memorial Library at Yale was intentionally designed to look like a European cathedral, but not to the glory of God. It was built with the funds set aside for a spectacular new chapel, but by 1924—the year the library was conceived—mandatory chapel had fallen out of fashion at Yale. The extraordinary and in some ways astonishing library building, which opened in 1931, was meant to lift up the secular idea of knowledge and learning, and to be sure no expense was spared in its design and construction. The long central corridor along which one proceeds toward the circulation desk was intended to look like the nave of a cathedral, and it does. From some distance the circulation desk looks for all the world like an altar, which was intentional, and above it is what the architect openly called his "altar mural," which portrays a woman who looks very much like Mary, but who is in fact Alma Mater, a personification of the university.

If one makes a right at this juncture, one finds oneself walking along an open cloistered walk featuring four bas relief sculptures on corbels. Three portray students at their desks, but none are studying. One listens to his radio, another ogles a pinup, and another is asleep next to a mug of beer. The fourth of these carved images, however, is of a student who is indeed studying, and who ever since he came into being under the carver's chisel in the late 1920s has been earnestly looking at the open pages of a stone book. On the left page are carved the letters U, R, and A, and on the right page the letters J and O, and below them, the letters K and E. The japery here committed to stone—"You Are a Joke"—may be read two ways. On the one hand it is perfectly puerile—ha, ha—as if it might instead have read "Ain't You Dumb? Huh-Yaw." But on another level, it is rather dark. It seems to say that if you really are intent on studying, ambitious young fellow, you might take care in how hard you do study—and in how far you wish to proceed in your studies. It seems to say that if you study well enough, you will discover something unpleasant that your less studious brethren have missed. You will discover that there is no meaning to life, nor any meaning at all in the universe—so that you yourself and your own life have no meaning but are rather merely a cosmic joke. So since you who have been studying at least seem to have wished to know, you may now know: You are the product of a random and meaningless evolutionary process that oddly enough has produced a creature who longs for meaning in a world without meaning. You will find that at the end of all your labors, if you keep searching for meaning you will at last come upon the grim notion that your studying—and all you do henceforth in your life—you do in vain. You will discover that you are not the beloved creation of a loving God, but are the random sputtering of a blind, deaf, and dumb cosmos, and that whatever noble ideas your young head holds about knowledge, wisdom, or love are specters, phantasms created by a blind process whose purposeless purpose is a perpetuation of your species. So you yourself are actually nothing. Messrs. Darwin and Freud and some others have made this quite plain. While we will not advertise this dark theme to those parents whose children may one day attend this august institution, we will at least here make a winking nod to it, here where you are standing now.

So this half-joking sculpture was subtle enough and hidden away so that many would not read so far into it. And yet it seems odd to find something saying what this carving seems to say here inside this

The lapidary—and almost impossibility bleak—distillation of a secularist worldview.

magnificent and important building, and carved in stone, too. The carving might well have gone another step, echoing Shelley's "Ozymandias," to read: "Behold thy end, ye foolish, and despair!" But it didn't wish to declare its sentiment too loudly.

Such places as Yale—or the innumerable other academic institutions that follow in Yale's disappearing footsteps—are very rarely explicit about the dark worldview that lies quietly in their secular hearts. And whether anyone is brave enough to declare it, it is nonetheless the default worldview of anyone who does not explicitly reject it. It is the worldview of the world in which we live.

But that worldview really is the worldview of those who have rejected God, whether out of irrational and peevish motives or from a sincere conviction that science has pushed God out of the equation. It is the mostly unspoken philosophy of the secular culture that grew out of these universities, and that in the forty years following the creation of that carving crept slowly outward beyond the elite universities and the cultural elites—but through them both—into the wider culture itself, until in 1966 it stepped out onto the brightly lit center stage that was the cover of *Time* magazine, asking "Is God Dead?"

Now What?

So by 1966—and by default ever since then—the cognoscenti determined without saying it openly that God really was dead, or actually never had existed, and the end of all of our yearning as a species had finally culminated in a very curious conclusion: an ending with a neck-wringing twist, as it were. They had concluded that at the very end of all of our searches for meaning throughout the centuries lay an answer we had not anticipated. It is an answer that is really a non-answer. It is a conundrum, or a paradox, but not in anything like a happy way. In fact, it seems to be a cosmic joke played on us by an indifferent universe, one that cannot even enjoy our humiliation, which is somehow even more humiliating. We have no one to reproach. But we feel the humiliation nonetheless, which is of course strange and seems to be part of the unfunny joke. But that is the sum of it. It is a ghastly joke of perfect meaninglessness.

What are we to do about it?

Well, for one thing we can reject it with every atom of our being. Have we not seen that there is enough evidence to do so? Because there is much more evidence than merely enough. There is enough evidence to leap toward the God who created the universe and who created us. But before we talk about that, let's pretend we haven't found such evidence. Let's think about those before 1966—and the many more after—who were unaware of the other side of the story, of even the possibility of a happy ending. What did they do in response to the grim news that the God they thought existed did not, and that we were alone in the universe? What was that journey like toward something, that ended in nothing?

For many of us who drank the cultural Kool-Aid along these lines, the journey toward meaning or God was something like walking hopefully along a trail in the woods. It was growing darker and darker, but we continued, hoping at the end of the long trail on which we had been walking since before we could remember to find a homey cottage with some lights on and someone there to welcome us—a friend whom we hadn't known but who knew us and loved us, who had been expecting us all this time. As the darkness became almost complete, we at last glimpsed in the distance a glow, and carefully made our way toward it. But then at the end of this trail the flickering light that we had seen and walked toward turned out not to be the light of a welcoming cottage, but rather a frightening Jack-o'-Lantern set upon a dead stump, surrounded by marsh and swamp in every direction. The wicked-seeming conundrum frightens us. The orange and yellow grin is dead, the mockery of a smile, just as the head is the mockery of a human head, and just as every corpse is the mockery of a living human being. We are horrified that the final answer to our quest and question is a heart-stopping and blood-chilling non-answer.

And so we stand there frozen, unable to proceed further. We have found after our nearly endless searching that the meaning of life is that life has no meaning. And that our lives have no meaning. But what does that mean? Could the idea that our lives have no meaning itself have meaning? Can we create meaning? What exactly is meaning, now that we are on the subject? Why should we be so desperate for it? And what shall we do now, if not crumple to the damp floor and expire, never again to be heard from in the endless eons of the never-ending and perfectly dead universe, and what does it matter?

Most people faced with this grim conclusion really can't face it directly. It is really too much to take in. Only a few have come close to facing this horror directly and honestly. We see that Sartre tried, and that Camus did too. But even they in the end were not able to face it. They eventually believed that somehow it was not possible, that it couldn't be. They knew that no matter what they knew, something else told them that this idea of a world without God or meaning could not be the whole story. It could not be as they had thought. Most of us who see that grinning death's head at the end of the trail cannot face it head on either and turn away long before Sartre and Camus did. Like them, we know this cannot be the whole story. Can it?

Some in history—thankfully extremely few—like the Marquis de Sade have faced this idea of complete meaninglessness head on and extremely perversely have embraced it utterly, even wantonly. They decided that anything that might give them any pleasure or excitement was worth doing, including even raping and killing one's own children. De Sade monstrously wrote of this and celebrated it with a cynicism so hellish and dark that most sane people recoil in horror. But there really have existed a few like him who concluded that if there really is no good or evil in the universe, they would live out that reality, and even revel in it in their profoundly sick way.

Others, like Adolf Hitler, have determined that what de Sade essentially did—privately and for his own amusement—might be done on a greater scale. They would not merely write of it and share it with the world in books but would live it out in an epic way—not merely abusing a few powerless victims, but invading entire nations with tanks and rockets and torturing, murdering, and enslaving millions, seemingly thinking themselves as gods, beyond good and evil, who could simply do as they pleased. *Who will punish us?* they thought. *We are free and alone in the universe!* Many others have not been able to do such terrible things, but nonetheless took in the full horror of the situation and chose simply to end their own lives.

Most people of course cannot do any such thing. Why they cannot is another question. But what do they do instead? They look away from the ghastliness and the grim logic of it all and do the only thing they can: they split the difference between the bang and the whimper. They are not proud of themselves for living in half-measures, but they simply don't know what else to do. Most of us are like that, if we are honest.

So we—or they—must live our lives in a strange tension. They might darkly hint at the meaninglessness of life now and again, but they can neither face nor embrace it fully. They do their best to accept what parts of it they can and work to ignore the contradiction that is left over. Perhaps life has no meaning, but they will neither kill themselves in despair nor seize the dark logic of it and exultantly live out the wild Promethean possibilities, becoming drunk with such power as they might wrest from others. Either option is far too much, so they will instead do the easier thing and—as we say—split the difference between the bang of evilly exulting in it and the whimper of exiting the dark situation via suicide.

If they have chosen this middle path, they might think: *If life is short and does not continue into eternity and there is really no good or evil, I suppose I will do what I like in the meantime. I will seize the day and more or less live for pleasure and fun and try to get by as best I can. I won't pretend to be happy about it, for there is something inside me that doesn't like it very much, though I can't say what. I will not raise my children to be bold atheists, but neither will I raise them to believe in anything. I will raise them to make their own decisions on such big questions—whatever that means, and of course it doesn't mean much, since the answers have eluded me—so I will essentially raise them to raise themselves, if that means anything. Who knows? After all, who can know?*

But perhaps also, as a mild form of revenge upon the God who in the end proved not to be there when they sought him, they will never acknowledge him more than social convention dictates they must. And they will scorn those who stupidly pretend they know he is there when they know he is not, thinking, *Their faith mocks us in our pain and doubts, and disgusts us in its blind hope for what we know doesn't exist.* But most of the time they will drift along with the crowd that avoids these dullards and cringes at them. If necessary, they will cut such fools socially as a dowager viscountess cuts the demimonde on the mezzanine, because life is too short to pretend. Or something.

But many others have seen enough evidence to know that the meaninglessness of life and the absence of God could not be true. Like Sartre and Camus, they at some point—perhaps early in life, perhaps later—came to the conclusion that God really must be the answer, that he was there and he was worth pursuing and turning toward as they were able to do so. And yet they did not do so. Why? Dylan Thomas knew at least enough to hedge his bets. He sensed there might be something out there—perhaps God—and he simply would not surrender to the hints that we are alone in the universe. But he died before he had the chance to get beyond that, still hedging his bets. Many people know far more than he did that God really must be the answer and is—yet they don't turn to him. Why?

In many cases it really is simply the power of the cultural narrative and the price that must be paid if we go against it. Many who have power in our culture—and in the various worlds in which we live our lives—have made clear that talking about things like the meaning of life or the existence of God too earnestly is embarrassing and socially unacceptable. They have bought into the false cultural narrative or aren't willing to look past it—and if they have anything to say about it, we won't look past it either.

So we have to be honest: What others think matters to most of us. And most of them have bowed to the cultural narrative and will do their part to see that we do too. Cultural narratives and paradigms are powerful. They have always been. Five hundred years ago things were dramatically different. Those in power believed in God. And if you dared speak against faith in the God of the Bible—or didn't talk about him as they thought you should—you might not only lose social status. You might be tortured and burned alive. Historically speaking, those in power are generally able to determine which beliefs are allowed and which are not. So even today in the so-called free cultures of the West, where freedom of speech and religious liberty are enshrined in our laws, we know that it's not that simple, that there are cultural forces at play that still have the power to shut most of us up. Will you let them?

Because as it happens, you have power, too. You have the power to speak the truth or to be silent. But if you don't speak the truth when you are able, you yourself become complicit in the false paradigm. Will you participate in silencing the truth? And if you are quiet about what you know to be true, are you not perhaps worse than those who genuinely don't know it to be true?

So don't you—who now know so much more than you need to know about these things—have some responsibility in all of this? Of course, you already know that you do. You get to be a part of giving others genuine hope in the genuine God who is the author of life and hope and goodness and truth and beauty. It is what you were created to do, but perhaps until now you didn't understand this as you do now. That only means that you can now live as the one who made you made you to live. You can begin now. And this is not merely a poetic or a nice idea; it is true. The God of the universe wants you to spread goodness and truth and beauty wherever you go, to his glory. There are people whose lives you will touch, whether you know it or not.

So now you know. Have we missed anything?

The Witness of Beauty

Dylan Thomas somehow knew—because he allowed himself sometimes to think with his feelings, which often can go wrong but sometimes go right—that the world in which he lived could not be without God. His innate sense of justice and beauty and his love for his father seemed to him compelling evidence that despite everything, there must be something more.

There are moments in which most of us experience something that speaks to us of something else, that points us beyond ourselves to something greater and that gives us the idea that despite all the darkness around us, there is goodness and truth and beauty and poetry and even justice in the universe, all of which seem to hint at the others and beyond to God himself.

Many things in each of our lives have been hints and clues that there really is a God, that what we think is not merely our own crazy idea but is in fact the truth. In this book we have shown that science in a way never dreamt possible has on several fronts pointed so vigorously and overwhelmingly to God that to look away from this evidence would be not merely tragic but a kind of betrayal. We cannot look at such things and then shrug, as if they require nothing of us. Truth is not so easy to come by, and when we do come upon it, we have a responsibility to it. Truth and goodness and love all require something of us.

And the archaeological record, too, is nothing less than extraordinary. No one a hundred years ago dreamt that we would have continued to discover things that supported the historicity of the Bible, but we have. It has been an astonishing run, and it continues this minute. The illogic of the atheist position on several levels has never been quite as easy to see—or to see through. How can we shrug at such things?

But there is another thing that speaks to us of God, and that is beauty. We hardly know what beauty is, but why does it often break our hearts, as if it were a door that opens up to another world?

In the summer of 1943, Cephalonia—the Greek island where my family has lived since the fifteenth century—was occupied by German and Italian troops. My father was sixteen. When the war began, he left the island's capital, Argostoli, for the safety of our family village Mavrata sixteen miles east, but now and again he would return. That summer he found himself in Argostoli for a few days, and each evening would go with his friends to the main square to eat and drink and socialize. One of those nights, after midnight, they suddenly heard the music of a trumpet from a distant rooftop. They sat, transfixed, and listened as its sonorous melody swam sinuously through the black night above their heads, until every soul there who heard it was stunned into silence and pierced by its beauty.

They later learned that the trumpet player was a German soldier, standing on a roof overlooking the square. The song he played that evening was Enrico Toselli's "Mourning Serenade," and its haunting beauty struck everyone so powerfully amidst the atmosphere of occupation and war that my father has never forgotten it, always saying that it was the single most beautiful thing he ever experienced. But what could it be about those notes embroidering the air that somehow wordlessly spoke to everyone about the meaninglessness and pain of war, and that pointed everyone who heard them beyond the ramparts of their present difficulties toward something so beautiful and glorious and true that many of them wept as they sat and listened? How could mere sounds do that? What was it exactly that had the ability to point everyone listening toward something ineffable and overwhelming and heartbreaking?

Something similar occurs at the end of the 1991 Lawrence Kasdan movie *Grand Canyon*. It happens after the ensemble of characters have managed to make their way through a litany of unpleasant and sometimes threatening circumstances in the grittier parts of crime-ridden Los Angeles during the course of a long night. At the end of these difficulties, they all somehow find themselves together the next day, standing at the lip of the Grand Canyon, raptly taking in the overwhelming grandeur of that greatest of geographical fissures, struck dumb with awe. Somehow the sublime beauty of what they are looking at seems to be the answer—or a door to the answer—that they have all been longing for during the difficult course of the story. But what can it be about that mere absence of rock—about that hole a mile deep and eighteen miles across—that could cause those characters and the movie audience staring along with them to be so utterly arrested and smitten? Why does the grandeur and beauty and sheer vastness of what they are looking at point beyond itself? And to what does it point?

Something similar to these things once happened to me. Half a century after my father listened to that trumpet that night in Cephalonia I was there myself. I was in Mavrata, the village where my family has lived for so many centuries. It was late August, and at the end of the day, I took a walk and eventually found myself on a very high cliff overlooking the sea.

Perhaps what happened had something to do with the fact that I was young, and perhaps it had something to do with the fact that I knew my father had been young there and had seen the very things I was looking at all those years before. But what particularly struck me that day as I stood there on that cliff overlooking the Ionian Sea was something I could not recall seeing before: It was the sun and the moon strangely close to each other in the sky in front of me, floating like perfect orbs just beyond my reach. One was to my left, roughly at eye level, and the other to my right at the same level. The air was deadly quiet. Now and again I heard birds singing. It was very still and pleasantly warm, and those few moments looking at these two heavenly spheres hanging there as if for me alone were as transcendent as any I have ever experienced. The colors of the sea below and before me and the fairytale beauty of the sun and the moon in such magical proximity to each other simply undid me. It was more beautiful than almost anything I can remember, a moment that pointed beyond itself, to eternity.

But what is beauty? Why does it seem to have a moral quality and to point to something beyond itself? Is that real or is it just something I imagine? Why does there seem to be a poetry and beauty in the sun and moon and stars? And why did God make the silver moon and the golden sun appear precisely the same size to us? Did he have beauty and symmetry in mind when he did that? Or did that just happen? Why does it feel like it means something? Why does beauty like that break our hearts and make us want to weep, as though God himself had appeared to us and wrapped his arms around us and told us he loved us and wanted us to live with him in paradise forever and ever? Why does extraordinary goodness break our hearts? And why do innocence and vulnerability sometimes break our hearts? What do all these things say to us about the nature of the universe and about who we are in it?

Everything Means Everything

Does not the idea that we long for meaning tell us something—or everything—about who we are and how we are made and by whom? Does not our deep longing for meaning in our own lives and for the meaning of life itself not tell us that we were created for meaning, and that without it we can hardly live?

In his incomparably beautiful book *Chance or the Dance?*, author Thomas Howard talks about these things. The book is written in some of the most gorgeous prose I have ever read, and in a series of short essays it provides a critique of what Howard calls "modern secularism" by contrasting it with the "medieval

Christian view." He is really only contrasting atheism and a simple biblical view, but Howard reckons that the Christendom of Medieval Western Europe was the fullest cultural expression of the latter. I am inclined to agree with him, and with C. S. Lewis, too, whom Howard met and from whom he got many of his ideas (just as I knew and loved Tom and got many of my own ideas from him).

In the book he asks some of the questions we have been asking here. But his central question is whether the modern secular view—which is atheistic, materialistic, and reductionist—is correct, or whether the biblical view is. Can it be that there is only matter and more matter and nothing more than matter? Can it be that the music of that midnight trumpet in the midst of war was merely sound waves pointing to nothing, but which those who heard them imagined were pointing to something? Can it be that the Grand Canyon is just a big hole, and that our reaction to it is the reaction we have been pro-grammed to have through eons of evolution, but which really means nothing except that some chemicals have been released in us for reasons we don't know yet and that make us feel a certain way for reasons we also don't know yet? In *Chance or the Dance?* Tom Howard says no. He says that everything actually means more than what it is, and he says that everything in creation somehow points beyond itself, and ultimately points all the way to God.[1]

---

[1] To be a bit more specific, Howard shows how each single thing in creation is more than what it is and points outward. For example, he says, when one looks at a Borzoi one inescapably sees some-thing regal and princely about the animal. It is not just a dog in a different shape than other dogs. It has a quality that really evokes regality and princeliness and is meant to evoke those things. It is not only in our own minds. God has put those qualities in it. In making it, God is saying some-thing more. According to Howard, God has given us innumerable pictures of other things throughout his creation. When one sees a hyena or a buzzard, one is typically repulsed. Somehow these creatures speak to us of death, both in their scavenging behavior and in their outward appearances. Hyenas skulk. But the Borzoi prances and struts. It cannot help doing so. Howard says that our general response to all these things is not random, but actually points to other things and other qualities—that these animals, to some extent, are living pictures of those other quali-ties. So a lion is thought of as the king of the jungle because he really does bear a stamp of king-ship, and a lamb is thought of as gentle and innocent because God is speaking to us about gentleness and innocence through the lamb, which he has created. Does the lion's mane suggest a crown, and was that God's idea in creating the lion, or did we borrow the idea of crowns from lions? Or both? Howard says that these creatures did not accidentally evolve into things that suggest this and that but were created by God specifically to suggest this and that.

If a secularist believes that nothing points beyond itself, nor "means" anything, we could say they believe that "Nothing means anything." But how might one sum up the Christian view? What is the opposite of "Nothing means anything"? Would it be "Everything means something"? Perhaps. And if "everything means something," then it follows that "Nothing means nothing."

So let's settle on the first of these, since it implies the second. "Everything means something." But Tom Howard in his genius says that even that is not quite enough. He says that the polar opposite of the dreary secular view "Nothing means anything" would really need to be "Everything means everything." Or better yet, to capture the inescapably exultant reality of the idea, "Everything means everything!" In other words, the opposite of a Godless and dead universe where meaning does not exist is a universe so entirely suffused with meaning that not only does everything mean something, but everything means everything. Everything in creation somehow points to everything else in creation.

Somehow—in God's impossible economy—everything is connected. Somehow. Through him. And because the good and beauty and truth in each thing points to him, it reflects off him and points back to every other good and beautiful and true thing that exists. It is a dizzying concept, and it is so magnificent that even those of us who believe life has meaning don't often think about how much meaning it has because it can be too much to take in. It can be unbearably beautiful and heartbreaking. It undoes us. But it is meant to undo us, too.

Because God who has made us in his image has created all of creation to point us to himself in every conceivable way. We are not incidental to what he has done. We are central to it. Which makes us see that his love for us is so impossibly and unimaginably great that it really is infinitely too much for us to bear. If he did not shield us from it in some way, it would really and truly undo us. It would destroy us. Imagine a goodness so good and a beauty so beautiful and a truth so true and a light so white and so impossibly and blindingly bright that apart from God's infinite love and mercy sheltering us from it, we could not bear it even for a moment. And then imagine a God who shows us his infinite love and mercy precisely so we can bear it—and not just for a moment, but for all eternity.

Is God Dead?

Two thousand years ago in Jerusalem others asked this question. Back then—and again more recently in our own time—the facts seemed to say that God was dead. That he must be. There could be little question of it. Most people in Jerusalem back then felt obliged to acknowledge it. And many people feel obliged to acknowledge it today. In Jerusalem two thousand years ago, some concluded it very reluctantly and sadly, while others declared it triumphantly. The same is true today. In each case, the facts rather strongly suggested that God was dead. But as it happens, God—back then and again now—has revealed things to us that we did not know before, that we could not have known before, that we couldn't have even imagined. And based on these new things, then and again now, we can say something deeply and heartbreakingly beautiful and true: God is not dead. He is alive.

Rejoice.

Appendix

The op-ed, "Science Increasingly Makes the Case for God," was published in the Wall Street Journal *on December 25, 2014. Since then, it has garnered over 600,000 Facebook shares and more than 9,250 comments, making it unofficially the most popular article in the* Wall Street Journal's *history.*

SCIENCE INCREASINGLY MAKES THE CASE FOR GOD

In 1966 *Time* magazine ran a cover story asking: "Is God Dead?" Many have accepted the cultural narrative that he's obsolete—that as science progresses, there is less need for a "God" to explain the universe. Yet it turns out that the rumors of God's death were premature. More amazing is that the relatively recent case for his existence comes from a surprising place— science itself.

Here's the story: The same year *Time* featured the now-famous headline, the astronomer Carl Sagan announced that there were two important criteria for a planet to support life: The right kind of star, and a planet the right distance from that star. Given the roughly octillion—1 followed by 27 zeros—planets in the universe, there should have been about septillion—1 followed by 24 zeros—planets capable of supporting life.

With such spectacular odds, the Search for Extraterrestrial Intelligence, a large, expensive collection of private and publicly funded projects launched in the 1960s, was sure to turn up something soon. Scientists listened with a vast radio telescopic network for signals that resembled coded intelligence and were not merely random. But as years passed, the silence from the rest of the universe was deafening. Congress defunded SETI in 1993, but the search continues with private funds. As of 2014, researchers have discovered precisely bubkis—0 followed by nothing.

What happened? As our knowledge of the universe increased, it became clear that there were far more factors necessary for life than Sagan supposed. His two parameters grew to 10 and then 20 and then 50, and so the number of potentially life-supporting planets decreased accordingly. The number dropped to a few thousand planets and kept on plummeting.

Even SETI proponents acknowledged the problem. Peter Schenkel wrote in a 2006 piece for *Skeptical Inquirer* magazine: "In light of new findings and insights, it seems appropriate to put excessive euphoria to rest.... We should quietly admit that the early estimates ... may no longer be tenable."

As factors continued to be discovered, the number of possible planets hit zero, and kept going. In other words, the odds turned against any planet in the universe supporting life, including this one. Probability said that even we shouldn't be here.

Today there are more than 200 known parameters necessary for a planet to support life—every single one of which must be perfectly met, or the whole thing falls apart. Without a massive planet like Jupiter nearby, whose gravity will draw away asteroids, a thousand times as many would hit Earth's surface. The odds against life in the universe are simply astonishing.

Yet here we are, not only existing, but talking about existing. What can account for it? Can every one of those many parameters have been perfect by accident? At what point is it fair to admit that science suggests that we cannot be the result of random forces? Doesn't assuming that an intelligence created these perfect conditions require far less faith than believing that a life-sustaining Earth just happened to beat the inconceivable odds to come into being?

There's more. The fine-tuning necessary for life to exist on a planet is nothing compared with the fine-tuning required for the universe to exist at all. For example, astrophysicists now know that the values of the four fundamental forces—gravity, the electromagnetic force, and the "strong" and "weak" nuclear forces—were determined less than one millionth of a second after the Big Bang. Alter any one value and the universe could not exist. For instance, if the ratio between the nuclear strong force and the electromagnetic force had been off by the tiniest fraction of the tiniest fraction—by even one part in 100,000,000,000,000,000— then no stars could have ever formed at all. Feel free to gulp.

Multiply that single parameter by all the other necessary conditions, and the odds against the universe existing are so heart-stoppingly astronomical that the notion that it all "just happened" defies common sense. It would be like tossing a coin and having it come up heads 10 quintillion times in a row. Really?

Fred Hoyle, the astronomer who coined the term "Big Bang," said that his atheism was "greatly shaken" at these developments. He later wrote that "a common-sense interpretation of the facts suggests that a super-intellect has monkeyed with the physics, as well as with chemistry and biology.... The numbers one calculates from the facts seem to me so overwhelming as to put this conclusion almost beyond question."

Theoretical physicist Paul Davies has said that "the appearance of design is overwhelming" and Oxford professor Dr. John Lennox has said "the more we get to know about our universe, the more the hypothesis that there is a Creator... gains in credibility as the best explanation of why we are here."

The greatest miracle of all time, without any close seconds, is the universe. It is the miracle of all miracles, one that ineluctably points with the combined brightness of every star to something—or Someone— beyond itself.

Bibliography

Agresti, James D. *Rational Conclusions*. Documentary Press, 2009.

Barr, Stephen M. *Modern Physics and Ancient Faith*. Notre Dame, Indiana: University of Notre Dame Press, 2006.

Bassett-Brody, Lisette. *Etched in Stone*: *Archeological Discoveries That Prove the Bible*. Washington, D.C.: WND Press, 2017.

Berlinski, David. *The Devil's Delusion*: *Atheism and Its Scientific Pretensions*. New York: Basic Books, 2009.

Bruce, F. F. *The New Testament Documents*: *Are they Reliable?* Grand Rapids, Michigan: William B. Eerdmans Publishing Company, 1981.

Collins, Steven, and Latayne C. Scott. *Discovering the City of Sodom*: *The Fascinating, True Account of the Discovery of the Old Testament's Most Infamous City*. New York: Howard Books, 2013.

Davies, Paul. *The Cosmic Blueprint*: *New Discoveries in Nature's Creative Ability to Order the Universe*. Radnor, Pennsylvania: Templeton Foundation Press, 2004.

Dawkins, Richard. *The God Delusion*. New York: Bantam Press, 2006.

Denton, Michael. *Children of Light*: *The Astonishing Properties of Sunlight That Make Us Possible*. Seattle, Washington: Discovery Institute, 2018.

———. *The Miracle of the Cell*. Seattle, Washington: Discovery Institute, 2020.

———. *The Wonder of Water*. Seattle, Washington: Discovery Institute, 2017.

Doane, John L. *Let God Be True: A Christian's Guide to Origins Science*. Wise Sheep Books, 2014.

Federer, William J. *Miraculous Milestones in Science, Medicine, and Innovation: And the Faith of Those Who Achieved Them*. Fort Myers, Florida: Amerisearch, Inc., 2020.

Gibson, Shimon. *The Final Days of Jesus: The Archaeological Evidence*. New York: HarperOne, 2009.

Gingerich, Owen. *God's Planet*. Cambridge, Massachussetts: Harvard University Press, 2014.

Gonzalez, Guillermo, and Jay W. Richards. *The Privileged Planet: How Our Place in the Cosmos Is Designed for Discovery*. Washington, D.C.: Regnery Gateway, 2004.

Gould, Paul M., and Daniel Ray, eds. *The Story of the Cosmos: How the Heavens Declare the Glory of God*. Eugene, Oregon: Harvest House Publishers, 2019.

Guillen, Michael. *Amazing Truths: How Science and the Bible Agree*. Grand Rapids, Michigan: Zondervan, 2015.

Hitchens, Christopher, and Richard Dawkins, Sam Harris, and Daniel Dennett. *The Four Horsemen: The Conversation That Sparked an Atheist Revolution*. New York: Random House, 2019.

Kennedy, Titus. *Unearthing The Bible: 101 Archaeological Discoveries That Bring the Bible to Life*. Eugene, Oregon: Harvest House Publishers, 2020.

Lennox, John C. *God's Undertaker: Has Science Buried God?* Oxford: Lion Books, 2009.

———. *Gunning for God: Why the New Atheists Are Missing the Target*. Oxford: Lion Books, 2011.

Mammen, Neil. *Who Is Agent X?: Proving Science and Logic Show It's More Rational to Think God Exists*. San Jose, California: Rational Free Press, 2009.

McGrath, Alister, and Joanna Collicutt McGrath. *The Dawkins Delusion?: Atheist Fundamentalism and the Denial of the Divine.* Downers Grove, Illinois: InterVarsity Press, 2007.

McGrath, Alister. *The Twilight of Atheism: The Rise and Fall of Disbelief in the Modern World.* New York: DoubleDay, 2004.

Meyer, Stephen C. *Return of the God Hypothesis: Three Scientific Discoveries Revealing the Mind behind the Universe.* New York: HarperOne, 2021.

Moreland, J. P. *Scientism and Secularism: Learning to Respond to a Dangerous Ideology.* Wheaton, Ilinois: Crossway, 2018.

Mumma, Howard. *Albert Camus and the Minister.* Brewster, Massachusetts: Paraclete Press, 2000.

Overbye, Dennis. *Lonely Hearts of the Cosmos: The Story of the Scientific Quest for the Secret of the Universe.* New York: HarperCollins Publishers, 1999.

Parker, Andrew. *The Genesis Enigma: Why the Bible Is Scientifically Accurate.* New York: Dutton, 2009.

Pearcey, Nancy R., and Charles B. Thaxton. *The Soul of Science: Christian Faith and Natural Philosophy.* Wheaton, Illlinois: Crossway Books, 1994.

Ross, Hugh. *Improbable Planet: How Earth Became Humanity's Home.* Grand Rapids, Michigan: Reasons to Believe Press, 2016.

———. *The Creator and the Cosmos: How the Latest Scientific Discoveries Reveal God.* Covina, California: Reasons to Believe Press, 2018.

———. *Why the Universe Is the Way It Is.* Grand Rapids, Michigan: Baker Books, 2008.

Schroeder, Gerald L. *Genesis and the Big Bang: The Discovery of Harmony between Modern Science and the Bible.* New York: Bantam Books, 1992.

———. *The Hidden Face of God: Science Reveals the Ultimate Truth.* New York: Touchstone, 2001.

———. *The Science of God: The Convergence of Scientific and Biblical Wisdom.* New York: Free Press, 2009.

Simmons, Richard E., III. *Reflections on the Existence of God: A Series of Essays.* Birmingham, Alabama: Union Hill Publishing, 2019.

————. *Reliable Truth*: *The Validity of the Bible in an Age of Skepticism*. Birmingham, Alabama: Union Hill Publishing, 2019.

Stiebing, William H., Jr. *Uncovering the Past*: *A History of Archaeology*. Buffalo, New York: Prometheus Books, 1993.

Strauss, Michael G. *The Creator Revealed*: *A Physicist Examines the Big Bang and the Bible*. Bloomington, Indiana: WestBow Press, 2018.

Thaxton, Charles B., and Walter L. Bradley, Roger L. Olsen, James Tour, Stephen Meyer, Jonathan Wells, Guillermo Gonzalez, Brian Miller, and David Klinghoffer. *The Mystery of Life's Origins*: *The Continuing Controversy*. Seattle, Washington: Discovery Institute, 2020.

Wells, Jonathan. *The Myth of Junk DNA*. Seattle, Washington: Discovery Institute, 2011.

Wiker, Benjamin, and Jonathan Witt. *A Meaningful World*: *How the Arts and Sciences Reveal the Genius of Nature*. Downers Grove, Illinois: InterVarsity Press, 2006.